HARRY ALTMAN

BUFFALO'S MASTER SHOWMAN

HARRY ALTMAN

BUFFALO'S MASTER SHOWMAN

GLEN CASINO. TOWN CASINO. ONE MAN'S NIGHTCLUB EMPIRE.

Plus the Turbulent History of Glen Amusement Park and *THE INFERNO*

by Susan Fenster

Buffalo
History Books

Published by
BuffaloHistoryBooks
rickfalkowski@aol.com
BuffaloHistoryBooks.com

Harry Altman Buffalo's Master Showman
ISBN number: 979-8-9869824-5-8
1. Buffalo, NY
2. Local History
3. Historic People, Nonfiction

Written by: **Susan Fenster**
(716) 870-1667
sfenster@roadrunner.com
Facebook page: Harry Altman: Buffalo's Master Showman

Edited by: Michael Buckley
Interior Design by: Nancy Wise-Reid
Proof Readers: Mike Reid, Nancy Wise-Reid
Front Cover: Elfy Fenster
Back Cover: Nancy Wise-Reid

First Edition: November 2025
Printed in the U.S.A.

DEDICATION

For Elfy, Always

TABLE OF CONTENTS

ACKNOWLEDGEMENTS

This book took root on a quiet winter's day in 2020 after a walk along the winding paths of Glen Park. The Glen had been part of my story since I was a young child. Its amusement park was a summer treat, two or three visits each year that felt like a grand adventure compared to my city neighborhood. While my parents lingered over a pitcher of Iroquois in the beer garden, I roamed freely with a strip of ride tickets in hand ("22 for a dollar!").

By the summer after second grade, the amusement park was already in decline, hastened by the 1968 fire that destroyed the Glen Casino/Inferno. I still recall walking with my father past the charred footprint where the building had stood. To me, it was a curiosity; to him, it marked the closure of an era that had shaped his life after returning from the Korean War. My parents' scrapbook—stuffed with photographs, ticket stubs, and souvenir booklets from nights at the Town and Glen Casinos—kept those memories alive long after the nightclub era had vanished.

Figure 1 Author's parents Edward and Mary Chludzinski sit across the Town Casino table from the author's aunt and uncle, Dolores and Raymond Przybylski

Decades afterward, a winter walk revived those memories and set me on the path to the Williamsville Library. To my surprise, Altman's name barely appeared, and his years at the Glen were treated as little more than a brief interlude between the property's industrial past and its current incarnation as parkland. I later learned that subtle but enduring antisemitism among local historians likely contributed to his absence from the region's recorded history.

Yet primary sources revealed a fuller story: an ambitious entrepreneur whose mark on Buffalo's entertainment and philanthropic life was long-lasting, though largely erased by his Jewish identity in a time of deep antisemitism, whispers of underworld ties, and the disruption his entertainment venue brought to a quiet village. What started as nostalgia evolved into a broader mission, one that reached beyond the Glen of my childhood to encompass Harry Altman's life and legacy. This book is the result of that journey, and of the guidance and generosity of many others, to whom I now turn with gratitude.

We begin with Ron Urban, whose willingness to share facts and photos helped bring this story to life.

The Altman grandchildren—Steve Goldstein, Alan Riche, Brad Altman and Jeffrey Altman—offered invaluable context about the family's history. The same can be said of Harry Wallens' grandchildren, Marjorie and Jay, who graciously shared their personal memories.

Research was central to this endeavor, and I am especially grateful to Daniel DiLandro, SUNY Buffalo State Archivist and Special Collections Librarian, for guiding me through the extensive *Buffalo Courier-Express* archives at Butler Library. My thanks also go to Cynthia Van Ness, Director of Library and Archives at the Buffalo History Museum, and to the staff of the Grosvenor Room at the Central Library of the Buffalo & Erie County Public Library. I appreciate your efforts in helping me tell not only Altman's story, but also the forces and circumstances that shaped Western New York in the first half of the 20th century.

I likewise benefited from the resources of the Williamsville Historical Museum and the Buffalo Niagara Heritage Village. Nothing delights me more than sifting through the artifacts and fleeting traces of our area's past. Thank you for giving me this privilege.

When it comes to the Town Casino, I need to thank Donny Kutzbach and Arties Kwitchoff, owners of the Town Ballroom, who now operate a performance venue in the very space where Altman and Wallens operated the nightclub. Their deep respect for the building's history, and their kindness toward me, a self-described superfan of 681 Main, is much appreciated.

Many voices gave this narrative its richness and depth. Special thanks to Mary Lowther, Sam Weimer, Clark Bono, Robert Mock, Laverne DeAngelis, Carol Cardina Schmidt, Barney Goldstein, Margaret Phillips, Linda Bartash Dawley, Patricia Riedel, Glenn Hufnagel, Paul Hufnagel, Rick Lohr, Michael Fixler, Larry Altman, Patrick Hasburgh, and Larry Scheur.

The members of the Facebook group, "Harry Altman: Buffalo's Master Showman," enriched this project with their knowledge and recollections.

I am indebted to Bob Paxon, WNY music historian extraordinaire, for his generous assistance with the chapters on the music of the "younger set" (as Altman would have phrased it), particularly regarding Club Commodore, the Inferno, and Gilligan's. The appendix included in this book is largely due to his guidance and support.

On the publishing side, I thank Rick Falkowski, Publisher of Buffalo History Books; Michael Buckley, an exemplary editor; and Nancy Wise-Reid, who heroically formatted this book from title page to final footnote.

Personally, I was sustained by the spirit of friends who endured my long silences while I wrestled with this project. Heartfelt thanks to Lucy Conti Mitchell, John and Carol Ostroot, Mimi Shapiro, and Tom and Nancy Lasker.

The book is dedicated to The Kid, the unwilling accomplice in my Altman obsession, who endured each new story with barely a sigh. "I know more about the Altmans than my own family," she once declared—probably correct. Love you, Elfy.

Lastly, I remember my late husband, Alan (1944-2009), whose presence endures in memory. He set a standard of doing well and being kind, and even now, he seems to offer a gentle, affectionate nudge toward the same.

INTRODUCTION

During the 1940s and 50s, the Glen and Town Casinos were nationally prominent nightclubs that featured the most celebrated entertainers of the era. Names like Sammy Davis Jr, Jayne Mansfield, Vic Damone, Al Martino, and Johnnie Ray were just a handful of celebrities that Harry Altman brought to Western New York for "three shows a night."

Beyond the glitter and glamour is a story about the last-born son of impoverished Russian immigrants.

Beginning his career as a glove salesman traveling across the northeast with life-long friend and future movie mogul Sam Goldwyn, Harry Altman spends the early 1900s scraping by as an event promoter and the co-owner of marginally successful niteries, roller rinks and ballrooms throughout the region.

Just weeks away from personal financial ruin, and only months after the start of the Great Depression, Altman starts managing an eight-acre picnic grove in the heart of Williamsville, NY. Perhaps, he believes, he can turn a profit on this beleaguered parcel of property that had recently served as a "picnic grove" after years of industrial use.

Altman thinks it is worthy an investment of his time.

Using every trick in his promotional arsenal, he spends more than a decade experimenting with entertainment of all kinds in the Glen—roller rinks, carnival attractions, kiddie rides, ballroom dancing, and modest nightclub acts. By the early 1940s, he finds his winning formula with the construction of a 1,000-seat nightclub alongside a popular kiddie amusement park.

But financial success does not bring an end to his troubles. He continues to struggle under the strain of anti-Semitic rhetoric, pressure from members of Organized Crime, and his own personal demons.

Yet, he remains undeterred.

Williamsville in the early 40s is little more than a rural outpost, and Altman's patrons show a reluctance to drive to the Glen during the severe winter weather.

Deciding to expand the nightclub business in a more centralized location, he partners up with Harry Wallens to open the Town Barn (and, later, Town Casino) in downtown Buffalo.

If the Glen is gold, the Town is platinum. Its all-star performances are followed weekly by media outlets like *Billboard* Magazine and the nation's leading entertainment columnists.

But the center does not hold. Television, coupled by the growth of Las Vegas as the entertainment capital, ends the lure of nightclub activity. By 1966, both Harry Altman and Harry Wallens have died. The Town Casino is sold to the Studio Arena Theatre, and the Glen to a Buffalo-based corporate conglomerate. In the fall of

1966, Altman's son-in-law, David Goldstein, decides to lease the casino and transform it into a rock and roll venue.

The newly-branded property—the Inferno—is a huge hit among area youth who are there to hear the likes of Wilmer & the Dukes; Sly & the Family Stone; and the Bob Seger System (among dozens of other local and national acts).

But the building's legacy as an entertainment hotspot ends in September 1968 when the massive, all-wooden building goes up in (oh, the irony) an inferno.

I welcome you into the world of Harry Altman, Buffalo's Master Showman for nearly half a century. As with the telling of all great stories, we will start at the beginning when Samuel (Schmuel Tabaznik) and Dora (Dwosche Meshes) Altman left Grodno, Russia with their seven children to escape a brutal regime.

PART ONE—THE FAMILY

Figure 1 Family Photo Buffalo, NY 1908
Top row: Abraham, Joseph, Charles, Harry, Morris, Simon
Bottom row: Sarah (Altman) Banditson, Samuel, Dora, Augusta (Altman) Evans
Photo courtesy of the Harry Altman estate

————

People say you're born innocent, but it's not true. You inherit all kinds of things that you can do nothing about. You inherit your identity, your history, like a birthmark that you can't wash off…We are born with our heads turned back…

~ Hugo Hamilton, The Sailor in the Wardrobe

CHAPTER 1—FROM THE PALE TO PROMISE

Dwosche Meshes gave birth to her first child, a son named Alter, in 1866 when she was about fifteen years old. For Jews living in nineteenth century in Czarist Russia, early marriage and childbirth were not outside the cultural norm.

Adulthood arrived early in the shtetls, Jewish communities often beset by poverty and overcrowding. Jewish boys could be conscripted into the Russian Army as young as 12 years old, and girls were expected to shoulder the burden of household and childcare duties while still pre-teens.

Although Dwosche and Schmuel Tabaznik's marriage would not be officially recognized by Russian authorities until 1870, the Orthodox Jewish couple would have commenced their life together after a Rabbinical ceremony known as Kiddushin. This ceremony was deemed fully valid and binding within the Jewish community.

The Meshes and Tabaznik families made their home in the Grodno province of Grodno Governorate, a territorial division within the Russian Empire. Grodno, currently located in Belarus, was situated within the confines of the Russian Pale of Settlement "in which permanent residency by Jews was allowed and beyond which Jewish residency, permanent or temporary, was mostly forbidden."[1] These restrictions were set into motion in the late 18th century under the rule of Catherine the Great, Empress of Russia.

Figure 2 Partial Map of Russian Pale of Settlement at time of Tabaznik family's exodus from Grodno (1880s) Photo courtesy of the Harry Altman estate

While Jewish social, religious, and cultural life in Grodno was vibrant, Jews faced legal restrictions that affected virtually every aspect of their lives. These included limitations on where they could live, the types of jobs they could hold, and quotas on the number of Jews who could take part in certain professions. Restricted from living in cities, many settled in villages. Few Jews in the Pale of Settlement were farmers; a third worked in manufacturing and another third as tradesmen. The remaining group excelled in mercantile commerce, dominating in absolute numbers despite constituting just nine percent of the population.[2]

Figure 3 Main synagogue in Grodno where Tabaznik family worshipped
PD

In this challenging environment, Schmuel, who was a year older than his bride, trained as a *schuhmacher*, a craftsman specialized in making shoes and boots. Details about the couple's life in Grodno during their early years of marriage are sparse, but genealogical records reveal that the couple was committed to having a large family, aligning with the Jewish Orthodox belief where birthing children is seen as fulfilling a mitzvah (commandment). Over the course of the next 25 years Dwosche gave birth to a total of 13 children, only eight of whom survived childhood.

Large families were also pragmatically valued for the labor and support children offered, aiding parents in their later years. Factors like high infant mortality, scarce contraceptive options, and norms favoring early marriages extended women's reproductive years. Dwosche, for example, gave birth to her last child at the age of 41, marking a reproductive span of 26 years.

The Tabazniks lived as Jews during a particularly tumultuous chapter in Russian history. Antisemitism, present since the late 18th century, worsened dramatically during Tsar Alexander III's rule (1881—1894). Following his father's assassination—wrongly blamed on Jews—the May Laws of 1882 were introduced. This legislation intensified antisemitic policies, sparking widespread pogroms, and imposing even more severe economic limitations on Jewish people. Entire neighborhoods were looted and burned, and thousands of Jews were injured or killed by peasants and soldiers alike.[3]

Daily living was particularly difficult in Grodno. Historians have singled the region out as one that "epitomized Jewish-Russian poverty"[4] during that era. Faced with such dire circumstances, many among the younger generation saw emigration as their only escape from the suffocating conditions.

The phrase "To America!" became emblematic of the mass migration of Jews from Eastern Europe between 1881 and 1914. This period marked the largest population shift in Jewish history since the biblical Exodus. During these decades, over 2.5 million Jews left Eastern Europe, with approximately 2 million settling in the U.S.[5]

Desperate to seek freedom in the U.S., Jews defied the czar's emigration restrictions. Many escaped at night, evading Russian border guards and hostile gangs, while others bribed officials to secure safe passage to Western Europe.

Against this backdrop, Alter, the Tabazniks' first-born, decided to leave Grodno in 1885 along with his new wife, Basche (nee Banditson[a]). Alter and Basche's departure was a bid for survival. With merely a suitcase each, the couple, in their early twenties, likely made their way by train to Hamburg, Germany. It was there they would have purchased steerage tickets to New York Harbor's Castle Garden. The steamship on which they sailed was the Bohemia of the Hamburg America Line, which departed on November 11, 1885.

Figure 4 Simon and Lena left Europe on the steamship, Bohemia for NYC
PD

For both the Tabaznik and Banditson families living in the Pale of Settlement, the significance of Alter and Basche's escape from Grodno cannot be overstated. They blazed a trail for their immediate families, teaching them the intricacies of the journey, and creating a foothold in Buffalo, NY, from which the rest could build.

---

[a] The surname is spelled many ways in genealogical research. In Western New York, the name has been commonly converted to "Benderson."

Figure 5 Jews fleeing Europe from the Russian pogroms often travelled in steerage where conditions were overcrowded
PD

But first, the couple needed to endure an ocean voyage on a steamship, crammed in a steerage compartment with 1,200 other passengers. Constructed in 1847, the Bohemia's "third-class" accommodations originally served as a cargo hold on the ship's lowest deck. However, with the rise of transatlantic travel among new emigrants escaping the Russian Terror, the ship was redesigned. The large area was partitioned into sleeping quarters for passengers, who rested on narrow bunks or hammocks, often divided by gender. Privacy was scarce, and conditions were cramped, with limited access to fresh food and adequate sanitation.

On November 25, 1885, the young Tabazniks arrived in Castle Garden, in a domed shed that predated the Ellis Island complex, after a 14-day voyage. There, they received perfunctory medical examinations and were freed to roam the continent.

For their first night of freedom, Alter and Basche slept on the bare floor of the landing depot, awaiting the next step of their journey.[b]

As dawn broke on their first day in America, the Tabazniks resolved to leave their surname behind. Although the reason is not documented, public records confirm that the name change was not the result of a clerical error by a ship steward or immigration official. Both the ship manifest and Castle Garden records affirm that the Tabaznik name endured the journey across the Atlantic intact.

Figure 6 The Tabaznik family arrived at Castle Garden, the immigration processing center in Battery Park, NYC
Castle Garden served as a precursor to Ellis Island
PD

---

[b] A more extensive exploration of the Altman family genealogy can be found in the "Altman Family Tree," compiled by this author and available on Ancestry.com, accessed April 28, 2025, https://www.ancestry.com/.

The choice of their new surname most likely stems from Alter's given name. In Yiddish, "Alter" means "old one" naturally leading to "Altman," meaning "old man Allowed to reinvent their identities, Basche adopted the name Lena and Alter took his father's name, the Angelized version of Schmuel (Sam or Simon).[cd]

For the Tabazniks, New York City would not be their destination. Instead, they boarded a train from the Grand Central depot, leaving behind the city's overcrowded immigrant neighborhoods and high competition for employment. Buffalo was the most convenient western railhead from Manhattan with an established Jewish community.[6] The Altmans decided to settle there.

LIFE IN BUFFALO

The initial Jewish settlers who came to Buffalo in the mid-19th century were mostly from Germany. They brought with them advanced education and specialized skills in various trades. These early settlers quickly adapted to American customs and language. By the time Jewish immigrants from the Russian Pale began to arrive, the German Jewish community had established itself as respected merchants, business owners, and civic leaders. Although they were willing to assist the new Jewish arrivals, the influx of Russian immigrants was so substantial that the charitable support provided by groups such as the Jewish Relief Agency became strained. Consequently, families like the Altmans needed to rely on their own resources to survive.

The new Jewish refugees wanted to establish a neighborhood where the Yiddish language and Orthodox traditions could be conveniently practiced. Assisted by German Jews already settled in the city, many of these newcomers found housing on William Street, east of Jefferson, near the intersection of Madison and Monroe. This neighborhood became known as "Castle Garden," reflecting the immigrants' recent passage through the entry point at the New York port.

Over time, the community expanded along William Street to Michigan Avenue and spread north and south along intersecting streets. The area had previously been home to the German settlers, who left behind affordable housing rentals. On commercial streets, families could live above storefronts that accommodated Jewish bakeries, butchers, grocers, and sundries.

Most families in the Jewish quarter resided in two-story houses along tree-lined, grass-edged streets. The typical home layout included a kitchen, dining room, and parlor on the first floor, with three or four bedrooms on the second floor, providing a comfortable living arrangement for a couple like Simon and Lena Altman and their children.

---

[c] For clarity purposes, the book will refer to young Samuel as Simon.

[d] Following their arrival in New York, all the Tabaznik family members embraced the Altman surname, opting to Anglicize their given names or select entirely new ones that appealed to them.

However, as the number of new arrivals increased and poverty intensified, families often had to adapt their living arrangements to include multi-generational housing and accommodate paid boarders. This shift led to increased overcrowding in many homes, as space was reconfigured to meet the economic needs and realities of the households.

Between 1880 and 1910, Buffalo's east side became home to an estimated 10,000 Jews, making up more than three-quarters of the local Jewish community. This was an opportune time for these new settlers, as Buffalo was booming, with the population of the city increasing three times as fast as New York, Boston or Philadelphia.[e7]

The Erie Canal continued to serve as a vital transportation route for goods moving through the Midwest, Northeast, and Canada. The expansion of the railroad network, coupled with the rise in industrialization driven by Buffalo's access to raw materials and hydroelectric power from Niagara Falls, supercharged the city's economic and population growth.

The city's expansion fueled a surge in job opportunities along the waterfront, in factories, and within warehouses. This economic boom, though promising, also sparked intense competition for jobs, as immigrants from Germany, Italy, Ireland, and Poland poured into Buffalo, each determined to secure a foothold and build new lives in the rapidly growing city.

All the Altman men gravitated toward careers as wholesale and retail merchants. Some, like Simon, expanded their business enterprises to become tavern owners. Harry, being the youngest and most adventurous, ventured into several entrepreneurial endeavors before eventually settling into the restaurant and nightclub business.

The following provides a summary of how life unfolded for the Altman family shortly upon their arrival in the U.S.

SIMON (ALTER)

As the oldest son and the first to arrive in America, it was Simon's duty to secure a home for his parents and siblings who were planning their escape from Russia. Upon his arrival in Buffalo, Simon and Lena rented a home on Jefferson Avenue, and he began work as a fruit salesman while Lena raised their growing family. He later moved to Broadway, which would be the house where his parents and newly arriving siblings would first settle.

By 1900, Simon established a business in the Canal District, located along Buffalo's inner harbor at the terminus of the Erie Canal. The District was known for its bustling, less regulated environment, a natural fit for a recently arrived Russian immigrant accustomed to operating on the fringes of society and adept at navigating the edges of legal norms.

---

[e] Of the large cities, only Chicago was outpacing Buffalo in terms of growth.

Canal Street was only two blocks long but earned the reputation as "Wickedest Street in the World" for its position right on the waterfront. Canal Street is where the "Canal met the sailors from the lake."[8]

During its heyday[9], the District was home to 93 saloons, 15 concert-hall dives, and hundreds of dance-hall girls.[10]

Simon's storefront business at 162 Canal Street was a versatile establishment serving many functions, including a second-hand clothing store, pawn shop, saloon, and grocery. (And, if newspaper reports are to be believed, a popular place for thieves to fence stolen goods.)[f] Simon, Lena, and their eight children later moved from Broadway to live above the shopfront.

With Simon and Lena now settled, Jon and Sarah, Simon's oldest siblings, made their way from Russia in 1888. In the next year, Dwosche and Schmuel sailed from Hamburg in November 1889 on the steamship Coblenz, along with their four youngest children: Abraham, Gaile (Augusta), Hirsch (Charles) and Moses (Morris). The ship took a circuitous route, landing in Castle Garden after a two-week journey in steerage class. Everyone eventually headed to Buffalo, all adopting Altman as their last name.

The last of Dwosche and Schmuel's children was born roughly a year later on December 4, 1891—the first on U.S. soil. They named their sixth son, Harry.

As for Simon and Lena, their relationship ground to a halt sometime in the in mid-1910s. Simon eventually moved out of the family home, declaring himself as "widowed" in the 1920 census.[g] Proving ever the adventurer, he sold his downtown tavern to Paddy Lavin, a popular local lightweight boxer prior to 1916 and moved to Los Angeles to manage a health resort. He would remain there, with infrequent visits back to Buffalo for the remainder of his life.

---

[f] As reported in local newspapers at the time, the Altman brothers—Abe, Joseph, and Morris—along with their father, Samuel, were charged with criminally receiving stolen property, primarily textiles and shoes taken from boxcars by thieves.

[g] Although he listed himself as widowed in the census, Lena was still alive and would remain so for several years. Perhaps she was only "dead" to him.

Joseph (Jon)

Simon and Joseph's lives ran strikingly parallel. Upon arriving in Buffalo, Joseph mirrored his older brother's actions by marrying Rebecca Benderson, the sister of Simon's wife Lena.[h] Each couple eventually had eight children.

Like Simon, Joseph opened a secondhand storefront on Canal Street, followed by a grocery store on Commerce Street. Moreover, both brothers ventured into the saloon business, opening separate establishments in downtown Buffalo within months of each other. While Simon's "Altman's Buffet" at 15 West Eagle Street was a popular meeting place for pugilists and politicians of that era, Joseph's stint as a saloonkeeper at 117 Main Street would prove less successful.

Figure 7 Simon owned this popular tavern/restaurant on West Eagle Street
PD

It was at this juncture that the brothers' lives seemed to diverge, and indications suggest that a feud may have developed between them. The Canal District, known for its rough-and-tumble environment, presented significant challenges for Joseph, who encountered numerous legal issues, both criminal and civil. Many of the early newspaper stories in the U.S. about the Altman family featured Joseph embroiled in various legal skirmishes.

Joseph's first step toward independence began when he leased a "very old" building on Quay and Washington Streets in the District. He used the building to manufacture and store catchup, sauerkraut, sauces and "other condiments" under the corporate name of Eagle Preserving Company.[11] It became known in the neighborhood as "the pickle factory."[12]

---

[h] One of Joseph and Simon's sisters, Sarah Altman, also married into the Banditson family. In 1893, she wed Louis Banditson, who retained the family's original surname.

On November 11, 1908, newspapers covered the fiery destruction of the pickle factory on their front pages. The blaze was discovered by a watchman in the early morning hours. The *Buffalo Evening News* reported on page one:

> "Ten companies of firemen were at the building and the fireboats *Grattan* and *Hutchinson* had taken up their position at the pipeline at the foot of Washington Street. The flames were subdued, however, without the aid of the big boats."

> "For a time after the arrival of the firemen the flames raged fiercely, and it was feared that the fire would sweep through Main Street. Great signs seven feet high [that] had been erected in front of the windows and doors on the lower floor delayed the firemen in gaining entrance to the building and for a time greatly hampered their work."

No one was injured in the fire; several horses that were used to pull wagons survived unscathed.

Damage to the building owned by the Jackman Estate, along with its contents, was estimated at $12,000. Joseph filed insurance claims totaling $4,700 for his lost product (approximately $150,000 in today's value). Joseph had multiple insurance policies covering the contents of the building.

Joseph saw very little of that money. Eli Altman, son of Simon Altman, came forward claiming he had joined his uncle Morris at the factory on the night of the fire, asserting that Joseph had contracted Morris to ignite the blaze.

Joseph vehemently denied these allegations, contending that Eli's accusations were driven by a desire for revenge on Simon's part.[13]   As a consequence of Eli's claims, the insurance companies withheld compensation for Joseph's losses, leading him to file lawsuits for non-payment. This sparked a lengthy series of legal disputes. Throughout late 1909 and early 1910, Buffalo's newspapers frequently reported on two separate New York State Supreme Court trials about the fire at the pickle factory.

During the trial, Eli presented a detailed narrative of how the arson was executed. According to testimony reported in the *Buffalo Courier*, Morris had confided in him about his plan to set the building on fire and and asked for Eli's assistance. When Eli arrived at the pickle factory that evening, he called Morris on the phone because he had not shown up at the agreed time.

"He was in bed, but he got up and said he would be down in a few minutes."

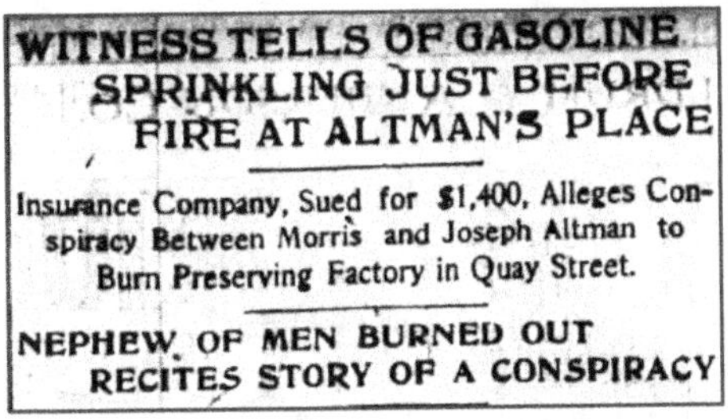

WITNESS TELLS OF GASOLINE SPRINKLING JUST BEFORE FIRE AT ALTMAN'S PLACE

Insurance Company, Sued for $1,400, Alleges Conspiracy Between Morris and Joseph Altman to Burn Preserving Factory in Quay Street.

NEPHEW OF MEN BURNED OUT RECITES STORY OF A CONSPIRACY

Figure 8 Pickle Factory Headline
Buffalo Courier, December 17, 1909, p6 PD

Upon Morris's arrival, Eli recounted how a keg of gasoline was rolled into the storeroom from the barn. Morris then filled a pail "more than once" and "sprinkled the gasoline around the room."[14]

Eli noted that he walked beside Morris during this process, which took about 20 minutes.

After the fire, Eli alleged that Morris offered him money for assisting with the arson, but he declined. Eli came forward to authorities after learning that Joseph was accusing him and Morris of setting the fire and was planning to have them imprisoned. By confessing, he hoped to clear himself of any culpability.[i]

This account was countered by witnesses who asserted that Eli had confessed to fabricating the story to retaliate against his uncle Joseph, purportedly at his father Simon's instigation.[j] Additional witnesses testified to corroborate Morris's alibi that he was playing cards at Simon's saloon that night and had no part in the arson.

The juries in both trials deemed Eli's testimony believable, siding with the fire insurance companies and rejecting Joseph's requests for compensation.

By the time the third New York State Supreme Court trial commenced, Eli had fled to Altoona, Ohio and refused to return to testify in Buffalo.[15] Instead, his statement was taken by deposition in Ohio and read before the jury. The *Buffalo Enquirer* reported that during this trial Eli "appears to have forgotten numerous essential details of the incendiarism,"[16] leading to a favorable verdict for Joseph in the amount of $600.[17]

For a fourth case held in Buffalo City Court, Eli returned to the court room to give his testimony "very reluctantly," the *Buffalo Courier* reported.[18] "I do not want to hurt my relatives," he said on the stand.[19]

But hurt them, he did. Not only did Joseph lose this fourth case, but eager reporters had filed stories with headlines like "Truth or Lie?"[20] "Chief Witness Has Bad Memory,"[21] and "Fire was Planned, Says Young Altman."[22] These stories resulted in the Altman family becoming widely known in the Buffalo community, but not in a favorable way.[k]

During this period, Joseph also found himself at the center of federal criminal prosecution that gained significant media attention. In 1909, he was charged, tried, and sentenced to six months in the Erie County Penitentiary[23] for "furnishing liquor to the Indians" from his downtown saloon.[24] At the time, federal policy treated Native Americans as wards of the state, a status that implied a need for government oversight, especially concerning alcohol consumption.

---

[i] It appears that neither Eli nor Morris was ever formally charged with a crime related to their alleged actions.

[j] The family conflict stemming from these events casts a long shadow. The rift was starkly evident nearly fifty years later, when Joseph's death notice, published on July 30, 1956, made no mention of Simon or Morris.

[k] Eli did not lose all his family connections; for many years, he worked as a cashier at Harry's Town and Glen Casinos.

At the time, the U.S. Attorney's office was engaged in what was called "a crusade" to prevent saloonkeepers from exploiting Native Americans' alleged propensity for liquor consumption. Joseph Altman was a target in their investigations.[25]

"We wanted to make an example of this man Altman," said U.S. Attorney John Lord O'Brian. "He is one of the most flagrant violators of the law in this respect." During Altman's trial, Blind Charlie Johnson, "a well-known Indian character on Main Street," was called as a witness. Johnson testified that Joseph had served him several drinks of whisky at his 117 Main Street establishment. Johnson identified Joseph by the sound of his voice, adding a poignant detail to the trial's proceedings.[26]

During Joseph's stint in prison, the government secured two other indictments against him on the same charge.

His legal problems continued after his prison release. In 1914 Joseph filed for bankruptcy before enlisting in the Navy during WWI. He eventually settled into the produce business, first on West Market Street and then at the newly opened Elk Market Terminal with his business partner, Jack J. Perna (Altman and Perna). This latest endeavor made him financially comfortable, and he, like many of his siblings, was a generous donor to various charities and war efforts.

Figure 9 The Elk Street Terminal shortly after it opened in 1916 PD

SARAH

Figure 10 Sarah (Altman) Banditson
PD

Sarah arrived in 1888 from Russia at age 10 and married Louis Banditson, five years later in 1893. Together they raised five children.

They were in the grocery business together for 35 years in the Clinton-Walnut section of Buffalo.

Sarah was one of the founding members of the Rosa Coplon Jewish Old Folks Home, an Orthodox Jewish "home for the aged" on Porter Avenue in Buffalo. She served Rosa Coplon in various capacities for several decades.

In addition to her charity work, she received press coverage when she was robbed at her Buffalo home on Mills Street in 1898.[27] Two men broke in and held her at gunpoint, ransacking her home before taking an "eight-day clock" and an accordion. Sarah's description of the robbers led to their arrest and retrieval of the items. The two youth, "known to be desperate characters"[28] pled guilty to first degree robbery. She was not harmed.

Her daughter, Lillian was married to Louis Schulefand, the uncle of Dick Shawn, a popular comedian and actor. Harry referred to Dick (given name, Richard Schulefand) as his nephew and promoted him as such during Shawn's appearances at the Town Casino. Ed Sullivan, renown television host, reported in his syndicated column that Harry had tried to dissuade Dick from working in the entertainment field: "You'll never get anywhere hanging around actors," Harry said. "And don't sit down with the chorus girls. Instead, go home and study. There's no money in being an actor even if you have the talent for it."[29]

Harry, who usually had an unerring eye for talent, missed the mark here.

ABRAHAM/ABE

Following in his father's footsteps, Abe, the fourth eldest child, became a shoe merchant and later expanded into men's clothing, a field in which his father-in-law, Lewis Goldstein, was also professionally involved.

During the latter part of the 1800s, Jews in the City predominated the wholesale and retail clothing trade. Of the 17 wholesale clothing firms in the Buffalo business directory, 14 were Jewish. At least 34 of the 88 retail clothing stores were owned by Jewish families who, when their business enterprises grew, included their relatives and former employees in their ventures.[30] Such would be the case with the Altmans.

From 1900-1924, Abraham and his wife, Mary, simultaneously operated seven men's clothing and shoe stores on Seneca, Genesee, and E. Chippewa Streets in downtown Buffalo. In 1922, Harry joined Abe and opened his first shoe store for women on Seneca Street (see Chapter 4) before ultimately deciding that his interests lay in the entertainment and restaurant businesses.

In December 1924, a massive fire on Seneca Street devastated several properties, including Abe's three-story headquarters, effectively ending his career as a downtown merchant. Following this setback, Abe and Mary transitioned into the fur trade, establishing Altman & Son Furriers on Richmond Avenue. Together, they raised three children.

Figure 11 Fire destroyed Abe's retail headquarters in 1924
PD

CHARLES (HIRSCH)

Arriving from Russia with his parents in 1888, Charles attended Buffalo schools before working with his brother, Abe, in the clothing business. He later switched careers, spending 50 years as a produce wholesaler at the Niagara Frontier Food Terminal alongside his business partner, Jacob Schwartz.[31]

He married Belle Berghash, another Russian immigrant living on Buffalo's east side, and they had one child, Adele. Upon Belle's death in 1952, Charles married Ida Secreto, a native of Italy. They lived at 296 Glen Avenue in Williamsville near Harry and his family.

AUGUSTA/GUSTA (GAILE)

Augusta was the second of two Altman daughters, arriving from Russia with her parents. Her marriage to Harry Evans became society news in December 1901. More than 500 guests attended "one of the largest weddings ever held" in the Jewish community at the Pine Street Synagogue.[32] The reception was held at Golden's Hall on Oak Street. Morris served as best man, and Joseph was a groomsman.

The *Buffalo Times* covered the story about the big wedding, referring to Mrs. Evans as "one of the belles of the East Side" and "a great personal beauty…with a wide circle of friends."[33]

Her new husband was "well known in Buffalo," serving for several years as a Russian, Polish and Italian interpreter in the Police Court "and a man of influence among his people on the East Side."[34] Evans became a deputy sheriff and later started the Evans International Detective Agency.

It was the Evans' family home where Dora Altman lived out her final years. The couple received Dora's inheritance, including the Altman family home on Clinton Street. The couple raised two daughters, both of whom were among the first women to graduate from the University of Buffalo Law School.

MORRIS (MOSES)

Morris was a toddler when he arrived in the U.S. from Russia with his family, making him the youngest Tabaznik to emigrate. He attended local grammar schools before beginning a career at Western Union in Buffalo. He was later promoted to another position in New York City. He ultimately returned to Western New York and founded the Morris Altman Produce Co., initiating a significant phase in his professional life as a produce wholesaler.

Figure 12 Morris Altman
Photo courtesy of the Morris
Altman estate

Morris was recognized as "a prominent east side commission merchant"[35] in a *Buffalo Courier* newspaper article announcing his marriage to Minnie Bergstein in 1911. Their wedding, held in Minnie's hometown of Pottsville, PA, just outside Philadelphia, was described as "one of the most brilliant marriages of the season." After their honeymoon, the couple returned to Morris's hometown and raised their family of four daughters.

In 1933, the *Buffalo News* referred to him as "the busiest man in Buffalo"[36] for his involvement in a broad range of charitable, civic, business, political, and religious organizations.[l] He considered his primary interest to be his work with the Rosa Coplon Jewish Old Folks Home, for which he served in leadership positions throughout his life.[m]

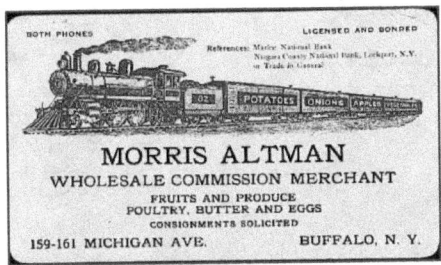

Figure 13 Morris's early business card
PD

---

[l] In the early years of his career, Harry worked hard to make a name for himself, but he often stood in the shadow of his older brother, Morris, a well-established figure in the community. At the time, Harry was frequently identified simply as "Morris's brother"—a reflection of the stature Morris had already achieved during that era.

[m] As previously noted, Morris's commitment to the Rosa Coplon Home extended to his family as well—his sister Sarah, who co-founded the organization, and his brother Harry, who contributed in his own way by regularly hosting free entertainment events for its residents at the Glen Casino.

Reflecting his family's challenges in Czarist Russia, Morris was dedicated to helping the poor and combating antisemitism throughout the region. Despite his activism, he remained a realist about the challenges facing his community: "In my opinion, prejudice against the Jews never will be exterminated," he remarked. "The Jew has been knocked from pillar to post throughout the ages, but he always carried on in the face of persecution. Rome, Syria, Babylonia, Egypt formerly ruled the Jew, and they have fallen, but the Jew has not."

Figure 15 Thelma was the first Altman to enter show business
Photo courtesy of Michael Fixler

Morris spoke about his father, Samuel, in an interview given in December 1941 when his youngest daughter, Thelma Altman (later Mrs. Robert Fixler)[n] had her inaugural appearance as an opera singer at the Metropolitan Opera Company in New York.

"[My] father was a religious Jew. I remember how he dressed at holiday time and went off to shul to pray. He sang for the congregation, but I do not recall that he had a particularly fine voice."[37]

The article noted that Morris "reads and writes Yiddish and expresses himself better in Yiddish than in English" even though he was raised in the U.S.

"My father paid plenty of rabbi fees for me and that's why I know Yiddish so well," he said.[38]

After a marriage spanning 40 years, Minnie died in 1951. He remarried in May 1953 to a widow, Rose Millis.[o]

---

[n] Thelma Altman (1919—2024) graduated from the Eastman School of Music in Rochester and performed as a mezzo-soprano with both the New York Opera Company and the Schenectady Choral Society. She joined the Metropolitan Opera in 1943 and appeared in more than 300 performances during her tenure, earning acclaim for her portrayals of Carmen in *Carmen*, Suzuki in *Madama Butterfly*, and Dorabella in *Così fan tutte*.

[o] Following his death in August 1953—just four months after his wedding—three of his four daughters filed a lawsuit challenging the will, which left the proceeds of his life insurance policy to his new wife. *Buffalo Evening News*, March 16, 1954, "Mrs. Altman Says Her Marriage Was 'Heaven on Earth'," 55.

DORA (DWOSCHE) AND SAMUEL (SCHMUEL)

After years of dire living in Russia, being separated from non-Jews by barriers of language, faith, and an array of brutally oppressive laws, neither considered themselves Russians, but referred to themselves through their ancestral lineage.[39] As noted by census takers through the years, if pressed to identify their country of birth, the first generation of the Altman family would state that they were "Russian Poles."

Upon his arrival in Buffalo, Samuel opened a shoe store on Main Street, learning English. Dora continued in her role as family matriarch, resistant to abandoning Yiddish as her primary language.

HARRY ALTMAN

"I understand poverty. I made my start as a shoe-shine boy on the streets of this city."

~ Harry Altman[40]

Harry was raised in Buffalo's East Side, a neighborhood that bridged the gap between the Eastern European heritage of his ancestors and the vibrant, modern American lifestyle. This area offered a welcoming transition for "green immigrants," helping them maintain their traditional customs while allowing them to "catch a glimpse of the other worldly outside."[41]

For many Jews in Buffalo, the East Side was a distinctly Jewish enclave. Newly arrived immigrants could purchase kosher food and navigate with the help of signs written in Yiddish and Hebrew. The neighborhood fostered a sense of community where Jewish organizations, residences, and businesses were interwoven, creating a network of support among friends and family.[42]

Typically, it was children who "first discovered the joys and sorrows of life in Grover Cleveland's America."[43]

A crucial element in adapting to new environments was the public school system. At that time, schools frequently suffered from overcrowding, inadequate lighting, and poor ventilation. Teachers often received below-average salaries and sometimes lacked proper training. Despite the textbooks being largely outdated, they played a significant role in the Americanization of children from homes where foreign languages were predominant.[44]

In the Jewish ghetto, hundreds of children—including the youngest Altmans—attended School 31 on Emslie near William. At the time, the school boasted the second-highest attendance in the state, with 2,800 students taught by 55 teachers. It was here that these children began to diverge from their family's cultural norms and embrace the wider opportunities America had to offer.

After completing eighth grade, Harry chose to leave formal schooling behind. For the next few years, he took on various odd jobs, building his skills and confidence. By the age of 18, he felt ready to leave Buffalo to pursue a career.

CHAPTER 2—NEXT STOP GLOVERSVILLE

The patriarch of the Altman family, Samuel, died on May 22, 1909. His obituary noted that "he was a well-known figure on Main Street," listed his eight children, but omitted his wife, Dora.[a]

The impact of his passing rippled through the lives of his eight children whose births spanned three decades. While the eldest six had married and moved on with their lives, Morris and Harry were still living at home. But not for long.

In 1910, a year after his father's death, Harry stepped onto a New York Central Railway car headed east to claim his fortune. He was just shy of his 19th birthday.

With the blessing of his mother, Altman accepted a job in Gloversville, NY to become a "commission merchant" for J. H. Danforth, a leading manufacturer of children's leather gloves.

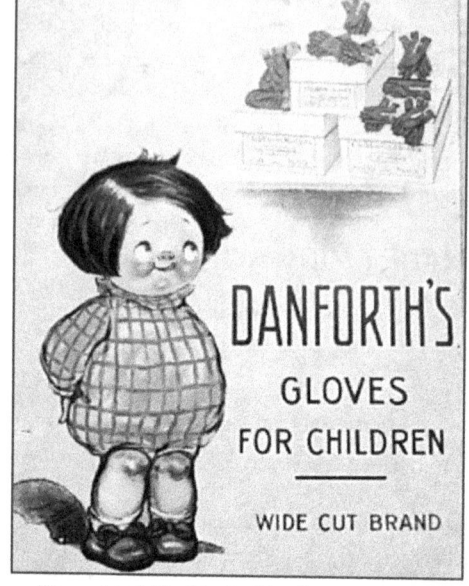

Figure 14 Ad for Danforth's Gloves for Children
PD

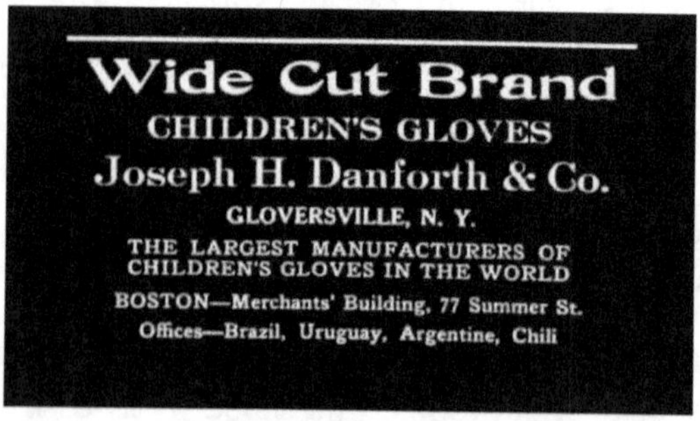

Figure 15 Danforth ad
PD

Gloversville, as the name suggests, was center of the glove-making trade, producing 90% of the gloves worn in the U.S. At the time of Altman's arrival in Fulton County within the Mohawk Valley region, a vast majority of the city's 15,000 inhabitants were involved in some aspect of the trade, earning it the title of "the glove-making capital of the world."

---

[a] Nevertheless, they are buried side by side in the Old Section of Brith Sholem Cemetery. Samuel's half of the gravestone bears the inscription: "An honest man, our father, rabbi, and teacher."

Residents of Gloversville (and the adjacent city of Johnstown) supported a wide array of craftsmen and laborers, melding together the unique talents of leather tanners, designers, cutters, sewers, and retailers. At the top of the hierarchy in the "Glove Cities" were the factory foremen, company executives and business owners.

Commission salesmen were seen as having unlimited earning potential, which is why Dora encouraged her youngest child to head to Gloversville. Widowhood had settled comfortably on her shoulders after years of estrangement from her husband, but she still relied on financial help from family members to stay in her home on Clinton Street where only Morris, 23 years old, remained. He, too, would soon leave Buffalo, heading to New York City for a promotion as a telegraph operator with Western Union.

For the first time in her life, at age 58, Dora would be living alone.[b]

Harry found early success at Danforth. Following his apprenticeship, Altman was assigned to the plum states of Indiana, Ohio and Michigan as his sales territory. The real-world lessons he learned during his subsequent nine-year career with Danforth would provide him with the tools he would need to succeed as an entrepreneur in the decades that followed. Those skills included persistence, perseverance, discipline, punctuality, confidence, determination, persuasion, and the art of negotiation. He would also find a mentor and lifelong friend in Gloversville, Samuel Goldfish (nee Szmuel Glebfisz).

Sam was an Eastern European export that had apprenticed as a glovemaker in England after fleeing the Jewish ghettos of Warsaw, Poland. Booking passage on the steerage ship Labrador in 1898, he arrived in New York City and made inquiries as to where he could ply his trade in glove manufacturing. Upon relocating to Gloversville, he started out as a floor sweeper before eventually finding work as a glove cutter while moonlighting as a student at Gloversville Business College.

Goldfish took advantage of every opportunity available to him. As noted in the blog "Fulton County Historian," by Samantha Hall-Saladino[45] Sam was known as "a hustler...willing to work smart, work hard, and use his brains to move ahead."

Altman had found the perfect role model to match his own energy and drive.

Figure 16 Goldwyn in the early years of his film career (1909)
PD

---

[b] In 1914, with the financial support of her children, she took ownership of the 386 Clinton Street house.

Goldfish faced failure in Gloversville when a glove company he had started with a friend went bust. But the setback only sharpened his resolve to succeed financially. He decided to set his sights on sales where he believed the "real money" could be made.[46] By age 30, he was earning $15,000 a year ($300,000 in 2025 dollars) at the Elite Glove Company before being promoted to vice president of sales.[47] After four years he convinced Elite to open a New York City office where he could go beyond selling clothing accessories and explore a "future in cinema."[48]

Altman was captivated watching his mentor chart a course to independence. Goldfish worked two jobs until he could bank enough money to break off permanently on his own. The key to financial freedom, Sam said, was applying the skills learned in sales to whatever one was most passionate about.

> *"No person who is enthusiastic about his work has anything to fear from life. All the opportunities in the world are waiting to be grasped by people who are in love with what they're doing."[49]*

Goldfish soon found himself in love with making movies, and by the early 1920s he would find enormous success.[c] After changing his name to "Goldwyn" in honor of the famous theatrical Selwyn family, in 1917 he formed Goldwyn Pictures before starting two of the largest Hollywood studios: Metro-Goldwyn-Mayer and Paramount.[d]

Meanwhile, back in Gloversville, Altman was second-guessing his choice of being a drummer (worker who "drums up" business) in a large geographical territory. During this era, long-distance travel primarily relied on steam-engine train service. Owing to budgetary constraints, Harry traveled in coach class, which offered only wooden bench seating, as he journeyed across the Midwest in pursuit of new sales opportunities.

Once a train arrived in the region, his options for local transport to his destination were sparse. He could either walk or opt for a horse-drawn carriage. In more urban areas, a streetcar might be an option. Although automobiles were starting to gain popularity, they were not financially feasible for a commissioned salesman like Harry, especially considering the limited availability of roads that could accommodate the Model Ts.

---

[c] Goldwyn's path to success was far from effortless. In his early years of film production, he came close to losing his entire life savings, recovering only through a mix of luck and strategic thinking. While many brief biographies tend to overlook these financial hardships in favor of highlighting his later triumphs, A. Scott Berg's *Goldwyn: A Biography* (New York: Alfred A. Knopf, 1989) offers a far more nuanced and complete portrait of his life.

[d] Altman would remain life-time friends with Sam Goldwyn, visiting the movie mogul whenever possible during his annual trips out west to book new acts.

Going door to door was the most efficient method for Altman to meet his sales targets, necessitating planned overnight stays at different hotels and boarding houses. Occasionally, hospitable locals would offer him a place to stay. The quality and availability of the accommodation varied from one location to another.

Hoping to jump-start a second career, Harry began thinking about moonlighting. Not wishing to leave the reliable income from Danforth, but wanting to utilize his connections in his hometown, he asked Danforth if he could relocate his base of operations to Buffalo.

Having demonstrated his value and adaptability, Altman received Danforth's approval for his return to Buffalo. Within a short time, he was back living with Dora on Clinton Street, taking overnight trips throughout his sales territory, and strategizing his next big move.

Altman made his initial foray into the entertainment industry by declaring himself the manager of Benjamin Finberg, a 14-year-old vocalist preparing for his inaugural public recital. Described by the *Buffalo Courier* on September 4th, 1910 as "possessing a voice of remarkable sweetness and a wide range," Finberg showed promise of becoming a distinguished singer. Interestingly, the article featured a photograph of Altman alongside the announcement, and not Finberg. This marked the beginning of Altman's pattern of discovering and promoting young musical talents in the local scene. Unfortunately, Finberg, like other early proteges of Altman, failed to progress in his singing career and eventually disappeared without any further public attention or success.

HARRY ALTMAN.
Popular young manager who will shortly present Benjamin Finberg, a talented young singer, in a public recital.

Figure 17 Altman with Finberg article 1910
PD

GOLDWYN AND ALTMAN

Years after both men had left the glove trade, Sam Goldwyn's influence on Altman remained strong.

Jack O'Brian,[a] a nationally syndicated Associated Press columnist, saw parallels between the two men, even referring to Altman as his "own private Goldwyn."[50]

Throughout his life, Sam's malapropisms—what O'Brian called a "a vocal stenography" that left "the listener to decode their meaning"—had become lore. Perhaps because English was his second language, or perhaps, as O'Brian opined, speech impeded "the quick expression" of his racing thoughts, he had become known by the national media for his humorous idioms.

Figure 18 Goldwyn as the titan of the movie industry
PD

Some of Goldwyn's most famous malaprops included:

"A verbal contract is worth about as much as the paper it's written on."

"Coffee isn't my cup of tea."

O'Brian noted that Altman resembled Sam in being "very intelligent" and having a conversational pace that "proceeds at a dead run, leaving tattered English in the wake of his thoughts."[51]

In his December 1946 column, O'Brian revisited his hometown and stopped by the Town Casino, which he whimsically described to his national readers as "a quaint little airplane hangar of a saloon seating 1,400 people."[52]

O'Brian also observed that people gathered "Altmanisms the way some folks collect first editions," highlighting Altman's unique way with words.

Here are a couple Altmanisms he found notable:

- "Excited to describe a new feature of his show, Harry made special note of the 'opening finale' before immediately running on to describe the first act."
- "Harry once yelled out instructions to his electrician: 'Turn the lights up louder.'"

Following an incidental fire in the building, he made sure to call the inspector "in a hysterical hurry" to assure him that there was no malfeasance. "You know, I don't go in for arsenic," Harry reportedly said.

---

[a] O'Brian was a native of South Buffalo's Old First Ward, reporting for the *Buffalo Courier-Express* before moving on to the *Associated Press* (AP) as its drama and movie critic. He was one of the first national television columnists, plying his trade for the *New York Journal-American* and later took over the "Voice of Broadway" column that was picked up by King Features Syndicate. He earned two Pulitzer nominations for his investigative reporting (wartime rationing system and the quiz show scandals) before dying in 2000 at the age of 86.

Harry Altman obscured the early history of his own career. In interviews he granted, and in the memorials written following his death, his origin story begins in 1923 with the opening of the Arcadia Ballroom.

In truth, he found success a full decade earlier, organizing large events under his own banner in 1912. By the time he hit 30 in 1921, he had become somewhat of a media darling, getting frequent mention in front page articles, and cavorting with business leaders and influential politicians.

Throughout this decade, he acquired the skills and connections that would later earn him the nickname "Mr. Show Business."

As later chapters will reveal, although Altman easily attained a measurable degree of success, maintaining it in an ever-changing world proved difficult.

CHAPTER 3—SHOWMAN IN TRAINING

arry's entrepreneurial journey began with a flyer he came across on a sales call. The advertisement, which promoted Mardi Gras celebrations in New Orleans, sparked an idea that fascinated him for many months. In 1912, Harry commenced a side gig as the general manager of "The Cabaret Club," an entity seemingly concocted by Altman on the spur of the moment. Its postal address was linked to the Ellicott Square Building in downtown Buffalo, in a suite of offices primarily associated with a carpet cleaning business.

Altman's first "Mardi Gras Carnival and Dance" was an event spectacular inspired by Michael Shea, whose Court Street Theater in Buffalo Harry frequented in his youth. From 1898 through the early 1930s, Shea operated a series of vaudeville theaters in Buffalo, making the city an important stop for variety-style entertainers traveling between New York City and Chicago.[a] Vaudeville entertainment featured musicians, singers, dancers, comedians, trained animals, and acrobats. They performed in continuous stage rotation throughout the day, starting late in the afternoon and lasting until the early hours of the morning.

Figure 19 Shea's Court Street Theater inspired Harry's love of vaudeville
PD

---

[a] It is interesting to note that Altman would later promote the Town Casino as the "most important nightclub outside of Chicago and New York City."

Figure 20 Photo of Michael Shea
PD

Shea, born in 1859, was a Canadian emigree whose impoverished parents eventually settled in South Buffalo. He began his career as a dock worker, iron worker and tavern owner before starting his long stint as an impresario and movie theater owner.[53] He catered his offerings to the working class, keeping ticket prices low and decorating each of his theaters in high-class style.

Altman adopted Shea's business strategy, setting low cover charges and menu prices to draw blue-collar customers to his nightclubs and restaurants. The venues were elegantly decorated, offering a variety of high-quality entertainment. During the years he operated the Glen and Town Casinos, for example, he often scheduled 1am performances (alongside the 8 and 10:30 PM offerings) to accommodate second-shift workers.

He selected the Broadway Auditorium for his first Mardi Gras event. It had been newly refurbished by the City of Bufalo for use as its municipal auditorium.[b] First constructed in 1858 as a National Guard arsenal, it was expanded into service as a drill hall and administration building for the Sixty-Fifth Regiment Armory before being decommissioned in 1907.

The Altman family had lived across the street from the mammoth structure at Broadway and William Streets when his family first settled in Buffalo. The auditorium could hold up to 12,000 patrons in its 47,000 sq. ft. of space, large enough to accommodate Harry's ambitious visions for the event.

Figure 21 Postcard of Broadway Auditorium
PD

---

[b] The building stayed in operation as a Municipal auditorium until 1940 when Buffalo Memorial Auditorium was opened.

The inaugural Buffalo Mardi Gras was set for the evening of Wednesday, December 4, 1912,[c] charging an admission fee of 25 cents for first-floor access while balcony viewing was free. Advertising promoted an indoor "grotesque" parade featuring patrons in costumes competing for cash prizes. After the awards ceremony, live music would play continuously from a stage at one end of the arena. Over its seven-year duration, the program expanded in complexity, showcasing a diverse array of musical acts, celebrity appearances, and kitschy contests.

To organize an event of this size required someone to manage the day-to-day tasks. Altman's travel obligations for Danforth made that an impossibility, so he decided to enlist a Buffalo-based business partner.

He did not have to look far. Harry Wallens was another Jewish immigrant who resided on Buffalo's East Side. Born in 1886 in Russia, Wallens was the second child of orthodox Jewish parents who would emigrate to the U.S. in 1890. After settling down off William Street in the Jewish quarter, Jacob and Bella (Michaels) Wallens would eventually grow their family to 12 children.

Jacob was a butcher by trade, starting out by selling kosher meat at the Clinton Street Market before opening his own sausage factory, J. Wallens & Sons on William Street.

The Harrys were neighbors and active in many of the same religious and community organizations. But it is believed that their mutual interest in boxing was what sparked their friendship.

Wallens (known by the nickname of "Sharkey"[d]) was a part-time boxing promoter, whose name frequently appeared on the sports pages as "the well-known east side enthusiast." He spent a lot of time at the Broadway Auditorium, a prominent venue for boxing matches for local fighters and others coming up in the national ranks.[e]

---

[c]While Mardi Gras is traditionally linked to the beginning of the Lenten Season, Altman did not adhere to this timing. His initial dance took place in December, and the following six events were scheduled around Halloween, seemingly to capitalize on the costume-wearing tradition shared by both holidays.

[d] Sharkey was a common nickname given to gamblers during that era. Wallens propensity for games of chance started early. He was arrested at age 14 with two other friends for shooting craps on Broadway. The judge released all three boys on a suspended sentence after their parents promised to "give them a good licking." ("Crap Shooters Brought into Court." *The Buffalo Enquirer*, April 14, 1902, 9.)

[e] One of the most famous boxing matches that took place at the Broadway Auditorium was the bout between heavyweight champion Jack Dempsey and challenger Tommy Gibbons on July 4, 1923. This fight, often referred to as the "Battle of the Century," attracted widespread attention and was considered one of the most significant boxing events of its time. Dempsey won the battle after the full 15 rounds were fought.

Altman would become seriously drawn to the sport of horse racing in the years ahead, but it was boxing that caught his interest early on.[f] Altman would be called upon by boxing clubs to organize their tournaments. The saloon owned by his eldest brother Simon, with whom Harry was close, was the watering hole for local pugilists, their managers, trainers, and fans. In fact, it was Paddy Lavin, a prominent local lightweight boxer (and a close friend of Wallens), who purchased Altman's Buffet at 15 W. Eagle when Simon left for California in 1916.[54]

Regardless of how their friendship began, the two Harrys established a business partnership in 1912 that generated financial returns and recognition for their work in event promotions. Although this initial collaboration was relatively short-lived, it laid the groundwork for joint ventures in the decades ahead.

During these early years, Altman was fueled by adrenaline and ambition. Being single, he could devote all his spare time to planning events, often sleeping on trains while covering his territory for Danforth. The Mardi Gras provided a crash course in various disciplines, including talent acquisition, advertising, securing sponsorships, managing ticket sales, negotiating contracts, obtaining leases and city permits, organizing food and beverage provisions, ensuring security, promoting the events, and hiring and retaining staff.

The learning curve was steep, as he faced a multitude of logistical and production hurdles throughout these years. The forthcoming section will detail his challenges, including navigating the disruptions of World War I and the Spanish Flu epidemic; dealing with a lawsuit from Wallens; enduring severe storms that disrupted events; and competing against a rival with superior financial resources and influence.

Throughout these challenges, Altman showed remarkable resilience and adaptability, continually finding ways to overcome the ever-shifting conditions. In contrast, Wallens faced a difficult period that took him more than a decade to overcome.

1912—THE START OF SOMETHING BIG

Beginning with his very first ever press release, Altman's natural talent for hyperbole to attract public attention was evident. It would serve him well throughout his career.

An article in the *Buffalo Times*[55] the City's inaugural Mardi Gras event was billed as "a mammoth joy fest...promising to be the greatest pleasure event in the history of Buffalo." The article forecast that "several thousand masqueraders" would parade through Broadway Auditorium, modeled after Mardi Gras events in New York and New Orleans. Up until this time, most carnivals were limited to parish halls on Fat Tuesday.

---

[f] Much later in his career, Altman was named in 1958 to the Golden Gloves Committee held at Memorial Auditorium.

The Buffalo parade would be led by Snuffy, the Cabman and his Funny Hack,[g] while lively tunes were to be played by the 65th Regiment Band led by Conductor Powell. Loving cups would be awarded as prizes for the best costumes, judged by local celebrities who would canvas the marchers as they paraded several times through the Auditorium.

A moonlight dance, "replete with electric scenic effects" operated by the electricians from Tech Theater, would be followed by a cabaret show of "first-class singers." At midnight, searchlights of variegated colors would illuminate falling confetti that was set to last 10 minutes.[h]

Altman kept public interest high by frequently announcing new performers for the program. On the eve of the ball, *The Buffalo Courier* reported that novelty acts Marie, the Country Woman; Narcissus, the Clown; and Spareribs, the Almost-Horse[i], were set to perform.

From an attendance perspective, the strategy was to attract the interest of large fraternal orders like the Orioles, Moose, Elks, and Eagles who could buy blocks of tickets, ensuring that attendance was not solely reliant on walk-in traffic.

When all was said and done, reviews of the initial event were mostly positive, and the attendance was respectable considering it was a first-time event being showcased in the large auditorium space.

Pleased with their efforts and results, show producers Altman and Wallens decided to give the event another go.

1913—LESSONS LEARNED FROM COMPETITOR CHALLENGE

Altman and Wallens started planning year two before Spareribs, the Almost-Horse, was returned to the barn. One of their first decisions was to move the date of the event to coincide with Halloween to attract more costumed dancers.

However, planning came to an abrupt halt when Altman and Wallens received troubling news from Mayor Louis Fuhrmann: the City planned to host its own Mardi Gras event to celebrate the official opening of the municipally owned Broadway Auditorium.[j] The evening celebration was scheduled for May 1913 and would include a large outdoor grotesque parade from downtown Buffalo to the Auditorium, followed by a Mardi Gras carnival in the large hall.

---

[g] Snuff was a public performance act that typically drew large crowds on Buffalo's Main Street.
[h] Altman boasted that a special device for the confetti shower had been flown in from New York City. The promise of this spectacular confetti event was featured in every local newspaper.
[i] A stage name for a pony. Interestingly, the "almost-horse" term became popular in the 1930s for thoroughbreds who finished a close second in the race. "True Blue, an almost-horse, ended his racing career today at Saratoga."
[j] The auditorium had been operating for several months as an event venue prior to this official opening.

Patrons would be charged 25 cents per person to attend the carnival, the only ticketed event of the inaugural's week-long festivities. So confident that the parade and carnival would be a success, that City leaders hinted that Mardi Gras would be added to the City's yearly programming schedule.[k]

Altman was not pleased; the feeling of powerlessness was not to his liking. His newly created enterprise was being usurped by a governmental entity with deep pockets and expansive influence. Harry's visits to City Hall to meet with Mayor Fuhrmann and other officials, lobbying to hire Altman and Wallens as event planners for the event, were ignored.

Returning empty-handed from these meetings taught Harry a valuable lesson. He made a promise to himself to work toward ensuring that his future endeavors would not suffer from his lack of political clout. True to his word, over the years he forged close friendships with members of both political parties and became a trusted confidant to mayors, legislators, and other political figures throughout the region. These efforts would eventually yield significant dividends.

However, for the time being, all the Harrys could do was wait on the sidelines to observe how the City's Mardi Gras Parade and Carnival would unfold.

Newspaper articles published prior to the event reported that Councilman Charles L. Willert, key organizer of the "grotesque parade" would serve as Grand Marshal. He would lead revelers on a winding one-mile course starting at Niagara Square and ending at the Broadway Auditorium where marchers could disperse or, if they had the money, enter the building for a night of dancing, dining and refreshments.[56]

Unfortunately for Willert, his plans for the night of the event did not materialize as expected. By early evening, it was estimated that "50,000 men, women and children" lined the parade route for the 7:30 PM start time. Some key roadway intersections became impassable; sidewalks were "lined with unbroken walls of humanity."[57]

Added to the chaos was the onset of darkness and inclement weather.

"The task of forming a grotesque parade in the dark and getting it under way would put the patience and ability of the man who wrote the book of tactics to the test," *The Buffalo Evening News* opined, "And Councilman Willert….is no West Point graduate."[58]

When the parade stepped off "sometime after 9 PM," bystanders found it "impossible to describe"[l59] partly because night had now fallen and it was pitch black, but mostly because a driving rain had caused many groups of marchers to fall out of line and abandon the parade.

---

[k] It is interesting to note that the City's Carnival committee voted to ban the throwing of confetti in the auditorium. Altman's confetti-spewing machine was apparently not well liked by the maintenance staff.

[l] Alongside Willert were 30 aides on horseback, as well as large guard of mounted policemen, making walking behind the animals treacherous in the rain and the dark and the….

"The number of participants dwindled by the time the procession reached Main Street," *The Buffalo Evening News* reported. Judges requested that the marchers loop twice around the Auditorium's outdoor reviewing stand, hoping to get a full view of all the participants.

Participants entering the Auditorium perked up a bit if only for the fact that it was dry and there was light. As the carnival was so far behind schedule, only 1,500-2,000 revelers elected to pay the 25 cents, disappointing the planners who had anticipated a much larger crowd.[m]

Hyer's Marine Band and the Buffalo Municipal Orchestra provided music as men and women in wet costumes danced in what was described as a "brilliant court of red, white and blue, surrounded by many towering columns similarly decorated and connected by festoons of bunting." Howard D. Herr, auditorium custodian and chairman of the decorating committee, was the only hero of this night.

All the chaos and subsequent negative publicity proved to be good news for the Altman-Wallens camp. With only five months until the rescheduled dance date of October 30th, the pair wasted no time in planning the "Real Mardi Gras" on Halloween. To broaden its appeal to a wider demographic, the Harrys added the subtitle "The People's Ball," encouraging patrons from all social classes to attend.

WALLENS AND ALTMAN.

MANAGERS OF THE MARDI Gras festival and masquerade ball to be given at the Broadway audi torium Thursday night.

MAYOR TO OPEN MARDI GRAS

Figure 22 The Harrys appear in the papers for the very first time
The Buffalo Enquirer, October 1913
PD

"We are preparing to the largest crowd which ever attended a dance in this city," Altman and Wallens announced in a joint press release.[60] The party, they promised, would surpass the prior year's inaugural event with 5,000 revelers. The estimate was based on the volume of advance tickets that "presages a crowd that will tax the capacity of the great hall."

A photo of the two men was featured with a *Buffalo Enquirer*[n] article along with the promise that the eight-hour dance would be "the most novel event of the fall and winter season in Buffalo."[61] The article stated that the grotesque parade would remain indoors, and loving cups of yesteryear would be swapped out by "valuable prizes" for the costumed winners.

---

[m] Events earlier in the week had filled the Auditorium (9,000+).

[n] While most of the local newspapers covered the event, the *Buffalo Enquirer* took special notice, cross-promoting appearance of "cartoon favorites" (Mutt & Jeff, the Jiggs family, etc.) that appeared in their regular comic strips. Altman would convince the paper in later years to become the media sponsor of the event.

Many popular features would be returning. People paying the 25-cent admissions fee could march in the parade and glide at the moonlight dance. Audiences willing to sit for free in the balcony could "watch the antics of the masqueraders without participating in the revelries,"[62] hear the cabaret singers who travelled from New York, and see the "snowstorm" of midnight confetti.

New to the program was the much-publicized competition that would decide who was the "champion tango dancer of the city." It was made clear in all the promotions that only "the real tango" would be allowed and "indecent variations will not be permitted."[63]

Fulfilling his earlier promise to always be within the circle of influence, Altman persuaded Mayor Louis Fuhrmann to be present to greet the guests. He was joined by a "large delegation of prominent political candidates" who would "mingle with the great throng of merrymakers"[64] throughout the evening.

Reviews of the Mardi Gras were very favorable. *The Buffalo Times* reported that "an exceedingly large crowd attended the dance," and "everybody who danced or went to see others dance expressed themselves as having a great time."[65]

Figure 23 Mayor Louis Fuhrmann became Harry's first political ally after his own efforts fall short PD

With year two behind them, the Altman-Wallens partnership was gaining the reputation of being the region's prominent event organizers. But Altman, it was soon discovered, wanted more.

1914—Business Expands; Nerves Fray

In early 1914, Altman accepted the job of organizing Crystal Beach's "Grotesque Parade and Carnival" scheduled in August°. Lauded in the promotional articles as "Harry Altman of Mardi Gras fame" by the media sponsor[66] this was the first time Altman would be paid by a third party for his planning services.

The parade was an annual promotion for the Canadian resort. Each year, hundreds of Western New Yorkers donned their jovial costumes to take part in a parade through downtown Buffalo. In high spirits, they would march their way from Niagara Square to the Commercial Street dock where they could embark on a free boat ride on the Canadiana to the Ontario, Canada amusement park. Once arriving at the Beach, costumed participants would march past the reviewing stand where judges awaited. Once that formality was completed, the revelers dispersed throughout the park to spend money at the carnival and amusement park.

° Erie Beach, Crystal Beach's major competitor, would also host a Mardi Gras parade that year sponsored by *The Buffalo News*.

Key to Altman's success was the recruitment of a large contingent of members from Sprudel organizations, with every local chapter having representation in the parade. Sprudels (German for "Sparkling") were popular, member-based social clubs that originated in German neighborhood bars and taverns. Their sole purpose was "to have a good time,"[p] attracting membership in some groups to total more than 300 members.

Media reports estimated that more than 1,000 marchers participated in the Crystal Beach parade, and "fully a crowd of 50,000" watched from the downtown Buffalo streets. The event was reportedly an uncategorical success, but it marked the start of cracks in the Altman-Wallens partnership. While Altman was frantically organizing the summertime activity, it fell on Wallens to do much of the heavy lifting for the October dance hosted by the partnership.

On a more favorable note, they began year three by signing a newspaper sponsor, *The Buffalo Enquirer*, and strategically selecting the date of the event to coincide with the weekend when 2,000 undergraduates—"real live college students!"—were in town for the Syracuse-Carlisle football game at Federal League Park.[q]

Campus leaders indicated that "almost all of the college students will join in the grand dance," as reported by the *Buffalo Courier*. "They promise to make things lively, too, and when the sophomores and freshmen meet on the floor there are bound to be some doings for the entertainment of Buffalonians who have never seen a real college hazing."[67]

Hal Chase, lauded by the Harrys (and Babe Ruth) as "the greatest first baseman" to ever play the game, agreed to be a judge of the costume parade. At this point in his career, Chase was playing for the Buffalo Blues of the Federal League.[rs] League Secretary Jack Kelly would also be on hand to cast his vote.

Landing the *Buffalo Enquirer* as sponsor was fortuitous for the Harrys as it gave them guaranteed

Figure 24 Hal Chase during his days with the Cincinnati Reds (1915), after leaving the Buffalo Blues
PD

---

[p] Due to the Sprudels' popularity, members became a factor in social and political life in Buffalo for several years. "Bitter Fights in Some Wards," *The Buffalo Courier*, September 12, 1921, 12.

[q] Syracuse played against the Carlisle Indian Industrial School, the foremost boarding school for Native Americans (1879-1918). It was Pop Warner's thirteenth and final year as coach for the Carlisle Indians who lost the game 24-3 before a crowd of 9,000.

[r] The Buffalo Blues (1915) was the last of three major league baseball teams to be based in Buffalo.

[s] He was later traded to the Cincinnati Reds where he ran into trouble for betting on games that he was playing in. But during his appearance in Buffalo, he was a golden boy.

promotional placement for the Mardi Gras in one of the region's largest daily newspapers. More importantly, it set the stage for Altman's friendship with William J. Connors Jr., whose father owned the *Enquirer*. Through a series of mergers and buyouts, the Connors family later formed Buffalo's *Courier-Express* newspaper, the City's morning daily. Connors, Jr. would help propel the Glen and Town Casinos to regional prominence through extensive reporting of the two venues.[t]

Although Altman and Wallens anticipated attracting college students and baseball enthusiasts to the Mardi Gras, it was ultimately the Sprudels who proved to be pivotal to their success. Sprudel organizations were pleased by how well the Crystal Beach parade turned out and purchased large blocks of tickets for the Broadway Auditorium event. For their loyalty, Altman chose leaders of the various Sprudel chapters to serve as the grand marshals.[68]

Spurred on by strong ticket sales, Altman decided "at a late hour" to host an outdoor parade. The night-time event would travel along Michigan, Seneca, and Main Streets, with floats and four marching bands on hand to take part.[69]

Successful ticket sales also meant that Altman and Wallens could increase their spending on the costume prizes. They announced in the media that they had purchased "diamond rings, solid gold watches and other valuable articles to induce the masqueraders to don their funniest attire."[70] The booty would be on display at a "prominent Main Street jewelry store."[u]

At event's end, the reviews were exceptional with *The Buffalo Enquirer* calling the Broadway Auditorium dance "one of the gayest affairs ever in that great hall."

"To Harry Altman and Harry Wallens…much credit must be given," *The Buffalo Enquirer* reported. "[T]hey gave the great throng of dancers all they promised and are to be congratulated upon their efforts to please."[71]

The partnership had survived Altman's solo career effort, but 1915 would prove even more challenging. It would eventually prove too much for Wallens. The 1915 Mardi Gras marked the final celebration of their original partnership.

1915—WAR ON MANY FRONTS

Dark clouds loomed as World War I escalated in Europe. With the U.S. maintaining neutrality and Canada aligned with the Allies, *The Buffalo Enquirer* canceled the August parade at Crystal Beach.

"Because of the war it was found impossible to convene this year's big funny parade at the Canadian summer resort, but not to be deprived of the chance to get the fun-makers of the city together, *The Buffalo Enquirer* has made arrangements to

---

[t] While in Altman's presence, Connors, Jr. would be physically harmed in 1937 by a member of Buffalo's undercover crime family. Altman received more serious injuries in the attack that was targeted at him. (See Chapter 14).

[u] The store was owned by a member of Altman's inner family circle, and it initially functioned more like a pawnshop.

hold the big grotesque parade in the Broadway Auditorium in conjunction with the Mardi Gras carnival."

Although the summer event was canceled, Harry Altman's ties to Crystal Beach remained strong. His memorable impact on John E. Rebstock, the amusement park's owner, during the previous year led to Altman's appointment in Spring 1915 as manager of the theater on the Ontario resort's midway. This position represented another step in Altman's independent career, providing him with valuable experience in managing amusement park operations.

Figure 25 Crystal Beach Theater
Photo courtesy of Rose Ann Hirsch

Altman's hiring by Rebstock had an almost immediate effect on his life. He announced just days later that he was leaving J.H. Danforth and manufacturing children's gloves for his own company.

It was a bold move. Danforth not only provided the factory-made product but also offered all the back-office support. Altman would now be the captain (and only participant) of his own glove-making enterprise.

Wallens was making personal progress, as well. On March 16, 1915, Wallens, 28, married Lillian Moskowitz, 18.[72] Lillian was the daughter of John and Lena (Niederman) Moskowitz, Hungarian immigrants who briefly settled in New York City before moving to William Street in Buffalo.

After the wedding, Lillian would move with Harry to a home on Cedar Street, right next to his family. In addition to his business partnership with Altman, Wallens worked as an ice dealer when he was first married.

While Wallens put the Mardi Gras Parade and Carnival in motion, Altman was preparing for opening weekend at the Crystal Beach theater on May 22nd. Declaring the music of Irving Berlin as the theme, Harry hired six boys to perform a minstrel show that would be presented between Charlie Chaplin and other silent movies. The boys would sing early Berlin hits such "Alexander's Ragtime Band," "When I Lost You," and the comic, ragtime love song "I Love a Piano."[73]

During the summer, Altman tried different promotions to attract patrons to the movie house, including amateur nights with $25 awards and vaudeville entertainment featuring local talent. These promotions achieved moderate success.

As soon as summer ended and the park closed for the summer, Harry returned to Buffalo to work alongside Wallens to get the Mardi Gras Parade and Carnival ready for November 1st.[v]

Since *The Buffalo Enquirer* covered all expenses for this year's Mardi Gras, there was no need for ticket sales. Consequently, Altman implemented a badge system to verify which pre-registered guests could access the Broadway Auditorium. However, Wallens was skeptical about this system, concerned it might enable "undesirables" to infiltrate the event and cause disruptions.

To ease Wallens' concerns, Altman took proactive steps by issuing warnings in the newspaper, aimed at deterring potential troublemakers. The notices stated, "Individuals unable to behave appropriately will be kindly asked to leave. Measures are in place to prevent the entry of undesirables." Additionally, private detectives and police officers were to be on duty throughout the event, ensuring a smooth and secure celebration.[74]

The concerns turned out to be unfounded, at least according to *The Buffalo Enquirer*, which described the parade as "a spectacle." All 3,000 participants carried "giant sparklers" that stayed lit from the starting point to the Auditorium. Leading the march was the magnificent White Buffalo, a 3,000-pound statue that had been used to promote the Buffalo Industrial Exposition in 1911. It was dramatically showcased amidst a "blaze of fireworks" and aerial bombs fired from the truck that carried it.[w]

---

[v] Details of Altman's short-lived stint as glove-making executive are lost to time but future interactions with J.H. Danforth would indicate very little progress had been made by this solo effort.

[w] Considering the amount of firepower in the parade, it is no surprise that the grand marshal was Dr. Arthur E. Campbell, a superintendent in the Buffalo Fire Department.

Figure 26 The Mardi Gras introduces its first major entertainer, Emma Carus, a celebrated American contralto singer and actress who rose to fame in vaudeville and Broadway
PD

According to the newspaper, onlookers packed the parade route from downtown to the Broadway Auditorium, standing five to six rows deep.[75] As the parade participants reached the venue, they were welcomed by a vibrant carnival atmosphere. Emma Carus, who was performing at Shea's Theater at the time, greeted the attendees with enthusiasm.[x] Rex, the carnival king, made a grand entrance at midnight, flanked by performers from the Garden Theater acting as his royal entourage.

The Buffalo Enquirer reported that Altman, known for his flair for the dramatic, arranged for one of the city's largest U.S. flags to be draped from the girders of the Auditorium. This set the stage for a spectacular visual as "thousands of rolls of confetti" showered down while a 100-member chorus performed "America the Beautiful."[76]

As would be revealed publicly a year later, *The Buffalo Enquirer's* glowing portrayal of the evening was largely a fabrication. In truth, the event was riddled with issues from start to finish, a reality that only surfaced during Altman's promotional efforts in 1916. These revelations quickly captured front-page headlines.[77]

Trouble started right at the parade's kickoff. Altman, who had been preoccupied with his work at Crystal Beach, had forgotten to secure an agreement with International Railway (IR) to halt streetcar service on Main Street during the event. Consequently, a streetcar collided with the truck carrying both the eagerly awaited White Buffalo statue and the fireworks, an incident reported nearly a year later as having "significantly diminished the splendor of the celebration."[78]

Furthermore, the parked streetcars along Main Street became a visual obstruction for hundreds of onlookers, preventing them from enjoying the parade.

The situation at the carnival proved disheartening as well. "Thousands of people" were turned away from the Auditorium when a brawl erupted at the main entrance.[79] Reflecting Wallens' previous concerns, the allure of a free event attracted many unregistered individuals. These attendees overwhelmed those who had badges, forcing their way into the venue.[80]

---

[x] Carus, a vaudeville superstar, appeared at Altman's behest. Carus's telegram accepting Harry's offer was reprinted in the local papers.

Altman took the failures as learning opportunities. In the year that followed, he proactively communicated with the media about the measures being implemented to prevent the issues that had spoiled the previous year's event. He announced that registered participants would now use a back entrance on Milner Street, which would keep them out of public view and help manage the crowd more effectively. Security measures were significantly strengthened. Moreover, he negotiated with the local transit authority to halt Main Street traffic during the parade to avoid vehicle collisions and improve the viewing experience for spectators along the parade route.[81]

For Wallens, the issues that marred the 1916 parade appeared largely preventable, if only Altman had listened to his advice instead of focusing solely on his own projects. Wallens, who had taken on the bulk of the preparations, was further exasperated by Altman's failure to halt streetcar operations during the parade, an oversight he had previously warned against. This, combined with ignored security concerns at the Auditorium, led to the brawl that prevented thousands from participating in the carnival, deepening Wallens' disillusionment with their partnership.

Feeling aggrieved and seeking to dissolve their partnership, Wallens demanded his share of the profits accrued over their years of collaboration. Altman, however, had plans to reinvest these earnings to grow the business. With no formal agreement beyond a handshake to guide their dissolution and unable to reach a settlement, Wallens found himself with no choice but to initiate legal action against Altman. He filed a civil lawsuit in the New York State Supreme Court (Equity Term, Case No. 16-2350) on an unspecified date, marking a contentious end to their partnership.[82]

Altman, meanwhile, remained dedicated to his ambitions as an event producer, eventually establishing his own corporation, the Mardi Gras Company, and hosting events at the Broadway Auditorium and other venues in Western New York.[83] He was disappointed when his one-year contract with Crystal Beach was not renewed. He was eventually forced to return to J.H. Danforth, covering his old three-state territory.

The time had come for Harry to begin building a solid financial foundation to support his aspirations of settling down and beginning a family.

1916—RAIN FORCES CHANGE OF PLANS

On January 4th, *The Buffalo Courier* announced that Altman was engaged to Annabelle Rosen, daughter of Mr. and Mrs. Henry Rosen of Toledo.[84] The large territory that Danforth had assigned had not only provided Harry with a comfortable living, but it also offered him the opportunity to find a life partner. The announcement mentioned that the wedding was scheduled for later that spring, but, in fact, would not be held until three years later. Harry had business to attend to.

Because Wallens no longer provided logistical support, the front office staff at *The Buffalo Enquirer* was assigned to handle the day-to-day operations of the Mardi Gras.

With his job at J.H. Danforth keeping him frequently on the road, Altman's efforts while in Buffalo were focused on generating enthusiasm for both the parade and carnival. On the evenings he was not traveling, he actively participated in monthly meetings with various fraternal, civic, sports, and social clubs, urging them to incorporate the Mardi Gras into their annual lineup of special events. Using his persuasive sales skills, Altman showcased the latest attractions planned for the event, referencing a "sensational surprise" he had secured on a "recent trip to Chicago."[y] In addition, he crafted an innovative scheme where participants could vote for their preferred organization via a ticketing system, with the winning groups receiving cash and gold prizes.

The hard work appeared to pay off. A record number of tickets were sold, and many of the organizations got to work building floats and encouraged their members to march in the parade.

In response to the negative stories being published about last year's mishaps, Altman sent out dozens of press releases promising a "gorgeous street pageant" and a carnival that would feature a popular talent he had recruited from Chicago.

Planned for the forefront of the parade that was going to be attended by "throngs of people" was a "replica of a Roman charioteer, led by a tandem team of show white horses," with the chariot driven by the Mardi Gras queen, Isabelle Ermatinger.[85] Ermatinger was celebrated as "one of the most handsome girls in the City," and promised to add a touch of grace and beauty to the event.[86z] Also expected to be in attendance were "three bands of large proportions, three drum

---

[y] This promotional tactic quickly became a trademark of his career. Local reporters often reported on Harry's Hollywood talent scouting trips. On each occasion, he would tantalize them with promises of "big news" for the Town Casino crowd but deliberately withheld the juicy details. He had a knack for leaving everyone eager for more details.

[z] Altman's announcement that he secured a sensational performer during a trip outside Western New York would become a staple of his promotional strategy during his entire career as a showman. Whether it was New York, Chicago, Las Vegas or Los Angeles, he always gave the impression that he was making important deals whenever he left the area on vacation or a business trip.

corps…and a number of grotesque and attractive floats that would accompany the 3,000 marchers"[87] during their procession through the City's east side.

Altman's efforts to promote the event paid off, attracting large crowds to the downtown parade route in eager anticipation of the festivities. However, inclement weather intervened, with persistent rain escalating to a torrential downpour just minutes before the parade's scheduled start, necessitating its cancellation. Undeterred, Altman swiftly adapted, organizing an impromptu indoor parade at the Broadway Auditorium, featuring 3,000 costumed marchers. Despite the last-minute venue change, Altman hailed the event as "wildly successful," demonstrating his ability to pivot effectively and maintain the spirit of the celebration under challenging circumstances.[aa]

Not everyone was happy that the parade had been cancelled. Weil's Sprudels, the fraternal order of Eagles, and a few other organizations decided to move forward with an unsanctioned event, not wanting to disappoint the spectators who were waiting along the parade route. In total, a few hundred marchers, without a police escort, walked through the streets in their "grotesquely decorated costumes." Additionally, a few water-logged floats came along for the ride, adding a surreal touch to this impromptu procession.

"Their appearance was but a taste of what would have been witnessed under favorable conditions," *The Buffalo Enquirer* wrote.

Inside the Auditorium, Altman welcomed with much fanfare his special guest star from Chicago: Capt. Adrian C. Anson, once a "tower in professional baseball" having played 27 consecutive years in the major leagues.[88] Even in retirement, Anson maintained popularity, owning several businesses in Chicago and a semi-professional baseball team. However, after facing financial difficulties that nearly led to bankruptcy due to his team's expenses, Anson turned to the vaudeville circuit in hopes of recovering from his debts. His appearance in Buffalo was part of this new venture.

Figure 27 Adrian Anson "Cap" Anson, baseball's first superstar, turned to stage work after retirement to recover business losses
PD

[aa] He would also publicly recall how the City of Buffalo's Mardi Gras event faltered after the unfortunate decision to proceed with the parade in the rain.

The fact that Anson could not sing, dance or act did not seem to detract from his show biz popularity. Audiences were eager to see baseball's first superstar. Using a monologue created for him by a devoted baseball fan and showman, George M. Cohan, Anson toured the U.S. playing the role of a living sports legend. His two daughters, Adele and Dorothy, often accompanied him on stage, running props and cheering their father on with little ditties they performed.[89]

Anson's appearance at the Mardi Gras coincided with his week-long appearance at Shea's Theater.

"He is well known in Buffalo and has many friends in the city, the 'old boys' remembering him when Buffalo was in the National League," *The Buffalo Enquirer* stated.

His whereabouts at billiard halls and golf courses while in Buffalo appeared in the feature and sports pages of the daily papers.[90]

Altman's efforts in coordinating the successful event were praised by the event sponsor: "General Manager Harry Altman (sic) was the busiest man at the carnival. The handling of such a vast crowd, the arrangements and the absolute fairness and courtesy extended to all, was the...subject of much favorable comment,"[91] *The Buffalo Enquirer* reported.

This Mardi Gras year proved to Harry that he could recover from past setbacks and successfully navigate a dramatic change of plans. He would need this boost in confidence heading into war time and a worldwide pandemic.

1917—ALTMAN'S EVENTFUL RISE DURING WARTIME

President Woodrow Wilson's declaration in April 1917 that the U.S. would enter World War I against Germany marked a significant shift from the nation's longstanding policy of isolationism. This policy change concluded a period of intense debate within the U.S. about its role on the global stage, reflecting growing concerns about national security, and economic interests that were increasingly tied to global developments.

The decision to enter the war, however, was not merely a selfless act by the U.S. government. It was also influenced by several strategic factors, including the need to protect American ships and citizens from German submarine attacks, which had escalated in the years leading up to the declaration. Moreover, the interception of the Zimmermann Telegram, in which Germany proposed a military alliance with Mexico against the U.S., played a critical role in swaying public opinion and governmental decision-making toward intervention.

With the abandonment of U.S. isolationism, a wave of patriotic fervor swept across the nation, permeating homes and businesses alike. Flags were proudly displayed, Liberty Bonds were purchased, and Liberty Gardens were planted, symbolizing the country's unity and determination to contribute to the cause.

As Congress debated Wilson's war resolution, *The Buffalo Evening News* urged readers to "put out the flag in every business place and home in Buffalo...now is the time to give evidence of your patriotism."[92]   During the coming weeks, "numerous patriotic displays—rallies, mass public meetings, parades, etc.—would be held to show support for the government and to raise the community's spirits."[93]

While the military drafted and trained soldiers for overseas combat, farmers increased their yield, and factories manufactured munitions to sustain and protect U.S. troops on the European battlefield.

Community fundraising went into high gear; by the end of the war, Liberty Loan Bonds sold to the public raised half of the defense department's budget. Buffalo's aggregate total reached $226 million, exceeding its goal by more than 7%.[94]

For a professional organizer like Altman, who had success in coordinating large-scale events, the U.S.'s entry into the war resulted in a boom for business. His photograph was regularly printed on newspaper front pages promoting the latest events he organized.

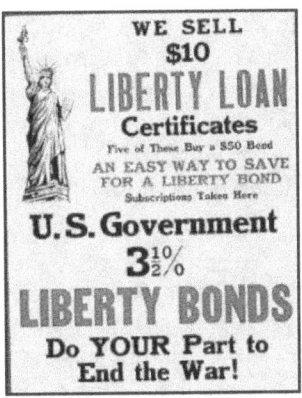

Figure 30 Liberty Bond PDs

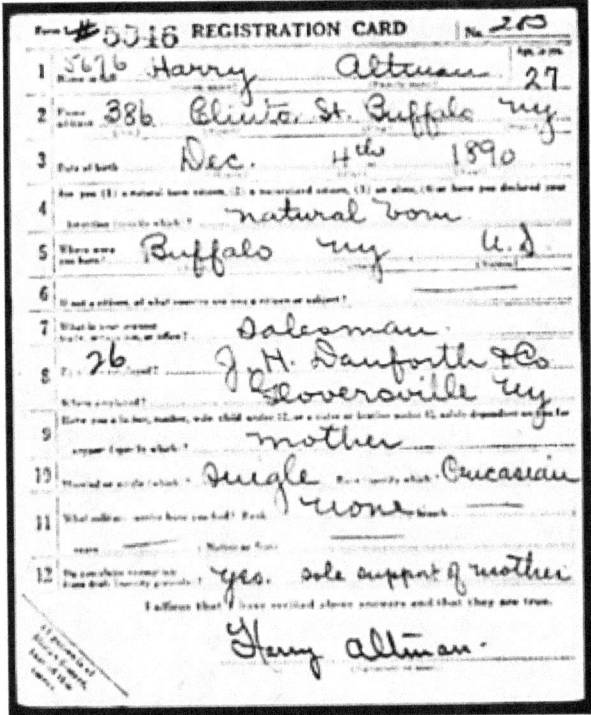

Figure 29 Altman's WWI Draft Card Buffalo Enquirer, May 1917 PD

HARRY ALTMAN, General manager of Buffalo Mardi Gras Co., which will hold a Hallowe'en masquerade ball at Broadway auditorium next Wednesday evening.

Figure 28 Newspaper photo of Harry Altman, General Manager of Buffalo Mardi Gras Co. PD

Conveniently, his job at J.H. Danforth took a backseat since leather was largely unavailable for consumer products. Glove manufacturers who could retrofit their operations were supplying goods for the war effort.

Harry did his patriotic (and legal) duty by registering for the draft. He listed his address as 386 Clinton Street, Buffalo (his mother's house), and his occupation as salesman for the J.H. Danforth company. He stated on the registry certificate that he was the "sole support of mother," which exempted him from military service.

The large German population of Buffalo was either supportive or silent about the American war effort; nevertheless, anti-German sentiment was rife.[95] Mayor Fuhrmann,[bb] son of German immigrants, did his best to alleviate the tension in the community. At a patriotic event in Elmwood Music Hall, he proclaimed that "Regardless of racial antecedents, there is and must be only one kind of Americans in America ... Americans who are willing to make every sacrifice of life and treasure necessary in the common effort to uphold the integrity of our country."[96]

Despite the strain of the war effort, popular entertainment remained freely available throughout the region. Plays, theater, music, and other amusements helped soften the hard edges of reality that now faced the nation.

The first order of business for Altman was organizing a May 1917 fundraiser for the Red Cross Base Hospital being mobilized for eventual deployment to France near the German border. Buffalo's chapter was tasked with raising $75,000 to support the battlefield hospital. More than 900 guests attended the event at the Broadway Auditorium, raising $5,000. Altman had secured the first public performance by The Cantors of Buffalo who were backed by a 20-piece[97] orchestra. The vaudeville-style fundraiser included variety acts by comedians, singers, and musicians.[98]

Entertainment for the troops was also in high demand. Altman was hired to help organize a large vaudeville-style show for the officers' training camp at Fort Niagara. The festivities in Sept 1917 featured 30 entertainers from local theaters and restaurants, all of whom volunteered their talents to the effort. *The Buffalo Enquirer* sponsored the event.

"The government is making an effort to give the boys a substitute for the old canteen and other forms of entertainment that [had] proven to be obnoxious in the past," *The Buffalo Enquirer* reported.[99]

Social events held in the general community were being hampered by the rapid decline in male participation due, in large part, to the draft, as well as the long hours required in factories serving the defense industry. Attracting a largely female audience to an event was critical, so Altman got to work developing special promotions. On September 13, 1917, *The Buffalo Enquirer* announced it would again host its annual Grotesque Parade and Mardi Gras Ball in early October.[100]

[bb] Fuhrmann's attempt for a third term was unsuccessful, partially due to prevailing anti-German sentiment. He was defeated by George Buck, an Anglo-American who was educated at Yale Law.

"Patriotism" would be the theme of the Broadway Auditorium event."[101] The Altman-inspired "Liberty Girl" contest received extensive publicity in the press. Registered contest applicants were featured with a story and photograph in the newspapers leading up to the event. The winner would be determined by a popularity contest at the carnival. The crowned "Liberty Girl"[cc] would win $50 in gold, and a fully paid trip to Spartanburg, South Carolina to deliver money, tobacco and other items to Buffalo soldiers stationed at the military training center at Camp Wadsworth.

Based on newspaper reports at the time, the parade proved a success despite the "nasty drizzle" as "massive" crowds lined the route as early as an hour prior to its start. Not surprisingly, participation by the Spruedel organizations declined, but many other civic groups filled the void, marching along with several bands, floats, decorated automobiles, and drum corps.

For reasons known only to him, Altman decided that the sounds of bombs would announce the start of the parade, accompanied by "a red fire display never before equaled in the city" that would continue along the entire route.[102]

One hundred and seventy-one dollars (and two Socialist Party buttons) was raised for the Soldiers' Smoke Fund by passing the hat among the spectators. Leading the parade was Miss Liberty (not to be confused with "Liberty Girl"), dressed in a gown composed of $3,000 in bills of various denominations.

That evening, the costumes drawing the most admiration featured two young siblings, aged 5 and 8, who were dressed as a Red Cross nurse and a wounded soldier. The soldier costume included a sign on the boy's back stating, "Somewhere in France," adding a poignant touch to their outfits.

The carnival had the usual line up of cabaret singers, food, drink, and dance music. The celebrity guests featured singer Jack Norworth[dd] and actress Lillian Lorraine, stars of the revue, "Odds and Ends of 1917," which was playing at the Teck theater that week.[103]

Altman took the opportunity to poll the "thousands" of participants at the "very successful Mardi Gras" to decide whether to host a masquerade ball in three weeks' time, keeping alive the Halloween tradition. The voters supposedly gave Harry the green light, prompting him to quickly pull together the costumed ball at the Broadway Auditorium on Oct. 31st. The event ended up being a mere shadow of its former self with low attendance, and only $250 in Liberty Bond prizes to sweeten the costume prizes. As custom dictated, cabaret entertainment and dancing continued throughout the evening.[104]

Despite a poor turnout at the Masquerade Ball, Altman remained resolute and planned one final event for 1917. He "engaged his competent corps of assistants"[105] to organize "The Grand Ball" on December 13th, which featured exhibition dances by A. Patton Gibbs & Joy Gardner, culminating in a "moonlight" dance. However,

---

cc Mrs. Michael Algase, wife of a popular Newsboy.
dd Norworth was a vaudeville singer who wrote "Take Me Out to the Ballgame."

with no media sponsorship and the public weary from a year of war and frequent events, the Broadway Auditorium was notably underattended that evening.

As the New Year dawned, Altman decided he would need time to re-group, hoping for better times ahead.

1918—A YEAR OF UNEXPECTED EVENTS

While Altman was devising his next strategy, Wallens, having lost his lawsuit against Harry, teamed up with John Banks to launch a cabaret named Belvedere Café on West Eagle Street in Buffalo. This venue, one of Buffalo's early cabarets, offered intimate dining with live entertainment.

Despite its popularity, the Belvedere Café's tenure was brief. Wallens and Banks often found themselves at odds with the city's Police Chief and Mayor due to violations of the Blue Laws. Tensions escalated significantly on New Year's Eve 1918 following a robbery in the basement. Reports indicate that a woman lured two male patrons downstairs, where they were then robbed by an armed assailant. Wallens and Banks decided not to call the police, choosing, instead, to handle the matter themselves. However, the victims filed a police report, which led to the assailant's arrest and ultimately gave cause for the City to revoke Belvedere's liquor license later that year.

Following the Belvedere's closure, Wallens turned to dealing in liquor, a daring choice of profession as the start of Prohibition was approaching. Before the Volstead Act even went into effect, Wallens found himself in legal hot water. In December 1918, he and Max Jacobson, who ran a liquor store on Seneca Street, were apprehended in Detroit for flouting Michigan's dry laws.[ee] Authorities found 24 pints of whisky in their hotel room.

While Wallens faced escalating legal troubles that foreshadowed a tumultuous decade ahead, Altman turned his attention to more hopeful horizons. As news emerged that the "War to end all Wars" was approaching its end, Altman meticulously planned a significant city-wide celebration. He envisioned starting with a grand military parade down Main Street, where thousands of spectators would cheer, grateful that the conflict had concluded. The procession would eventually reach the Broadway Auditorium, where returning soldiers would be warmly greeted by the women who had been waiting for their safe homecoming.

The event was set to be the biggest event Harry had ever organized; one he hoped would be remembered in the annals of the City's history. Timing was all important. He monitored the war effort and listened to the rumors about when the armistice would be signed, and victory declared by the allies.

Hope for peace hung in the air all spring and summer. By fall, the tension grew as headlines proclaimed the allies' triumphant battles on the western front. As the

---

[ee]Michigan led the way in the temperance movement in the United States, banning the manufacture and sale of alcohol in 1919.

seasons began to shift, so did the peoples' mood as the first symptoms of the Spanish Flu were being reported throughout Buffalo. Areas of the country where the deadly pathogen had already made its presence found the only defense against this virile threat was social isolation and the restriction against large public gatherings.

Harry's plans for a grand victory celebration dimmed as the public health crisis took hold. Patience, never Harry's strong suit, would need to be nurtured in the face of the pandemic.

THE SPANISH FLU

The 1918-1919 Spanish Flu epidemic was a worldwide phenomenon, taking the lives of more than 50 million people—far exceeding the military and civilization casualties in WW I.

Figure 31 Spanish Flu
PD

The Spanish Flu is believed to have originated in March 1918 at a military training camp in Kansas where crowded living conditions and poor infection control measures allowed the virus to propagate. From there, the disease was spread by soldiers deployed to Europe and other military installations throughout the country.

In early summer, civilians were becoming infected by the dangerous contagion. It crept into Buffalo in September 1918, before running rampant through the densely populated neighborhoods, leaving a trail of despair and urgency in its wake.

On October 4th, Buffalo Mayor George Buck closed all schools, places of worship, and other public spaces: "[More than] 1,700 new cases were reported on the first day of the closure order, with 53 new deaths. Casket makers could not keep up with demand; their usual capacity was 30 per day, but the number of epidemic deaths alone far surpassed that."[106]

By the end of October, the Buffalo epidemic crested with more than 22,000 cases reported and 1,800 deaths,[107] a mortality rate of 8%.[108] Its primary victims were the very young (under 5 years) and healthy young adults (20- 40 years of age). Symptoms came suddenly and were severe, leaving little time for the afflicted to seek treatment or quarantine, rapidly overwhelming local healthcare providers.

Altman's Mardi Gras Company which had been scheduled for October 31st was postponed until November 7th due to the "invasion of the Spanish influenza in Buffalo."[109]

"This will in no way change the plans of the management," Altman said. "The Halloween feature will be maintained." He would co-brand the event "The Dance of the Allies," emphasizing a patriotic theme.[110]

Harry would ultimately end up cramming multiple themes into the title: "Dance of the Allies: The Biggest Masquerade Carnival Ever."

TWO DANCES, ONE WAR

Fortunately for Harry, the progression of the epidemic seemed to align with his planned date of November 7th. Although new influenza cases were still being reported each day, local health and civic leaders officially declared the Buffalo epidemic at its end on November 1st. While the disease's deadly impact had been profound, the time it spent in the Buffalo region was relatively short-lived.

Altman also rescheduled the large military parade that would consist of 500 naval officers, 300 soldiers attached to the motor convoy service, detail men on horseback, a band, and a drum corp. They all would march from the McKinley Monument in downtown Buffalo to the Broadway Auditorium to "join the other merrymakers" at the "biggest Masquerade Ball" ever held in Buffalo.[111]

Figure 32 Military Parade Down Main Street
PD

To ensure that the Army and Navy men would enjoy the festivities, Altman had newspaper stories published with the headline: "Girls Wanted for 'Dance of the Allies.'"[112]

"All that is needed to make this dance a great success is plenty of girls," said Lieutenant Donnelly, commander at the naval barracks. "The boys are ready for a big time.... They are a fine bunch of young men and Buffalo's girls will find them the best dancers they ever saw."[113]

Seemingly blessed by the gods, Altman's timing appeared to work out perfectly. On the morning of November 7th, newspapers throughout the country began to report that the armistice had been signed. Altman's plans to bring his Victory Day events sprang to life.

That evening, the sailors marched, and the soldiers rode their military vehicles through Buffalo's east side to the Broadway Auditorium. Altman estimated that a crowd of 10,000 lined the one-mile parade.[114] Inside were costumed contestants vying for prizes, and several hundred women were there to greet the servicemen.

The "Dance of the Allies," featuring Webb's Jazz Band, was successful, but it would not formally commemorate the war's conclusion. Sparked by a misunderstanding or miscommunication from Europe's western front, the war had not ended as the newspapers had earlier reported. November 7th would forever be known as the "False Armistice Day."

Harry was not put off by the blunder, although it was widely reported that the public was confused and disappointed once the truth was clarified.

In Altman's eyes, the real armistice day would give him an opportunity to host yet another dance. He immediately got to work, sending out press releases hedging his bets that the war would end on November 11th: "Victory Dance Next Monday If Peace is Declared."[115]

The Buffalo Enquirer wrote: "If peace is declared Sunday night or Monday morning, a 'victory' dance will be held Monday evening …under the auspices of the Mardi Gras Company which conducted the very successful 'Dance of the Allies.'"[116]

Altman is quoted in the article: "We believe that the thousands who celebrated the false peace rumors last Thursday night will be more than eager to enter into a patriotic outburst when the genuine news is given out."[117]

Altman assured the public that the short timeline to complete the "extensive preparations" for the second dance would not be a problem. Blossom Seeley, a vaudevillian singer who was headlining at Shea's Theater that week, would lead the indoor Victory March, and Webb's Jazz Band would be "re-engaged" to provide the music.[118]

WEBB'S JAZZ BAND—ALTMAN'S FIRST HOUSE BAND

Altman's legendary success as an impresario relied primarily on his uncanny ability to spot budding stars before they hit the mainstream. His first notable discovery traces back to 1919, when he stumbled upon Harry E. Webb and his jazz ensemble.

Born in Buffalo, Professor Webb (an honorary title bestowed upon those with exceptional musical prowess) initially honed his craft busking alongside fellow jazz musicians in downtown Buffalo, pulling an audience for selling Liberty Bonds in Lafayette Square. Altman convinced the quintet to make their indoor debut at Broadway Auditorium at the 1917 Mardi Gras, catapulting Webb's quintet into the limelight, where they quickly garnered a devoted following.

By all accounts, Webb was the director of Altman's first house band.

Guided by Webb's leadership as both violinist and director, the band showcased talents including Ray Brost/Henderson on piano, John Webb on drums and saxophone, Joseph Colby on banjo, and Harold Sturr on saxophone.[119] Evolving into Webb's Novelty Band, celebrated for its fusion of music and comedy, the group garnered widespread acclaim across Western New York and southern Ontario.

Figure 33 Photo of Harry E. Webb
PD

The newly rebranded "Harry Webb and His Entertainers" landed a coveted RKO vaudeville circuit contract following a successful stint at Lowe's. After several three-year contract extensions, Webb ended his entertainment career just before World War II at the Hippodrome Theater, sharing the stage with luminaries such as Bob Hope and Ken Murray.[120]

In later years, he would become renowned for his portrait and commercial photography, owning a studio in New York City.[121]

ARMISTICE TERMS SIGNED BY GERMANY AT 5 O'CLOCK
HOSTILITIES CEASE 11 A. M.

Washington, Nov. 11.—The world war will end this morning at 6 o'clock Washington, 11 o'clock Paris time. The armistice was signed by the German representatives at midnight. This announcement was made by the state department at 2.50 o'clock this morning.

GERMAN PEOPLE HAVE SPOKEN NEW WORD AND OLD GERMANY IS GONE

William, Kaiser and King, Strip ped of His Power

A FUGITIVE IN HOLLAND

Virtual Ending of Greatest Con flict in History Has Come With Dramatic Swiftness

REVOLT, FAMINE, ANARCHY

IF THE ARMISTICE IS SIGNED WILL OUR WAR PROGRAM BE CHECKED

Would Such a Course Be Safe for the Military Arm?

DIFFERENCE OF OPINION

Some Men in Congress Believe When Armistice Is Signed En trenchment Should Begin

MILITARY MEN AGAINST IT

IN TERRIFIC FIGHTING THE AMERICANS ON SUNDAY TOOK STENAY ON BANK OF MEUSE

German Ex-Emperor Is Now in Holland

BRITISH HAVE CROSSED FRANCO-BELGIAN FRONT SOUTH OF THE SAMBRE

They Have Advanced Four Miles East of Renaix

IN GUNFIRE OF BRUSSELS

Figure 34 Headline Announcing the War Over
News & Record, November 11, 1918
PD

On the morning of November 11th news of the real Armistice was broadcast, and spontaneous celebrations erupted across the country. Twelve hours after the announcement, Altman and team had the Broadway Auditorium ready for the celebration.

The Buffalo Enquirer declared the dance a "success with 8,000 lovers of dancing enjoying themselves to the utmost."[122]

A key moment of the event was the "grand, high executioner at the hanging of the Kaiser, which caused much merriment."[123] Following the "disposal" of his imperial Majesty, "the hall was darkened and the band struck up 'the Star-Spangled Banner,' while a powerful spotlight was thrown upon a large oil painting of President Wilson," reported *The Buffalo Enquirer*.[124]

"When the national anthem was concluded the crowd broke into the greatest cheering ever heard in the hall. It lasted for five minutes."[125]

While Altman would be extolled for his successful nightclub operations in the decades to come, orchestrating two highly successful and well-attended events in less than 10 days may be the high point of his career. At the age of 26, he demonstrated formidable leadership qualities, tirelessly working around the clock, relying solely on the earnings from his latest success for investment. He emerged as a singular force of nature, showcasing his ability to manage large-scale events at a significant venue, leveraging the political and business networks he had diligently nurtured.

And the year was not even over yet. His dance card remained full.

CURTAIN CALL FOR A BANNER YEAR

On December 3rd Altman organized a benefit for the Kehillah of Buffalo. Titled the "Victory Celebration—Chanukah Festival," the Broadway Auditorium was again selected as the venue. Patrons paid 50 cents, with proceeds going to various Jewish charities.[126] The event featured vaudeville performers, musical acts, and moonlight dancing throughout the night.

Nine days later on December 12th, he was back at the Broadway Auditorium to host the "Dance of the Aces," sponsored by the Aircraft Club of the Curtiss Aeroplane & Motor Corporation.[127]

It was a prestige event to celebrate the most important U.S. aircraft manufacturer of the war. Founded by aviation pioneer Glenn Curtiss in Hammondsport, NY, the company moved its headquarters to Buffalo just prior to the war, employing 18,000 workers. The company was instrumental in building a variety of aircraft for the Allies in World War I, most famously the Curtiss JN-4, known as the "Jenny." This biplane was widely used for training U.S. and Canadian military pilots.

The program for the event was much more eclectic than Altman's usual fare. In addition to seven vaudeville acts and the music of the omnipresent Webb's Jazz Band, the first showing of a film featuring the "daring exploits of American 'aces'" in France was presented.[128] An exhibition drill of the Tenth Division, Motor Transport Corps. proved to be a crowd favorite, as was the appearance of a German Albatross airplane that had been shot down inside the French lines.[129]

Four thousand Curtiss employees were on hand that night, joined by hundreds of members of the public who paid the 50-cent admission charge.[130]

For Harry personally, December ended on a joyous note. Using his contacts in the entertainment community, he hosted a "a farewell social gathering" for his bride-to-be, Annabelle, and her mother at his brother Abe's home on Walnut Street. Mother and daughter were planning their return home to Toledo after being the houseguests of Morris Altman and his wife on Bird Avenue.[131]

Harry acted as master of ceremonies in presenting Webb's Novelty Entertainers, and various vaudeville performers. Dancing and refreshments were offered to family and friends, capping off a spectacular and eventful year for Altman.

1919—ALTMAN'S PERPETUAL CALENDAR

The year commenced with the wedding of Harry Altman and Annabelle Rosen on February 25, 1919 at the home of Annabelle's parents on Franklin Avenue in Toledo, Ohio.[132] Annabelle was the daughter of Henry and Rachel (Jacobson) Rosen, both Russian immigrants. For 60 years, her father owned and operated Henry Rosen and Co., a scrap iron and waste dealer. The Rosens had eight children and were the co-founders of the B'nai Israel Congregation in Toledo.

Rabbi J.M. Silberman from B'nai Israel solemnized the wedding. The groom was 27, and the bride, 23. Annabelle had seven bridesmaids, including her two sisters, Nettie and Bess. Following the reception, the couple left for an "extended eastern trip,"[133] and were expected to return home to Buffalo on April 1st.

Altman asked Henry E. Hyman to serve as his best man. Hyman, like Harry, had a strong sales background and high aspirations. Just a couple years earlier Henry

USE YOUR
CREDIT

TO INTRODUCE OUR CONFIDENTIAL
CREDIT SYSTEM

We Are Offering to the Public for SATURDAY ONLY
1 Genuine Leather Roll—18 Piece French
Ivory Manicuring Set for

$7.48

Only One to A Customer

Just Pay   EVERY
A Small Sum $1 WEEK
Down   OR SO!

Diamonds, Watches and Jewelry

Court Jewelry Shop, Inc.
24 COURT STREET
Corner Court and Pearl   Opposite Denton, Cottier & Daniels

Figure 35 Court Jewelry Shop
PD

had started the "Hyman Arcade Company," selling coin-operated movie projectors that played short films or "vaudeville" acts.[ff]

Hyman's father, Edward L. Hyman, was also in the entertainment industry, having been employed for years by Michael Shea. He would eventually become a vice president of the distribution unit of Paramount Pictures.[134]

In August 1919, Harry and Annabelle would invest in another business, joining with Albert Miller[gg] to open the "Court Jewelry Shop" at 24 Court Street, Buffalo. At the beginning, the store was little more than an upscale pawnshop, later evolving into a reputable jewelry store. Its presence was a convenient downtown headquarters for Altman's many event activities. He used the space for back-office tasks like distributing contest entries and admissions tickets for Mardi Gras.

Altman granted his first newspaper interview on September 27th to the *Buffalo Enquirer*.[135] The article portrayed him as the area's leader in event production, noting that "thousands had attended the four big dances" held under his auspices in the fall of 1918.

He stated in the interview that the Mardi Gras Company "has established a fair reputation in Buffalo," and he announced plans "to energize the dance-loving community with provisions that cater to those seeking to enjoy dancing in an appealing and congenial environment."[136] Just a month earlier, Harry announced his newest initiative: Saturday night dances at the Elmwood Music Hall. These affairs, he assured people, would be "conducted on a high standard" and that only "the best jazz dance music and a variety of other entertainment will be given."[137]

Mardi Gras Co. Has Ambitious Plans on Foot

Next Thursday Night's Sixth Annual Ball But a Forerunner of What is to Come Later On.

"The plans of the Buffalo Mardi Gras company, which will hold its sixth annual "Mardi Gras ball at the Broadway auditorium next Thursday evening, are more ambitious than ever before," said Harry Altman, general manager, last evening. "The thousands who attended the four big dances held under the auspices of our company

Figure 36 Altman's First Newspaper Interview
PD

[ff] Henry's career trajectory ultimately took a turn and he went into retail sales of clothing and other soft goods. Henry would later marry Catherine, a home economics teacher in the Buffalo Public Schools, and settle into a life in retail sales management. It is not known whether he maintained a close relationship with Harry and Annabelle through the years.

[gg] Miller was the husband of Lena (Altman) Miller, daughter of Harry's older brother, Joseph.

The Elmwood Music Hall was a new venue for Altman. Like the Broadway Auditorium, it had been a military arsenal prior to its conversion in 1899 to a public event space. The building, located at the northeast corner of Elmwood Avenue and Virginia Street, served as the City's premier setting for musical performances until it was demolished by the Works Progress Administration (WPA) in the late 1930s.[138][hh]

Figure 37 Elmwood Music Hall
PD

The special guest star for opening night, September 14th, was Lieutenant John W. Bolton and his celebrated war band. Bolton's band, known in Europe as the 55th Pioneer Infantry Band, was the official band of the Third U.S. Army at Koblenz and had entertained troops in the trenches in France. This was the band's first public appearance.[139]

With two venues now to promote, Harry began experimenting with various cross-selling techniques. Selected to publicize Fox Film's "Most Beautiful Girl" contest, he required applicants to register at a Saturday night dance at the Elmwood Music Hall, while the judging was to take place later at the Mardi Gras Carnival in the Broadway Auditorium.

On October 2nd, Altman hosted 6,000 patrons at the Mardi Gras Ball in the Broadway Auditorium. It was promoted as the fall season's first, big public dance.[140]

[hh] Kleinhans Music Hall would replace it in the annals of Buffalo music history when it opened in 1940 on Symphony Circle.

Webb's, as expected, provided the music on the "unusually warm night," and the "Fox Film Beauty Contest" attracted the attention of "thousands of Buffalo's young men who were unable, because of the war, to attend last year's affair."[141]

As the crowd cheered the newly crowned beauty queen, "Miss Hazel Berkebeil, 19, of Bailey Avenue, Buffalo," an audience member stepped forth from the crowd.[142] He whispered to Harry that Hazel was not an amateur contestant but, in fact, a veteran performer on the vaudeville circuit. Altman later learned that Hazel's real name was Olga Paradofska, a Russian émigré, who had been hailed as a "phenomenal child coloratura-soprano" in advertisements published throughout the U.S. Olga had appeared in prestigious halls like the Orpheum in Los Angeles singing classical music alongside her brother, Alado, an accomplished piano accompanist.[143]

Altman, upon learning of the alias, never broke stride. The loving cup was swiftly handed off to Hazel/Olga with the round-trip ticket to New York City for a Fox screen test.

At the event, Harry predicted "a high future for her." However, the beauty contest turned out to be the last time the young singer and her brother were mentioned in public records.

During this era, Altman's work ethic and dedication to his craft were unparalleled. Throughout the latter half of 1919, he managed to produce an impressive lineup of 12 large-scale events over a span of just four months. This feat not only showcased his exceptional organizational skills but also his passion for bringing people together through memorable and meaningful celebrations.

Just two weeks after the Mardi Gras Ball, Altman returned to the Broadway Auditorium for the Halloween Masquerade Ball.

"The plans of the promoters are more ambitious than ever before," *The Buffalo Enquirer* stated in its October 18th edition. "It will be recalled that the flu epidemic prevented the holding of last year's Halloween dance, so the management is doubling its effort this year."[144]

More than 4,500 people attended the event that featured, among other performers, Howard Thurston who was a renowned large-scale magician specializing in elaborate illusions.

For the first time, Altman did not rely on entertainers already in town to headline, instead going to "considerable expense" to hire the magician, while noting that his negotiations skills had scored a triumph: Thurston agreed to pay for his own electricians and mechanics.[145]

Figure 38 Howard Thurston
PD

A parade led by Professor Webb led the costumed participants along a short outdoor route near the Auditorium. Five hundred dollars in prizes were awarded for the best costumes.[146] The band ended the night at 2 AM with "Home Sweet Home."

Altman's last public event for 1919 featured Sergeant Frank J. Gaffney, a Lockport-born Medal of Honor Recipient,[ii] who was the special guest at the Peace Dance/Armistice Day Celebration on November 11th in the Broadway Auditorium. It was Gaffney's first public appearance since he arrived home from WWI, and he was in full dress uniform wearing decorations from nearly all the allied countries. Accompanying him were several local members of his former company.[147]

Gaffney received his military honors following an incident while on patrol near Ronssoy, France. He was an Army private then, and the only member of his squad that had survived a ruthless attack. Now alone on the front lines, he discovered several Germans placing a heavy machine gun in position and killed the crew with his automatic weapon, capturing the gun and bombing several dugouts. He held the position until reinforcements came. As a result of his heroism, 80 Germans were captured.[jj]

Also appearing at the event was Olive Thomas (Pickford), a popular Hollywood silent-film actress, model, and member of the Ziegfeld Follies.[kk] She presented the loving cup to the couple winning the "Upstairs and Down" fox trot contest. Webb's provided the music.

To end the year, Harry and Annabelle welcomed Little Miss Altman[148] on November 18th. The family were living on 783 Potomac Avenue in Buffalo. They named the baby Natalie Adele.

Figure 39 Olive Thomas
PD

1920—PROHIBITION TAKES THE STAGE

Within the span of 12 months, Altman surrendered to domestic life, and was now supporting both his wife and their newborn baby

After relentless hard work throughout the latter half of 1919, Altman was finally taking a moment to pause to enjoy his new family. It was during this time that his employer, J.H. Danforth, came calling. Now that the war was over, the company had resumed manufacturing consumer goods and needed Harry back on the road.

---

ii Gaffney's story is the subject of the book "He Charged Alone," by John Strasberg, published by LuLo (June 19, 2022).

jj Gaffney's war medals are on display at the Niagara County Courthouse.

kk Olive died a year later after ingesting her husband's topical syphilis medication. She was 25. This was one of the first big Hollywood scandals; her husband was actor/director/producer Thomas Pickford, brother of Mary Pickford.

Since the last time Altman and his sample case had traveled to the Midwest, he had become a seasoned business owner, single-handedly leading a team of per diem workers to produce spectacular events under tremendous time pressure.

After a few false starts in previous years with the Gloversville company, Harry was finally ready to commit to a new business arrangement. As reported in the trade paper *The Glover Review,* he announced in January 1920 that he was "opening his own account" with his long-time employers.[149] Under this arrangement, he would now purchase leather goods directly from the company at wholesale prices, allowing him to retain the full profit margin upon their sale. This marked a significant shift towards independence and financial self-reliance.

This new "on account" arrangement offered a financial advantage but also bore some risk. His ability to correctly predict the volume of the product he could sell would be vital as excess inventory could prove financially ruinous if buyers were scarce.

Filled with the assurance that comes from recent triumphs, he reentered the world of glove sales as an independent traveler. Departing from Buffalo in late January, he set off on an eight-week sales trip, returning with substantial earnings.

His success was noted in a small, front-page item in *The Buffalo Enquirer.*

Figure 40 Jack Yellen
PD

"Harry Altman returns from a two months' trip on the road selling gloves and cleans up so much in commissions he is thinking of leaving his partner at the Court Jewelry store. We hear Jack Yellen the songwriter is in town, and that he is looking for Harry to back his next musical comedy. Jack is in on a new hit on Broadway and they will clean up big."[150]

This small article hit several sweet notes for Altman. It referenced to his jewelry business, his success as a glove salesman, and his friendship with Jack Yellen who also grew up in Buffalo's east side (they were one year apart in age). Yellen had found success early in his career, becoming one of the most popular lyrists in the 20th century, writing such hits as "Happy Days are Here Again," "My Yiddishe Momme," and "Ain't She Sweet."

It should be noted that as Yellen gained national recognition, he never strayed from his origins. He remained active in Buffalo with various Jewish philanthropic organizations throughout his career. Altman often participated in these endeavors, serving most commonly as chairman of the entertainment committee.

Figure 43 Sophie Tucker
PD

While the article humorously suggested that Yellen was seeking financial assistance from Harry, it cleverly associated Altman with a rapidly ascending Broadway star. Harry would continue to capitalize on his relationship with Yellen. Yellen appeared at Harry's request at area fundraisers like the Navy Relief Show during WWII (where Yellen entertained "51,454 persons in the big Best Street bowl"[151] (Civic Stadium)), and prompted Sophie Tucker—for whom Yellen had written many best-selling hits—to headline at both the Glen and Town Casinos.[II]

Altman spent most of 1920 either on the road selling children's gloves or working to organize the annual Mardi Gras event from the west side home he shared with Annabelle and Natalie.

Broadway Auditorium was again the site of the October 6th Mardi Gras, promoted as the event that "opens the winter dance season."[152] There was no parade, but a costume contest was held with $500 in prizes. To spur on ticket sales, a special door prize was added—a round-trip ticket and hotel accommodations to NYC to see the Ziegfeld Follies.[153]

The entertainers for the event were Webb's Novelty Band and Lieutenant John W. Bolton's "popular overseas band."

Figure 41 Broadway Auditorium postcard
PD

For the event, Altman had the floor of the Auditorium scraped and polished to make it "one of the smoothest dancing surfaces in the city." A dance platform could be raised to the level of the balcony so a "close up" of the latest dance steps could be seen from every vantage point.[154]

Despite Prohibition's dampening effect on party-going, the carnival achieved modest success. But Harry could read the writing on the wall and decided to limit his event planning operations. No longer willing to self-fund events, he decided to work only on a flat-fee basis for non-profit organizations looking to host large fundraisers.

He was on to what he hoped were bigger and better things.

[II] Harry Wallens was Yellen's first cousin, another example of how closely knit the Jewish community was in those years.

CHAPTER 4—BETWIXT AND BETWEEN

JOINING THE FAMILY BUSINESS

At the start of 1922, Harry decided to end his tenure with J.H. Danforth for good. He decided, instead, to join forces with his brother, Abe, a well-known figure in the Seneca Street business district, selling men's clothing and shoes.

Together, they launched Bankers' Shoe Stores at 51 Seneca and 12 East Chippewa Streets, focusing on women's footwear. Harry took on the role of managing the day-to-day operations. Meanwhile, his other family venture, the Court Jewelry Shop, was forced to shut down abruptly when a severe windstorm tore off the storefront's facade, along with causing extensive damage throughout the city.[155]

Figure 42 Bankers' Shoe Stores
PD

Over the next couple of years, Harry balanced his time between the shoe business and his passion for event planning. Although he no longer managed the Mardi Gras, he continued to assist various nonprofit sponsors with the annual event, and volunteered as the entertainment director for numerous community organizations.

In early December 1924, Harry branched out on his own to open another women's shoe store, the Lafayette Boot Shop, situated downtown at Main and Lafayette Square beneath the Buffalo Trust Company. His sister, Augusta Evans, was his investor for this venture.[156] The attorney overseeing the incorporation was Abraham N. Carrel, who would become a key figure in Harry's future business endeavors.[157]

LAFAYETTE BOOT SHOP

The grand opening of the Lafayette Boot Shop on December 14th was a great success, as Harry Altman combined his retail expertise with his event-planning skills. Large crowds gathered to see the "Al Jolson's Show Girls," who were hired to model the latest footwear styles.[158]

Figure 44 Altman hired Al Jolson show girls from the Shubert Teck to promote his shoe store, likely paying for their appearance since there was no theater cross-promotion
PD

Figure 43 Ever the showman, Altman used Miss America's appearance at his new Arcadia Ballroom to cleverly cross-promote the shoe store
PD

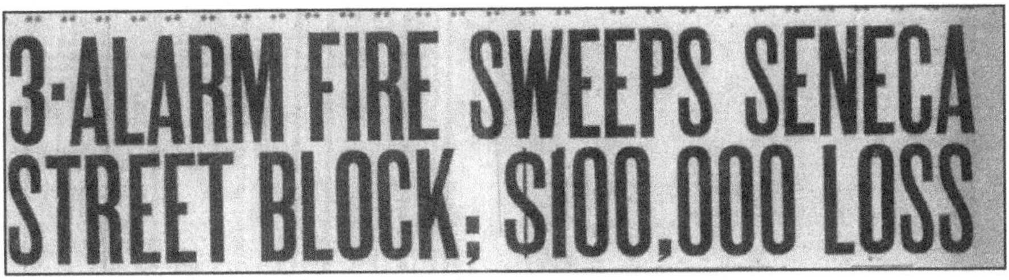

3-ALARM FIRE SWEEPS SENECA STREET BLOCK; $100,000 LOSS

Figure 45 The Buffalo Post, December 31, 1924
PD

Harry's decision to expand beyond the Seneca Street business district proved timely. Just weeks after the Lafayette Boot Shop's grand opening, a devastating fire—one of the most dramatic the area had seen[159]—razed several storefronts and warehouses along Seneca Street. The fire resulted in $100,000 in losses and destroyed most of Abe's business ventures.

In the wake of this setback, the Lafayette Boot Shop became a focal point in Harry's business operations. He used the store as a hub to distribute pre-sale tickets for events at the Broadway Auditorium which helped him boost retail traffic.

During this period, Harry and Anabelle welcomed their second daughter, Hermine, in November 1925. About a year later, the Altman family matriarch, Dora, died in December 1926 at the home of her daughter, Augusta. By then, Dora had lived in the U.S. for 40 years, witnessing all eight of her children marry and begin to assimilate into their new country.

Meanwhile, Harry was growing restless. His natural inclination towards entrepreneurship led him to delegate the general management of the Lafayette Boot Shop to Harry Kessler, allowing him time to pursue other endeavors.[160] He would eventually sell the store outright in November 1928 to Johnnie Fenton after Altman's career in hospitality began to take off.[161] The timing of the sale was fortuitously prescient, as the Stock Market Crash of 1929 struck just months later, leading to the store's financial demise.

This would not be the last encounter with the Fenton family. In less than two years, Altman would secure the intellectual property of Johnnie's more prosperous brother, Nate, when he launched his own version of the Palais Royal. Later, Harry Wallens would partner with another member of the Fenton family in a real estate venture that ultimately bankrupted them both.

Enter Hospitality: Bramson's Café

Harry's entry into the restaurant industry brought him into contact with an influential social circle centered around one of Buffalo's notable landmarks. The Iroquois Hotel, owned by the famed hotelier Ellsworth M. Statler in the late 1910s, was renowned for its luxury, exceptional service, and appeal to high-end patrons. This 11-story building was conveniently located a short distance from Statler's flagship hotel, which was nearing completion at Niagara Square.

Figure 46 Iroquois Hotel
PD

Figure 47 Home of the Bramson's Café
PD

Statler's tenure owning the Iroquois Hotel was brief, as his main objective was to shut it down upon the completion of the Statler Hotel in 1923. This decisive strategy aimed to remove his primary competition and allowed him to hire the Iroquois Hotel's best personnel.[162]

Statler's plans soon changed. Albert H. Bramson, formerly an executive with Statler's organization, quickly took action to transform the vast space into a commercial office building. Because it would not compete with his new hotel property, Statler agreed to hold the mortgage on the newly named Bramson Building while Albert launched an ambitious public stock offering to fund the conversion to commercial space.[163]

As Bramson maneuvered to put the fiscal puzzle pieces in place, he persuaded Max Helfman, a 35-year veteran of the hospitality business and the popular manager of the Olde Iroquois Restaurant,[164] to join him. Bramson sought to have a third-party establish a separate company that would own and operate the dining space that occupied three quarters of the building's first floor.

Helfman, an active member of the Temple Beth El, approached Altman to invest in what would become known as Bramson Café. With Helfman overseeing daily operations, Altman accepted the presidency of Bramson, Inc., joining forces with investors Matt Bramson and Sam Polis.[165]

Under Altman's direction, the restaurant underwent a complete makeover, adopting a "Baronial" design, featuring a striking mural painted in a "vibrant Mardi Gras theme" by Albert Kowalski.[166]

Figure 48 Mayor Frank X. Schwab
PD

On April 12, 1924, more than 200 guests showed up on opening night to enjoy dinner, a musical revue, and a night of dancing by the Bramson Orchestra. *The Buffalo Courier* reported that Buffalo Mayor Frank X. Schwab[a] provided the opening remarks in a "room filled with flowers."[167]

Altman told the newspaper, "The opening was a tremendous success, exceeding my expectations. I'm confident we'll satisfy our customers."[168]

Bramson Café did not last long. Competition from the Hotel Statler's recently opened restaurants proved insurmountable. Despite aggressive marketing and a menu featuring seven-course dinners and five-course lunches,[169] Bramson Inc. went into involuntary bankruptcy four months after its opening, accruing debts of more than $22,000 (roughly $400,000 in 2025 dollars).[170]

The financial fate of the Bramson family followed a similar downturn when the stock offering failed and control of the property reverted to Statler in April 1927.[b] Statler kept it in operation as commercial office space, renaming it the Gerrans Building in tribute to H. Montgomery Gerrans, the Iroquois Hotel's first owner who Statler said was "known as one of the great hotel greeters in the world."[171]

---

[a] Schwab and Altman had a mutual admiration society. Frank consistently promoted Harry's events, while Harry reciprocated by backing Frank's political aspirations. Altman even supplied vaudeville entertainers for Schwab's major fundraiser at the Statler during the 1928 GOP primaries for Governor.

[b] Albert H. Bramson was later convicted in Cleveland of mail fraud and conspiracy charges in connection with sale of oil royalties' certificates. "Heights Man Found Guilty in Oil Land Promotion Fraud," *Plain Dealer*, January 18, 1942, 11.

Statler died in 1928, less than five years after his flagship hotel was completed. The Garrens Building was demolished by the Statler Corporation in 1940, ultimately making way for One M&T Plaza.

Despite the Hotel Statler's role in the closure of the Bramson Cafe, Altman continued to select it as the venue for various charity events in its early years. It was also the site of the high society wedding of his daughter Hermine to her husband, David Goldstein, in 1944. Later, when his nightclubs gained popularity, the hotel became the preferred accommodation for many of the headline entertainers performing at the Town Barn, Town Casino, and—to a lesser degree—the Glen Casino.

Importantly, the Bramson Café offered Harry his initial exposure to restaurant management, a field of endeavor that quickly captivated him. Energized by this new passion, he and a newly found partner swiftly began planning what would emerge as his boldest venture yet in the entertainment industry.

CHAPTER 5—SERIAL ENTREPRENEURSHIP (1925-1935)

Driven by sheer ambition, Harry Altman was a powerhouse of activity, spending up to 18 hours a day juggling multiple business ventures.

No sooner had one business contract been finalized than Altman would show up at his lawyer's office with another, proudly waving a document he proclaimed was "The Best Idea Yet!"

Several of the early enterprises persisted for a few years, but the majority were attempted and subsequently discontinued within months, or even weeks. Old newspaper ads and musty business filings serve as the only evidence of the many projects that ran hot out of the gate before turning to ash.

Harry's approach to business was that of a serial entrepreneur. If the monthly receipts did not prove financially viable, the business was cast aside or, more likely, recast to suit the needs of the latest trend in entertainment. Altman favored leasing buildings with large, open floor plans that could easily be converted into a dance hall or a roller rink or a restaurant/nightclub—whatever Harry thought would pay the bills and attract the money of business partners who could fill the coffers.

For much of this era, he would hopscotch along Main Street in downtown Buffalo, leasing different commercial buildings, sometimes for only a year, to accommodate his various business ventures. He had a small group of investors that he mixed and matched according to the scale of the project and the financial risk each investor was willing to take.

In the early 1920s, Harry shifted his focus to ballroom dancing, capitalizing on its popularity as an affordable form of entertainment during Prohibition and the Depression. Patrons eagerly embraced dancing as a cost-effective way to enjoy themselves during these economically challenging times. The music of the era went far beyond staid waltzes to include lively, upbeat rhythms that celebrated the peace and stability following the victory of a brutal world war.

ARCADIA BALLROOM

In Harry's own origin-story narrative, he frequently identified the Arcadia Ballroom as his first show business venture. This portrayal was echoed by journalists such as Bob Sokolsky, a critic for *The Buffalo Courier-Express*. In his column "In the Spotlight," published two days after Harry's death, Sokolsky wrote: "From that day in 1923(sic) when he opened the Arcadia to the summer of 1965 when he sold his beloved Town Casino, Harry carried on an open affair with show business itself."[172]

BEAUTIFUL *ARCADIA BALLROOM* · BUFFALO'S BEST

Figure 49 The Arcadia Ballroom—indoors
PD

In fact, the Arcadia—where the seed of possibility for a career in nightclubs was first sown—opened more than 15 years after Harry had orchestrated his first Mardi Gras. He spent that decade and a half tirelessly honing his entrepreneurial skills and cultivating the connections necessary to successfully launch his debut venture into the nightlife scene.

The Arcadia Ballroom marked a distinct shift in Harry Altman's business career. Unlike many of his earlier endeavors, the ballroom was not a fresh start. He was there to help rescue the faltering business.

Like the Bramson project, the building that housed the Arcadia at 640 Main Street[a] had architectural import. Built in 1914, architect Edwin Austin Kent designed the Otto-Kent Building.[b] He was prolific during this area, also designing the Cornell House at 484 Delaware Avenue, the Unitarian Universalist Church on Elmwood Avenue, and the original Temple Beth Zion on Delaware Avenue, among others. Architecturally, the Otto-Kent Building is a standout for its Neo-Gothic architecture, characterized by its ornate facade and detailed stonework.

Figure 50 Otto Kent Building
PD

---

[a] Now known as "Theater Place," adjacent to Shea's Buffalo
[b] Kent was the lone Buffalonian who perished on the Titanic in 1912. He reportedly stayed on the ship to help other passengers leave safely. His body was recovered from the ocean near Halifax. He is now buried in Forest Lawn Cemetery.

In 1925 the first floor of the building was leased to Edward Scott, a prominent area roller rink operator, for a total rental fee of $100,000 over five years[173]. He immediately went to work reconstructing the wooden floor on the first floor of the three-story building. He also installed a huge organ that would help entice what he hoped would be the "thousands of Buffalonians who find relaxation and enjoyment in this well-known pastime" of roller skating. The floor space was sizeable: 23,500 square feet, roughly half an acre.

The Grand Central Rink, as the enterprise would come to be called, did not last long. In April 1926, the rink was damaged by a fire started in a radio shop housed in adjoining space. Scott decided then to convert the space to a ballroom.

By September 1926, the necessary repairs were made and the "Arcadia Ballroom" opened under the management of L.O. Beck, a nationally known ballroom operator.[c] Newspaper advertisements promised a "dance palace" that would provide "Toe-Tickling Tunes to Tempt Terpsichoreans" (straining, as they were, to create an alliterative slogan that might slide off a dancer's (terpsichorean's) tongue).

The price for admission and all-evening dance was 75 cents. Carl Fenton's Orchestra ("direct from NYC") was the main opening night attraction.

Beck held the management position for only six weeks before Scott introduced new "local" management and overhauled the pricing model. Moving away from a general admissions fee ("social plan" pricing), Scott implemented the "park plan." This approach, favored by amusement park dance halls, consisted of a minimal entry fee coupled with a small charge for each dance in which participants chose to engage. The strategy was designed to appeal to theatergoers and late diners interested in a few dances before returning home. Additionally, it provided a cost-effective option for spectators just wanting to sit and watch the dancers while enjoying refreshments available for purchase in the ballroom.

Figure 51 Arcadia Ballroom Grand Opening
PD

---

[c] Beck helped build ballrooms throughout Ohio in Cincinnati, Toledo, Cleveland, Akron and Canton.

While attendance saw some improvement in 1926 with the hiring of local management, the revenue figures were still disappointing. At this crucial time, Barneth Satuloff, the president of Temple Beth El and owner of the Otto-Kent building, stepped forward.[d] He enlisted Altman's help to revitalize the project. Accepting the challenge, Altman took over operations at the Arcadia in March 1927. He used his expertise in booking unique entertainment to promote the ballroom and attract more visitors to the building.

Figure 52 Wes Barry PD

One of the novelty performers Altman hired early on[174] was "Wes Barry and his All-Star Act."[e]

Wes, known for his "beet-top" hair and a "million freckles," was a former child actor from the silent film era who was attempting to transition into sketch comedy on stage. To draw larger crowds for Barry's run at the Arcadia, Altman promoted a special free matinee for children, and their accompanying adult, to sample the talents of the All-Star Act. Determined to ensure the event's success, Altman planned to include a competition that would name "Buffalo's champion freckled face kid." He widely promoted this contest through press releases and advertisements, leaving nothing to chance.

Harry's efforts were successful. *Buffalo Courier-Express* reported that even kids without freckles were awaiting Barry's appearance.[175]

"Wes Barry came to Buffalo for the first time yesterday, full of enthusiasm and pleased with the opportunity of seeing Niagara Falls," *The Courier-Express* stated. "Freckles Barry is grown up and married, but ostensibly and apparently, he is still the wistful boy star of Hollywood. Freckles Barry is filling a three-day engagement.[176]

As he would become known for later at the Town and Glen Casinos, Altman would frequently adjust the admission pricing strategy at his venues to maximize both audience size and revenue. On weekends, patrons could opt for either the park plan, paying 25 cents for admission and an additional 5 cents per dance per couple; or choose the "social dancing plan," which allowed unlimited dancing for a flat fee of 50 cents all evening. The strategy was so successful at the Arcadia that Altman tried to patent this combination pricing structure, but to no avail.

---

[d] In addition to his real estate investments, Satuloff was also the owner of Satuloff Brothers, the area's largest poultry concern at the Elk Market Terminal.

[e] The All-Stars included the Lucas Sisters, "twinkle-toe artists" (which was taken to mean professional dancers), and Jimmy Long and his 10-piece harmony band.

Harry's adeptness at event promotion culminated in his becoming a co-owner of the "New Arcadia Ballroom" alongside Scott and Satuloff in January 1927.[177] As Altman crafted the overarching business strategies, a succession of general managers handled daily operations. Under his guidance, the ballroom, with seating for 1,000 spectators around the dance floor, saw further enhancements.

Captain Warmack's Algerians, celebrated for being "a peppy orchestra with distinction and charm," were installed as the house band.[178] To maintain a continuous musical ambiance, Altman introduced a novel setup: whenever nationally recognized orchestras played at the Arcadia, he arranged for a second stage at the opposite end of the venue. This allowed the music to flow seamlessly throughout the event. Additionally, the venue began to feature more novelty acts, including vaudeville performers and renowned dance duos, giving them a spotlight on stage.

Billboard Magazine took notice of the Arcadia in November 1928 when the dance hall featured a "battle of music" between two nationally prominent jazz bands: the Bert Stock Orchestra against Charley Boulanger and his Georgia Melodians.[179] The success of this experiment led to a series of what became known as the "jazz battles."

Bill Coleman (1904-1981), one of the most important jazz trumpeters of the swing era, wrote in his autobiography "Trumpet Story"[180] about playing in a jazz battle at the Arcadia as a member of the Lloyd Scott Orchestra, an important all-black band of the era.

Figure 53 Bill Coleman
PD

He wrote:

"During a one-week engagement Lloyd Scott was hired to fill-in for Warmack's orchestra at the Arcadia. It was the first time they were engaged to play in a dance hall that engaged two orchestras at the same time. The alternating band was an all-white orchestra of 12 members, the Buffalodians,[f] who were well known in the eastern States."

"Jazz battles did not exist then like the ones that would become famous a few years later; still, it was a jazz contest every night," Coleman wrote. "We were not as well known in Buffalo as the Buffalodians who had played in the City for years, but we blew enough to have a big majority of the people applauding for us after each number. The Buffalodians were throwing their best numbers at us, and we were throwing our best numbers back at them."[181]

Coleman also noted that, "Buffalo was the first city that I went to during the Prohibition era that was wide open...the saloons were open 24 hours a day."[182]

The Arcadia was operating successfully until August 1928 when Altman and Scott announced their decision to leave Main Ballroom, Inc., the entity managing the Otto-Kent, to start a new venture at 681 Main Street.[183] This would be the first enterprise Altman operated at the future site of the Town Ballroom. Altman and Scott's departure left Satuloff as sole owner of the Arcadia.

Their departure was prompted by Satuloff's negotiations with Greyhound, which was looking to transform the first floor of the Otto-Kent building into its downtown Buffalo hub. Indeed, by 1930, the space leased by the Arcadia had been converted into the Greyhound Union Station,[184] the second largest motor coach terminal in the eastern U.S.[g]

---

[f] The Buffalodians, a spirited jazz and dance band active in Buffalo during the early 1920s, was known as the original Yankee Six. Led by violinist Jack McGlaughlin and featuring a young Harold Arlen (then Harold Arluck) on piano, the group recorded for Okeh and Columbia Records before disbanding in 1926. Decades later, the name Yankee Six reappeared in Buffalo, unrelated to the original group. This later Yankee Six, led by drummer Eli Konikoff, became known during the 1950s and 1960s for its Dixieland jazz performances at both the Town and Glen Casinos. Though they shared a name—and a city—the two Yankee Six bands belonged to entirely different musical eras.

[g] A decade later, in 1940, Greyhound would build a new terminal across the street at 672 Main Street which would remain in operation until 1972. It would later become a police substation and is now home of the Alleyway Theater. When Greyhound left Otto-Kent in 1940, the first floor of the 640 Main Street building would be converted to leased storefronts, and Harry Wallens would rent space there for his Glass Bar Restaurant and his Midtown Bowling Center.

In the wake of this transition, Altman ramped up his promotional efforts for his new enterprise. He invited WMAK radio listeners to select the name of the new ballroom at 681 Main. Alongside Scott, Harry also involved two more partners, his brother, Charles Altman, and attorney Abe Carrel.[185]

WMAK listeners would select "The Ritz" as the name of the new ballroom.[186]

THE RITZ

Altman had a preference for the name "The Ritz," which he adopted widely throughout his career after legally registering it in 1928. His first ballroom in Glen Park was dubbed "The Ritz Barn," and he carried this name over to a dance hall he later managed briefly in Rochester.[187] Furthermore, he extended the Ritz brand to at least three dance halls in downtown Buffalo, launching each in rapid succession. This consistent use of thematic naming played a key role in establishing Altman's foothold in the dance hall sector during that period.

Figure 54 Abraham N. Carrel, an early Altman investor and becomes his personal attorney Photo courtesy of University Archives, Special Collections, University at Buffalo, SUNY

Figure 55 The Ritz Grand Opening
PD

The original Ritz at 681 Main Street was an exciting project for Altman, offering him the chance to completely renovate the space. Claiming a "substantial investment of $150,000"—about $2.8 million today—Altman, with more imagination than means, remade the property into what he proudly called, "The Spanish Dance Mansion."

The *Buffalo Courier-Express* described The Ritz's décor as "in a Spanish style" with the color scheme of subdued gold and blue. "The furnishings and wall decorations are of the same motif. The ceiling represents a blue sky with concealed lights forming rolling clouds and twinkling stars."[188]

In advertisements, the ballroom was promoted with the tagline: "Time pleasurably flits when you dance at The Ritz."

The opening night of the ballroom on October 26, 1928 was reported by *The Courier-Express* to be "a smashing success."[189] "The capacity of the ballroom was exceeded, with several hundred people being denied admission."[190]

Mayor Frank X. Schwab was on hand to give the signal to start Art Landry's orchestra, a popular 1920s dance band and Victor recording artist. Landry, a clarinetist and saxophonist, also served as the master of ceremonies for the event.

In the humor column, "The Daily Hammer," published in *The Buffalo Times*, editor "K.N. Ocker," took a tongue-in-cheek approach to the proceedings:

> *"At the opening of The Riz ballroom tonight Harry Altman and Eddie Scott will sport Spanish costumes for the event. Neither of them needs the regalia because everyone in town knows they are master bull throwers."*[191]

The excitement of opening night was short-lived. On Monday, Altman discovered that burglars had broken into the ballroom through a skylight and used explosives to blow open the safe in his office. The thieves made off with $3,000 in cash, which represented the entire earnings from the opening weekend. The safe was opened using either dynamite or nitroglycerin, indicating a well-planned heist by the gang.[192]

Harry, despite being deeply affected by the intrusion and subsequent revenue loss, maintained a composed and resilient demeanor in front of the public. Interviewed by *The Buffalo Times* on the eve of Thanksgiving, Altman reported in "The Daily Hammer" column that he was thankful "that those safecrackers took only money and were kind enough to leave me the ballroom."[193]

PALAIS ROYAL

Nate Fenton (nee Fernandez) exemplified the type of philanthropist Harry Altman aspired to become.

A Brooklyn Jew of Holland/Dutch Portuguese descent, Fenton built a small restaurant empire in New York City, Long Island, and Buffalo. In the early 1920s, his Palais Royal fine dining establishment at 752 Main Street in downtown Buffalo featured eight-course dinners accompanied by the likes of Jimmie Morgan's Orchestra, a regional favorite that performed music popular of the era, including jazz, swing, and dance.

Fenton promoted the Palais Royal as "Buffalo's Greatest Show Business Restaurant."

But it was Fenton's philanthropy that made him a standout, often featured in newspaper articles extolling his generosity. When he died in January 1924 of cancer at age 65, the city mourned. "Thousands of Buffalo's poor and needy lost a philanthropic friend," *The Buffalo Enquirer* wrote in his obituary.[194]

Figure 56 Palais Royal interior
PD

One of his principal charity events was the annual Nate Fenton Christmas dinner for "the poor and down-and-outers" that he held each year at the Broadway Auditorium.[195] Everyone enjoyed the "real turkey and trimmings," while every child received a pair of new shoes, mittens, and underclothing.[196] Fenton also established a soup house on North Division Street that fed hundreds of unemployed who had been going hungry.

Despite being a generation younger, Harry saw himself reflected in Fenton. They were both business savvy businessmen of Jewish heritage, members of Temple Beth El and the Elks, and had limited educational backgrounds, relying instead on their street smarts.

After Fenton's death, the Palais Royal Restaurant struggled to survive without its popular proprietor. The Stock Market Crash of 1929 sealed its fate. Seizing on the failure of the Fenton enterprise Altman rebranded 681 Main ("The Ritz") as the new Palais Royal.

Forty years later, Altman's obituary in the *Buffalo Courier-Express* made mention of this quick change, calling out Altman's agility to alter course during "the free spending era of the 20s" when jazz, blues singers, torch singers, sweet and hot music all become popular.[197]

Needing additional capital to rebrand The Ritz, Altman recruited two new partners, both veterans of the saloon business: Bernard Elliott and Harvey "Speedy" Anderson. While Altman, Scott, and Carrel had reputable business pedigrees, the new recruits had extensive law violations in connection with owning drinking establishments.

Elliott[h], who would go on to invest in many future Altman projects, operated Elliott Brothers Tavern at 194-198 Pearl Street, and the Grand Island Ferry Saloon. Buffalo newspapers of the era (1910-30) reported on Elliott's frequent citations for various law enforcement violations by local police and the New York State Liquor Authority.

Speedy Anderson, a boxing manager and saloonkeeper at 6 Elk Street, received front-page news coverage during his federal trial for selling and transporting 1,000 cases of whiskey. [198] The court found him guilty, sentenced him to prison, and fined him $500; his three-month sentence was overturned on appeal. Anderson was later implicated in a rum-running operation on Grand Island.[199]

By bringing Elliott and Anderson into his group of investors, Altman inadvertently drew unwanted attention, prompting the police to watch the new Palais Royal closely. It was not long before law enforcement raided the restaurant.

On January 2, 1930, 20 dry agents rushed into the Palais Royal as "the orchestra was rollicking strains of the fox trot" and the "dance floor was awhirl with couples."[200] The front-page article in *The Buffalo News* reported that the raid threw the "patrons and employees" of Buffalo's "gayest and most widely known cafes" into a "near panic."[201]

"Everybody in the restaurant thought the raiders were bandits and that a wholesale robbery was being staged." *The Buffalo News* reported. "Ten or 15 minutes were required to quiet the fears of the guests and attaches of the place and convince them that the visitors were federal officers."[202]

Business was immediately suspended, but the agents detained the guest for five hours to investigate every person who was in the building when they arrived.[203]

"Every nook and cranny of the restaurant was scrutinized," the paper reported.

Altman, Elliott and Abe Bergson, the headwaiter, were ordered to appear before Richard H. Templeton, U.S. District Attorney for questioning. [204] Anderson, who was not at the Palais Royal when the place was raided, did not join them.

In the end, it amounted to nothing, as no incriminating evidence against the restaurant management was found.

By October of that year, the ownership team was downsized. The Ell-Alt Restaurant Corporation, now consisting of Altman, Elliott and Carrol, took over the operation of the Palais Royal.

---

[h] Elliott was close friends with Paddy Lavin (nee Patrick Stynes), the former boxer who bought Simon Altman's tavern before he left for Los Angeles. Ellott served as Lavin's pall bearer after Lavin "met death" when an auto he was driving "turned turtle" during a visit downstate. He was 34. "Pay Last Respects to Patrick Stynes," *The Buffalo Times,* September 20, 1920, 20.

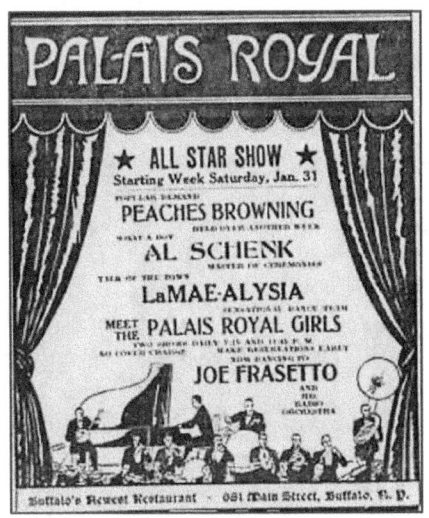

Following in Fenton's philanthropic footsteps, Altman and Elliott hosted the annual Christmas feast in 1930 for 1,700 "families who might otherwise have to do without Christmas dinner," at Palais Royal. More than 100 employees of the restaurant donated their services to the cause.[205] This act of generosity helped propel Altman's career-long commitment to charitable causes. Just weeks later as the tragic impact of the Depression lingered on, he joined other downtown merchants in supporting the all-star show at Shea's Buffalo, benefiting the Mayor's Committee on Unemployment Relief. The Palais Royal contributed by donating the services of its stage talent to the show.[206]

Figure 57 Palais Royal Menu
PD

These charitable events fueled Altman's rising star, but there was a dark side to his success during this era. The safe-cracking incident at The Ritz in October 1928, followed by the police raid at the Palais Royal in January 1930, marked the beginning of the most challenging decade of Altman's career. During this period, he faced escalating violence, severe financial pressures, and the destruction of several commercial properties by fire.

Yet, despite these devastating setbacks, he soldiered on.

PALAIS ROYAL—THE SUMMER HOME

Downtown Buffalo dining establishments often suffered financially during the hot summers. Without commercial-grade air conditioning patrons were hesitant to don their finest clothing to dine and dance in the suffocating heat.

To address the problem, Altman and Elliott decided to rent out a large ballroom on the breezy banks of Lake Erie just south of Buffalo. In the spring of 1932, they inaugurated the "Summer Quarters of the Palais Royal" at the location previously occupied by The Alhambra nightclub on Old Lake Shore Road/Route 5 in Athol Springs.

Figure 58 Alhambra advertising
PD

The property, developed in 1922, was built to accommodate 1,000 "Buffalo Beach" bathers with its numerous changing rooms and storage lockers on the lower ground floor. Above, 1,000 patrons could dance in its spacious hall. Resembling a Moroccan castle from the exterior, the original investors lost control of the property after a bank foreclosure that occurred shortly after a severe storm destroyed the below-ground changing rooms.

One original investor, Edward Antonucci, a native of Genoa in northwest Italy, was determined not to give up. He decided to reopen the venue solely as a nightclub. Due to his lack of hospitality experience, Club Alhambra struggled to achieve significant success. Nevertheless, the building attracted the attention of Altman and Elliott who were looking to lease property that would serve as Palais Royal's summer home.

In early 1932, Antonucci handed over the keys,[i] and on May 14th, the Palais Royal of Athol Springs opened to rave reviews. However, the good press was short-lived.

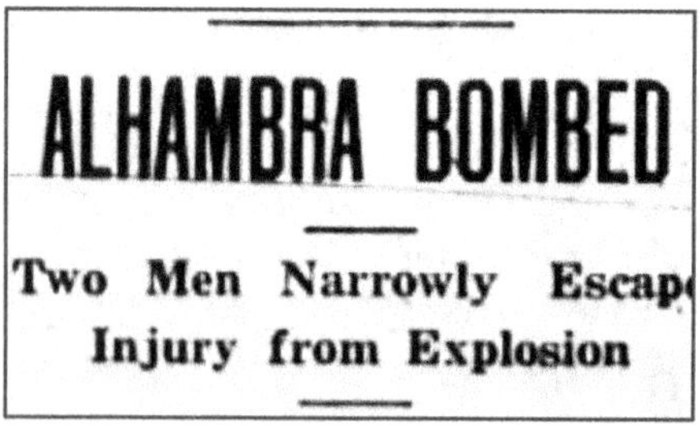

ALHAMBRA BOMBED

Two Men Narrowly Escape Injury from Explosion

Figure 59 The Sun and Erie County Independent
May 26, 1932
PD

Just one week later, at 5 a.m. on May 21st, a bomb ripped through the building, nearly killing two attendants from Buffalo, Anthony Areno and Michael Pascoe, who were asleep inside.[207]

Elliott told police it was fortunate the boys were on the upper floor, as they had previously "been sleeping in quarters adjacent to the kitchen, right alongside the part of the building that was bombed." The young men initially reported to police that they thought the boiler had exploded.[208]

The dynamite ordnance that caused the explosion heavily damaged the west wing of the building, shattering a dozen windows, ripping plumbing from the wall and floor of the men's room, and wreaking "extensive damage to the kitchen." The blaze that resulted from the explosion was quickly extinguished.

Police estimated the damage at $25,000. Elliott reported no conflicts or issues with any individual or group that might have planted the bomb. After his investigation, Sergeant William L. Ireland of the New York State Troopers stated that the bomb had been placed in a niche in the wall and detonated by electrical contact.

"Somebody will probably get a letter in a day or two which will throw some light on the matter," Ireland said.[209]

No one ever called or wrote as per official reports.

---

[i] Antonucci would never return to the nightclub business. He would go on to start "Buffalo Wholesale Millinery" in downtown Buffalo and would hold the patent on the artificial poinsettia. He died in 1968.

There is no way to know these many years later if Altman or Elliott ever discovered who bombed their nightclub, but the incident raises several possibilities. Could it have been linked to those who cracked Altman's safe at the Arcadia? Was the nightclub interfering with liquor trafficking from Canada, given that the lakeshore area was a key entry point? Could it have involved members of Buffalo's organized crime, with whom Harry would become increasingly entangled? Or was it something else entirely?

The explosion would only disrupt nightclub operations for a week, as Altman ordered construction crews to work around the clock to repair the damage.

As the summer home of the Palais Royal returned to working order, Altman was frantically busy making other plans for the fall of 1932. Despite it being the depths of the Depression, Altman would be involved with three separate Main Street dancehalls that September, in addition to other projects:

Palais Royal (downtown): When it was time to leave its summer home, the dancehall operations did not return to 681 Main Street.[j] Instead, the Palais Royal moved into 722 Main Street, designed to resemble yet another Spanish garden in elaborate decoration. It would remain at 722 Main Street until the end of Prohibition in December 1933.

Navigating the intricate maze of corporate ownership from this point forward is complex. After the bombing, Abe Carrol exited the business venture. Altman and Elliott frequently swapped the title of president across a series of corporations. They eventually relocated the Palais Royal for a third time in 1934 to 2700 Main Street, near Hertel Avenue.

In 1935, Altman took over the property as "The Ritz," maintaining his naming tradition. The business was short-lived and quickly shut down. Shortly thereafter, the building was converted into an automobile dealership, signaling the end of its brief era as a dancehall.

Trianon Ballroom: Located at 725 Main Street, across from the Palais Royal, the Trianon Ballroom was opened in 1931 by owners by Altman, Elliott, Satuloff, and Scott. Initial press releases announced that the dancehall had been renovated at a cost of $100,000 and boasted a capacity of 3,500 patrons.[210] Despite the decorative refresh, the ballroom lacked flair and seemed to follow the same formula as other nearby Altman properties. Consequently, it struggled financially, forcing Altman to offer "bargain days" at 10 cents a dance to keep the large space occupied. The Trianon closed after only a couple of years.

---

[j] Altman began operating events for the Marathan Amusement Corporation at the Palais Royal, capitalizing on latest trend in dance entertainment.

Park Central Ballroom: Marketed with the slogan "Catering to the Best: Socking ol' Man Depression," the dance hall initially launched under different ownership in the fall of 1931. In January 1932, Altman, Elliott, and Scott took over the business at 2651 Main Street, near Fillmore Avenue, operating as Park Central Ballroom Inc. [211] Scott departed from the company after a year, leaving Altman and Elliott to manage the ballroom, implementing their "Park Plan" pricing of 10 cents per dance.

Lloyd Wolf and His Orchestra served as the initial house band, frequently performing at Altman and Elliott's other venue, The Palais Royal. In December 1932, Leroy Smith and His Chocolate Dandies replaced Wolf. Tommy Flynn also became a regular guest performer, with Altman securing midnight simulcasts on WBEN-AM.[k] Despite these efforts, the ballroom ceased operations in 1934 due to Altman's insolvency.

Palais Royal/Alhambra: After its initial season, Altman and Elliott co-branded the business as Palais Royal/Alhambra under the Lake Shore Amusement Corporation. It would continue its summer operations beginning in 1934 with Elliott as the primary shareholder until the company filed bankruptcy in 1937. Joseph DiMaria would later take ownership of the building where he would operate Club Alhambra to more than moderate success. By the 1950s, it became a popular roller rink. In April 1954, fire destroyed the building and 400 pairs of rental skates. During the firefighting efforts, a fire truck also sank. Today, a sign commemorating The Alhambra stands at the original location.

Figure 60 Alhambra Program
PD

---

[k] A Cleveland native, Flynn caught Altman's attention and quickly rose to prominence under his enthusiastic promotion. Later, Flynn married Alice Funk, daughter of the owner of the Dellwood Ballroom, Altman's competitor. Flynn would later step in to manage the Dellwood.

Glen Colosseum. Having expanded his business into the southern tier, by 1933 Altman began to spread his wings toward the north. He opened the Glen Colosseum, an evening dance hall and afternoon roller rink, at Park Avenue and Hawley Street in Lockport, NY. *The Lockport Sun & Journal* ran an article about the newly renovated space featuring a new orchestra stage, "with the varied colors of the open work columns" and a "background with its sparkling silver."

Altman operated the business for only one season. Evening dancers during that period were put on notice to be "properly groomed" and to conduct themselves "in the right way" to assure the public of pleasant evenings. "Men wearing sweaters will not be permitted."[212]

The building's existence as an entertainment spot ended when Harry's magic touch failed him in Niagara County. In less than a year, the Colosseum closed its doors; yet another auto dealership took over the space months later.

CHAPTER 6—DANCE UNTIL YOU DROP

W hile ballroom operations were becoming the foundation of Harry's business success during this period, his ambition led him to explore new opportunities. He was particularly drawn to the dance marathon craze that was sweeping the nation. Lacking the initial expertise and capital, Harry cleverly leveraged the investments of others to learn the ropes.

Starting in the mid-1920s, endurance dancing marathons swept across the U.S., attracting dancers and spectators alike. Local promoters organized these events and set the rules for competition. By 1928, when Altman first got involved in the marathon business, the record for continuous dancing was 77 hours. In marathons structured with 45-minute dance periods followed by 15 minutes of rest, the record had soared to 356 hours (nearly 15 days), a mark set that year at Madison Square Garden.

Figure 61 In Chicago, couples drag themselves across the floor, dancing past exhaustion in a marathon where survival matters more than style
PD

While Altman never achieved a world record at any of his events, his ability to draw both enthusiastic dancers and paying spectators added to his growing list of achievements.

For the dancers, marathons provided multiple revenue streams. They could win by outlasting competitors and winning the prize money; participating in mini contests held throughout the marathon; collecting tips ("silver showers") thrown by spectators; and securing sponsorships from local businesses. At the height of the craze, many dancers even quit their day jobs, finding that the marathon circuit offered enough income to support them full-time.

Harry Altman's first venture into marathon competitions came in 1927 when he sponsored a dance team led by Harry Gordon, a "veteran Buffalo hoofer," in the Crystal Beach Marathon.[213] Gordon, a regular patron of Altman's ballrooms, led the charge in organizing a strike against the marathon sponsor due to the contest's two-hour dance rule.

"That kind of grind would have had us all collapsing in two days," Gordon told reporters.[214] Though Altman was not the promoter of the event, he closely observed the negotiations and the inner workings that involved organizing such a spectacle. The dancers ultimately succeeded in their demands, resulting in the adoption of the 45-minute dance/15-minute rest rule.[215]

Six weeks later, armed with this new-found knowledge, Altman was ready to manage his first marathon competition.

Promoted as Rochester's first Marathon Dance competition, the event was held September 9-19, 1928 at Danceland in Sea Breeze Park.[216] Sponsored by Greystone Amusement Company, Altman served as a hired gun for the event. It was not an easy assignment from start to finish.

HERE AT LAST! SENSATIONAL!

MARATHON DANCE

Graystone Amusement Co. Presents
World's Championship Endurance

DANCE MARATHON!
— AT —

NATATORIUM

SEA BREEZE PARK

— Rain or Shine —

| Starts 8:30 P. M. | SUNDAY SEPT. 9 | Continues DAY AND NIGHT |

$1000 In Cash Prizes--$1000

Thrilling! Spectacular!
Dance Sprints! Don't Miss It!
Entertainment and Music Galore!
The Greatest Novelty Attraction Ever!
General Admission—50c

Figure 63 Marathon Dance
PD

Figure 62 Danceland
Photo courtesy of New York State Museum of Transportation
PD

The first hurdle was determining which venue on the property the competition would take place. Initially, the idea was to use the natatorium's outdoor swimming pool by draining the water and holding the marathon on the pool floor. However, logistical issues prevented this plan from materializing. Instead, organizers opted for an indoor wooden dance floor, providing a more comfortable environment for the dancers and shielding them from unpredictable weather conditions.

Before the competition began, each participant had to pass a rigorous physical examination. Doctors focused particularly on the health of the dancers' "lungs, hearts, and nervous systems" to ensure they could endure the demands of the marathon.[217] Out of the initial group of entrants, 20 couples were disqualified after being deemed physically unfit to compete.

In the end, 22 couples stepped onto the dance floor, representing Rochester, Buffalo and other cities from across the U.S. The average age of the competitors was a youthful 18, and many who signed up were marathon professionals.

The competition began with an enthusiastic audience of 600 spectators, many of whom stayed well into the early morning hours, curious to see how long the dancers would last. By 3 a.m., nearly 100 onlookers were still present.

In addition to the grueling dance requirement, a late summer heatwave proved to be a formidable opponent. On the second day, as temperatures climbed into the high 80s, three couples dropped out, unable to withstand the sweltering conditions. By the end of day three, with the temperature still hovering around 85°, an additional 10 couples bowed out, some collapsing from exhaustion, others succumbing to injury, or simply unable to endure the unrelenting strain.

The marathon continued to draw large crowds to Sea Breeze Park, each audience member paying 50 cents a day. By the evening of the second day, an astonishing 2,000 spectators had gathered to watch the dancers struggle on. At the 97-hour mark, only 11 couples remained on their feet.[218]

By day five, the event's nurse took an unusual but necessary step, corralling the exhausted participants into the natatorium showers to cool them down. The women danced through the showers in their section, while the men did the same on their side, briefly refreshed but still committed to the grueling challenge.

Adding a touch of romance to the already dramatic event, a love story unfolded on the dance floor. By day six, dancers Susie Monroe, a local from Rochester, and James Ross of Pittsburgh had fallen for each other, their growing affection evident to everyone in attendance. Altman, ever the sly observer, commented with a wink that "six days and nights of arm's-length companionship will lead to its logical conclusion" once the two had recovered from the punishing marathon.[219]

The charm of romance could not disguise the fact that marathon dancing can be a dangerous sport. Over the era when these competitions were popular, there were many published reports of dancers pushing their bodies to the brink, often collapsing from exhaustion or suffering serious health complications as they fought to stay on their feet (a knee falling to the ground was an immediate disqualification). There were some contestants who had psychotic episodes from the lack of sleep; a few even died from competing under the strenuous conditions.

Lengthy marathons benefited event promoters, who profited the longer the competition dragged on, drawing paying spectators and generating free media coverage. To keep the exhausted dancers on their feet, promoters employed various tactics to revive them, such as dunking participants in cold water and controlling access to stimulants like coffee and food—much to the amusement of the audience.

By the end of day five (143 hours) at Sea Breeze, Altman decided to change things up. With a large weekend crowd expected, he led the contestants to the natatorium to waltz inside the now-empty outdoor swimming pool.[220] Bleachers were set up around the pool to provide a clear view for spectators.

However, the experiment lasted only a few hours due to cold winds, fog, and complaints about the discomfort of dancing on the concrete surface.[221]

The next day, the Monroe County coroner visited after hearing reports about the health of the remaining three couples. After a quick physical examination, he concluded that some dancers were in "satisfactory" condition, while others were "questionable."[222]

In response, Altman decided that, after 10 days of marathon dancing, the event would conclude on September 19th as a precaution against further health risks to the dancers. The final day was heavily promoted in the media, and Altman took advantage of the heightened interest by raising the admission fee to a dollar.

After 220 hours, two couples remained to share the prize money, with each pair receiving $250.[223] This amounted to roughly 57 cents per hour—a respectable wage in 1927—along with any additional side prizes they had earned during the marathon.

Susie and James, the new love birds, came in third and did not receive a share of the prize money.

The winners appeared happy with their earnings, but Altman was not satisfied with the outcome. "The attendance was good, but my contract terms were terrible," he said.[224]

After returning to Buffalo, Harry chose to step away from organizing dance marathons himself, leaving that to other promoters. Instead, he focused on renting out his ballrooms for such events, allowing him to avoid the long hours while still benefiting from the income and publicity generated for his properties.

Although dance marathons continued after the Wall Street crash, the atmosphere shifted. Many participants were unemployed amateurs, drawn not only by the prize money but also by the promise of the 12 small meals served to contestants daily. The age range of dancers extended well into middle age, reflecting the harsh economic times.

In August 1932, Sea Breeze invited him back, and he must have secured better terms as he returned to Rochester. Press releases highlighted him as "the dance promoter who manages the Palais Royal, Buffalo's best nightclub during the winter months," and the "impresario of the Sea Breeze dance."[225]

Given the challenges of the Great Depression, admission fees were lowered to 25 cents for daytime entry and 40 cents in the evening.

The first day saw 31 couples take the floor. To prolong the marathon and maximize ticket sales, he introduced a new rule: if a dancer's partner dropped out, the remaining dancer could continue solo until another contestant left the competition. At that point, the two solo dancers, regardless of gender, could pair up for another shot at victory.

However, Harry encountered trouble when the Irondequoit police threatened to shut down the event on the first Sunday, citing Blue Law violations.[226] He managed to delay the closure by scheduling the court hearing two weeks later and instructing the dancers to walk instead of dance on Sundays, thus complying with the law.[a]

Knowing these delay tactics could not last indefinitely, and facing more pressure from law enforcement, he decided to conclude the marathon late on Saturday night after 19 days.

While the crowd expected the exhausted dancers to collapse, it was the Master of Ceremonies who gave out during the final week, having slept only two hours every 24 hours over the past two weeks.[227] With no emcee to carry on, Harry stepped in at 11:55 p.m. on Saturday, September 11th to declare the event over, just as the police were preparing to shut down the marathon.[228] Seven pairs of finalists shared the $500 first-place prize.[229] Ever the showman, Altman led a "grand march," guiding the winners in a three-lap parade around the dance floor before they dashed to a bed for their first proper sleep in 20 days.[230]

By 1932, the dance marathon craze was starting to fade, but Altman was not ready to give up. In November of that year, he founded the Marathon Amusement Company, Inc.[231] and introduced special promotions to revive interest in the events, including live performances during breaks and simulcasting the orchestra music on local radio. Over the next few months, two more marathons were held in Buffalo to mixed reviews.

The novelty was wearing off for audiences as the events dragged on for nearly seven weeks. Growing criticism from authorities and social reformers, who condemned the marathons as cruel and inhumane, further contributed to the fad's gradual decline from public favor.

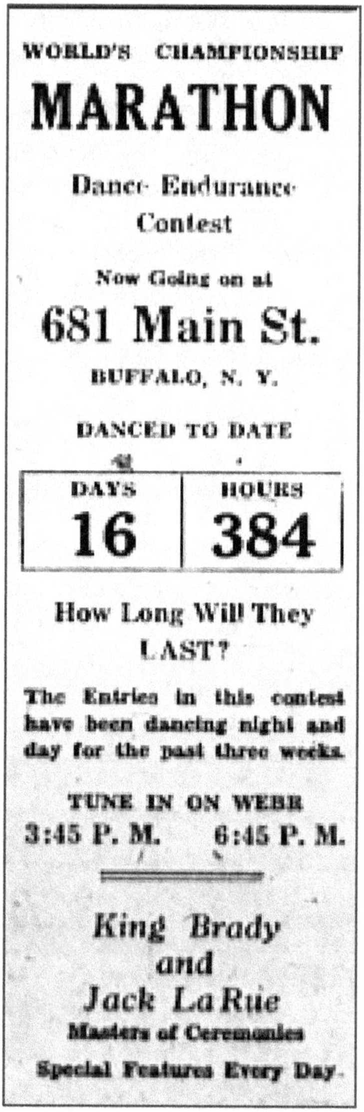

WORLD'S CHAMPIONSHIP

MARATHON

Dance Endurance Contest

Now Going on at

681 Main St.

BUFFALO, N. Y.

DANCED TO DATE

DAYS	HOURS
16	384

How Long Will They LAST?

The Entries in this contest have been dancing night and day for the past three weeks.

TUNE IN ON WEBR
3:45 P. M.   6:45 P. M.

King Brady and Jack LaRue
Masters of Ceremonies
Special Features Every Day.

Figure 64 Altman organized a marathon at 681 Main Street, the previous home of the Palais Royal, in December 1932 Advertisements were published daily to record the duration of the marathon PD

---

[a] It's worth noting that Harry's early career was often complicated by the Sunday Blue Laws. For this reason, he kept on retainer an experienced attorney to navigate these legal challenges.

CHAPTER 7—OUT OF THE SHADOWS: HARRY WALLENS

In 1936, Harry Wallens rejoined Altman's circle of influence, gaining part ownership in Sagamore Ballroom, Inc. at Main and West Ferry Streets in Buffalo. In addition to the two Harrys, Abe Carrel, Altman's corporate attorney and occasional partner, also became involved in the venture.[232]

Since his breakup in 1918 with Altman during the Mardi Gras business era, Wallens reputedly became involved in ventures that operated both within and outside the law. In 1923, in midst of Prohibition, Wallens became embroiled in a large-scale conspiracy involving counterfeit whiskey prescriptions, forged internal revenue stamps, and fake labels meant to mislead customers into believing bootleg whiskey was legally made. He was charged in Federal court after testifying before a grand jury.[233] The case took a dramatic turn in 1924 when a co-conspirator was implicated in selling bootleg liquor laced with wood alcohol. This toxic mixture was believed to have caused the deaths of 40 people across the Niagara Frontier, making front-page headlines for months.[234] The charges on Wallens were dropped before trial began due to a technical error by prosecutors.

During this period, Wallens listed his occupation as "real estate," reflecting his involvement in the March 1923 purchase of what was then known as the Jennie Williams Pratt Building at 625-627 Main Street. Hailed in the newspapers as "one of the most important real estate deals in Main Street property," no purchase price was publicly made available at the time of the sale "although it is understood that several hundred thousand dollars have changed hands during the transaction."[235] Joe Rothenberg was Wallens's partner in the purchase of the three-story floor building.

Development plans were never clearly outlined, and the Wallens-Rothenberg venture was short-lived. By 1925, just two years after the purchase, the property was sold for $350,000 to Arthur J. Block, president of the jewelry firm T.C. Tanke, Inc.[236] Block was a prominent presence in the business district, serving as president of the Main Street Association and other civic organizations.

Later in 1925, Wallens entered a new real estate venture with Harry Fernandez, brother of Nate Fenton (the original owner of Palais Royal) and Johnnie Fenton (to whom Altman sold the Lafayette Boot Shop). Together, Wallens and Fernandez founded the Walfern Corp., a real estate holding company that purchased a commercial building at 1333 Main Street in Niagara Falls, NY.[237] Fernandez did not stay around long; eventually, Wallen's brother Charles and attorney Max Yellen became corporate shareholders.

In 1930, Wallens diversified his business interests by opening Wallen's Corned Beef Shop, a deli and restaurant at 46 West Chippewa.[238]

Figure 65 Ad for Wallens Corned Beef
PD

Figure 67 Dinty Moore's Opening Ad
PD

His former real estate partner, Harry Fernandez, subsequently opened Dinty Moore's sandwich shop next door at 42 West Chippewa.[239] These businesses were opened in anticipation of the end of Prohibition, with the aim of legally selling alcohol at their locations.

PROHIBITION
ENDS AT LAST!

DECEMBER 5, 1933

BARTENDERS POISED FOR DRINKERS' RUSH

Figure 66 Prohibition Ends!
PD

When the Volstead Act was repealed in 1933, it was celebrated nationwide. *The Buffalo Courier-Express* reported the news on its front page.[240]

> *"Legal beer, palatable amber fluid of the pre-Volstead era, is back. While Buffalo slept last night and early this morning it was being bottled by the Iroquois brewery in Pratt Street at the rate of 200 pint bottles a minute."*
>
> *"This morning, hundreds of cases will be delivered to Buffalo homes and hundreds more will be delivered to large hotels and several downtown restaurants. The information that hotels and restaurants would receive shipments of beer came as a surprise. It was believed that the first day delivery would be only to homes."*
>
> *"The Statler, Buffalo Touraine, Lafayette and Markeen all will have bottled beer on sale this morning. So will Gerling's, Wallen's, Dinty Moore's, the Rosticceria and several other restaurants."*

Wallens, who was unable to personally secure a liquor license,[a] turned to Fernandez for assistance. Fernandez responded by merging the two adjacent storefronts on West Chippewa Street under the banner of Dinty Moore's, Inc., with Wallens stepping in as the manager of the expanded operation.

Figure 68 Advertisement after the merger of Wallens and Fernandez
PD

But adding the beer to the menu could not keep Dinty Moore's afloat. In July 1934, Fernandez, president and secretary of the corporation, filed for bankruptcy on behalf of the company, listing more than $9,000 in unsecured claims. Fernandez filed for personal bankruptcy less than a year later, nearly $25,000 in debt.[241]

The financial bloodshed continued when the bank foreclosed on Walfren's Main Street property in Niagara Falls in August 1934.[242]

Figure 69 Opening week ad in the Buffalo Jewish Review, January 1933
PD

The failures did not deter Wallens from starting another business. In April 1934, he launched a new venture, Wallens Brass Rail, a restaurant at 634 Main Street, Buffalo, next to the Greyhound bus station that was once operated by Altman as the New Arcadia Ballroom.[243] As he was on unstable financial footing, his wife, Lillian, was listed as owner. First opened as a corned beef diner, Wallens elevated the offerings to become a "fine restaurant" with an oyster bar.

In January 1936, Harry Wallens filed for bankruptcy in federal court, listing debts exceeding $300,000. Because the Wallens Brass Rail was owned by his wife, Lillian, the establishment remained open until 1939. Her ownership effectively shielded the business from her husband's financial collapse—a strategy Harry Altman would later employ himself when he took over Glen Park, naming his own wife as a corporate shareholder in the company.

After the Brass Rail closed, Lillian opened a new venture: Wallens Glass Bar Restaurant at 640 Main Street. Once again, the corporate records and liquor license were in her name.[b]

---

[a] The New York State Liquor Authority viewed Wallens's involvement in the Belvedere Café unfavorably, earning him a lifetime ban. In all future Wallens's family operations, his wife, Lillian, and/or his adult children held the liquor licenses.

[b] By the mid-1950s, Harry and Lillian's sons, Herbert and Burton, would be added to the corporate paperwork as noted on the NYS Liquor License permits.

Figure 70 Opening weekend ad dated July 3, 1940
PD

The Sagamore was a bright spot for Wallens during this period. The sophisticated ballroom was located at 1525 Main Street near the corner of East Ferry Street. The ballroom, co-owned with Altman and Abe Carrel, was promoted as the place "Where the Better Class Meet." The venue opened with a traditional Altman lineup. On its debut night, September 30, 1936, the entertainment included the Allan Brooks Orchestra, the house band at the Glen Casino, and performances by Larry Evans and Bobby (Riff) Robbins.[244]

The decision by Altman to invite local high school students to the venue brought a fresh spark and a bit of notoriety to the Sagamore.[c] The teens introduced a new dance called the "Jeep," and before long, the ballroom was hosting "Jeep" dance contests, drawing large crowds eager to learn the acrobatic swing steps[d]. This new dance quickly caught on with youth from Rochester and Syracuse, soon making a splash on the national dance scene.

Regrettably, the youthful energy that vitalized business at the Sagamore was quickly extinguished by a fire. On the same front page as King Edward VIII's abdication, newspapers on December 11th reported a two-alarm blaze that destroyed the building that not only housed the Sagamore, but also sporting goods and hardware stores. The total damage to the building and its contents was estimated at $50,000.[245]

FLAMES SWEEP BIG BALLROOM IN MAIN STREET

Firemen, summoned by two alarms and special calls battle to prevent spread

SMOKE AFFECTS SOME

First alarm sounded shortly after 2 a. m.; second call is sounded quickly

FIRE HOSES PAINT PICTURE—Spray from the numerous streams of water poured into the Sagamore ballroom at Main and Ferry streets early yesterday etched an artistic picture against the night sky. The blaze caused damage estimated by firemen at $30,000 to the two-story building.

Figure 71 Headline for Sagamore Fire
The Buffalo Courier-Express, December 11, 1936, p1
PD

Figure 72 Fire Hoses Paint Picture of Sagamore Fire
The Buffalo Courier-Express, December 11, 1936, p18
PD

---

c This seems to be the only instance—apart from the final years of the Town and Glen Casinos—when Altman targeted what he called "the younger set" as patrons for his dance halls. This exception occurred during the depths of the Depression, a time when any source of revenue was welcomed.

d Another attraction of the dance was the controversy it stirred among parents who were alarmed by the frequent broken noses caused by the energetic elbow movements.

Newspaper reports reveal that at around 11:30 p.m., a musician from the orchestra performing in the ballroom notified Richard Gordon, the ballroom manager, of a smoke odor. Unable to locate its source, Gordon placed water into sandboxes—a rudimentary fire-extinguishing method—as a precaution when the venue closed at 12:30 AM..[246] However, the sandboxes were proven ineffective. By 2 AM, the building was ablaze.

On December 20th, *The Buffalo Courier-Express* featured a front-page article about the "rash of fires" across Buffalo. Records indicated that 120 fires had occurred in 20 days, causing $250,000 in damage in the last 10 days alone.[247] Fire Commissioner William R. Castimore noted that the arson squad thoroughly investigated only one fire—the Sagamore's—finding "not the slightest reason to believe that the fire was deliberate."[248]

Altman tried to make light of the Sagamore fire, the second nightclub of his to go up in flames that year[e] by telling newspaper columnist Rod Reed: "The next ballroom will be made of iron."[249] The *Buffalo Evening News* also made note of the "ironic" publicity sign that remained outside the Sagamore for several months after the fire: "Sagamore Ballroom: Something Happening Every Nite."[250]

Whatever the financial cost of losing the Sagamore,[f] the fire did not diminish the strengthening bond between the two Harrys. Any lingering animosity between Wallens and Altman from their Mardi Gras days was now firmly in the past. While each continued to pursue some individual ventures, their shared focus shifted toward developing a downtown nightclub together.

With Wallens family successfully running Wallens Brass Rail in a space adjacent to the bus station, the two Harrys decided to set their sights on occupying the second floor of the Greyhound Building at 640 Main Street[g] for their next ambitious project.[h]

Stepping away from the traditional ballroom scene, the Savarin Café & Hickory Steak House became the first major effort by the pair to combine fine dining and entertainment in Buffalo's bustling theater district. The pair invested heavily in transforming the space, including spending $3,000 on a custom oven designed to broil steaks over hickory logs.[251] To add a modern touch, an electric elevator was installed to whisk patrons up to the second-floor venue.

---

[e] the Ritz Barn, later rebuilt as the Glen Casino, was destroyed by fire in July (see chapter 10).

[f] The Allan Brooks Orchestra certainly felt the financial pinch as their instruments were not insured.

[g] Altman, along with Scott and Sataloff, had previously operated the New Arcadia Ballroom in the space Greyhound now occupied.

[h] The Otto-Kent Building at 640 Main Street, across from where the Town Barn/Casino would flourish, housed a series of entrepreneurial ventures by Altman and Wallens, beginning with Altman's Arcadia in the 1920s. Greyhound's conversion of the first-floor space into a bus depot in 1930—and its departure a decade later—allowed the two men, both jointly and independently, to lease portions of the first and second floors well into the 1960s.

A *Buffalo Times* reviewer noted the fanfare surrounding the steaks:

"The new Savarin is making quite a fuss about its steaks which are cooked over hickory logs. I cannot say what hickory logs are supposed to do to set them apart from ordinary steaks, but I can report that they taste fine." [252]

Figure 73 Savarin Menu
PD

Altman announced that the restaurant would operate on an "all-day Bowery policy," offering continuous entertainment. Patrons could expect singing waiters, nostalgic tunes, and barbershop quartets throughout the day. The *Buffalo Times*[253] noted that "Every employee from the chef to the last bus boy, all the waiters and hat check girls, either sing or dance. There is not a non-performer in the place, except for Mr. Altman, who is reported to be studying up on 'Gunga Din.'"[254i]

Opening on October 3, 1935, the Savarin quickly earned a reputation for its lively variety shows. With three performances nightly, the venue featured a large orchestra and a rotating lineup of comedians, acrobats, dancers, and singers. Among its standout performers was Gloria Rondell, the mistress of ceremonies,[255] whose career soared when she was cast in Broadway's "New Faces of 1936," starring Imogene Coca. The Savarin thus became recognized as a launching pad for emerging talent.

Wallens, already a veteran of Buffalo's entertainment scene, earned a nod from the *Buffalo Times* for his earlier success operating the Belvedere on Eagle Street two decades prior. The paper remarked: "Mr. Wallens has returned to the business where he got his start, and he hopes to bring back to the new place some of the old-timers who first crashed the boards in Buffalo hot spots." "[256]

In February 1937, the atmosphere of the popular nightclub was suddenly disrupted by an outbreak of violence. Around 2 a.m., several armed individuals stormed the venue, launching a brutal attack on Altman with chairs and makeshift weapons.[257] During the chaos, employees and several prominent Buffalo citizens, including William J. Connors, Jr., the publisher of *The Buffalo Courier-Express*,

---

i "Gunga Din" is a famous poem written in 1890 by Rudyard Kipling and had a popular resurgence at the time due to an action-adventure film just released.

intervened. In a disturbing turn of events, Connors was hit in the head with a chair, a story that was later prominently featured on the front page of his own newspaper about the need for better policing downtown. [258]

Figure 78 Joseph "The Wolf" DeCarlo, Jr. PD

The Buffalo Evening News, the competing newspaper, reported that the motive behind the attack was to extort money from Altman to fund a notorious gangster's escape from the city.[259] This incident was reportedly part of a larger conflict involving Joseph DiCarlo Jr, a former capo under Mafia boss Stefano Magaddinowho was fleeing the city amidst a power struggle. Altman, whose ties to the entertainment industry made him reliant on mob favors for protection and other services, was caught in this conflict, presumably suffering injuries requiring a hospital stay.

The *Buffalo Times* reported on February 5, 1937, the day of the attack, that Police Commissioner James W. Higgins was stepping into the investigation.[260] The article detailed how 10 men, who "in typical gangster fashion," guarded exits while their leader assaulted Altman. The beating took approximately five minutes, and Altman was either "punched or hit with a sharp instrument" leading to his injuries.[261]

The police interviewed DiCarlo later that day, and he denied any knowledge of the incident. "He said he wasn't even there."[262] Detectives reported that no witnesses would come forward with a statement. Wallens, who told investigators that he was dozing in a booth at the nightclub "heard the scuffle but did not see it."[263]

The police commissioner said that he is of the opinion that "the incident has been exaggerated out of proportion 'by the newspapers."[264] Ultimately, no one filed a formal police complaint.

"If Joe DiCarlo was in on it, I would be very much surprised," Commissioner Higgins told the paper. "I have known him many years and his father[j] before him, and it would be more like him to stop a fight than to start one. He is more likely to be a peaceful, law-abiding citizen than some of the well-known guests who were in there."[265]

---

[j] Joseph DiCarlo, Sr. was head of the mob in the region before Magaddino assumed the role.

This was not the last time DiCarlo's associates targeted Altman's property. The feud persisted, even leading to the disruption of a wedding reception of an Altman family member at the Statler and the after party at the Town Barn (See Chapter 14).

Fortunately, there was better news on the horizon. Savarin's popularity by patrons caught national attention. In 1937,[266] *Billboard* praised the venue, writing:

"Now in its second week of the season, SRO (Standing Room Only) has been the order at this popular downtown spot. A steaming hot band and excellent floor show have been the teasers. The Harrys Altman and Wallens hold the reins here."[267]

Later in December of that same year, the nightclub launched its "Black and White Revue," featuring Hollywood's "Sunshine Sammy Davis" in his debut performance at an Altman venue.

Figure 74 Sammy, age 9, as a member of the Will Mastin Trio
PD

Figure 75 Savarin Ad Promoting Sammy Davis
PD

Despite initial ticket sales for Davis, audience numbers over the next few weeks soon began to decline overall. In an effort to rejuvenate attendance, Altman shifted the show's format towards burlesque. By early February 1939, the Savarin introduced a new floor show starring Vnette Vnette,[268] who emulated the performance style of the renowned Ziegfeld Follies star, Anna Held. Promotional materials highlighted Vnette Vnette's act as a spectacular exhibition of "Adolescent Feminine Pulchritude,"[k] centering on a provocative "milk bath" scene, aiming to draw larger crowds with the promise of a bold and daring performance.[269]

---

[k] Loosely translated: admiring the physical beauty of a young women her teenage years.

Anna Held's original act, immortalized in press coverage, featured her emerging from a trap door, encased in a "glass temple." She was adorned with a gold headdress and surrounded by little more than a few leaves.[270] Anna Held, ever the show woman, later confessed: "I'm an exhibitionist at heart, I guess, and I really enjoyed it."[271] The "milk," she revealed, was merely a thin layer of white paint swished along the side of the tub.

Despite the publicity surrounding Vnette Vnette's performance, the spectacle could not rescue the Savarin; the venue abruptly closed a few weeks later. *The Buffalo Courier-Express*, published by William J. Connors, Jr., a victim of DiCarlo wrath, cited multiple reasons for the venue's demise:

> "A feeble season...bad breaks...and the whimsy of the stay-outs and going-places people...any or all of these rendezvous' traits might have been responsible for locking up...the fun and food during the last week."[272]

After the Savarin nightclub closed, Altman and Wallens went their separate ways for a time. This period marked an era of introspection for Altman, who was nearing his 50th birthday and had been tirelessly pursuing success since his first train ride to Gloversville at 19. The career challenges he faced went beyond economics; threats to his business and personal safety were escalating, the evidence all pointing to a singular, ominous source.

Yet, he remained hungry to make it big in the entertainment world. As the Sagamore burned and the Savarin floundered, Altman had put into motion the transformation of a former picnic grove, located 10 miles from downtown Buffalo, into a nightclub and small amusement park. The unique endeavor brought its own set of headaches, but Harry's filing for personal bankruptcy in 1934 caused him a different kind of pain. Its public reporting in the newspapers not only damaged his credit but tarnished his hard-earned reputation.[273] Due to the foreclosure on their home, the Altmans had to move into a hotel that Harry managed for a brief time before taking ownership (according to newspaper records). He also was forced to take on other salaried jobs to provide for Annabelle and their three young children.

Altman had chased spectacle since staging his first Mardi Gras in 1911. Selling gloves had once paid the bills, but only the stage stirred his ambition. By the depths of the Depression, his circle of respectable investors had mostly vanished, undone by their own financial misfortunes. What remained were men he had long avoided: flush with cash, well-connected, and dangerous. He had felt their scorn before, but after years of relentless work with little to show for it, he began to realize that accepting their help might be the only way left to stay in show business.

PART TWO—GLEN PARK

Figure 76 The Williamsville Glen, 1916
Photo courtesy of the Williamsville Historical Society

————

"And that is how change happens. One gesture. One person. One moment at a time."

~ *Libba Bray, The Sweet Far Thing (Gemma Doyle, #3)*

CHAPTER 8—BIG PLANS, BIGGER SCANDAL

In 1919, more than 600 members of the Benevolent and Protective Order of Elks (BPOE, Lodge 23) hosted a summer event at the Conshafter Picnic Grove, which was the name of the recreational area of Glen Park during that era. As a newspaper covering the event reported, it was "the first outing of the herd" since WWI broke out.[274]

"Every one of the antlered boys who could get away from business took advantage of the occasion," the paper stated. Participants "ate, drank and made merry" and "not an untoward incident marked a perfect's day pleasure."[275]

It was at this picnic that Harry Altman, a very active member of the Elks, came upon Glen Park for the first time. His story was told in a July 1, 1960 *Buffalo Evening News* article[276] chronicling his rise to the top of the entertainment field:

> *"The young businessman stood on a bridge over Ellicott Creek, looked onto the grounds and announced to his benevolent and protective colleagues: 'I'd like to own this park someday.' There was a lot of laughter at the speaker's expense. His ideas were big, but they had no visible means of support."*
>
> *"Harry was a small café owner at the time, barely making ends meet. But the future would be kind to him: There has been a lot of laughter in the grove ever since, but not necessarily at [Altman's] expense."[277]*

Altman's dream of operating Glen Park became a reality 15 years after the memorable Elks picnic. During that time, much had changed, symbolized by the steady flow of Ellicott Creek beneath the bridge at the park's eastern edge. Altman's opportunity resulted, in part, due to Louis Conshafter surrendering the park after starkly violating the community's moral standards.

CONSHAFTER'S DOMINANCE IN BUSINESS

In 1911 when Louis Conshafter, age 47, decided to purchase a swath of vacant land in the heart of Williamsville, he was already a member of the city's power elite, short-listed for the county's top job in his profession. His C.V. included a listing in the "Who's Who in Buffalo,"[278] and the honor of receiving "prominent mention" in the esteemed *"Illustrated Buffalo."*[279]

The Williamsville Glen benefited from his wealth and influence. He assisted in helping to return the property to its natural state after it was depleted during an extended period of industrial use. Less than a decade after purchasing the Glen, he had converted a section of the Glen into Conshafter's Picnic Grove, a popular recreational destination for visitors seeking a quiet sanctuary along Ellicott Creek nearest Glen Falls.

By the time the roaring 1920s rolled around, Louis, now in his late 50s, should have been hailed as a senior stateman. Instead, a secret he had been harboring among his circle of friends would cause his world to come crashing down. When his private life became public in 1924, it was front page news, destroying his reputation and causing his expansion plans for the Glen to come to a full stop.

Figure 77 Photo of Louis Conshafter Courtesy of "Illustrated Buffalo" (1890)

He came from humble beginnings. Louis was born in 1863 to Charles [Auguste] and Maria Magdalene [Heinrich] Conshafter, émigrés from Alsace, France. He was born in the U.S., the fifth of 10 siblings. Soon after his birth the family moved to Manitoba, Canada where they remained for several years before returning to the rural outskirts of Buffalo. Louis's father was a cabinet maker, owning and operating a wood shop in Clarence, NY. Louis joined him by learning the craft.

In the mid-1800s, cabinet makers often provided caskets and coffins to men whose task it was to "undertake" the interment of the deceased's body into a burial plot. The undertaker earned his revenue from charging a fee for his service and a mark-up on the wood-paneled box.

Up until that time, funerals were no-frill affairs. Families prepared their loved one for their final resting place by bathing and grooming the body before dressing them in their best personal day clothes or nightwear. Wakes were short, solemn affairs, held in the deceased's parlor or bedroom. Mortuary science was in its early development, so a room would be cooled by ice if a delay in burial was required.

Rather than sell the funerial cabinets to a middleman, Louis decided to become an undertaker himself. It was a trade that required no formal training. With the backing of his father, he forged ahead.

Louis's first major foray into the undertaking business was seeking the city's contract to bury its paupers ($9.50 for children under 10; $14.50 for adults).[280] The year was 1885 and it was a bold move for him, being that he was relatively new to the profession and still working with his father in Clarence. Just a year prior he had been expelled for membership in The Buffalo Undertakers Association (BUA) for failure to pay dues.[281] The organization had created a monopoly in Buffalo, encouraging vendors not to sell to undertakers who did not agree to the pre-approved fee schedule. Independent to his core, Conshafter decided to go it alone, prepared to manufacture the caskets and buy other funeral supplies from vendors not on the BUA's approved list.

Louis's prime competitor for the City pauper bid was J.B. Sackett, president of the BUA. Sackett's bid came in slightly higher than Louis's. Despite having won the bid based on cost, Conshafter's selection was not a foregone conclusion. The Buffalo Common Council called both sides into City Hall to negotiate a deal.

According to the report in *The Buffalo Daily Republic* (July 1885), a "solemn cortege of determined men bent on the capture of pauper bodies" entered the chambers. "A war of words was expected," and everyone stopped what they were doing to "hear the fun."[282]

The audience was not disappointed. One "prominent member of the city government" said that he considered BUA practices "a damned outrage…I tell you the undertakers own the dead."[283]

"You have no way of telling how badly you are being cheated," he said. "They hatch up their plans in secret and the people are at their mercy."[284]

A "well-known citizen" noted that Conshafter was starting to do "big business on the East Side," charging lower fees to poor families who were unable to pay BUA pricing. He predicted that Louis would prevail in winning the bid.[285]

"Old man Conshafter is a hard-headed German, as stubborn as you will find, and I think he will win this fight."[286]

In the end, both sides were forced to compromise. The City gave the contract to the BUA, with the stipulation that they charge the lower fees set forth in Conshafter's proposal. Conshafter would be included on the list of undertakers called on to bury the city's paupers.[287]

One of the primary points of contention during the bidding process was that Louis was not yet a Buffalo resident. To overcome that objection, he swiftly packed up his belongings in Clarence and moved to the city with his new wife, Wilhelmina [Minnie] Rippel, in 1886. The couple purchased a home at 483 William Street near the corner of Cedar Street. Their only child, a daughter, Lillian, was born in 1887. Louis and Minnie were 24 years old.

At the time of Louis and Minnie's arrival in the city, the population was booming. The ethnic group that predominated on the east side were Germanic Catholics and former residents of Alsace, a neighboring region of France. Louis's familiarity with the language (German/French) and the various religious and cultural customs gave him an advantage when starting out there. Compared to the waves of immigrants that followed, the residents in Buffalo's German Village were more prosperous, well-educated, and skilled at a variety of trades. In addition to sharing a common background, Louis's personality was reportedly well suited for the job.

"This peculiar calling requires a temperament and disposition possessed by few," "*Illustrated Buffalo*" said of Conshafter. "To him is entrusted the superintendence of the funeral ceremony and all pertaining to the last sad rites of the dead, and success is only awarded to those who, possessed of a sympathetic nature, have a due regard for their sacred duties."[288]

Figure 78 Eugene V. Debs (1855-1926) A founding member of both the Industrial Workers of the World (IWW) and the Socialist Party of America PD

As his undertaking business grew, the Socialist movement was gaining ground in the U.S. Louis found himself drawn to the economic model espoused by its charismatic leader, Eugene V Debs. Conshafter considered Debs a "firm friend,"[289] so much so that when the industrial labor leader passed through Buffalo in September 1898, Debs stayed at Conshafter's William Steet home. The event made front page news.[290]

In 1899, Conshafter decided to put the Socialist economic model to the test by helping establish the Co-Operative Funeral Association of the State of New York.[291] Louis's partial failure to secure the City of Buffalo contract convinced him that he needed to try and level the playing field for all undertakers. The Co-Op promoted less-extravagant funeral rituals than those being performed among the "Delaware Avenue" elite, thereby saving families money. Members were also required to publish their price lists to allow consumers to make better educated decisions.[292]

The initial meeting of the organization was held in Conshafter's William Street home; he was elected first Vice President.[293] Within a short time, Co-Op members saw their overhead reduced in some cases by 70% because of being able to bulk-purchase funeral products at discounted prices. The success of the organization solidified Louis's leadership role within the profession and earned him a spot on the shortlist as Chief Undertaker in all of Erie County.[294]

As Conshafter climbed the ranks, his friendship with Debs proved unsustainable. While Debs continued to embrace his "equality of men"[a] argument throughout his five campaigns as the Socialist Party candidate for U.S. president (1900-1920), Conshafter was increasingly attracted to a more radical and less egalitarian viewpoint.

By the turn of the century, Conshafter's business was booming. The death rate in the City of Buffalo was spiraling upward due to the lack of effective infection control measures in overcrowded neighborhoods as immigrants streamed into the region. Life expectancy at birth was a mere 43 years. Germ theory had not yet been discovered by scientists, nor had effective vaccines. In some circumstances, nascent medical techniques made treatment more dangerous than staying home and suffering from the harsh diseases rampant at the time.[b] Ruinous injuries also resulted in fatalities, as did the risky practice of giving birth. By some estimates, between 1 and 1.5% of women in 1880 died of pregnancy-related complications, with the lifetime risk (due to attempting multiple births) pegged at 4%.[295] Just being a child at the turn of the century was hazardous to one's health. It is estimated that in some urban areas 30% of children died before their first birthday, and 4.3% before their fifth, primarily due to contamined food, milk and water.[296]

As Conshafter's coffers grew, he began building an investment portfolio —a not-so-Socialist endeavor. Newspapers during that era ran articles about Louis's holdings in new energy companies (mostly oil and gas),[297] and his ever-growing real estate portfolio that included multiple residential lots in the burgeoning suburbs of Buffalo.

He also seemed to enjoy a bit of luxury. In 1910, the *Buffalo Morning Express* featured an article about his purchase of a new Reo, four-cylinder touring car for $1,260 ($40,000 in today's dollars).[298] In 1911, he placed a successful bid for purchasing a portion of Glen Park from Benjamin Miller's estate.

---

[a] Eugene V. Debs, the influential American socialist and labor leader, consistently argued for the equality of men in his speeches and writings. His stance was rooted in the idea that all people, regardless of class or occupation, are fundamentally equal and deserve equitable treatment and opportunities.

[b] Tuberculosis, pneumonia, diphtheria, heart disease, cholera, malaria, scarlet fever, and dysentery were the leading causes of death during this era.

Brief History of Williamsville and Glen Park

Glen Park is a picturesque eight-acre property situated along Ellicott Creek in Williamsville, NY, a charming village within the Town of Amherst. The park is notably home to Glen Falls, a 27-foot waterfall where the creek tumbles over the Onondaga Escarpment.

Williamsville's foundings date back to 1798 when it was first surveyed by the Holland Land Company. The Village's early success can be attributed to its strategic location at the intersection of Ellicott (formerly Nine Mile) Creek and the Great Iroquois Trail, the main byway between Buffalo and Albany. Ellicott Creek was crucial for the early settlers, providing waterpower for the 30 mills that lined its banks. These mills produced essential agricultural byproducts, helping to establish a strong residential and economic presence in the region.

Williamsville's historical significance was further highlighted during the War of 1812. General Alexander Smyth, after an unsuccessful attempt to invade Canada in the winter of 1812, stationed his army of 5,000-6,000 troops in Williamsville. A year later, 250 soldiers from Fort Niagara Army Hospital were moved to a makeshift hospital in Williamsville due to the threat of advancing British troops. Eventually, the Williamsville facility was designated a general military hospital, treating 1,100 patients.

The presence of the troops and their support personnel boosted the local economy, leading to the establishment of taverns, stores, and other businesses in the frontier settlement.

Figure 79 1880 Map of Glen Park. Creek and tailrace flows varied with natural conditions and demands of area water mills
PD

The park itself, located just north of the intersection of Main Street and Ellicott Creek, is bordered by Glen (formerly Bear and Bridge) Street to the north, Ellicott Creek to the east, Spring Street to the south, and Rock Street to the west. Historically, the park's water levels were significantly influenced by local milling operations, which necessitated the construction of dams and channels to control the creek's flow. Unlike the current man-made features in today's park, the original landscape was level with the creek and prone to frequent flooding due to its low position at the base of the escarpment. These floods erased signs of early habitation, destroyed vegetation, and removed traces of Native American presence in the area.

The discovery of limestone deposits along the Onondaga Escarpment initiated industrial quicklime (calcium oxide) production in the early 19th century. This quicklime, used as stone mortar for major construction projects, significantly enhanced Williamsville's role in the regional economy. By the 1800s, the area around Glen Falls transformed into an industrial hub, leveraging the reliable power source provided by the falls.

The Williamsville Mill [c] originally built by Jonas Williams in 1811, played a crucial role in quicklime production during this era.

Figure 80 Built in 1811 atop the escarpment overlooking Glen Park, the Williamsville Water Mill complex (shown here circa 1950) still stands on its original site. It was spared significant damage during major fires that broke out below in Glen Park in both 1936 and 1968
Photo courtesy of the Town of Amherst

Perched atop the escarpment above Glen Park, the grist/flour mill was sold by Williams to Juba Storrs & Co. in 1814, shortly before Erie Canal surveyors discovered local lime deposits. The company capitalized on this discovery by opening quarries to extract lime throughout the village, operating the mill to pulverize the stone, and building kilns to finalize production. It utilized the western ridge of the Glen (along Rock Street) to quarry limestone and build a furnace/kiln operation in the Glen, further industrializing the property.

Another notable feature of the Glen property was the tailrace, a channel that directed water away from the Williamsville Mill after it passed over the water wheel. This tailrace meandered along a path parallel to the creek on the east side of the property and west of the creek, with its flow volume adjusted based on the mill's operational needs. The channel was designed to eventually reconnect with its original source downstream.

---

[c] Constructed by Jonas Williams in 1811, the Williamsville Water Mill is the only remaining building from what was once a sprawling industrial district in Williamsville. Located at 56 Spring Street, the mill is recognized as both a local and national landmark.

To fully understand what followed in the decades ahead, it is important to picture the land as it once was: flat and open from Rock Street to the creek, from the base of the escarpment to Glen Avenue. There was only a slight incline at the west end—just enough that someone could, and once did in the Altman years, accidentally drop a beer keg and watch it roll toward the water. Today, it is hard to reconcile that industrial past with the Glen Park we now know: a tranquil, carefully contoured green space with duck ponds, footbridges, and rows of gentle firs. Its natural beauty, shaped in part by human hands, has softened its history. But beneath the serenity lies a stage once set for a very different act.

The quarry continued to operate when Louis Conshafter, the first person to realize the recreational potential of the Glen, purchased a section of the property in 1911. Conshafter's Picnic Grove extended between the tailrace and the creek, allowing the western-most section to continue industrial operations.[d]

Figure 81 Early 1900 map of Williamsville Glen courtesy of the Williamsville Historical Society. Conshafter's holding consisted of the property located between the Mill's tailrace on the west and Ellicott Creek on the east

PD

---

[d] The historical details of the Village and Glen during the pre-industrial and industrial era can be found in a book by Sue Miller Young, *A History of the Town of Amherst, New York, 1818—1965* (Amherst, NY: Town Board of Amherst, 1965) that details the geological history of the era. Other invaluable resources include: Joseph A. Grande, *Glancing Back: A Pictorial History of Amherst, New York* (Amherst, NY: Amherst Museum, 2000) and the Village government's website at "History," Village of Williamsville, accessed June 2, 2025, https://walkablewilliamsville.com/government/history/

The reasons behind Louis's decision to purchase the Glen are unclear. However, it is likely that he perceived potential in the land, which had been reduced to a desolate state resembling a big mud puddle due to extensive industrial use over the years.

The waterfall on the eastern border of the park was not quite the showstopping feature that it is today. The visual impact was tempered by the demands by the mills upstream of the property. During a dry summer when the mills were running at full capacity, the waterfall was reduced in volume to little more than a trickle. The land on the west border of Conshafter's Glen—the area between the tailrace and Rock Street—remained industrial with a quarry and kilns dotting the property.

Once Conshafter signed the deal to buy the land, he purchased some picnic tables and park benches to encourage recreational use. Soon, he added a swing set. His most urgent need was for the land, stripped bare by earlier floods and industrial use, to return to its natural splendor.

To create a revenue stream, in 1915 Louis constructed an enclosed pavilion for dancing, a popular activity during WWI. Dancehalls served as venues for soldiers returning from overseas to interact with local women who had been engaged in factory work and affected by the war's austerity measures. Income at the pavilion was generated by the cost of the dances (10 cents each), often featuring Balduf's Orchestra.

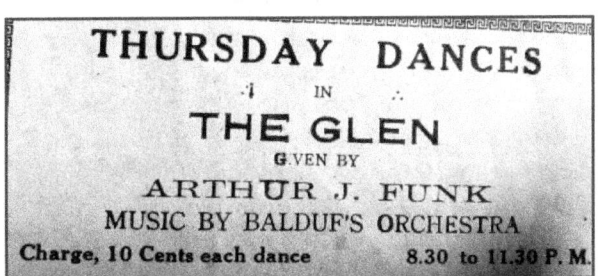

Figure 82 Dances —10 Cents each
PD

Arthur J. Funk offered classes at the pavilion and a summer dance party on Thursday evenings.

As word spread, the Glen started to attract families and younger children to the park-like setting that was emerging. An essay, "Our Day's Outing" by Grace Hirsch, age 10, of 100 Timon Place in Buffalo, was published in 1915 in the *Buffalo Evening News*.[299] It provides a snapshot of what it was like at the Glen during that time:

"It was a beautiful day and papa decided he would take us to the country. So, we packed a large basket of lunch and started off. There were about 20 of us including my two little cousins."

"We boarded a Jefferson car, transferred to the Main car and rode as far as City Line, then we changed for Williamsville. It was about 10 o'clock when we reached our destination which was at Williamsville Glen. Then our fun started."

"It was a beautiful place. There were many swings and we tried them all. We ran through the thick shrubs and bushes and went wading in the creek. Then we got very hungry and were ready for our lunch."

"We ate until we could eat no more, all kinds of sandwiches, cookies, salads and fruit...We went to a farm house for our milk which seemed to taste so much sweeter than we got in the city.

"We were very tired but still hated to leave the place but dusk was drawing so we started for home. I don't think we shall ever have such a good time again."[300]

Conshafter was also having some success renting the Glen to civic organizations looking to host large outdoor events. There were two publicized gatherings of note at the Glen during the later part of the 1910s.

The first was in August of 1917 when Conshafter invited his old friends from Branch One of the Socialist Party to have its annual picnic there. A.I. Shipcaloff, Socialist Assemblyman from Brooklyn, was the special guest in attendance for the gathering. A press release at the time promised "dancing, games and all sorts of amusements," along with Women's Club's "splendid clam chowder."[301]

The second event was the annual summer gathering of the Elks, an occasion that would go on to become legendary in Altman lore.[302]

END OF AN ERA

By the early part of the 1900s, the ethnic composition of the East Side neighborhood where Conshafer lived and ran his "mortuary and warespace" was undergoing significant changes. The area, once predominantly German, was now home to Russian Jewish immigrants fleeing the pogroms of Eastern Europe. Families like the Altmans were among those settling into the community, now commonly known as "Castle Gardens" or the Jewish Quarter.

In other parts of the east side, newly arriving peasants from Poland were establishing a foothold, while in the western half of the City Italians were closing rank and creating their own communities. African-Americans, who already had a small presence in the City near Michigan and William Streets, began arriving in record numbers from the agrarian South, hoping to obtain factory jobs. Also growing in number were the Irish who joined their brethren in South Buffalo where they had settled after helping build the Erie Canal.

Immigrants arriving during the early part of the twentieth century generally remained separated by ethnic group, creating a patchwork design across the city. Their differences in language, customs, religion, and political beliefs made it difficult for them to meld into an interwoven tapestry.

A change in the status quo affected men like Conshafter who made a comfortable living as a member of the city's predominant ethnic group. Younger men of Anglo-Saxon origin also had their livelihood threatened as jobs on the lower rungs of the economic ladder became competitive. As a result, tensions rose throughout the region as the influx of new immigrants started to put a strain on existing resources.

Figure 83 The Conshafter family gathers for a Glen Park picnic
From left: John, Frank, Charlie; Sadie (Conshafter) Fischer and her husband, Phillip; Louis;
Mabel (Conshafter) Hicks; William Conshafter; and David Hicks
Photo courtesy of John Conshafter

Conshafter was also experiencing much sadness on the home front. Daughter Lillian, Louis's office bookkeeper, died in February 1916 at the age of 29. Wife Minnie died in 1923 at the age 60. The couple had been married for 37 years.

By the early 1920s, Louis shifted his focus from the funeral business to developing the Glen. He expanded the park by acquiring the western end of the Glen, stretching from the tailrace to Rock Street. In the *1922 Buffalo Business Directory*, he described his profession as "entertainment."[303]

This new venture seemed to be flourishing; by 1924, Louis was regularly hosting large-scale events. Notably, in July of that year, he organized a banquet for 600 guests at the 25th annual Western New York firemen's convention held at the Glen.[304]

This event, however, would mark the last widely publicized gathering at the Conshafter-owned picnic grove.

THE KLAN EMERGES

Based on what is known of his political interests, Louis Conshafter must have been an easy recruitment target for the Ku Klux Klan (KKK).

While some of the secret society's rites and rituals were like those used by the Reconstruction Era Klan (1865-1876), the second wave (1915-1930) was in many ways markedly different. It was now a well-run "fraternal organization," spewing hate beyond the Southern states. While blacks remained a target, the KKK extended their wrath to foreigners just arriving in the U.S.[e]

Nationally, the second wave of the Klan appealed mainly to rural, under-educated, impoverished whites in northern and midwestern states. Their high-profile acts of terrorism like cross-burnings and solemn parades down main streets were reflective of the outrage they felt against the influx of foreign-language immigrants who were competing with them for the same low-income jobs.

In Buffalo, however, the KKK membership profile was remarkably different. The Knighted Order attracted the white, Protestant, professional class who believed that Catholics and weak Prohibition enforcement were the root cause of moral decay among the middle class.[f]

The Klan positioned itself to make members feel that their anger was not motivated by "racism, resentment or a false sense of victimhood." Instead, the core myth of the Klan lay in the notion that it represented the "defense and manifestation" of America's true character.[305] In other words, the members could justify their actions on the grounds of patriotism, not bigotry.

Wearing the white robe, hood, and regalia synonymous with the movement, Klansmen in the 1920s are on record for having barged into WNY churches during worship services. Their leader would interrupt the sermon to read a letter declaring the group's devotion to Christianity and Prohibition. Upon departing, each Klan member would deposit a donation in the poor box. This soft-peddling tactic was an

---

[e] Many historians believe that the 1915 release of "Birth of a Nation," a silent epic drama film, played a significant role in the resurgence of the Ku Klux Klan in the months that followed. The film was shown in 1917 at the Glen Theater in Williamsville.

[f] One of the most comprehensive accounts of the Ku Klux Klan's history in Western New York is Shawn Lay's *Hooded Knights on the Niagara: The Ku Klux Klan in Buffalo, New York* (New York: New York University Press, 1995).

attempt by the Klan to be seen by the public as "civil action" crusaders, not the hooded thugs of yesteryear.

When these "civil actions" ultimately proved ineffective however, the vigilante behavior for which the KKK was previously known remerged to terrorize the whole of WNY.

Conshafter certainly fit the local KKK membership profile as a member of the white, Protestant, professional class. He was also on record for being anti-Catholic, quoted as saying:

"Someone in the organization (KKK) should bomb the next President of the U.S. if he appoints any Catholics to office."[306]

His sentiments were echoed by fellow Klansman Albert C. Acker who expressed a desire to "shoot some of these damn Knights of Columbus."[307]

At the time of the Klan's resurgence, Conshafter's business was declining due to his inability to provide funeral/burial services for many of the new arrivals into the city. He found himself either disqualified because of religious restrictions, or not being able to establish inroads within the closed-knit, ethnic communities. In this new paradigm, Louis and the other Angelo-Saxons were considered the outsiders.

Louis had shown himself eager to identify with a political/socio-economic movement as demonstrated by his earlier participation with another group, Debs-style Socialism. But the KKK's radical stance more closely aligned with his personal agenda. In fact, the KKK and the U.S. Socialist Party became heated adversaries during this period, rallying for societal reform from opposite ends of the spectrum. The Socialist philosophy was to provide equal opportunity for every stratum of society—as in the motto, "One for all." The Klansmen zeroed in on their own self-interests: "All for one."

The KKK kept members busy with a host of "parades, cross burnings, picnics, weddings, Konclaves, and the more mundane biweekly meetings." These events allowed them to "socialize, discuss local conditions, and decide upon a course of remedial action."

"Lonely men could find companionship; frustrated men could articulate their grievances."[308]

And Louis Conshafter was both of those things: Lonely following the deaths of his wife and young daughter and immensely frustrated by his drop in status and funeral home revenue.

At its peak, KKK membership in WNY totaled 4,000. While Louis undoubtedly profited from being one of only three undertakers listed in the local chapter directory, he has left an ample historic footprint to assume that his involvement was more than pecuniary.

Conshafter was at his most vulnerable during this era, devastated by personal loss and on unstable financial footing. How else can you explain how an otherwise ordinary, well-established businessman be persuaded to join a notorious secret society that pandered to the darkest impulses in America?

The Klan had a presence in the area as demonstrated in July 1923 when approximately 3,000 knights and "neophytes" conducted their "spectacular ceremonial" chartering of the "Williamsville unit of the hooded order" at Main Street and Transit Road. Hundreds of automobiles gathered at the scene after nightfall to shine their ghostly headlights on the ritual.[309]

While there is no evidence to suggest the local Klanvern lit up the night skies at Conshafter's Glen, it can be imagined that Louis would have hosted a picnic for the "Invisible Empire" on this Williamsville property.

What is known, however, is that local Klan members mobilized again in March 1924, when they raided the Auto Rest, a well-known roadhouse at Transit Road and Main Street. The establishment was run by Minnie Clark—widely known as "Jew Minnie"—a rumored paramour of Giuseppe DiCarlo, Buffalo's reigning mob boss. By the time of the raid, ownership of the roadhouse had officially passed to DiCarlo's son, Joe "The Wolf" DiCarlo, though Minnie clearly remained in charge. The Auto Rest was a popular hotspot during Prohibition, drawing crowds despite its controversial associations.[g]

The night of Saturday, March 15th started out normally with a roadhouse full of 150 patrons enjoying a jazz band.[310] Just after midnight, a guest reported seeing red flares being ignited around the building before 50 white robed and hooded men entered. Ordering the patrons to stand, they demanded the band play the National Anthem after which an older Klansman delivered a warning against the continued sale of alcohol:[311]

"It is the understanding of the Invisible Empire that this place is running in violation of the law and under the protection of the authorities. In the Invisible Empire, there is no such thing as partiality or protection. The Klan stands for law and order, and if this place is run on an orderly basis, no one will be molested. But if the owners persist in running it in violation of the law it will be closed."[312]

Following the request that a second song be played— "America" —the Klan members departed.

Interviewed later, Minnie said that the visitors "acted like gentlemen and molested no patrons in the place." For that reason, she did not object to the demonstration.[313]

One local publisher was unimpressed with the shakedown: "We do not for one moment believe that the Klan is even slightly interested in the enforcement of law. Bent on having an excuse to wear their silly disguises in the same dramatic fashion that the immature detective displays his tin star, they scrutinize hopefully rather than regretfully, every situation which may provide them with the opportunity to pose as guardians of the community and to parade in their clown clothes."[314]

Eventually, the roadhouse raids throughout the area ceased when armed guards were stationed at each of their doors.

---

[g]See Chapter 12 for more information about the mob.

By planning the raids on the outskirts of the City, the Klan was making an effort to avoid adding heat to the rising ire of its Mayor Frank X. Schwab.[315] Schwab, a former brewery owner who ran on the anti-Prohibition platform in 1921, was incensed with the presence of the KKK and put into motion a plan that eventually resulted in causing the "Invisible Empire" to disappear on the Niagara Frontier.

****

After months of increasing activity by the Klansmen, Schwab recruited a former Vice Squad officer to infiltrate the organization. The efforts of "special patrolman" Edward C. Obertean and a second undercover officer eventually led to the theft of the Klan's membership list from inside the organization's headquarters in the Calumet building on Chippewa Street.[316] Many of the Klan's members depended on the secrecy of their involvement to keep them on good standing in the city. The directory was ordered posted in the lobby of the Buffalo Police Headquarters, and thousands of people lined up to read the names. Eventually, a pamphlet was published with the names and put on sale.[h] The breakdown of anonymity was the beginning of the end.

Louis Conshafter's name was listed in the KKK membership directory under the Undertaker category.

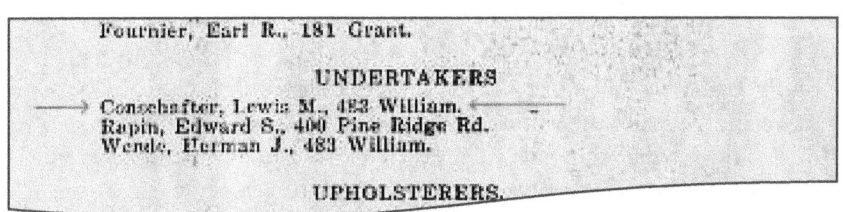

Figure 84 Louis M. Conshafter is listed in the Klu Klux Klan's WNY membership directory as a member
Courtesy of the Buffalo History Museum

By August 1924, the Klan was in its death throws.

'People boycotted clan businesses; employers dismiss individuals whose names appeared on the list; and one individual, many believe, committed suicide after killing his wife and two sons rather than face his friends."[317]

The presence of the KKK in Buffalo might have been chalked up to an intense grudge match between two political factions if the bullets had not begun to fly, resulting in the death of two men—one from each side of the divide.

---

[h] The entire membership directory is digitized and available at NYHeritage.org.

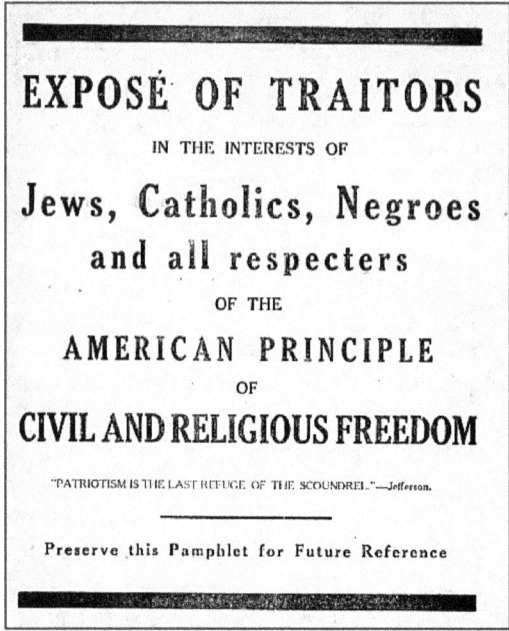

Figure 85 The KKK membership directory cover
(1924-1925)
Courtesy of the Buffalo History Museum

Following the release of the membership list, national Klan leaders sent Thomas Austin, a Klan investigator, to Buffalo. It did not take him long to finger Obertean as Mayor Schwab's informant. In August 1924, Austin drove along with two Klansmen to confront the special patrolman at his home in North Buffalo. Obertean escaped the scene in a car driven by a friend, but Austin gave chase.[318]

Nine gunshot blasts were exchanged on Durham Street in Buffalo where both cars were pulled over to settle the dispute. The firefight resulted in the death of Obertean and Austin, and the end of the Buffalo Klan's resurgence in Western New York.[319]

The national KKK organization continued for a time. Ultimately, the greatest threat to its existence did not come from outside the organization, but from within. As millions of dollars accumulated in their coffers from the payment of dues ($10) and the sale of uniforms and regalia (for which they had a monopoly), in-fighting for control among the leadership ranks caused a massive fissure. Eventually, the leadership ranks imploded, taking down Klaverns in communities throughout the country.

As for Conshafter, he officially retired from his funeral business following the publication of the KKK directory. He was forced to sell Glen Park and ended up taking off to foreign ports (five trips to Europe and one around the world). While on a vacation to Germany, the former woodworker purchased a hand-carved, solid walnut casket[320] in which he was buried in 1940 after dying at the home of his Eggertsville brother. He was 76. The casket's 600-pound weight required eight pall bearers to carry it and the lid needed to be removed to fit into the hearse.[321]

In accordance with his wishes, there was no minister to oversee the funeral. The members of Mystic Star Lodge No. 512 (Independent Order of the Odd Fellow) took charge of the service.[322]

He is buried in the Pine Hill, Cheektowaga cemetery alongside his wife and daughter.

CHAPTER 9—FRESH FACES, SHATTERED FUTURES

Whoever Louis Conshafter was—or how he came to a place in his life where he could embrace the prejudiced views of the KKK—he did usher in the entertainment era at the Glen. Under Louis's guidance the property had emerged as a recreational destination. He had cleared the land, built the dance hall, and established a catering service for large-scale picnics.

With Louis out of the picture in the far reaches of the globe, it offered the Cardina Brothers—James and Thomas—the opportunity to take on the task of becoming the property's official steward.[a]

Born to parents from Frosolone, Italy,[323] both boys were Buffalo natives from a family of six children. James, the eldest, was born in 1875. Thomas came along six years later. Both men were barbers by trade and serial entrepreneurs by temperament. Together, alone, and with other family members, they owned confectionary stores (299 Parkside Avenue, Buffalo, is one example) as well as delicatessens and small restaurants.

In the 1920s, their main source of income came from a small chain of movie theaters in Buffalo. The eldest brother, James, had purchased the Kensington Theater on Grider Street (often called "Little K" or "Grider-Kensington") back in 1916.[324] Originally a 445-seat venue, he invested $150,000 for a major renovation in 1923, the same year he also built the Varsity Theater at 3165 Bailey Avenue near Delavan.[325]

Figure 86 Thomas Cardina
Photo courtesy of Carol (Cardina) Schmidt

Their expansion accelerated in 1925 when, after managing the Glen Theater in Williamsville for G.A. Nichols, they decided to buy the theater. Glen Park was added to their property portfolio following Conshafter's expulsion.

Renovations on both Glen properties began almost immediately. The Glen Theater underwent a significant overhaul, including increased seating capacity, the construction of a new atrium, and a refreshed Tudor-style façade.[326]

---

[a] For folks who believe in karma, there is satisfaction in knowing that two sons of Italian immigrants – and in the decade to come, the son of Russian Jews –would find success at the Glen after a Klan member was essentially run off the property.

In the Park, the Cardina brothers—"two of Williamsville's most progressive businessmen of the younger school"[327]— re-laid the ballroom floor to a smooth "piece of ice" and enlarged it to become "one of the largest...dance halls in Western New York."[328] In a May 25, 1925 article in *The Buffalo Times*, it was reported that dance music was provided every evening at the Glen by "the celebrated Varsity Eight, one of the best known and most competent musical organizations in Buffalo." The orchestra had earned a reputation for the "perfection of its timing and the sweetness of its harmony."[329]

The reporter wrote raptorially about the Williamsville Glen: "Its graceful falls and its rustic surroundings have aptly been described as one of the prettiest spots in Western New York."[330] "Tucked away among trees and rocks and ravines, hardly more than a stone's throw from Main Street...the Glen is not only one of the best equipped outing spots in this section of the state, but one of the most accessible as well."[331]

By 1927, Thomas and James announced in an advertisement that the Glen offered "every facility to help make you merry."[332] The attractions included a roller rink, merry-go-round, big dining room, playground, and concessions. By then, visitors could buy "special steak and chicken dinners" every Sunday during the summer months.[333]

Concurrent with all this frantic activity, James signed a long-term lease to operate the Capitol Theatre on Niagara Street in Niagara Falls.[334] Built in 1926, the theater seated 1,400 people and was originally designed as an event venue. Key to its claim to fame is the fact that one of only two known concert recordings of Hank Williams Sr. was recorded at the Capitol.

For the Cardinas, the end came suddenly, as it did with many commercial enterprises following the Stock Market Crash of 1929. Their real estate properties were foreclosed on by the banks, including Glen Park and the theaters they owned. Standing in the wings were two men primed to begin new chapters of their lives: Menno Dykstra and Harry Altman. They would pick through the ruins left behind by the Cardinas and launch successful, lifetime careers.

When the Cardina business portfolio was set to be auctioned off in the late 1930s, Harry Altman emerged as a strong candidate to secure its purchase due to his extensive experience in event management and a proven ability to assemble investment teams. At the time, he was nearly destitute, nearing personal bankruptcy.

Reflecting on his struggles, Altman remarked, "I had a stake in a shaky joint called Palais Royal back in town. There were times when I had to borrow $5 from the head waiter just to take something home for the family."[335]

In a *Buffalo Evening News* article, Altman recalled being captivated by the idea that the Glen could be acquired for relatively little money due to the sharp decline in property values during the Depression.[336] Although he acknowledged that the land was little more than "a mud hole with tables," he recognized its potential. However, without access to funding to begin operations at the park, he had to get creative and scrape together enough money to place an ad in *Billboard* under the headline: Wanted: Concessionaires for New Park Venture."[337]

Altman told *The Buffalo Evening News* that the ad attracted three interested concessionaires, who paid $500 in total for the rights to operate at the park. With that seed capital, he was able to incorporate Amherst Amusements Corporation in 1931. and lure a handful of investors to expand the business.[338]

This version of events, which Altman often shared with reporters, presented a story of ingenuity and resourcefulness. However, the reality was more nuanced. As Altman's grandson, Steve Goldstein, later explained, Altman devised a clever strategy to demonstrate his financial capability to his investors. By presenting the accounting records of concessionaires he did not own, Altman created the impression that he had the necessary revenue stream to continue park operations.[339]

In the end, it was not money that built Glen Park—it was illusion, timing, and nerve.

MENNO DYKSTRA

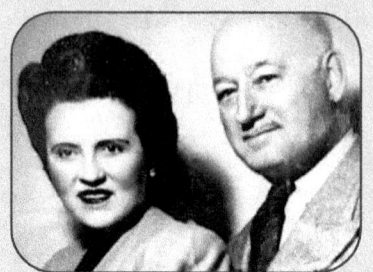

Figure 87 Edna and Menno Dykstra
Photo courtesy of Maron (Dykstra) Carubba

While Altman focused on securing Glen Park during the Cardinas' bankruptcy, Menno Dykstra stepped in to take over the Glen Theater, located at 5606 Main Street, just a short walk from the Park. He also secured the Kensington Theater at 525 Grider Street, formerly owned and operated by the Cardina brothers.[340]

The Glen Theater reopened on Easter Sunday, 1931, marking the beginning of a remarkable four-decade run under Dykstra family stewardship.

Menno and his wife, Edna (Frank) Dykstra, moved into an apartment above the theater, where they raised their only child, Robert. Edna served as the box office cashier, a role she held for 25 years while Menno managed daily operations and booked the films.[341]

GLEN Theatre
WILLIAMSVILLE
TALKING PICTURES THAT PLEASE
— ADMISSION PRICES —
ADULTS 25c — CHILDREN 10c
— ANYTIME —
Under Management of
Mr. and Mrs. M. H. Dykstra
PROGRAM WEEK OF JUNE, 7th, 1931.
SUNDAY, June, 7th,
Continuous 2 to 11 P. M.
WARNER BROS. Present
The LIFE OF THE PARTY
With WINNIE LIGHTNER
CHARLES JUDELS & IRENE DELROY
A deliciously daring comedy that will make you laugh and gasp all in the same breath.
CHARLIE CHASE Comedy
"DOLLAR DIZZY"
Serial "PHANTOM OF THE WEST" Chap. 7
"STEIN SONG" Screen Song

Figure 88 Promo card from first screening by Dykstras (1931)
Photo courtesy of Maron (Dykstra) Carubba

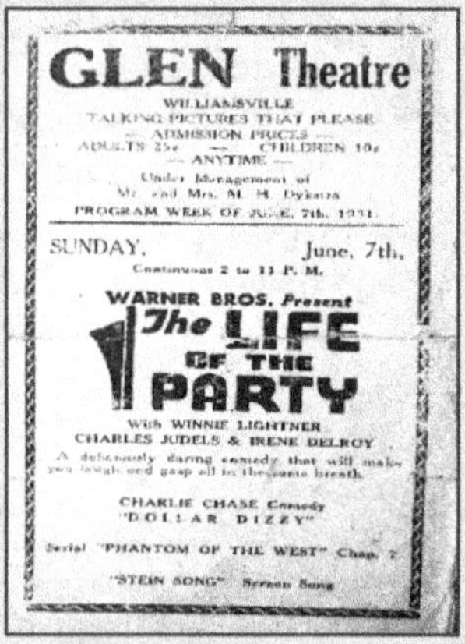

Under their care, the Glen weathered the Great Depression and World War II, offering affordable entertainment when people needed it most. Menno kept the theater current, introducing "talkies," showing Hollywood features, and occasionally running newsreels and serials that drew loyal crowds.

In 1941, the theater underwent a major renovation—a sleek Streamline Moderne makeover[b]*—which modernized the facade and briefly rebranded the venue as "The New Glen Theatre."*[342]

Throughout the 1940s and '50s, the Glen thrived. Menno estimated weekly attendance at more than 2,000 patrons, with weekend double features drawing families, packed Saturday matinees delighting kids, and teenagers on dates filling the back rows—earning the theater its affectionate nickname, "The Pit" (short for "passion pit").

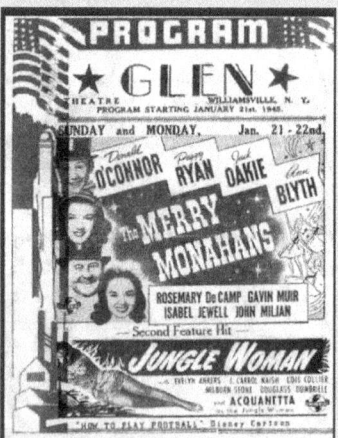

Figure 89 Theater program from January 1945
Photo courtesy of Maron (Dykstra) Carubba

---

[b] The Streamline Moderne is a later period of the Art Deco style.

Figure 90 Photo courtesy of Maron (Dykstra) Carubba

By the late 1950s, with television, drive-ins, and multiplexes pulling audiences away, Menno chose to retire. In 1959, he leased the Glen to Miracle Films, Inc., a national chain known for fine art and revival cinemas.[343] The theater transitioned from a neighborhood second-run house to a dedicated art cinema, joining a national circuit showcasing silent classics, foreign films, and offbeat features.

In 1965, reflecting its new identity, the theater was officially renamed the Glen Art Theatre.[344] Around this time, local theater impresario Fred Keller took over management, expanding its cultural footprint with a small bookstore and art gallery in the building.[345] The Glen Art hosted everything from Bergman and Fellini films to avant-garde pieces and vintage comedies.

Its biggest commercial triumph came in 1966, when the French film "Man and a Woman" became a sensation, running for 57 consecutive weeks—the longest film run in Buffalo's history at the time.[c]

But after nearly 50 vibrant years, tragedy struck in 1970. In September, Menno died at age 78. Just two months later, in November, a devastating fire engulfed the Glen Theater.[346] Firefighters from Williamsville and neighboring towns battled the blaze, complicated by the building's patchwork construction and hidden voids in the roof from decades of remodels.

Trapped on the upper floor, Edna Dykstra, then 77, was rescued by firefighters through a window.[d] Other tenants escaped down the stairs. During the chaotic effort, a misdirected blast from two fire hoses injured a firefighter's eye.[347]

Though the fire was eventually subdued, the damage was irreparable.

Today, the Glen Theater lives on in local memory as a beloved landmark. Longtime Williamsville residents still trade stories—sneaking candy in from the corner store, watching reels change mid-show, and gathering in "The Pit." Once a humble neighborhood movie house, the Glen became a cultural beacon, remembered with affection, nostalgia, and pride.

---

[c] "Fred Keller Brought TV to Buffalo and Art Films to Main Street but His Heart Belongs to Theater" *The Buffalo News*, November 20, 1994, 16.

[d] Edna Dykstra would live another couple of decades, dying in her centennial year (September 1, 1992).

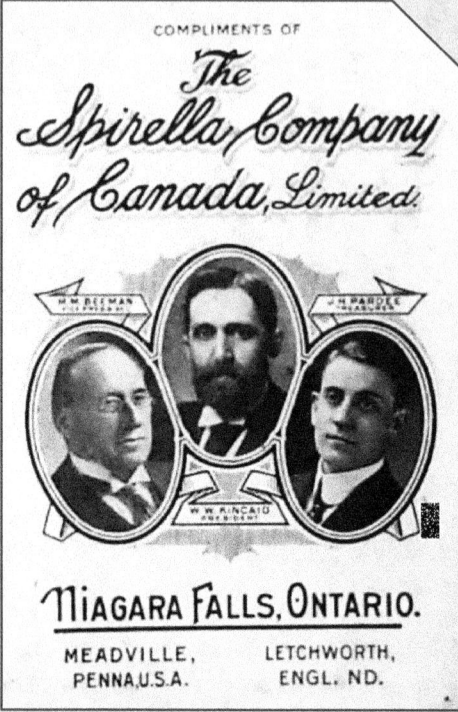

COMPLIMENTS OF

The *Spirella Company* *of Canada, Limited.*

NIAGARA FALLS, ONTARIO.

MEADVILLE,   LETCHWORTH,
PENNA,U.S.A.   ENGL. ND.

Figure 91 Pardee's success at Spirella helped fund his purchase of Erie Beach in 1925
PD

As Altman's plans for managing the Glen took shape, he accepted a salaried position at Erie Beach, a nearby amusement park entering its final season. The park closed after the 1929 stock market crash, and its downfall—and the toll it took on owner J. Homan Pardee—left an impression on Altman. Despite Pardee's considerable wealth, prominence, and influence, he was not shielded from the sting of failure or the depths of despair.

With a lineage that traced back to 16th-century Normandy, Pardee built his personal wealth as the co-founder of Spirella, a corset manufacturer in Meadville, PA, that later achieved international prominence by manufacturing surgical supplies and other elastics.[348] His involvement with Erie Beach began when Spirella's factory relocated to Niagara Falls, NY, followed by the unexpected death of the park's high-profile owner, Frank V.E. Bardol, at the age of 56.[349] In 1925, Pardee seized the chance to acquire the 300-acre amusement park from the Bardol estate for $1.5 million—a record real estate transaction for the Canadian/Niagara Frontier at the time.[350] The purchase was seen as a prudent investment as Erie Beach saw upwards of 20,000 visitors daily during the peak summer season.

Though Erie Beach is now largely forgotten, it was once considered the "Atlantic City of Southern Ontario," boasting amenities such as a 65-room hotel, 4,000-foot beach promenade, a 3,500-capacity stadium, the world's largest swimming pool,[e] 100 midway attractions, and an airport.

---

[e] An entertain feature Altman coveted and would seek to emulate without success in later years.

*Figure 92 Erie Beach had what was advertised as "the world's largest swimming pool,"
a feature Altman would long covet for the amusement park's he managed
Photo courtesy of the Buffalo & Erie County Public Library*

Two ferries transported patrons from the U.S. to the shores of Fort Erie, where the Sandfly Express, an open coach train, took them the final three miles to the park.

Erie Beach's primary competitor, Crystal Beach, located a few miles west in Ridgeway, Ontario, was smaller but fiercely competitive. Its owner, George C. Hall, employed clever promotions to draw visitors to its sandy beach, modern midway rides, and iconic roller coasters.[351]

Once the Depression began, the local economy could not support having two large amusements parks in the region. Thanks to Hall's agile promotional strategy and ability to successfully reorganize after a 1931 bankruptcy filing, Crystal Beach survived largely intact and continued operating for five more decades before closing permanently in 1989.

While Spirella would remain viable well into the mid-20th century, Pardee never recovered from the high-profile failure of Erie Beach. On November 15, 1931, he died of carbon monoxide poisoning in his mansion's garage six months after the park closed, at the age of 52.[352]

By the time of Pardee's death, Harry had already weathered his share of entrepreneurial battles—and many more lay ahead. Yet his perseverance, tireless work ethic, and deep cultural roots would carry him through the turbulent times to come.

CHAPTER 10—ALTMAN TAKES THE REINS

arry's history in Glen operations began in September 1930 when Amherst Bank foreclosed on the Cardinas' loan for the property.[353] Within six months (March 1931), Amherst Amusement Corp. was incorporated; shareholders were Annabelle Altman; Bessie (Violet) Gallagher, the stewardess of the Palais Royal (1931); and Helen Newman, a Williamsville resident.

In the early 20th century, it was a common but not strictly legal practice to use real individuals' names as "placeholders" in corporate filings. Due to less rigorous regulatory oversight at the time, this method was frequently adopted by new businesses looking to protect the real investors for privacy or strategic purposes. These placeholder names appeared in the initial incorporation paperwork, which had to be publicly filed. Once that requirement was met, any subsequent changes—such as replacing those names—were handled privately and did not become part of the public record. Crucially, those individuals used as placeholders needed to be trustworthy and loyal to the actual owners, especially in executing day-to-day business operations.[354]

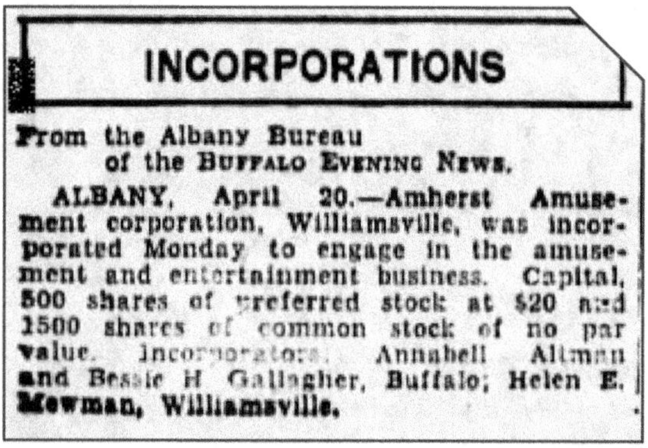

INCORPORATIONS

From the Albany Bureau
of the BUFFALO EVENING NEWS.

ALBANY, April 20.—Amherst Amusement corporation, Williamsville, was incorporated Monday to engage in the amusement and entertainment business. Capital, 500 shares of preferred stock at $20 and 1500 shares of common stock of no par value. Incorporators: Annabell Altman and Bessie H Gallagher, Buffalo; Helen E. Newman, Williamsville.

Figure 93 Amherst Amusements Incorporation Announcement
The Buffalo Evening News, April 21, 1931
PD

When Amherst Amusement was formed, Harry was on the brink of personal bankruptcy—a reality that came to pass in 1934. Listing three placeholder names in the incorporation documents appears to have been a strategic move to safeguard the business. The women selected as proxies were trusted for their dependability and willingness to follow instructions.

Amherst Amusement does not appear on records as the owner of the park's real estate. However, its role in securing an alcoholic beverage license and being named in lawsuits suggest the company likely owned and operated the park's above-ground assets. Early on, these included a dance hall, roller rink, and facilities for preparing and serving food and drinks.

Harry quickly announced the launch of his company, informing the press just two weeks after its March 1931 incorporation about his new role as general manager of Glen Park.[355] Coverage in local newspapers highlighted his ambitious plans to invest $150,000[a] in developing an amusement park and enhancing the picnic areas. The re-opening was slated for May, just two months later. He noted that the financing was sourced from "Buffalonians who have formed the new corporation."[356]

In his announcement, Harry also disclosed the names of five corporate board members: Edward Scott, a previous investor of Altman's; Mrs. Rose Murray, a recent widow and a GOP committee member for the 4th district; Carl Shuman; Frank Hughes; and Kenneth Clay.[357]

In April, *The Buffalo Courier-Express* unveiled details about Harry's newest ideas for the Glen.[358] Drawing inspiration from the "world's largest swimming pool" at Erie Beach, Altman planned to construct a state-of-the-art pool, with a 200-foot sand beach along one side. "The sand and water will be sterilized and cleansed daily," Altman promised. The plans would also include dressing rooms, showers, a first aid room, and a team of lifeguards to ensure safety.[359]

"The pool will be conducted in a high-class manner," Altman said.[360]

While the pool idea never came to pass, Altman's investors did spend money in that first year tearing down some of the "old shacks" on the property that he declared were "eyesores," rebuilding the floor of the skating rink to create an "elaborate" dance hall (naming it the Ritz Barn), and establishing a small midway using rides owned by concessionaires. Promotional advertising also placed emphasis on the natural features of the park including "the beautiful waterfalls and giant willow trees."[361] Altman's days of laying asphalt were still in the future.

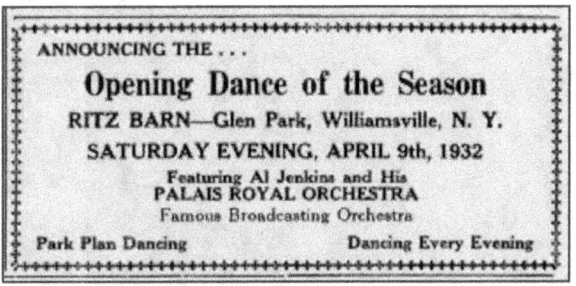

Figure 94 Advertisement from 1932 promoting The Ritz Barn, the precursor to the Glen Casino
PD

Park gates opened in May. Trouble followed soon after when the Village of Williamsville refused to issue a license permitting the dance hall to open on Sundays.[362]

---

[a] One hundred and fifty thousand dollars was the figure Altman seemed to favor whenever he announced projected investments to the press. In truth, it would be years before that amount—equivalent to about $3.5 million today—was ever spent cumulatively on Glen upgrades.

The village took the stance that Sunday dancing was "contrary to the desire" of local property owners near Glen Park. Allowing them to "dance the waltz and fox trot on the Sabbath" would have "a detrimental influence on young people in the community."[363] As midnight approached on the first Sunday of Glen Park's operation, tensions escalated. Despite earlier warnings to management that Sunday dancing would not be permitted, a crowd of 1,500 people was still on the dance floor when Mayor Harry M. Abel, Police Chief Edwin H. Evans, and Village Attorney Phillip J. Snyder arrived at 11 PM on Saturday night to enforce the rule.[364]

"The officials did not attempt any forcible intervention, leaving it to Mr. Altman and his associates to deliver the unfortunate news," reported *The Buffalo Courier-Express*. The crowd responded with boos and jeers directed at the village officials, but by midnight, the pavilion was cleared, and the orchestra was dismissed for the night.[365]

Figure 95 Interest in Col. Rogers' efforts to break the flagpole sitting record made national news
Photo courtesy of the Rogers' Estate

"There was a spirited exchange between Amherst Amusement attorney [Abraham N.] Carrel and the village officials, but the encounter ended without any physical altercations."[366] Carrel would prevail shortly thereafter in the courts, and by Decoration Day the Ritz Barn was a seven-day operation.

Altman's first year managing Glen Park culminated in a national media event when Arthur (Colonel) Rogers, aged 50, broke Shipwreck Kelley's flagpole-sitting record at the park, remaining aloft for 57 days and two hours.[367] According to *Billboard* on September 12th, "Rogers came down on Labor Day and danced a jig."[368] His endurance was tested during a "terrific electrical storm" one night, which caused about $100,000 in damage to nearby buildings and crops.[369] Altman reported that the contest drew large crowds to the park, and Rogers eventually made pole-sitting his permanent career, finding it "more profitable" than carpentry.[b]

According to his family, Rogers, who was born in Vermont and lived on Shirley Avenue in Buffalo, eventually lost his eyesight, which they attributed to the constant sun exposure from his pole-sitting stints.

In his operations summary in *Billboard,* Altman proudly stated that "Glen Park can be counted among amusement parks which made a profit in 1931." *Billboard* noted, "This park had been considered a bloomer [failure] until Mr. Altman assumed charge last year."[370]

Under Altman's direction, all the concessions, refreshment stands, and small buildings were painted in "gay, bright colors" to evoke a festive, Coney Island-like atmosphere.[371] "The Ballroom was the main attraction, and thousands congregated there nightly," Altman said. "I can safely say we did the largest business of any...ballroom in this part of the country. We only hope that we can do as well in 1932, as I know we were one of the few parks that made money this year."[372]

During the early years of Altman's Glen Park management, the area alongside Ellicott Creek had a carnival-like atmosphere.

Rides and games provided by concessionaires took over much of the property, allowing Altman to do what he did best—promote special events that were meant to attract a curious crowd. His creativity knew no bounds, and he was rewarded for his efforts by receiving free publicity in the many newspapers published during this era.

In the depth of the Depression, free admission to the Glen attracted patrons from throughout Western New York. Harry served "fair food" (10 cent sandwiches) and beverages (large pitchers of beer for a quarter) from several small shacks that dotted the property. Guests were welcome to bring their own picnics and eat at tables supplied by Altman. For families tight on a budget, there was a playground with a sandbox where children could expend their energy while parents rested only a few yards away.

Decades later during a zoning dispute with the Village of Williamsville, Harry became enraged when a local resident called him a "carnival man." But in the early years, a carnival atmosphere was indeed prevalent.

---

[b] Flagpole sitting was a 1920s fad in which participants perched atop poles to test their endurance—or chase fame. For sponsors, it served as a publicity stunt to draw attention to a location. The craze faded with the onset of the Great Depression.

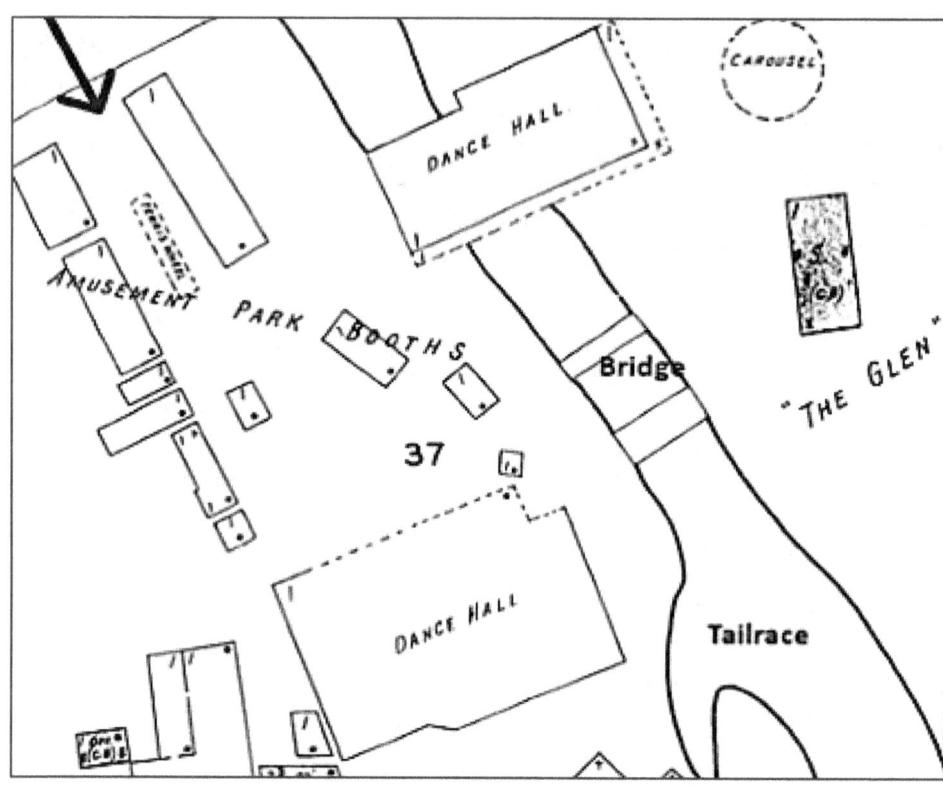

Figure 96 This 1932 Sanborn map of the Glen shows only structures relevant to fire insurers—
buildings and the circular carousel
Author annotations identify key features such as parking, entrance, bridge, and water
PD

1932—THE ROAR OF THE WEDDING CROWD

Ritz Barn opened in April featuring Al Jenkins and the Palais Royal Orchestra.[373] The property at the time was coming into its own as Altman began to take over from what the Cardinas left behind. The dance hall, roller rink, food and concessions were in operation; it would still be another decade until the amusement rides, east of the tailrace, would become prominent.

The remainder of the park began operations in mid-May. The opening weekend included special events involving wrestling bouts, leg races, quoit pitching (like horseshoes), and pie eating contests. Schepp's Comedy Circus was provided as a free attraction, along with the Hilton Sisters, vaudeville performers who were one of the first set of female conjoined twins to become national celebrities.[374]

Figure 98 The Hilton Sisters would be frequent guests at Altman's Glen Park
PD

Altman pushed the boundaries of convention when he hosted an outdoor wedding in a lions' cage that was set up in the Glen as part of the circus. Dorothy Douglas and Lincoln A. Scott, dancing partners appearing at the Palais Royal, said their solemn vows in the presence of five huge, lumbering, growling African lions under the control of trainer William C. Schulz.[375]

Figure 97 Altman, far left, watches the lion in the foreground with a pensive gaze, while the groom, far right, stands ready for the ceremony to begin
Photo courtesy of The Buffalo Evening News

There is an online video clip of the ceremony featuring a wedding party of several bridesmaids and groomsmen entering the large lions' enclosure. Altman is seen giving away the bride, with best man duties handed over to Irving Fox, Harry's general manager for the dance marathon company.[c] While clearly an Altman publicity stunt, the bridegroom appeared to be onboard:

"We live a queer, interesting life. So, we decided to marry the same way," Lincoln A. Scott told a *Buffalo Evening News* reporter.[376]

Town of Amherst Justice of the Peace Alvin K. Ouchie kept the ceremony short and sweet to avoid agitating the beasts. Once the vows were complete, more lions swaggered into the cage, "snuggling against the knees of the bride" who posed for photos with the groom.[377]

"Well," said Justice Ouchie. mopping his brow, "I suppose the next wedding ceremony I perform will be for a couple standing on their heads in the midst of Niagara Falls!"[378]

Not all news was good. The Amherst Amusement Company faced its first public lawsuit when Matthew G. Michaels, a welter-weight boxer from Cheektowaga, was awarded $231 in damages he suffered while visiting the park. As noted in *The Buffalo Courier-Express*,[379] he was in the process of swinging a mallet on a rubber pad to ring the bell when the mallet head broke off and hit him in the leg. He claimed that he had to "abandon his career" as a prizefighter due to the injuries.[380]

At the end of year two, Harry reported to *Billboard* that there was a downturn in revenue from 1931, but the park was still running in the black. The dance hall stayed open until October, continuing to draw good business.

1933—ALL IN THE FAMILY BUSINESS

Park operations during the next two seasons ran smoothly, with large-scale organization picnics becoming a key feature. The New York Central and Nickel Plate Railroad Athletic Associations held their events at the park for at least two consecutive years. In 1933, the gathering attracted 1,800 participants, and by the following year, Harry, taking a personal interest, counted 9,000 attendees himself, proudly announcing the impressive turnout.[d381]

The roller rink was renovated and would be the first of several rinks operated by the Altman family in the coming years.

---

[c] The couple were legally married at the event and went on to perform in venues across the country.

[d] To get a sense of the massive numbers of patrons who visited the park, visit "The Critical Past" website. There is a one-minute film clip showing hundreds of patrons enjoying the Park as part of an event hosted by area firefighters.

In 1933, the Park hired its first manager, James (Jimmie) Phillips. Annabelle, now a mother of three after the birth of their son Robert in 1930, stepped up to serve as the "assistant park manager," helping to oversee operations. She would become pivotal to the long-term success of the Glen.

Their daughter, Hermine (Altman) Goldstein, recounted in a 1976 article in the *Amherst Bee* that her mom worked 15—17-hour days behind the scenes supervising the help and running the office.[382]

Hermine still remembered the first time she saw the park. Harry had picked her up from elementary school to drive her to Williamsville.

"'I've got something to show you,'" he said, when she jumped into the car. She remembers that there was only a monkey cage (known colloquially as "Monkey Island") and maybe one or two rides in the Glen.[383]

"During the Depression times, it was one of the few places where people could afford to go for entertainment," Hermine said. As the children got older, the Altman children were expected to pitch in and work in the park.[384]

Natalie, the older Altman daughter, worked the hardest, Hermine said. "She worked as head cashier.[e] I was selling tickets when I was 16."[385]

1934—BANKRUPT BUT NOT DEFEATED

For Harry, bankruptcy had always seemed like a distant storm on the horizon, until the dark clouds finally rolled in during February 1934. At 43 years old, he was a seasoned serial entrepreneur who had faced and survived many economic downturns. However, the devastating impact of the Great Depression, combined with his desperate attempts to revive multiple businesses in hopes of igniting a spark of recovery, led to his inevitable downfall.

Harry's approach to this pivotal moment was nothing short of masterful.

Drawing on the expertise of the legal brain trust he had cultivated over the years; he skillfully navigated the Federal bankruptcy process to prevent crippling repercussions. The key player in crafting his legal strategy was Abe Carroll, his close friend and former business partner.

At this critical juncture, Harry had much at stake. The first step in his plan was filing for personal bankruptcy, leaving Annabelle and Amherst Amusement

---

[e] The basement of the Altmans' Williamsville home at 74 Mill Street, just yards away from the Glen, became the counting room for all the money collected at the Glen after 1940. Annabelle, with the help of Natalie, oversaw the operation. Many park employees recalled seeing large, heavy bags of coins from the games being carried to the house. Ken Fritz, manager of the Smothers Brothers, recounted a visit to the basement around 1963 where he, Tommy, and Dick were offered a bag of coins each as a token of appreciation after a successful one-week run. Initially hesitant to take the money after considering the difficulty of lugging the heavy bags onto a plane, they were relieved when Harry suggested a local bank that would exchange the coins for cash. In the end, all three left the house with bags in hand and headed straight to a Main Street bank.

Company free from encumbrance. Upon filing in Federal bankruptcy court, he listed himself as a "manager" with personal debts totaling $15,500, and assets of $0.[386] By 1934, Altman's Inwood Avenue home had been foreclosed on by the bank, and he and Annabelle had taken residence on East Depew Avenue in Buffalo and, subsequently, the Mansion House in Williamsville.

The second step of the plan was to ensure that his business interests were kept at arm's length. While he no longer owned shares in the companies he had operated during the ballroom and dance marathon era, there was significant public interest in his purported acquisition of the Glen Park operations after the Cardinas went bankrupt in 1931.

It took three years, but in 1934 ownership of the Glen property was finally settled. The newly formed Williamsville Amusements, Inc.[387] assumed the Cardinas' loan from Amherst Bank, thereby becoming the owner of the property—a role that appeared to be its sole function. This corporation retained ownership of Glen Park until 1965, when the property was purchased by the Emprise Corporation. The shareholders of the new property, Valentine O'Grady, Irving Greenberg, and Lee A. Healy, were all attorneys.[388] There is no evidence to suggest that they had close ties with Altman, but they did share a common profession and a particular focus: all were actively involved in debt collection, seeking recompense from individuals on behalf of either merchants or the U.S. Government. It seems that their primary role was to act as nominal shareholders, although it remains unclear whom they were protecting from public disclosure.[f]

Among the three, O'Grady was the most distinguished. He graduated from the University of Buffalo Law School and held an undergraduate degree from Yale. His career included private practice, serving as a referee for the New York State Compensation Board, and a former deputy collector for the Bureau of Internal Revenue. He also pursued political office.[389]

Irving Greenberg's early life was notable. In 1925, at 18 years old, he was arrested for manufacturing moonshine at his mother's home on Eagle Street, taking over the business from his father who left for Canada.[390] Greenberg later earned his law license, established his practice in the Morgan Building, and by mid-century he had a general law practice focusing primarily on debt collection cases.

Lee Healy, another University of Buffalo Law School graduate, was a general practice attorney specializing in collections and bankruptcy cases. His initial office was on Niagara Street before moving to the Ellicott Square Building. Healy made headlines at the end of his life when he was found dead in police lock-up after being arrested for public intoxication. Later reports indicate that the medical examiner attributed his death to natural causes, specifically alcoholism and edema.[391]

---

[f] The practice of using proxies would occur again in 1941 when Amherst Amusements was dissolved, replaced by a new company, Williamsville Amusements.

1935—SUCCESS SHINES ON THE GLEN

By 1935, Glen Park was beginning to hit its stride. The ballroom, a centerpiece of the park's entertainment offerings, had undergone a complete refurbishment, embracing an "elegant Spanish style of decoration that added a touch of exotic flair to the venue."[392] The reopening of the dance hall season was marked by the lively tunes of Gordon Robinson and his Orchestra,[393] who were well-received by enthusiastic crowds.

The era of the "Big Bands" was in full swing, and Glen Park capitalized on this musical craze. The sounds of swing and jazz resonated through the newly decorated ballroom, drawing large crowds eager to dance the night away.

The amusement park maintained a steady attendance, supported by large group picnics from local organizations. To enhance the entertainment, Altman hired the Bench Bentum Aquatic Revue, featuring Jerry O'Brien's daring 116-foot dive into a flaming water tank.[g] The show, set against a Spanish galleon backdrop, also included Miss Bench Bentum, a five-time national diving champion, and her team performing impressive dives from the ship's rigging into the concealed tank below.[394]

Harry was a happy man, reporting to *Billboard* that the Park had "the biggest season to date" in years.[395]

Figure 99 *Ad for Bench Bentum Aquatic Revue*
PD

---

[g] The danger was real. A year earlier, O'Brien misjudged the twist while diving into the water while performing in Yonkers, NY and crashed into the bottom of the tank.

GLEN PARK
WILLIAMSVILLE, N. Y.
Starting WEDNESDAY
The
Sensational **HILTON**
Novel **SISTERS**
Amazing IN PERSON
Thrilling VAUDEVILLE'S
GREATEST ACT

FAMOUS AMERICAN

SIAMESE
TWINS
Joined Together
at Birth
—THEY—
DANCE
PLAY
SING
Free Parking
Free Admission

Two Big Wrestling
Matches Free Wednesday,
Saturday and Sunday

Figure 102 Ad for Hilton Sisters
PD

The year 1936 started on a high note with the return of the Hilton Sisters, the famous conjoined twins known for their captivating performances as singers, dancers, and musicians.

Meanwhile, the Allan Brooks Orchestra,[396] now the Glen's first house band, took center stage in the ballroom, adding to the lively atmosphere at the venue. Harry even arranged for WGR radio to broadcast the orchestra's music four times a week throughout the summer, ensuring widespread exposure. However, as the July 4th weekend approached, things took a sudden and unfortunate turn.

On Wednesday, July 1, 1936, just hours before the busiest weekend for the park began, fire swept through the Glen Park dance pavilion during the early morning hours, destroying the dance hall, three concession stands and the photography gallery.[397]

The fire at the Ritz Barn, which backed up along the escarpment below the Williamsville Mill, took seven volunteer fire companies to get under control. When the trucks arrived, a column of black smoke was pouring "into the still morning air."[398]

Dance Pavilion Burns to Ground

Figure 101 Front page
Photo courtesy of The Buffalo Evening News,
July 1, 1936

Glen Park Blaze Burns Pavilion, 3 Resort Stands

General Alarm Calls All Town of Amherst Apparatus as Flames Threaten Williamsville Business Section.

Figure 100 Front page headline
Courtesy of The Buffalo Evening News,
July 1, 1936

Figure 103 Eggertsville Fire Department continues to quell flames the next morning of the fire
Photo courtesy of the Eggertsville Fire Department

The night watchman at the park, Deputy Sheriff Albert Zimmerman, said he smelled smoke two hours before the pavilion burst into flames, but could not identify the source.[399]

"Firemen said the fire seemed to have made the most headway in the orchestra corner of the pavilion when they arrived, and they concentrated their first efforts there," *The Lockport Sun & Journal* reported.[400] "Valuable musical instruments owned by the Allan Brooks Orchestra, including a new piano, were destroyed."

In addition to fighting the flames in the Glen, firefighters spent a concerted effort to ensure the fire did not spread to the Williamsville Mill, above the Glen on the escarpment.

The property damage was estimated at $12,000, with insurance covering everything except Brooks' musical instruments valued at $4,000. To help the Orchestra financially recover, a fundraiser was held at the Glen a few weeks later.[401]

Figure 104 Eugene Braun (left), member of the Eggertsville Hose company inspects the aftermath of the fire with Altman
Photo courtesy of The Buffalo Evening News

*Figure 105 Ad Announcing Glen to
Continue Operations
PD*

Despite the setback, Altman pushed forward with his July 4th holiday plans. He quickly hired a crew to clear the debris as soon as it cooled and set up a temporary ballroom in the roller rink. Musical instruments were rented to ensure the Allan Brooks Orchestra could still perform.

To attract crowds to the Glen for the pivotal Fourth of July weekend, Altman announced a series of free events. The world-famous snake charmer, Maji, would appear with her live snakes, and additional attractions included wrestling, boxing, the picnic grounds, Monkey Island, and a spectacular fireworks display.[402]

A little more than two weeks after the devastating Ritz Barn fire, Altman moved forward with plans to create something even grander: the newly-named Glen Casino, an 1,000-seat ballroom that he believed would become a landmark.[403] However, before construction could begin, Altman would have to navigate the challenging and often contentious approval process before the Williamsville Village Board. The hearing before the Board would evolve into a full-blown public spectacle, complete with an unexpected reveal that stunned the crowd and the Village Board members.

The Village Board trustees, still nursing grievances from the feud over Sunday dancing at the park, were not going to make things easy. They considered voting against the necessary building permit due to the anticipated increase in noise and traffic that it would bring to the area. Neighborhood residents, including a sizable contingent from the Randall Memorial Baptist Church,[h] were also up in arms.

The Village Board meeting on July 21, 1936, just three weeks after the fire, set the stage for a heated confrontation.[404]

The church members, led by Sunday School Superintendent Milton Hoover, expressed their frustration with what they described as the "awful goings-on" at the property. Hoover emphasized that the noise and parking difficulties caused by Glen visitors were disruptive to their worship services and made it nearly impossible for parishioners to find a place to park near the church.[405]

---

[h] The church was then located at Main and E. Spring Streets, on the escarpment, not far from the overlook to Glen Park.

George A. Terharr, the superintendent of the Williamsville Post Office, launched a scathing critique of Chief of Police Edwin H. Evans. Terharr accused Evans of failing to control the behavior of park patrons and insinuated that Evans, who owned a house on Glen Avenue directly across from the park, had a financial interest in the business as Evans would not allow the previous owners—the Cardinas—to expand their business.[406]

"He and his department are responsible for the noise and parking issues,"[407] Terhaar said.

Evans, visibly stung by the accusations, defended his actions and his integrity. "I have no interest in the park beyond maintaining law and order," Evans stated firmly. "I have been policing the park for three years, handling traffic, and watching over the Glen, and there have been few arrests and very few occasions for an arrest. The park is orderly, well-conducted, and closes at very reasonable hours."[408]

Altman, who had remained calm throughout the heated exchanges, finally spoke up. He reassured the gathering that he took their complaints seriously and was committed to making improvements. "I am about to invest another $65,000 into the property," he announced. "I am only trying to make a living in a decent and respectful way. I have hired special officers, I close my dance hall at 12:30 a.m., and I will not tolerate any rowdyism."[409]

As the meeting dragged on, the board prepared to vote on the issue. The atmosphere was tense, with many expecting Altman's plans to be blocked. But just as the vote was about to be called, Harry made a surprising revelation. He casually informed the board that he already had the building permit in hand. The Village Clerk had issued it after the Zoning Board approved it, believing that most of the Village trustees would vote in favor of the permit.[410]

A brief but intense argument broke out over the finer points of parliamentary procedure, but it was clear that the game was over. Altman walked out of the meeting with the permit in his possession, victorious despite the opposition.

Figure 106 The Mansion House was demolished in 1955, it was located in the plaza where Talbots now stands, just West of the Glen Park Tavern
PD

The year 1936 was pivotal for Harry Altman as he worked to rebuild his shattered finances. While still managing the Glen, he took over daily operations of the Mansion House restaurant, which had recently been rebranded as the Rainbow Room. The stately, three-story limestone hotel at 5495 Main Street, built around 1827, had long stood as a village landmark. Its first floor housed two bars and an elegant dining room; above was the famed third-floor ballroom, rumored to rest on springs. More likely, the bounce underfoot came from a lack of central support beams—an architectural quirk that only added to its mystique.

The 1930s were a tumultuous period for the historic property, which cycled through a series of short-lived owners. In 1937, after William J. Madden declared bankruptcy just weeks into his tenure, Altman seized the opportunity. Though fresh off his own financial collapse, he transferred the liquor license from the now-defunct Sagamore Ballroom that had been destroyed by fire in December 1936 to legitimize the operation of the Rainbow Room 89.

During this critical period, following the fiery destruction of both the Sagamore and the Ritz Barn, the Mansion House provided Altman with a much-needed financial foothold. He drew on his industry connections to bring Glen Casino orchestras into the venue, forging a vibrant cultural link between the two properties. Altman, financially liable to pay the lodging for out-of-town performers, received discounted rates, while he and his family, having lost their home to foreclosure, lived in the Mansion's second-floor quarters.

But Harry could not stay settled for long. A. Irving Milch, the bankruptcy receiver for the Edgewater, offered him the position of manager at the Grand Island amusement park (see on page 142). The opportunity aligned perfectly with Altman's long-term plans for the Glen and proved too tempting to refuse.

"I will not have the time to devote to the operation of the restaurant," Altman told the Amherst Bee. "I enjoyed being at the Mansion House and meeting so many local people, and I hope that the same splendid support will be continued for the new owners."[411]

The Altmans promptly left the Mansion House and moved into a residence at 74 Mill Street, near the corner of Glen Avenue, a property they would occupy for the next 30 years. Initially, Harry and Annabelle leased the home from Dr. F. M. Gipple, later securing the financial means to purchase it outright through a mortgage. Conveniently located just steps from the Glen, the new home kept the family close to the center of Harry's business operations.

Meanwhile, the Mansion House continued to struggle, passing through several owners in the years that followed and failing to recapture its former success. It was ultimately demolished in 1955.[412]

1937—A NEW BALLROOM EMERGES FROM THE ASHES

The new Glen Park Casino, rebuilt after the fire, had its pre-opening event in April 1937.[413] The Allan Brooks Orchestra was on hand with their new instruments, and the ballroom was "beautiful, as all get out," according to Altman.[414]

The official opening was a sell-out on April 10th, with a crowd exceeding 2,000. *The Lackawanna Herald* reviewed the new venue, which it called a "mecca for amusement seekers throughout Western New York."[415]

> *"The Casino is modern Spanish in motif, and the interior is one of the most magnificent ever conceived for a dance hall. Executed by Peter Klein studios of New York City and Buffalo, the interior...gives perfect acoustics."*
>
> *"As one enters the doors his attention is directed to the large bandstand, located in the center of the big building. Lighted indirectly, the fabulous tropical flowers on the back of the stand appear almost radiant. From the bandstand extends a ceiling that is both unusual and colorful. Numerous circles conceal panels of indirect lighting which bathes the dancers in lights of various hues."*
>
> *"The side walls are more daring and original than the ceiling. Brilliantly lit colored stripes melt into the cleverly hidden lighting panels, producing a radiant effect. The promenade is done in the same manner, with a long row of lights running from end to end."[416]*

In 1937, Altman decided that the roller rink, situated in a large building that ran parallel to Glen Avenue near the bridge. could be repurposed into a more profitable event center. Originally named "The Glen Barn,"[i] it offered a casual setting, perfect for hosting performances and gatherings that did not require the grandeur of the Casino. Outside the building was a popular outdoor beer garden.

Figure 107 Hill-Billies Promotional Card
PD

---

[i] In the 1950s and early 1960s, it would be become better known as "The Family Inn."

In its first year, it hosted "Old-Fashioned Barn Dances" with the "World's Greatest Square Dance Band," the Hornellsville Hill-Billies.[417] Altman used the Barn strategically throughout the years, ensuring Glen Park had a venue for every type of entertainment.

While the new Glen Casino received a lot of publicity, *Billboard Magazine* reported that the "dance business" was still off by 45% from the prior year. *Billboard* stated that to attract more business, Harry was experimenting with different styles of music, featuring two house bands in a single month to observe their popularity with the audience.[418] He discovered that his patrons "prefer sweet syncopation to the shag and jeep stuff," noting that the audience eagerly danced to the smooth rhythms of Bunny Wilson but only listened passively when "Peanuts Holland's sepia syncopations" took the stage.[419]

Altman was also starting to bring in big-name acts, with the most successful night of the year being Benny Goodman's performance at the Glen Casino. More than 1,700 patrons paid $1.50 each,[420] resulting in a $2,550 gate[j] for the evening.[k] Goodman's "vigorous thumper of voodoo boilers"—Gene Krupa—would be the featured act at the Glen in May 1938 after leaving Benny to form his own band.[421]

Figure 108 Caricature of Benny Goodman
Photo courtesy of The Archives & Special Collection Department of SUNY Buffalo State

---

[j] Roughly $56,000 for the night in 2025 dollars.
[k] Goodman would return to the Glen on July 5, 1938, bringing along his regular "Caravan" broadcast that was distributed nationally on CBS radio. The Benny Goodman Quartet/Trio would play "I Hadn't Anyone till You" and "I'm a Ding Dong Daddy (from Dumas)."

SAMMY AND JOEY ON THE EARLY ROAD TO STARDOM

The year 1938 saw two future super-stars (and fellow rat-packers) featured at the Glen: Sammy Davis Jr and Joey Bishop.

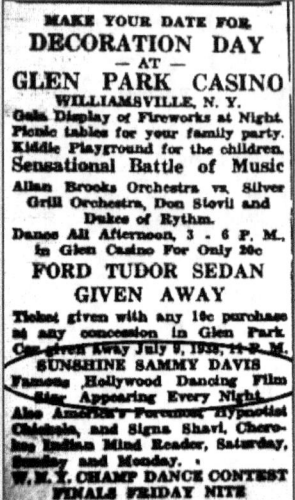

MAKE YOUR DATE FOR
DECORATION DAY
— AT —
GLEN PARK CASINO
WILLIAMSVILLE, N. Y.
Gala Display of Fireworks at Night.
Picnic tables for your family party.
Kiddie Playground for the children.
Sensational Battle of Music
Allan Brooks Orchestra vs. Silver
Grill Orchestra, Don Slovil and
Dukes of Rythm.
Dance All Afternoon, 3 - 6 P. M.,
in Glen Casino For Only 20c
FORD TUDOR SEDAN
GIVEN AWAY
Ticket given with any 10c purchase
at any concession in Glen Park.
Car given away July 9, 1938, 11 P. M.
SUNSHINE SAMMY DAVIS
Famous Hollywood Dancing Film
Star Appearing Every Night.
Also America's Foremost Hypnotist
Chislolu, and Signa Shavi, Chero-
kee Indian Mind Reader, Saturday,
Sunday and Monday. ·
W. N. Y. CHAMP DANCE CONTEST
FINALS FRIDAY NITE

*Figure 109 Advertisement -
Sammy Davis*

Sammy's appearance in May would be the second time Davis appeared at an Altman club.[i] Now age 12, Sammy was a seasoned performer, starting in show business at three years old with his father, Big Sam, and family friend, Will Mastin. Mastin and Big Sam had had been "flash dance" performers in vaudeville revues and on stage between film reels in movie theaters.[422] Adding a child to the act and rebranding as the "Will Mastin Trio" provided them with a promotional advantage in a competitive field of itinerant performers. Additionally, Sammy demonstrated exceptional talent as a showman at a young age.

The trio never hit the big time during this period, but they were well respected in the industry for their "clean act," strong stagecraft, and powerful dancing. Billed as "Sunshine Sammy Davis" the "Famous Hollywood Dancing Film Star," the young dancer appeared at the Glen during Decoration Day weekend.[423] Just prior to his Glen appearance, he had performed in two short films in Los Angeles making him a "Hollywood star." The trio was leading mostly a hand-to-mouth existence during this time, living in low rent, segregated boarding houses.

During their early years in Buffalo, the Mastin Trio stayed at the Vendome Hotel, a two-story building at 175-177 Clinton Street between Michigan and Pine.[424] The Vendome was known for attracting popular musicians from across the country and was notably listed in the "Negro Traveler's Green Book," a guide that helped African Americans find welcoming accommodations in a largely segregated country. As the racial climate evolved and Sammy rose to fame, he began staying at the Statler Hotel during his frequent performances at both the Town and Glen Casinos.

In a May 1955 interview with The Buffalo Evening News, conducted in his suite at the Statler, Davis paid homage to his early visits to Buffalo as "Sunshine Sammy Davis" and his enduring friendship with Altman. Davis described his time at the Vendome as "the nearest thing to a home I remember."[425] However, despite their extended stays in downtown Buffalo, he admitted, "I was never still long enough to go to school in Buffalo...But I learned in burlesque houses and honky-tonks. Yes, I suffered...but it was necessary."[426]

---

[i] Sammy's first appearance booked at an Altman venue was six months earlier at the Savarin in December 1937. Davis, then 11, appeared there in the "Black & White All-Star Revue," performing three times per night (7 PM, midnight and 2:30 AM).

Just when vaudeville was disappearing and nightclubs were coming into their own, Sammy was drafted into the Army during WWII. He was placed in a newly desegregated unit and confronted severe racial prejudice. Upon being honorably discharged in 1945, he returned to the Will Mastin Trio, to whom he would remain loyal all his life. In fact, he continued to pay appearance fees to both his dance partners long after their retirement from show business.[427]

In terms of racial tension, Sammy faced one of his greatest challenges in the Spring of 1952, just as his star was ascending upon the national stage. Buffalonians would provide strong support for the embattled star during this period, thereby earning Davis's enduring gratitude.

The incident in question occurred when he was performing live on The Colgate Comedy Hour hosted by Eddie Cantor before a prime-time audience. Television viewers witnessed Davis become a "break-out star," showcasing his celebrity impressions and phenomenal tap-dancing routines.

The subsequent events displayed on television screens sparked significant discussion among the show's viewers nationwide. Eddie, a former vaudevillian and now famous television comedian, rushed the stage during Sammy's performance to pat the dancer's brow with a handkerchief. At the end the of the routine, Eddie placed a congratulatory arm across Sammy's shoulders.[428]

Figure 116 Sammy was a frequent performer at both the Town and Glen Casinos. Here he is pictured at the Town Casino signing autographs with two of Harry Wallens' grandchildren among the crowd of excited kids
Photo courtesy of Marjorie Wallens (first in line)

This interaction between the white/Jewish Cantor and the black/Jewish Davis enraged many outspoken viewers. Worried sponsors led NBC to threaten cancellation of the show; Cantor's response was to book Davis for two more weeks.[429]

Cantor won this battle, but Sammy faced an uncertain future, unsure how the racial backlash might affect his upcoming nightclub tour.

This was the backdrop to when Sammy and his dance partners headed into Williamsville six weeks after the Eddie Cantor appearance. Contracted by Altman for a one-week engagement at the Glen Casino, Sammy was boldly advertised by Altman as "Eddie Cantor's protégé."[430] The people of Buffalo rallied around him, filling the venue night after night and turning the planned one-week run into a triumphant two-week engagement.[431m]

Figure 110 Sammy and Charles Tyrrell - a vocalist and occasional emcee at the Town Casino
Photo courtesy of Kevin Tyrrell

In a 1955 interview with The Buffalo Evening News, Sammy reflected on the pivotal role the Glen Casino audience played during a challenging time in his career: "I can't find them all to thank them, with the exception of Harry Altman, a pioneer Sammy Davis recognizer," he said. "I thank him often and always will."[432]

Altman responded in kind that year, calling him a "lifesaver" for club owners: "For his age (27), he's the greatest entertainer of the day, the guy who can keep a club owner in business."[433] During his 1955 appearance, Davis set an all-time attendance record at the Glen, breaking Jimmy Durante's record.

Another future Rat Pack member made an early appearance at the Glen in 1938, though his experience was far less glamorous than Sammy Davis Jr's. Joey Bishop took the stage as part of The Three Bishop Boys, a comedy trio from South Philadelphia. Booked in Buffalo the week before the Jewish High Holy Days, the group earned just $45 for the week—split three ways.[434] While Davis would later recall his debut at the Glen with fondness, Bishop's first brush with the venue ended quite differently: the trio wrapped their engagement with an unexpected stint in jail.

---

[m] In addition to hosting The Will Mastin Trio in June 1952 at the Glen, he invited them to return to the Town Casino in December of that year where they sold out more shows.

"There was this guy's daughter who was in love with one of the kids in the trio," Bishop told the Buffalo Courier-Express in 1962. *"And Altman, who apparently was pretty close to the young lady,* " *took a dim view of the whole thing.* "[435]

Harry incorrectly thought Joey was the girl's love interest, so when he discovered her plan to run away with Joey, he decided to step in. "Actually, she was in love with another kid named Sandy, and they had plans to meet at the bus station," Bishop explained.[436] *"Harry, who was [like] the mayor of Williamsville, had us jailed to keep us from leaving Buffalo. I spent Yom Kippur in the can.* "[437]

Eventually, all was forgiven, and Joey and the other members of the group were released. Joey remained a lifelong friend of Harry's, returning to play the Glen periodically throughout the years.°

Figure 111 Joey Bishop
Photo Courtesy of The Archives & Special
Collection Department of SUNY Buffalo State

---

n Steve Goldstein, Harry's grandson, identified the would-be runaway as Natalie Altman, who was then 19 years old.
° Years later, Joey Bishop told columnist Jack Allen that The Three Bishop Boys' 1938 appearance in Buffalo was only their second nightclub booking. Although he admitted he does not enjoy traveling for club dates, Bishop said he continued to perform in Buffalo "out of appreciation to Altman." "O'Brien Debuts Tonight as Series Regular," *The Buffalo Courier-Express*, October 14, 1960, 8.

EDGEWATER: ALTMAN MOONLIGHTS

In 1938, the Edgewater Amusement Park on Grand Island was in receivership, and A. Irving Milch was tasked with helping creditors recover defaulted funds and reverse course. Milch assigned Altman as General Manager to lead the park's revitalization.[438] In his announcement of the new hire, Milch praised Altman's record of "having developed Glen Park into one of the finest amusement parks between New York and Chicago."[439]

Located on Grand Island's East River, Edgewater had been owned by the Voetch family since 1886, when William E. Voetch transformed his farmland into an entertainment destination with numerous attractions including a hotel, grand dance hall, amusement rides, carnival games, and outdoor activities like boating, swimming, fishing, and baseball. With no bridges connecting the island, visitors relied on steamships to link this remote getaway along the Niagara River.

Figure 112 Edgewater Amusement Park, circa 1920
PD

The park's fortunes began to decline during the Great Depression, compounded by the construction of the Grand Island Bridge in 1935, which changed travel patterns. The isolation that once benefited Edgewater became a disadvantage. William E. Voetch, the founder's son and the driving force behind the park's later expansion, died in 1936, leaving the park's future in doubt. Bankruptcy loomed.

Harry's plan was to add a large Roman-style swimming pool[p] to the offerings at Edgewater, as well as construct a new ballroom.[440] The Buffalo Courier-Express noted that Harry had attended the annual National Association of Amusement Parks, Pools, and Beaches convention to gather new ideas to enhance Edgewater's offerings.[441]

Harry did his best, creating an atmosphere of fun with the limited funds made available. He encouraged Niagara Boat Rides to start a ferry service between Tonawanda and Grand Island from the newly opened Grand Island Terminal.[442] For just 35 cents round trip, visitors could board The Griffon and sail directly onto the pier at Edgewater Park. From there they could enjoy "acres of new amusements, spacious picnic grounds, cool breezes, good swimming, dancing, and great food."[443]

The plan to construct the Roman-style swimming pool was not carried out, and the existing ballroom stayed the same. Despite Harry's dedicated attempts to enrich the park's event offerings, the financial state of Edgewater continued to decline. By the early 1940s, the amusement rides were sold, and the property passed into the ownership of Smith & Martin of New York City.[444] The hotel continued operating until part of it collapsed during an April storm in 1974 and was demolished in 1978.[445]

---

[p] Again, with the pool.

1938—GLEN EXPANDS TO WINTER GARDEN

More change was planned for the Glen in 1938. During the regular season, Altman expanded the park's attractions by constructing a wrestling ring in the concession area, where free exhibitions were held four times a week. Professional wrestling was immensely popular in the 1930s, and the Glen gained national attention when Iron Talun (aka Wladyslaw (Walter) Francizak Talun), a Lithuanian-born wrestler, set up his training camp at the park.[446] He was preparing for his first major U.S. bout against Danno O'Mahony, a title contender and Irish whip specialist.

Dubbed the "280-pound mastodon" and standing 7'2" tall, Talun trained at the Glen with a couple of "husky performers," *The Buffalo Evening News* reported.[447] Meanwhile, his opponent O'Mahony conducted his public workouts at Crystal Beach.

Iron Talun won the bout. His competitor claimed he lost because Talun wore hard leather heels on his ring shoes, causing him to suffer cartilage damage from kicks to his rib cage.[448]

After his wrestling career ended, Talun transitioned into acting, most notably playing the role of Goliath in the 1951 film "David and Bathsheba." In the movie, Gregory Peck starred as King David, and Susan Hayward portrayed Bathsheba.

Figure 113 Iron Talun at his fighting weight
Photo courtesy of the Talun Family Estate

The biggest change for the Glen came at the end of the summer season. Without a downtown nightclub to promote (Savarin had closed earlier in the year), Altman announced he would keep the Glen open through the winter, rebranding it as "The Glen Winter Garden."[449] The venue would not collect a cover charge or mandate minimum spending; Harry promoted it with the slogan "spend what you like."[450] Altman showcased a variety of on-stage talent at the Winter Garden, sometimes featuring as many as 15 acts in one night. For a time, he advertised the venue as "The Poor Man's Nite Club."[451]

Figure 114 Talun takes on Hollywood as Goliath
PD

Altman's newspaper ads guaranteed that Winter Garden shows would be "terrific,"[452] aiming to encourage patrons to brave the Western New York winter and attend the nightclub. In the 1930s and 1940s, accessing the Village of Williamsville meant traveling along Route 5 (Main Street), a rural two-lane road. Without the benefit of modern snow removal and road treatments, winter driving could be treacherous.

To ease concerns, the Winter Garden offered "continuous entertainment," eliminating the need for patrons to rush to make curtain time. They could drop in at any point of the evening to catch part of a stage show or dance to the sounds of Bernie Sandler, the Winter Garden's most frequently booked orchestra leader. Georgie Walker, the popular emcee of the era, ensured the night flowed smoothly by introducing acts, engaging audiences, and keeping the energy high.

Every holiday was a major event at the Winter Garden, celebrated in grand style by Harry and his team. Popular occasions like Halloween, Election Day, Thanksgiving, New Year's Eve (featuring a full turkey dinner for $2.25 per person), and Valentine's Day were heavily promoted and featured top talent. Harry took advantage of every promotional opportunity, such as the public wedding of Clown Quit,[453] a frequent performer, and Dorothy Mason, at center stage.[q]

Clown Quit (more commonly known by his later moniker, Quitsie) probably spent the most years on the Glen Casino stage than any other performer. Originally from Philadelphia, Victor Puree (1902-1971) began with Altman in the 1930s and appeared regularly until the late 1950s, traveling from his home in Newark to entertain in weekly shows.

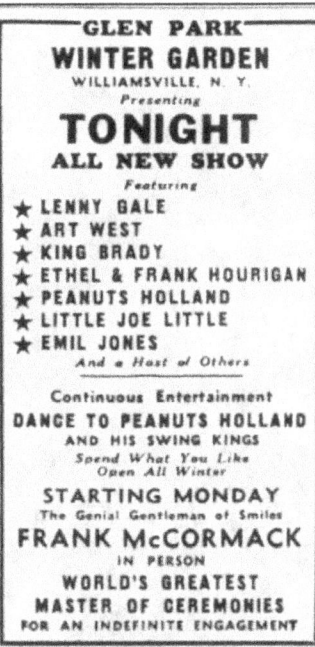

Figure 115 Winter Garden Advertisement November 4, 1938

Figure 123 Ad for clown Quits (Victor Puree) Wedding

---

q It was a real wedding, but not a long marriage. The couple would divorce a few years later and Victor would marry his second wife, Josephine Mavrich. They would stay together until his death in 1971.

FEATURING —
A NEW AMERICAN COMEDIAN

VIC "QUITSIE" PUREE

THE ALL AMERICAN SCREWBALL

Figure 116 1947 Quitsie Promotional Card
Courtesy of the Puree Family

Over its four years of operation, the Winter Garden provided consistent employment to talents such as Joe Howard, vaudeville singer and showman; Beatrice Kay, vaudeville comedienne and singer; Paddy Cliff, popular British tenor; and the Hilton Sisters, conjoined twins.

Altman's most notable event at the Winter Garden occurred at the conclusion of its final season when The Mills Brothers garnered substantial attention from the local media in January 1942. Though the Glen Casino continued operations during the summer months until the 1960s, the Winter Garden closed its doors as Altman and Wallens prepared to open their new downtown nightclub, The Victory Room, in February 1943.

RINK. FIRE. REPEAT.

Roller rinks remained popular during the Depression, offering an affordable form of entertainment. To recoup the revenue lost from closing the rink at the Glen, Altman opened a new location at the northeast corner of Main Street and Transit Road in Clarence. Named the "Haymow,"[r] Harry heavily promoted the roller rink alongside his advertisements for Glen Park, aiming to attract skaters to the venue located two miles east of the park. The Haymow, capable of accommodating 1,000 skaters, opened in May 1938.[454]

The skating activities at the Haymow were abruptly halted less than six months later due to a significant fire on November 14, 1938.[455] This incident led to extensive power outages and attracted numerous motorists drawn by the fire's illumination against the night sky. The blaze reportedly began at 11:30 PM in a small fruit stand and subsequently spread to the rink and the nearby F.C. Clark Candy factory.[456]

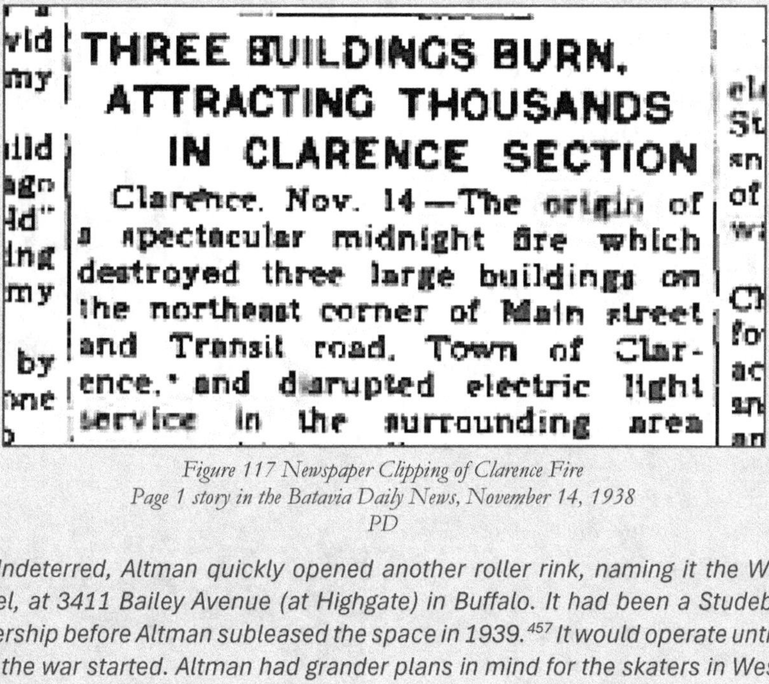

THREE BUILDINGS BURN.
ATTRACTING THOUSANDS
IN CLARENCE SECTION

Clarence. Nov. 14—The origin of a spectacular midnight fire which destroyed three large buildings on the northeast corner of Main street and Transit road, Town of Clarence, and disrupted electric light service in the surrounding area

Figure 117 Newspaper Clipping of Clarence Fire
Page 1 story in the Batavia Daily News, November 14, 1938
PD

Undeterred, Altman quickly opened another roller rink, naming it the Wagon Wheel, at 3411 Bailey Avenue (at Highgate) in Buffalo. It had been a Studebaker dealership before Altman subleased the space in 1939.[457] It would operate until just after the war started. Altman had grander plans in mind for the skaters in Western New York.

---

[r] A term used to describe part of a barn where hay is stored. Typically, it is located in the upper part of the barn, often above the animal stalls, keeping the hay warm and dry. Apparently, Altman was really leaning into the "barn" analogy during this era.

CHAPTER 11—BOOM TIMES AT THE GLEN

As the U.S. stepped into the post-war era in 1946, Altman appears to have secured substantial financial investment facilitating the advancement of his ambitious plans for the Glen. During this year, the Barn was expanded to accommodate up to 800 guests; new property was acquired to increase parking capacity; ride concessionaires were phased out in favor of attractions owned directly by the park; and a new park superintendent was appointed to oversee extensive improvements to the grounds.

The role of superintendent was assigned to Clyde V. Urban, who served as the park's architect and operations chief for the next 20 years.

His responsibilities included general maintenance, managing ride installations, supervising seasonal staff, enforcing safety protocols, and coordinating repairs and improvements across the property. Urban, a skilled construction carpenter by trade, directly contributed to reshaping the park's layout and infrastructure during its most expansive years. He supervised the construction of a stone retaining wall along Ellicott Creek to prevent seasonal flooding and a privacy fence that restricted views of the creek. Additionally, he built a small pedestrian bridge spanning the tailrace from the old mill. The bridge was one of the park's features that remained in place long after the Altman era ended.

Figure 119 Park Superintendent Clyde Urban
Photo courtesy of Ron Urban

In the early years of his employment, Clyde and his family—wife Olga and sons—resided in a house on Glen Park property. This situation lasted until the house's lot was required for the expansion of patron amenities. Urban's efforts helped transform property from a modest summer venue into a polished, self-contained amusement complex. For more than two decades, he was the park's quiet cornerstone, ensuring it ran efficiently, safely, and with a level of structural integrity that allowed it to thrive through periods of change and growth.

Figure 118 Photo of Urban House on Glen
Photo courtesy of Ron Urban

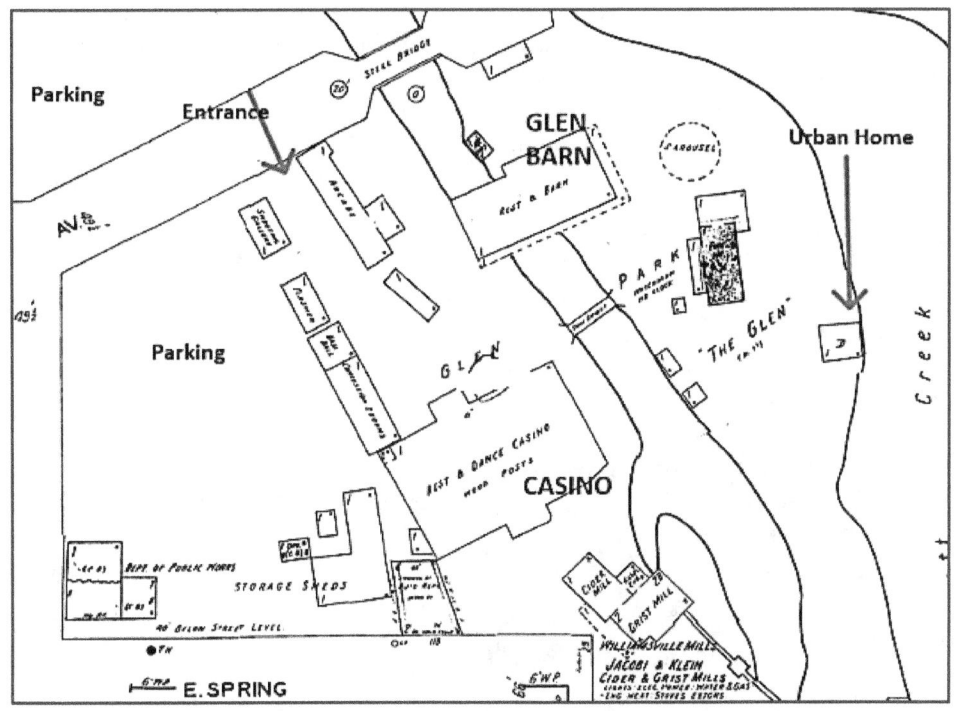

Figure 128 This 1940 Sanborn map of the Glen reveals several additions since the 1932 version, including the recently built Glen Casino and other new structures on the amusement ride side of the grounds
Author annotations highlight key features such as parking areas
PD

The period of expansion followed the establishment of a new corporate entity, Glen Park Amusements, Inc., in January 1941.[458] This new company acquired all above-ground assets, thereby superseding Amherst Amusements Corp., which had been incorporated a decade earlier with Annabelle Altman and two female associates as shareholders. Similar to the preceding Williamsville Amusements arrangement, the three shareholders listed for Glen Park Amusements—Barnett Snapp, and brothers Franklin and Albert Goldman—did not appear to be close associates of Harry Altman, although they had business connections to Altman's attorney, Abe Carrel, and his brother Hyman, who was Carrel's partner at their law firm.[459] It is reasonable to assume that these individuals served as nominal representatives for the actual owners or investors in this transaction.

Snapp and Albert Goldman, who were business partners,[a] owned the Retail Merchants Bureau (collections) and Retail Budget Co. (finance), both based in the

---

[a] In the decade to come, both men would be involved managing Buffalo prizefighters. with their most notable boxer, middleweight Henry Brimm, securing a draw against Sugar Ray Robinson in 1949.

~ 149 ~

Brisbane Building. In addition to his partnership with Goldman, Snapp was a serial entrepreneur involved in owning a drug store, heating manufacturing company, and a construction business. Franklin Goldman was an employee of Retail Merchants Bureau for many years, before joining the Lincoln Credit Bureau.[460]

In related corporate developments, Williamsville Amusements, the owner of the Glen property, transferred its mortgage from Amherst Bank to Marine Trust.[b]

AMUSEMENTS ON THE MIDWAY

The evolution of Glen Park's amusement rides was a gradual and ever-changing process, shaped by shifting ownership, seasonal upgrades, and the constant desire to keep things fresh for returning guests. Rather than launching with a full suite of attractions, the park expanded over time, swapping out older rides for new models at regular intervals.

Figure 120 Phil and Claire Morrot in 1932 at Glen Park
Photo courtesy of the Morrot family

In its earliest years, the ride concessions were operated by what early records indicate only as "Mrs. Rhinehart."[461] Later, most came under the direction of Theophilius "Phil" Morrot, a seasoned figure in the amusement world known for his expertise in rides and games concessions. Throughout the 1930s, he was a regular presence at Glen Park, renting space for his attractions during the park's peak summer seasons.

Morrot's ambitions extended well beyond Glen: in 1940, he took over management of Rialto Park in Olcott, New York, and by the end of the decade, he fulfilled a larger dream by founding Boulder Park (1949-1970) in Indian Falls, NY.[c]

---

[b] Seven years later, another loan was secured by Williamsville Amusements to purchase additional property adjacent to the Glen for a parking lot. This loan document is the only evidence indicating that the Altmans eventually came to own "at least two-thirds" of the shares in the real estate company.

[c] For more information about Morrot, Emilie's Carousel and Boulder Park, read Cyndy Hennig Hanks, *Boulder Amusement Park: The Biography of a Carousel* (Boulder, CO: Pruett Publishing Company) 2003

Among Morrot's most treasured possessions was a carousel widely considered one of the finest creations ever produced by the Allan Herschell Company. Glen Park had the distinction of hosting this masterpiece—later affectionately known as "Emilie's Carousel"—on two separate occasions, first in 1932 and again from 1937 to 1939.[462]

The carousel was a true original, designed by Morrot's sister, Emilie Morrot Bourgard, and built in 1919. It featured 32 elaborately carved horses and seven rare, hand-painted animals, including a giraffe, elephant, camel, lion, tiger, a reindeer adorned with real antlers, and a striking polar bear. Its presentation was equally spectacular: more than 1,000 electric light bulbs ringed the cornice, their glow reflected in mirrored panels set between oil paintings of pastoral Western New York landscapes.[463]

Tragically, Emilie's life was cut short by the very carousel she had helped bring to life. In 1930, while stooping to retrieve a dropped ticket, she was struck by the knee of a passing Black Charger horse and fatally injured[464]—a poignant reminder of the risks that often-accompanied early amusement technology.

Figure 121 Emilie's Carousel shown here at Olcott Beach in the early 1900s
Photo courtesy of Frederick Fried archives

The carousel's story did not end there. After decades of operation at Morrot's Boulder Park, it was eventually acquired by a private collector and dismantled in the early 1980s. The unique animals Emilie had designed became highly sought-after pieces of Americana, sold individually at high-profile auctions. In 1989, it was purchased by a collector for what was then an astonishing $121,000.[465]

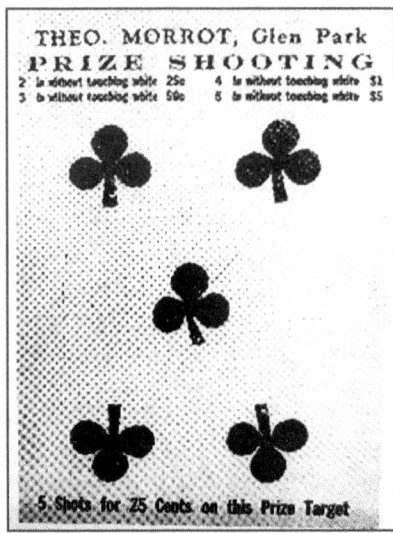

Figure 122 Besides operating amusement rides,
Morrot also rented out game booths
The target shooting attraction even used real
ammunition
Photo courtesy of the Morrot family

Other classic rides Morrot contributed to the Glen included the area's earliest versions of the Ferris Wheel, Kiddie Airplane Ride, and Kiddie Auto Ride.[466]

Among Morrot's contributions, the Pinto Plane ride stands out not only for its popularity but for the unique problem it posed. Acquired in 1935 and brought to Glen Park in 1937, the ride's lightweight airplanes would fill with rainwater during storms. To drain them, Morrot would tip the planes upside down when the ride was not in use. Unfortunately, the park's security guards found another use for them: removing the planes from their chains and paddling around on Ellicott Creek in the makeshift canoes. Morrot, both practical and exasperated, finally drilled holes into all six planes to prevent the aquatic mischief.[467]

Figure 123 The pinto plane rides (on land) with Lucille Morrot (center) and her friends
Photo courtesy of the Morrot family

By the mid-1940s, the rides were no longer leased from concessionaires. Instead, the park's management company, Amherst Amusement, began purchasing and maintaining its own attractions. The early company-owned lineup included a Merry-Go-Round, a Kiddie Ferris Wheel, a Kiddie Auto Ride, a Funhouse, and an Aeroplane Swing.[468]

Figure 124 Kiddie Ferris Wheel; Plane Ride; Swing Ride; Jet Ride
Photos courtesy of Ron Urban

Over the decades, the specific placement and identity of the rides became a topic of nostalgia-fueled debate among former parkgoers. Memories blurred, in part, because Glen Park frequently refreshed its lineup. Altman and Urban were known to buy and sell rides annually, creating an ever-changing landscape of entertainment.

To keep the experience lively and interesting, the amusement park periodically rebranded itself with new theme. At various times, the grounds were transformed into *Frontier Land* or *Western Corral*, evoking pioneer settlements; *Circus Land*, complete with whimsical decor and costumed clowns; *Storybook Land*, where fairy tales came to life; and *Action Land* and *Kiddies' Corral*, both emphasizing fun and fantasy for younger audiences.

These thematic changes were not limited to scenery. Even the ticket booth might be reimagined as a stagecoach, while ride operators were expected to dress the part—donning pith helmets, cowboy hats, or circus-themed attire depending on the season's motif. In some cases, live performers roamed the grounds in character, creating a fully immersive experience that transformed Glen Park from a local amusement spot into a rotating stage for childhood adventure.

Figure 125 The Urban children line up at the stagecoach themed
ticket booth at the Glen
Photo courtesy of Ron Urban

THE CAROUSEL THAT GALLOPED THROUGH HISTORY

At Glen Amusement Park, one of the most remarkable treasures was not hidden, but overlooked—blending seamlessly into the joyful chaos of summer crowds and carnival sounds.

For years, Harry Altman had relied on rides and games from concessionaires to entertain his guests. But in the mid-1940s, the first major amusement ride was permanently placed in the park: a vibrantly painted, all-wooden carousel featuring 34 horses, a lion, a tiger, and two chariots was acquired from a small amusement park in Rochester, NY.[469]

Figure 126 Thousands of families enjoyed the Glen Park carousel during its quarter-century on the property
Photo courtesy of Rose Ann Hirsch

For nearly 25 years, the three-row merry-go-round and its accompanying Wurlitzer band organ created golden memories in a prime location beside Ellicott Creek.

Unbeknownst to Altman, the true provenance of the carousel remained a mystery during his lifetime. Its historic significance only came to light after the park closed when a Williamsville business owner, suspecting there might be a hidden gem beneath the layers of aging paint, purchased the ride.

With the help of carousel historians, the machine's true identity was revealed in 1973: it had been crafted around 1903 by the E. Joy Morris Company of Philadelphia, home to some of the finest master carvers of the Golden Age of American carousels.

Once removed from the Glen, the carousel underwent a full restoration by a craftsman on Grand Island, NY, and was subsequently leased to the Skylon Tower in Niagara Falls, Ontario. There, it delighted thousands of visitors to the amusement park in the basement of the tower.

By the mid-1980s, the Skylon Amusement Park closed, and the carousel was sold to a collector in Ohio. What followed—sparked by personal tragedy and a rising market for antique folk art—set the stage for its eventual auction and the dispersion of its parts.

What follows is the full story of this legendary ride, which entertained families across the Northeast for more than 80 years.

THE GOLDEN AGE

The years 1880-1930 are considered the Golden Age of wooden carousels[d] in America.[470]

It is estimated that during that time 5,000 hand-carved, hand-painted merry-go-rounds were built in the U.S. Their existence was derived in large part from the artistry of 14 major carvers, mostly displaced European immigrants skilled in furniture making and ship building, who settled throughout the northeast.[471]

The Depression took a financial toll on amusement parks and carousel manufacturers. An impoverished carousel owner considered himself fortunate if he could off-load the ride to a secondary market. Many of the machines were destined to be stored away in old warehouses/barns or destroyed in their entirety.[472]

"So little was thought of the value of the wooden horses that the demolition crews would often be told to burn them in bonfires," said Arlan Ettinger, co-founder of Guernsey's auction house where many premier carousels were later sold.[473]

When prosperity returned after the war, the amusement parks returned to prominence in the U.S. But by then, metal (and later, fiberglass or resin) had become the preferred medium for forming the carousel mounts, molded into shape in factories that no longer relied on expert woodworkers to create the fine artistry.

The fact that a "Golden Age" carousel survived to service patrons of Glen Park was a minor miracle. The machines that were not intentionally destroyed had often become victim to weather catastrophes or permanent ruin due to hard use and too little maintenance.[474]

---

[d] The terms *carousel* and *merry-go-round* are generally used interchangeably, despite some collectors insisting that distinctions—such as the direction of rotation—determine which term is correct.

The vast majority, however (80 percent by some estimates), were lost in fires started by the primitive, one-cylinder gas engines that ran them, a kind of self-immolation.[475]

Today, only 150 wooden carousels from the Golden Age are said to exist.[476]

THE CAROUSEL'S ORIGIN STORY

Failure to find vital records has shrouded the earliest histories of many of the existing carousels.

The origin story of the E. Joy Morris ride featured at the Glen remains somewhat of a mystery to carousel historians.[e] Missing are photographs of the machine dating back to the early 20th century, and vital sale and maintenance records are thought to have been destroyed long ago for being inconsequential.

What researchers can confirm is that the carousel was crafted by the E. Joy Morris company circa 1903.[477]

Company founder Edward Joy Morris II, the son of a wealthy U.S. Congressman, became enamored with the amusement industry in the 1880s while managing his family's vast real estate holdings. In 1898, he formed his own amusement device company with his three brothers and began to build water chutes, toboggans (roller coasters), and carousels.[478] Living in Philadelphia where many of the master carvers honed their craft, Morris set out to develop a distinct carousel style that would distinguish him from competitors.

Carousel historians have identified his work through three distinguishing features,[479] all of which were present in the Morris carousel that was eventually placed in Glen Park.

Realism. The outer row standards (the most elaborately decorated figures) are big, graceful, and well-formed, with pretty heads and arrow faces. Morris provided touches of realism whenever possible, taking great pains to detail well-carved bone structure, veining, teeth, and other anatomical features.

---

[e]For purposes of writing this book, much effort was taken to determine the provenance of the EJ Morris carousel that resided at the Glen. The origin of the carousel has been the subject of debate among carousel historians since is removal from the park in the mid-1970s. With valued assistance of Linda Bartash Dawley, a carousel historian from Rochester, NY, and Rick Lohr, great effort was made to access public records, obtain documents from private collectors, and interview E.J. Morris experts. The goal was to identify whether the Glen carousel is the famed "PTC #4" as asserted by Earl Corey, the full carousel's last owner. The result of our findings is not absolute, but the research clearly points to the Glen carousel mounts pre-dating the existence of the PTC #4 machine. Details of the entire history of the carousel is included here for readers interested in Glen Park, and for carousel enthusiasts who keep track of each carousel's chronology.

Whimsicality. Relying on imagination and innovation, he added small touches to the carvings to delight riders. On the Glen carousel, for example, an outside row horse had a dog's face peeking out from under the saddle trapping. Carved alongside the cantle of another Glen horse were individual bearded gargoyles. There are many examples of this style of playfulness throughout his work.

Detail. Carving intricate detail on all the mounts was an important hallmark of Morris's style. Traditionally, the only tricked-out ponies were on the outer row where they could be seen by passersby. Morris encouraged his craftsmen to lavishly embellish all the mounts, creating sumptuous works of art on every figure of the carousel.

Figure 127 E.J. Morris circa 1903, about the time the Glen carousel was crafted PD

Morris's influence on carousel craftsmanship ended in 1903 when he took ill and decided to sell his roller coaster patents and inventory of 200 crafted mounts to the Philadelphia Toboggan Company (PTC) for a sum of $30,000 (nearly $1 million in 2023).[480] PTC was a nascent company at the time, best known for building "toboggans" (i.e. roller coasters). Morris's inventory allowed the company to jump-start its carousel division; within a short time, PTC was able to assemble and sell its first four, three-row carousels.[481]

The Glen carousel dates to this ownership transition. Based on the known timeline, it was either (1) one of the last produced at the E.J. Morris workshop; or (2) one of the first assembled by PTC (most probably #4 of the initial series). For researchers dedicated to tracking the journey of each Golden Age carousel throughout history, this origin story has been an ongoing quest.[482]

The carousel's earliest known home was likely Erie Beach Amusement Park in Fort Erie, Ontario.[483] As discussed in Chapter 9, Altman had been hired in May 1930 to oversee musical programming at the park, and it is entirely possible he encountered the carousel in operation during that season. When Erie Beach went bankrupt at the end of the summer, the ride was sent across the river to North Tonawanda for an extensive overhaul.[484]

There, it came under the care of the Allan Herschell Company, one of the most prolific amusement ride manufacturers of the 20th century. Renowned for their beautifully hand-carved carousels and rugged kiddie rides, Herschell's work was a fixture at carnivals and amusement parks across North America.

During the renovation, the company replaced the original frame with one built by Herschell-Spillman and downsized the wheel, reducing it from four rows of horses to three. The previously stationary inner-row animals were fitted with mechanisms to make them rise and fall, creating motion across all tiers.[485] New center panels and elaborately painted rounding boards were added, giving the carousel a refreshed and more modern profile—one suited for the next chapter in its long and storied life.[486]

The newly refurbished carousel, while still substantial in size, was smaller in circumference (50 ft vs. the original 60 ft) and more easily dismantled. The hope was that these two features would attract the interest of operators who were not running amusement parks on big plots of land.

Its new stature was a perfect match for Ellison Park in Rochester, where it first appeared in 1937.[487] Owner Lloyd O'Laughlin did not provide a roundhouse for the carousel but rather placed the machine under a tent-like canopy. During the off-season, the mounts and canopy were dismantled and stored in a concession stand.[488]

O'Laughlin eventually sold the ride to Altman in the mid-1940s. During that same period a Wurlitzer band organ (145B) was obtained from a Lockport dealer. That band organ provided the background music at the park for nearly 30 years.[489]

Figure 128 Ron Urban enjoys a ride on Glen's menagerie lion
Photo courtesy of Ron Urban

According to Ron Urban, son of Glen Park superintendent Clyde Urban, the carousel spent its early years "more or less in the open" to the elements. In the 1950s, Clyde raised a roof above it, put up surrounding walls, and installed gates for riders to enter and exit. Each winter, the mounts were dismantled and re-painted in the maintenance barn. This painting process was not restorative; the pigments from earlier winters were left on each mount and a new coat applied.

HISTORICAL DISCOVERY

*Figure 129 These infamous "22 for $1" ride tickets confirm the amusement park
stayed in operation through the 1971-72 season*
PD

The next transition for the carousel occurred in 1972 when Glen property owner, Emprise, decided to close the Glen Amusement Park.

While the roundhouse remained intact on the property, the mounts on the carousel were removed in late 1972 and stored in the Family Inn (renamed The Old Barn) to await their fate. By all accounts, the carousel's ponies were in rough shape after decades of service at Glen Park. To add insult to injury, vandals also spray-painted parts of the machine during its final days in the roundhouse.

The carousel would have burned with the rest of The Old Barn in 1973 if Rick Lohr had not stepped in and purchased it from the Emprise Corporation in 1972. Tipped off by a former employee of the Glen as to its availability, Lohr said he had a sense that a gem might be hiding beneath years of haphazard paint jobs.[490]

Lohr was a Williamsville native who owned and operated International Chimney Corporation (ICC) on S. Long Street in the Village. ICC has a national reputation for helping preserve important historical structures. The company performed work that moved the Cape Hatteras Lighthouse; the Meyer-Peace House in Charleston; a 130-year-old railway roundhouse in Saratoga Springs; and the Block Island lighthouse in Rhode Island.[491]

In the Village of Williamsville, Lohr's historic perseveration efforts involved the landmark Lehigh Valley Railroad depot on S. Long Street near his offices. By purchasing the property in the 1970s, Lohr ensured that the depot would escape the wrecking ball. In the years that followed, the Western New York Railway Historical Society bought the property from Lohr for half-price with the added benefit of an interest-free loan.[492]

As the carousel's new owner, Lohr looked for clues to determine the carousel's provenance. He hired professional carousel restorer Vincent Staley who, over a period of 14 months, painstakingly removed 26 coats of paint from each of the mounts. What he discovered was a carousel "exquisite in detail," dating back to a master carver from the Golden Age.[493]

Lohr set about gathering the opinions of prominent carousel historians who all identified it as the work of E. J. Morris (the so-called "Undiscovered Master") at the turn of the 20th century.

Staley work was not done after he stripped off the paint from the mounts. He had to make necessary repairs like returning teeth on the snarling lion, and restoring missing bits of ears, arms, and legs on many of the horses. Using historical reference material, he was also tasked with repainting the 34 horses, two chariots and menagerie (tiger and lion). [f][494]

In place of the old music machine, Lohr's father-in-law, Joseph Marquis, restored an original Wurlitzer organ for the project.[495]

THE LAST TURN OF THE WHEEL

By 1975, the refurbishment was complete. Lohr decided to lease the carousel to the amusement park in the basement of the Skylon Tower in Niagara Falls, Ontario.

"Being indoors would greatly extend the life of the 80-year-old carousel," he said.[496]

Advertisements promoting the Skylon Amusement Center featured full-color photos of the E.J. Morris carousel, as it was a key attraction to the park along with a full-sized Ferris wheel, Bumper Cars, Tilt-A-Whirl, and a wooden Go-Kart track.[497]

Figure 130 Restored ride mount from the Glen, shown here during its display at the Skylon
Photo courtesy of Rick Lohr

---

[f] Taking artistic liberty, Staley converted two of the horses to zebras (a decision that has permanently altered the menagerie configuration.)

The public enjoyed the carousel for another decade, until Canadian Pacific Hotels—the owners of the Skylon Tower—chose to sell the building and shutter the amusement park. Rather than place the carousel in storage, Lohr opted to sell it outright.[g] The buyers, Ohio entrepreneurs Earl and Rogene Corey, acquired the piece at a pivotal moment in the carousel industry. Just three years earlier, Guernsey's auction house in New York City had hosted the first major sale of carved wooden figures from the Golden Age, signaling a surge in collector interest[498]

Arlen Ettinger, Guernsey's co-founder, personally handled that first sale after being approached by a collector whose daughter had been injured in a car accident.

"The family was underinsured and needed to raise money to pay her medical bills," Ettinger said.[499]

The man had started on his path to collecting carousel horses in his youth when he witnessed workmen dismantling the abandoned inventory of a former Philadelphia amusement park. They were torching whatever they could burn, so the youngster asked if he could have the wooden carousel carvings. The workmen agreed.

An empty barn on his family's property was used to store his collection which, over time, numbered 96 figures. After talking to Ettinger, Guernsey's decided to hold its first carousel auction, hoping to make a total of $30,000 (roughly $300 per mount).[500]

After a successful promotional campaign that included media coverage by *The New York Times*, the money raised by the auction generated around $1 million.

Thinking the results of the sale an anomaly, Ettinger assembled another sale. Again, the final net tally was many multiples over the pre-sale estimate.[501]

The feeding frenzy for Golden Age carousels was on.

Figure 131 E.J. Morris and the Coreys were featured in the March 1989 issue of The Carousel News & Trader
PD

Some collectors were interested in buying an entire carousel, but most were willing to pay top-dollar for individual mounts that they could display in their homes and offices. "Dispersing the machine" (i.e., selling the individual components) netted far more money than trying to the sell the sum of its parts.

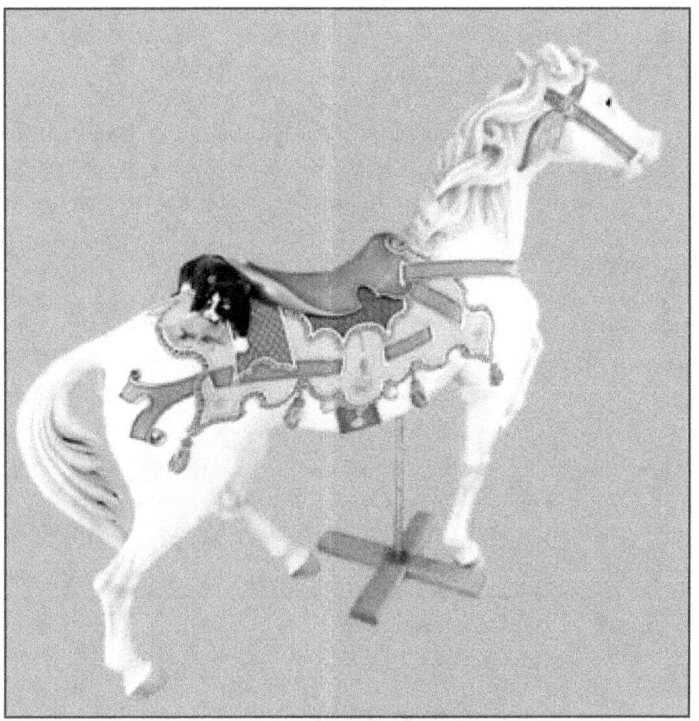

Figure 132 Photo of a Glen carousel horse at auction
Note the whimsical kitten on the back of the saddle
Photo courtesy of Guerney's Auctions

The fact that the Coreys were keeping the E.J. Morris off the auction block was good news and was noted in carousel trade journals of that period.[502] Full-color photos of the carousel were often accompanied by articles featuring Earl and his carousel-loving wife.

Buoyed by dreams of "feather-weight children" spinning with delight,[503] the future of the Glen carousel seemed secure in the hands of the Coreys.

But that vision dimmed when Rogene was diagnosed with cancer. She died on December 3, 1988, bringing their shared dream to an unexpected and heartbreaking end.[504]

Corey, stricken with grief, decided to divest much of Rogene's collection. He hired Ettinger to handle the sale of the carousel on April 22, 1989, at a spectacular auction held at Passenger Pier 88 in New York City.[505]

The lux auction catalog promoting the sale was titled, "A Carousel Fantasy: An Extraordinary Array of Some of the Most Imaginative Carvings in the Carousel Field." The multi-page catalogue was dedicated to Rogene: "Whose love of the carousel has been an inspiration to us all."[506]

In addition to the E.J. Morris machine, the auction put up for sale a Herschell Spillman menagerie from 1915; a Niagara Falls, Ontario carousel from Maple Leaf Village; and many original posters from the Enquirer Job Printing Company featuring the Barnum & Bailey Circus.[507]

The E.J. Morris carousel was divided into 28 lots. None of the mechanical elements were included in the sale, nor were the prized mounts. Estimates for few the most valued horses (the standers, outside-row animals that are most elaborately carved) were expected to sell anywhere between $25,000-$60,000 each. Prancers were appraised between $9,000-$10,000. Only one of the chariots was included in the sale, eventually selling for $2,750 (above its estimate). The lone menagerie animal, a "zebra" jumper, was sold over its estimate at $17,600.[508]

Bidding was brisk that Spring afternoon, and by the time the gavel fell for the final time the E.J. Morris carousel had raised $327,000 ($780,000 in 2025 dollars). Two of the priciest standard horses were returned to Corey because they did not meet their reserve price.[509]

Once acquired for a modest sum on the second-hand market, the carousel horses Altman installed to delight families later became coveted collectibles—an irony he might have relished, as they generated returns long after their last ride.

Figure 133 Front cover of Guernsey's Auctions catalogue featuring the E.J. Morris carousel, once a centerpiece at both the Glen and Skylon Tower
PD

NOVELTY ACTS ABOUND

Altman's deep affection for vaudeville ensured that his shows regularly featured an eclectic mix of novelty acts—from hypnotists to animal trainers with every kind of domestic creature imaginable. One standout attraction was the ice show, performed on a 20-foot circular refrigerated platform, a dazzling feat of stage engineering. The following are just a few of the more unusual performances that lit up the early years at the Glen.

Grandma and Shorty Sprouse

Who could resist a hillbilly band fronted by a headline-making May-December romance? On Independence Day weekend in 1946, 78-year-old Mattie Large Lyons and her brand-new husband, 18-year-old Delbert "Shorty" Sprouse, took the stage at the Glen Barn.[510] Shorty played bass, Grandma sawed the fiddle, and at least three other musicians rounded out the group as they toured together.

Figure 134 Grandma and Shorty Sprouse
PD

The local press could not get enough of the story of Grandma Mattie, a widow with 10 children from two previous marriages, and young Shorty, who had spent the past four years working as her farmhand. "He couldn't pass up my good cooking and cornbread," Grandma quipped, adding, "After a while, we just sort of felt a heap of loving for each other, so we got ourselves married."[511]

Records suggest the couple remained married for at least 11 years.[512] As for children? There were none. "Shorty doesn't want none," Grandma explained, without a hint of regret.[513]

FERDINAND THE BULL

Ferdinand the Bull, the beloved star of Munro Leaf's classic children's book "The Story of Ferdinand," first captured hearts in 1936 with his refusal to fight in the bull ring—choosing instead to sit quietly and admire the flowers in the ladies' hair. Illustrated by Robert Lawson, the tale became a nationwide sensation, its pacifist message resonating deeply with readers young and old. Just two years later, Walt Disney brought the gentle giant to life in the animated short "Ferdinand the Bull," which went on to win an Academy Award and ignite a full-blown case of "Ferdinand mania" across America.

Riding the wave of this cultural phenomenon, Texas showman Herman "Tex" Mosely set out to turn fiction into fact. Inspired by the story, Tex began training a real bull calf—whom he, of course, named Ferdinand—starting when the animal was just three months old.[514] As Ferdinand grew (tipping the scales at 1,620 pounds, although promotional flyers often upped the ante to 2,000), Tex turned him into a one-of-a-kind touring sensation.

Ferdinand's life was anything but ordinary. He stayed in hotel rooms, lived in basement dressing rooms, and traveled the nightclub circuit alongside county fairs and civic events.[515] In September 1943, Ferdinand and Tex made a memorable stop at the Glen, delighting audiences with their unique act that blended novelty, charm, and a surprising dose of showbiz polish.[516]

Figure 145 A determined Glen Casino patron gives it her all atop Ferdinand, with Tex Mosely standing immediately to the right
In the background, Lenny Paige cues the action
Photo courtesy of the Lenny Paige estate

Described as "gentle as a pet cat,"[517] the real-life Ferdinand wowed crowds with a repertoire of tricks: he could bow, kneel, lie down, or perch all four hooves on a small stand with theatrical grace. A crowd favorite involved bringing brave volunteers onstage to ride him—though most slid off his broad back to roars of laughter.[518]

Ferdinand's fame eventually led him to Hollywood, where he appeared in seven feature films, a string of comedy shorts, and numerous live performances. Through it all, he remained true to his storybook spirit—sweet, calm, and camera-ready. In an era hungry for spectacle, Ferdinand stood out not for his might, but for his gentle nature—earning a legacy as America's real-life Ferdinand, the bull who charmed the spotlight without ever needing to charge it.

HAIL, CESAR

In 1942, Don Romero—billed by Harry Altman as the younger brother of Hollywood actor Cesar Romero[519]—was a last-minute addition to the Glen's entertainment roster. Promoted in newspaper stories as the "Handsome Don from Hollywood," the Latin dancer's appearance was framed as a favor born from Harry's supposed friendship with the famous star.[520] As part of his act, Don would invite audience members to join him on stage for an impromptu dance.[521]

But genealogical research later debunked the claim: Cesar Romero had no brother named Don. His only brother, Eduardo, was not in show business and had begun losing his vision at a young age. Even by Altman's standards of exaggerated flair, this promotional ploy pushed the boundaries of truth.

BURIED ALIVE

Another sideshow event that Altman often talked in later years was the fellow who liked to be buried alive. "But something went wrong with his secret air gimmick, and the volunteer fire company had to come and dig him out."[522]

ACROBATICS

In April 1945, the Glen spotlighted a truly unforgettable duo: Myra Jeanne, the astonishing performer who walked on her elbows while gripping a foot in each hand, shared top billing with the legendary one-legged tap dancer Peg Leg Bates.[523] (Not to be confused with Peg-Leg Castle, the equally unforgettable one-legged unicyclist who rolled onto the scene later that same season.) Outside of the headliners, Altman's entertainment lineup often featured acts reminiscent of carnival sideshows—unconventional, attention-grabbing, and designed to draw a crowd.

GAMES

Jack Gilbert, a veteran concessionaire on the carnival circuit, joined Altman in 1948. By then, Altman had grown disenchanted with leasing out concession space at the Glen. It was Gilbert who persuaded Altman that they could manage all game concession operations themselves. Altman gave Gilbert a one-year trial to prove himself, which extended into a decade-long partnership without a formal contract.

Gilbert explained to *Billboard* Magazine: "What good is a contract if people are dissatisfied? It's such a personal business; everything must be on a friendly basis."[524]

One of the games Gilbert helped introduce to the Glen was Bingo. In the mid-1950s, New York State prohibited Bingo games as they were considered games of chance rather than skill. For Altman, seeing his nightclub sitting empty during daylight hours was a challenge—and an opportunity. By 1956, he and Gilbert began testing the limits of the law, quietly introducing Bingo sessions at the club. It was a calculated risk. The games drew daytime crowds, filled otherwise idle seats, and spurred the sale of game cards and refreshments—all while skirting the edge of legality. For Altman, it was a savvy move: part business instinct, part showman's flair, and fully in character.

Sammy Davis Jr played his first-ever game of Bingo at the Glen.[525] In a 2016 *Buffalo News* article, columnist Mary Kunz Goldman recounted an eyewitness account from years earlier: Davis, unfamiliar with the rules, initially struggled to keep up to play the game. But with a little coaching, he quickly caught on—and before long, he was reveling in the excitement of calling out a win.[526]

"He yelled 'Bingo!' louder than anyone ever had," Kunz Goldman wrote. "Then he leapt up and began tap dancing. That the prize was small, tiny compared to his pay at the Glen Park, did not bother him one bit. He was celebrating, and he made sure everyone joined in."[527]

At the time, legal restrictions forced Bingo at the Glen to operate under the radar. Advertising was minimal, limited to discreet signs within the park and word-of-mouth among regulars. When there was any suspicion that outsiders, particularly reporters, were taking notice, the game was swiftly rebranded as "Darto, a game of skill."[528] Despite the name change, the gameplay bore a striking resemblance to the banned Bingo. To avoid legal repercussions, cash prizes were replaced with certificates that could be redeemed for merchandise. A single coupon might fetch a modest trinket, but those who played frequently and saved up could walk away with more substantial rewards, like a table-model television for 105 coupons.[529h]

As early as 1954, unease about the Glen's operation of Bingo games surfaced in a Letter to the Editor published by *The Buffalo Evening News*.[530] The anonymous writer expressed concern that a private, for-profit enterprise was profiting from games of chance—while charitable and nonprofit organizations were barred from doing the same. The letter questioned why local churches or civic groups were not given the opportunity to "swell their reserves" by hosting Bingo events of their own.

> *"Where is the 'civic pride' of our village fathers? Hiding behind 'see no evil, hear no evil and speak no evil?'"*[531]

A reporter from *The Buffalo Evening News* visited the Glen on two separate occasions to take part in a Bingo session, causing a stir with management.[532] Although there was no attempt to disguise the game as "Darto," a trio of singers suddenly emerged for an impromptu performance on a six-foot stage. After delivering three quick songs, "they put on their coats and left," *The Buffalo Evening News* reported. "The management then gave all the customers a free game." Typically, Bingo cards cost a dime each.[533]

The Bingo wing of the casino was built to accommodate up to 225 players, though attendance varied—one day drawing around 75 participants, and just over 100 on another, according to the reporter's account.[534] The room was filled with an impressive array of prizes, from modest knickknacks to full-sized refrigerators. Special games upped the stakes, offering winners matching sets of men's and women's watches or a stylish pair of lamps.

It was noted that during sparsely attended sessions the games were called more slowly, allowing fewer games and prizes to be distributed—a strategy to mitigate lower earnings. Conversely, busier sessions saw a rapid pace of play that barely allowed the reporter time to place down his markers on the Bingo boards.[535]

Payment for a successful win at Bingo was merchandise instead of cash prizes. Gilbert was responsible for managing its daily operations. When Bingo was legalized in 1957, and the system of trading merchandise for prizes was phased out, Gilbert decided to "chuck everything" and relocate to Arizona, following the advice of Harry's son, Bob.[536] Before leaving, Gilbert sold his equipment and remaining merchandise but stayed in Buffalo for an additional year to ensure the outstanding

---

[h] Another local entrepreneur found a way around the Bingo restrictions by inventing the game "I-Got-It," a regional favorite still played at lawn fetes and fairs. Patrons are provided with red bouncing balls that are thrown into a box with a Bingo-like grid. The first person to score a Bingo wins a certificate for a prize. This game, apparently, can be considered one requiring skill. Another game comparable to "I-Got-It" is "Fascination" which had a large following at the Glen. Many people recall Glen employee, Jimmy Moser, calling the game: "Roll the ball under the chevron, under the glass and into the hole. Five in a row wins!"

coupons were redeemed, of which there were many.[537] In total, patrons presented 300-400 coupons valued at $2 each for cash. Once all the redemptions were complete, Gilbert left Buffalo and began investing in Phoenix real estate.[538]

Visitors entering through the Glen Street gate were immediately drawn into the park's bustling games area, a lively stretch lined with booths promising prizes and instant thrills. Two popular attractions allowed guests to place a nickel on one of 24 numbered squares. A flashing light would eventually stop to reveal the lucky winner, who would walk away with a doll or toy.

But not everyone saw the fun as innocent. At one point, a local magistrate ordered the temporary shutdown of the toy and doll stands, arguing that their mechanics constituted a form of gambling, a violation of local law.

Over time, the game offerings evolved, reflecting changing tastes and regulatory pressures. Still, a few staples remained etched in memory. Among them were the ever-popular Skee-Ball and the Shooting Gallery. One of the most fondly remembered attractions was Fascination, often advertised as "Bingo with a ball." Its rhythmic gameplay and the unmistakable voice of longtime booth caller Jimmy Moser left a lasting impression on generations of parkgoers (on page 257).

GLEN PARK ZOO

One of the most memorable—albeit, short-lived—attractions at the Glen was a petting zoo.

Figure 135 Donnie and Dottie Denneen feed the zoo animals in 1954, clearly enjoying the moment
Photo courtesy of Patti Denneen Walker

The venture began in the spring of 1953 when Altman announced to the press that the park would feature a "new zoo for the entertainment of children," which would be "well stocked with animals."[539] From the outset, he made it clear that his collection was not meant to compete with the sprawling 23-acre Delaware Park Zoo in Buffalo.

"We just want [Buffalo Zoo curator] Abgott to know we're not invading his province as a competitor," Altman joked. "Ours is small, compact, and quiet."[540]

Over time, the zoo, which was located below the east wall of the Williamsville Mill, featured an assortment of animals, including white-tail deer, sheep, mountain goats, rhesus monkeys, llamas, and peacocks.

Figure 136 The zoo was located below the eastern wall of the mill. The door shown here served as an emergency exit from the Glen Casino
Photo courtesy of Ron Urban

Among the notable residents was a rhesus monkey called Clyde, named after park superintendent Clyde Urban. The human Clyde would occasionally stroll through the park with monkey Clyde perched on his shoulder, delighting visitors. Other memorable characters included Mike the Buck, who fathered several fawns, and the ever-entertaining llamas, notorious for their spitting antics.

Clyde's son, Ron Urban, who lived across the street from the park, helped care for the animals. He vividly remembered the day they arrived:

Figure 137 Glen Park Zoo animals
Photos courtesy of Ron Urban

"My dad and I went to Catskill Game Farm in Catskill, NY for the animals," Ron recalled. "We kept the goats and sheep in a separate pen where visitors could reach over to pet them. Guests could also buy animal crackers from machines to feed them."

During springtime, baby lambs and fawns were often hand-raised by the Urban family in a back parking lot near their house.

In all, the zoo experiment lasted four years.

Unlike buildings that could be shuttered, and amusement rides that could be partially dismantled and stored away, the animals needed attention all year. Ultimately, Altman chose to donate most of the animals, 29 in all, to the Buffalo Zoo, a gesture warmly received by curator Joseph Abgott.[541]

The space that had been occupied by the zoo would become the site of a popular small roller coaster that did not need daily care.

PARKING

Harry Altman was always in pursuit of more:

- ☞ More star power on his stages.
- ☞ More showtimes in his casinos.
- ☞ More patrons in his nightclubs.
- ☞ More parking spaces at the Glen.

Through careful, methodical effort, he usually got what he wanted.

Over the years, he fought mightily for adjacent land to be zoned for parking, an invaluable commodity for the suburban property. As automobile travel became more widespread, the popularity of the Glen Casino rose in tandem. During the day, visitors arrived by streetcar or bus along Main Street to enjoy the park's amusement rides and shaded picnic areas. But by nightfall, most patrons heading to the Glen Casino came by private car. Altman, ever attuned to audience needs, recognized that the success of a nightclub in a semi-rural village like Williamsville hinged on accessibility—and parking. To that end, he ensured Glen Park offered generous, always-free parking, tailored to accommodate the era's growing fleet of oversized, American-made automobiles.

Throughout the 1940s and early 1950s, Altman operated three parking lots along Glen Avenue, with a combined capacity of roughly 300 vehicles. Still, that was not enough. His promotional savvy came through clearly in his advertising, which boasted: "Free parking nightly for 1,000 cars." The wording was intentional—it did not promise space for 1,000 vehicles at once, but rather accounted for the turnover across the casino's three nightly shows. To keep traffic flowing and ensure safety between shows, Altman employed a team of lot attendants to manage the operation.

By 1956, however, with the Glen reaching the height of its popularity, Altman realized his parking solution was no longer sustainable. He petitioned the Williamsville Village Board to rezone land on the north side of Glen Avenue to build an additional parking lot. The proposed expansion—measuring 300 feet wide by 565 feet deep—would add approximately 169,000 square feet of new parking space, running alongside residential Mill Street.[542]

At the rezoning hearing in August 1956, more than twenty Mill Street residents showed up to protest. They voiced concerns that additional access to parking would add to the "carnival" atmosphere of the property: more noise, litter, and traffic. The result would negatively impact property values.[543]

Altman took personal offense to the "carnival" label.

"They're trying to drive me out of town," he told the board about the protesters. "I'm a good citizen and I expect to die here. I may even turn the park over one day to the village. That's how much I think of the community."[544]

To reassure officials and neighbors, Altman promised that parked cars would be kept at least 75 feet from the nearest homes. He also committed to hiring private security to deter vandalism.

Though opposition remained, several tenants from Altman's Spring Street apartments voiced their support, praising his contributions to the community and noting that better parking would improve traffic safety.[545] Still, some residents suspected that the parking lot was simply a cover for future expansion of the park's entertainment offerings.

Frustrated by the allegations, Altman offered to sign a legal guarantee that the new lot would not be used to expand the amusement park or nightclub.[546] After a month of deliberation, the Village Board approved the rezoning—with restrictive covenants to ensure that further development would be limited.[547]

What began as an eight-acre operation had, by this point, grown to nearly 11 acres as Altman quietly acquired adjacent parcels to support parking demand.

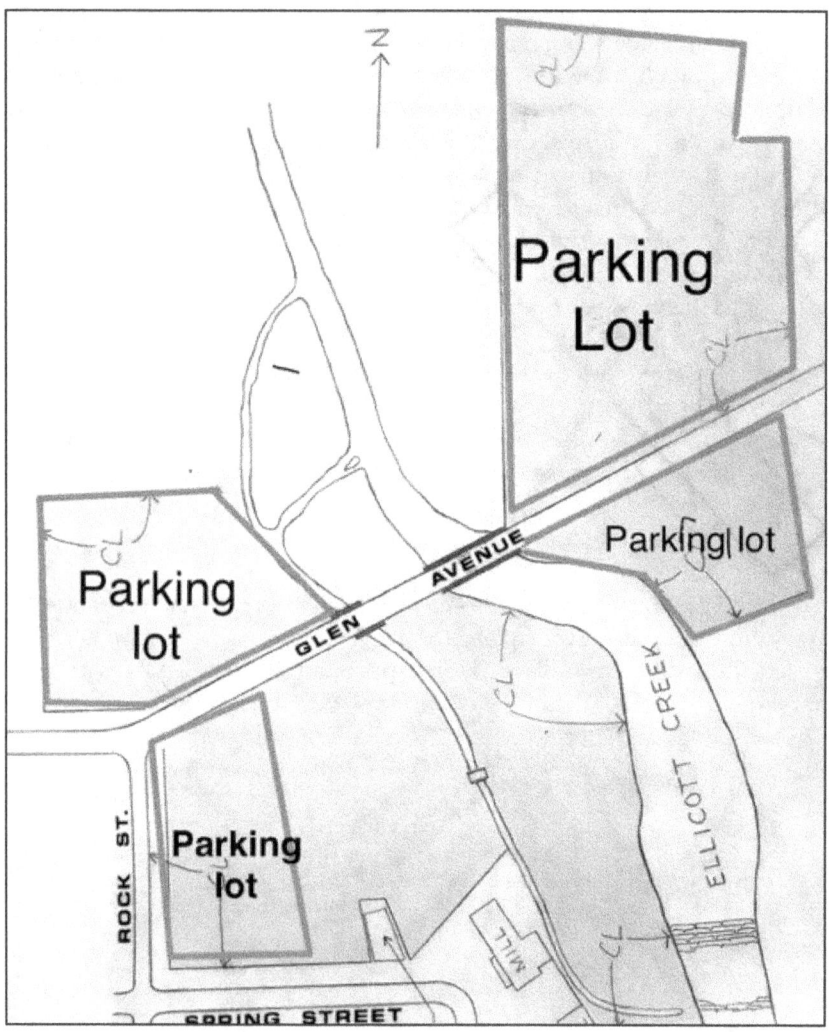

Figure 149 Today's parking at Glen Park is modest compared to the sprawling lots of the Altman era. Over time, Harry added acreage extending north toward what is now Amherst State Park. The shaded areas that are outlined indicate the full extent of the final parking layout

PD

CHAPTER 12—Downtown Nightclubs Emerge

T he dream of a thriving downtown Buffalo nightclub never died—it simply waited for its moment.

In January 1943, a new corporation named "H&H Inc." (short for "Harry & Harry") was formed.[548] This company would go on to allow Altman and Wallens the ability to operate three nightclubs—Victory Room, Town Barn, and Town Casino—which opened in succession. As was customary for businesses associated with Altman since the early 1930s, the two named shareholders on the H&H incorporation paperwork appeared to be proxies: Elliott L. Hose and Eileen Stone.[549]

A significant departure from past incorporation practices was the appointment of A. Irving Milch as the "attorney of record" for H&H. Milch was the bankruptcy receiver who hired Altman to be general manager of Edgewater Amusement Park (on page 142). His dual role as both a shareholder and legal representative for H&H was unusual, particularly given Altman's long-standing loyalty to Abe Carrel. Since as early as 1927, Carrel had been deeply involved in Altman's ventures, serving as his corporate and personal attorney in addition to being an occasional business partner.

In contrast, H&H, Inc. appeared to be well-financed—its Town Casino deal alone was estimated at $125.000.[550a] Altman's decision to turn to Milch instead of Carrel for legal counsel implied that H&H's funding came from sources outside his traditional circle of investors.

H&H, Inc. was incorporated in 1943, just two years after Glen Park Amusements, Inc. was formed to acquire the above-ground assets of the Williamsville property. Incorporation records and legal filings show that Milch served as attorney for H&H, and there is evidence he also provided legal representation to Glen Park Amusements following its formation. The close timing of the two incorporations; the use of proxy shareholders in both filings; and Milch's legal role in each corporation point to a likely convergence of interests operating behind the scenes. Together, H&H and Glen Park Amusements came to dominate much of the region's nightlife scene throughout the 1940s and 1950s, operating with distinct identities as the Town and Glen Casinos, yet seemingly shaped by shared financial interests and strategic direction.

Milch served as the legal linchpin behind both the Town and Glen Casinos. On the surface, he appeared to be the archetype of a mid-century attorney—measured, discreet, and respected, practicing real estate and estate law from a

---

[a] $2.2 million in 2025, well beyond the amount Wallens and in Altman could finance on their own.

modest office in Buffalo's Brisbane Building. After earning his law degree from the University of Buffalo, Milch began his career on a promising note, serving as assistant to Special Prosecutor Frank G. Raichle during the Buffalo City Affairs Investigation that uncovered extensive corruption in municipal government.[551] He married Florence Beck in 1930, and the couple had one son, James, in 1934. But personal tragedy struck twice in rapid succession: Florence died in 1950 at the age of 45, and Milch died suddenly of a heart attack in September 1951. He was also 45. Their 17-year-old son was now orphaned.

It was only after Milch's death that a more complex picture of his professional dealings began to emerge. In the final months of his life, he had served as legal counsel for David D. Levitt, a "self-styled former operator of games of skill and chance," who was indicted in U.S. District Court for income tax evasion.[552] Levitt had allegedly failed to report substantial income from a network of pinball and slot machines that quietly populated nightclubs, backrooms, and private clubs throughout the region.[553]

At the center of the case was Pioneer Amusements Corporation, a company believed to have been controlled by Levitt, operating out of 1472 Main Street since 1944. Pioneer distributed coin-operated gaming machines throughout Buffalo until its operations came to an abrupt halt following a police raid on March 31, 1951, part of a broader anti-gambling campaign. In the aftermath of the raid, Levitt disappeared and actively evaded a subpoena to testify before a grand jury investigating gambling and municipal corruption.[554]

At the time Pioneer Amusements was operating, both coin-operated slot machines and pinball machines were considered illegal gambling devices under New York State law. Slot machines had been explicitly banned statewide since 1934, following a wave of anti-gambling legislation during the Great Depression.[555] Though some machines were presented as games of skill or amusement-only devices, courts generally ruled against such defenses.

Pinball machines, too, were widely outlawed during this period. Starting in 1942 with a high-profile crackdown in New York City by Mayor Fiorello LaGuardia, municipalities across the state, including Buffalo, followed suit, citing concerns about organized crime's impact on the industry, and youth corruption. These machines were presumed to be games of chance, and enforcement often fell under local anti-vice campaigns. The legal status of pinball would not shift meaningfully until the mid-1970s, when courts began to recognize it as a game of skill rather than chance.

As such, Pioneer's inventory of coin-operated machines—whether slot or pinball—would have fallen into a legal gray zone at best, and outright illegality at worst, especially if payouts were involved. This legal climate helps explain the 1951 police raid and subsequent federal scrutiny of Levitt's financial practices.

When Levitt finally resurfaced after several months, he testified at his trial for tax evasion that Milch was not merely his attorney but a silent partner—holding a 50 percent stake in Pioneer[556] and another venture, Erie Services, incorporated in 1944.[557] Erie Services allegedly issued chattel mortgages on saloon properties, providing cash advances to bar owners, another potentially lucrative and legally gray enterprise. Levitt testified that Milch managed his personal financial filings as well, including preparing tax returns for 1946 and 1947, which Levitt admitted signing in blank.[558] Milch also received the cash collected from the gaming machines when Levitt was unavailable.[559]

Levitt was found guilty of tax evasion, sentenced to three years' probation, and fined $2,000.[560] In 1955, he and his wife settled with the IRS, agreeing to pay more than $44,000 in back taxes, penalties, and interest for unreported gaming income estimated at $68,000.[561b]

At the same time, reports from state and federal investigations noted that Buffalo's coin-operated machine trade had become a focal point for illicit earnings, particularly in connection with unlicensed gambling. While no formal link was ever established between Milch and any organized crime figures, the nature of the businesses he was tied to—machine distribution, off-the-books cash handling, and financial arrangements with bar owners—placed him at the edges of a system that investigators increasingly viewed as vulnerable to criminal exploitation. Milch's proximity of these ventures suggested a far more complicated legacy than his public reputation would have implied.

---

[b] Roughly $815,000 in 2025.

THE MOB

In mid-century America, owning a nightclub almost guaranteed a brush with organized crime—it came with the territory. Altman's interactions with local mob figures inevitably became interwoven with his expanding business and financial ventures. The appeal of high-profile entertainers, many of whom were managed by mob-connected agents,[562] only added to a nightclub's allure. Regular purchases of bulk inventory,[c] high-volume alcohol sales, dependence on union labor, and the constant flow of cash made such venues prime targets for criminal infiltration.

Altman's establishments, the Town Barn, Glen Casino, and Town Casino, were no exception. Evidence from news articles, FBI surveillance, and other records confirms that these venues were frequented by known mob associates, placing Altman's ventures squarely within the orbit of organized crime.[d]

Altman's ownership of ballrooms, niteries, and nightclubs coincided with what many historians regard as the golden age of the American Mafia, spanning roughly from 1920 to 1957.[563] Nationally, the Mob's rapid rise was fueled by the passage of the Volstead Act, which ushered in Prohibition and created an unprecedented black market for alcohol. January 16, 1920, the first day of Prohibition—is sometimes referred to as the birthdate of the modern American mob.[564] What had been loosely connected street gangs and criminal enterprises rapidly evolved into highly structured organizations. Bootlegging proved far more profitable than prior rackets such as black hand extortion, gambling, and fencing stolen goods.

Western New York became a hub of illicit activity during this era, due in part to its proximity to Canada and its favorable political climate. Buffalo's mayor, Frank X. Schwab, a former brewery owner, ran on an anti-Prohibition platform and won.[565] His administration's light-touch approach to enforcement allowed speakeasies to flourish, stocked with smuggled Canadian liquor and locally distilled spirits, often under mob control.

---

[c] Stephan Magaddino directly controlled two such supply companies, Camellia Linen and Power City Distributing (beer purveyor).

[d] One notable—though far from singular—example occurred in 1964, when a confidential informant reported to the FBI that they had attended the wedding reception of Victor Randaccio's daughter held at the Town Casino, which was then operating as a banquet facility. According to the Bureau's report, "After the wedding reception, 30 members of the party went on to the Glen Casino as guests of Harry Altman."

The foundation of organized crime in Buffalo[e] was laid by Giuseppe (Don Pietro) DiCarlo Sr., who was known in the media as "overlord of Buffalo's Italian Colony."[566] From the time he arrived in Buffalo from Sicily in 1908, until his death in 1922, DiCarlo ran the local mob and built up "powerful connections" with other Italian gangs across the country.[567]

Don Pietro's death at age 48 from natural causes left a significant void in Buffalo's mob leadership. With Prohibition entering full swing and enormous profits at stake, his top lieutenant, Angelo Palmeri, was forced to act quickly in naming a successor. Joe "The Wolf" DiCarlo, Jr., Pietro's 23-year-old son, had his sights set on the position, but was widely seen as too young and inexperienced.[568] "He's just a punk," one police officer told The Buffalo Courier-Express.[569f]

This is when Stefano Magaddino entered the picture. Born in 1891 into a prominent Sicilian Mafia family, Magaddino had already survived an assassination attempt in New Jersey and accepted Palmeri's invitation to relocate to Buffalo and take the reins. He had the experience and ruthlessness to lead; after emigrating to Brooklyn in 1906, he quickly gained a reputation for violence. As a leader of the feared enforcement crew known as the Good Killers, he was linked to multiple contract killings.

Under Magaddino's leadership, the Buffalo family evolved into one of the most powerful organized crime syndicates in the country. By the mid-20th century, the Buffalo crime family dominated a tri-border zone encompassing Upstate New York, Southwestern Ontario, and parts of Pennsylvania and Ohio, with notable reach into major Canadian cities like Toronto and Montreal.

Figure 150 Stefano Magaddino, one-time leader of the Buffalo mob PD

---

[e] His summary of Buffalo's mob history draws heavily on the scholarly contributions of three books by Western New York authors who have extensively documented the city's organized crime legacy:

Hunt, Thomas, and Michael A. Tona.: *Buffalo's First Family of Crime. Vol. 1.* Tonawanda, NY: Hunt & Tona Publications, 2013; Hunt, Thomas, and Michael A. Tona. *DiCarlo: Buffalo's First Family of Crime. Vol. 2.* Tonawanda, NY: Lulu Press, July 27, 2013; and Michael F. Rizzo, *Gangsters and Organized Crime in Buffalo: History, Hits and Headquarters* (Charleston, SC: The History Press, 2012). Thanks also to Lee Coppola—investigative journalist, former federal prosecutor, and former dean at St. Bonaventure University—whose work on the Buffalo Mafia provided valuable context and perspective.

[f] Joe, Jr. was handed ownership of the Auto Rest roadhouse in Williamsville that was raided once by the KKK (on page 108) and twice by Prohibition agents attempting to secure a conviction against DiCarlo for alcohol possession.

Operating from Niagara Falls, NY, Magaddino ran his criminal empire from behind the facade of a legitimate business: the Magaddino Memorial Chapel. This enterprise, combined with his nickname, "The Undertaker," reflected his ability to cloak violent operations in respectability. Under his leadership, the Buffalo Mafia expanded into bootlegging, loansharking, extortion, gambling, drug trafficking, hijacking, and labor racketeering. His influence earned him a founding seat on The Commission, the national governing council of La Cosa Nostra, giving Western New York an outsized role in national mob affairs.

For Altman, Magaddino's dominance meant navigating an entertainment landscape shadowed by criminal influence. Matters were complicated further by the volatile presence of Joe Jr. who was embittered for being passed over for the top leadership role. Although Magaddino attempted to placate him by naming him underboss, the gesture eventually backfired. DiCarlo ramped up his independent criminal activities, eventually drawing the ire of local law enforcement. He was labeled "Public Enemy #1" by Buffalo Police Commissioner Austin Roche in 1932.[570]

By 1945, tensions between DiCarlo and Magaddino had reached a breaking point. DiCarlo was demoted and eventually left the area, linking up with criminal outfits in Florida and Ohio.[571] His activities in Tampa, Miami, and Youngstown would later earn him the title of "syndicate lieutenant" from The Commission.[572]

DiCarlo's violent streak extended to Altman, as detailed in Chapter 7.

Altman was reportedly assaulted by DiCarlo in February 1937 at the Savarin, an incident that marked a clear escalation in their interactions. DiCarlo's influence would continue to echo through Altman's properties in the months that followed.

CHAPTER 13—VICTORY ROOM

With the incorporation of H&H, Inc. firmly in place, Altman and Wallens revived their partnership and ventured back into the nightclub scene in February 1943. They chose to lease space above the Greyhound Bus Station at 640 Main Street, previously home to the Savarin, launching their new establishment under the name "Victory Room" (also referred to in advertising as "Altman's Downtown Casino").

The term "Victory Room" was part of a broader wartime initiative that provided communal spaces for military personnel, workers, and civilians to socialize and unwind. These venues often featured entertainment like dances and music, aiming to boost morale and foster community solidarity during the war. This concept was integrated into the Victory program, which also included Victory Gardens and Victory Bonds.

Timing was everything when it came to launching the Victory Room. During the war years, gas rationing had cut deeply into attendance at Altman's other venue, the Glen Winter Garden, where its semi-rural location proved a growing liability. Even *Billboard Magazine* remarked that the Glen's distance from Buffalo could dampen nightclub turnout.[573] But Altman was not caught off guard. He had a new venue—and a press release—waiting in the wings: "Harry Altman, the Fun-King of Western New York[a]…moves his hilarity center from Williamsville's green grottos to the traffic center of downtown Buffalo, making his unique entertainment readily available by bus line or 'enroute to work,' fulfilling the new Traffic-Rationing requirements."[574]

Beyond the challenges of gas rationing, Altman faced mounting difficulties in staffing the new club, calling the hiring process "brutal."[575] Wartime shortages of basic supplies—everything from kitchenware to dining essentials—further complicated the operation, slowing progress to a crawl. Still, the show had to go on. To adapt, Altman made key compromises. The Victory Room abandoned Altman's usual three-nights-a-week format in favor of two 90-minute performances every night of the week, with a Saturday matinee. Between shows, guests were invited to dance to the sounds of Bono and his Orchestra, keeping spirits high despite the constraints of the time.

To attract audiences during war times, the club allowed women to enter free on Mondays, regardless of whether they had an escort. Paddy Cliff, a singer with a robust tenor voice reminiscent of Frank Sinatra, was particularly popular among female patrons. Other acts slated to perform at the Victory Room were former vaudeville performers and older entertainers not involved directly in the war effort.

---

[a]That same press release referred to Altman as the "Wowser of Williamsville" and the "Dazzler of Downtown."

HARRY ALTMAN
Your Host
Announces the
Opening of His

New Nite Club

the

DOWN TOWN CASINO

VICTORY ROOM
640 MAIN ST.

Next to Shea's Buffalo
TOMORROW NIGHT
THURSDAY, FEB. 11th
at 9 P. M.
with an ALL-STAR SHOW
featuring

LEON LA VERDE
IN PERSON

PLUS 15 OTHER STAR ACTS
The beautiful Cocktail Chorus
and Other Outstanding Acts

3 Floor Shows Nitely
8:15—11:15—1:45 A. M.

Music by
BONO and His Orchestra

Special A La Carte Plates at All Times
SATURDAY MATINEE at 1 o'CLOCK
Your Hosts:
HARRY ALTMAN—HARRY WALLENS
Phone CL. 9665-9718

Figure 138 Ad for Victory Room
PD

An early highlight at the Victory Room was a performance by The Three Stooges, who, surprisingly, did not receive top billing despite their burgeoning popularity nationwide. The group at the time consisted of Moe Howard, Larry Fine, and Curly Howard. This appearance would be the first of many regular engagements for the trio.

The club was a collaborative effort between the Harrys, yet it was prominently marketed as either "Harry Altman's Downtown Casino" or "Harry Altman's Victory Room," with both men listed as "hosts" in the postscripts. This naming strategy was primarily aimed at attracting patrons from the Glen Winter Garden. However, positioning Altman as the lead promoter would persist for the next quarter century.

Unbeknownst to the public, the Victory Room was not intended by the Harrys to be a long-term operation. It served primarily as a staging area for a more ambitious project. In October 1943, the club discreetly shut down, and the staff, along with all the sought-after kitchen equipment, relocated across the street to 681 Main Street.[576] This site, previously the Palais Royal, had been extensively refurbished by professional interior designer C. Theodore Macheras (who also designed the famed Chez Ami, and its revolving bar) into a more elegant, upscale venue named "The Town Barn."[b]

That address, 681 Main, would become the downtown anchor of the Harrys' collaborative business empire for years to come. And though the building itself would later endure a fate common to many of Altman's ventures, fire and reinvention, the partnership endured for the next quarter century.

---

[b] The name "Town Barn" was a deliberate nod to Glen Park's first nightclub, the Glen Barn.

END OF THE LINE FOR ROLLER RINKS

The war effort tested Harry Altman on many fronts, but only one setback landed him prominently in the Federal Register[577] and ended his roller-skating ambitions for good.

Altman had chased the roller-skating craze through the 1930s with mixed success. His first attempt, a rink on the Glen Park property, was quickly repurposed into a dance hall after the 1936 fire of the Ritz Barn. The Haymow at Main and Transit burned down shortly after opening. The Wagon Wheel Rink at Bailey and Wingate was ultimately dismissed by Altman as too small for serious skating.

Still undeterred, he took one more shot. In 1942, Glen Amusement Corporation began renovating the old Dellwood Dance Pavilion at Main Street and Kensington Avenue in Snyder, just two miles from the Glen, at a projected cost of more than $15,000.[578] Altman envisioned a full-scale, polished rink to capitalize on the wartime hunger for simple, wholesome recreation.

But federal wartime restrictions closed its doors before it even opened. The War Production Board ruled that the project was "diverting critical materials and labor" from the war effort.[579] As a consequence, construction was halted, leaving the rink incomplete under Altman's supervision.[580]

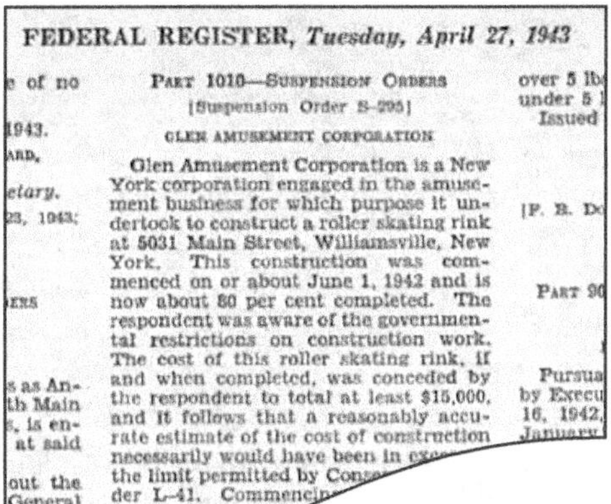

FEDERAL REGISTER, *Tuesday, April 27, 1943*

PART 1010—SUSPENSION ORDERS
[Suspension Order S-295]

GLEN AMUSEMENT CORPORATION

Glen Amusement Corporation is a New York corporation engaged in the amusement business for which purpose it undertook to construct a roller skating rink at 5031 Main Street, Williamsville, New York. This construction was commenced on or about June 1, 1942 and is now about 80 per cent completed. The respondent was aware of the governmental restrictions on construction work. The cost of this roller skating rink, if and when completed, was conceded by the respondent to total at least $15,000, and it follows that a reasonably accurate estimate of the cost of construction necessarily would have been in ex of the limit permitted by Con der L-41. Commencin tion constituted

Figure 139 Clipping from the Federal Register April 27, 1943
PD

By 1944, the building had been revived under new management as the Pal-a-Mar Skating Rink, a bitter reminder that sometimes even Altman's determination could not outmaneuver history.

Still, Harry could not entirely let go of his love for skating. When the mood struck, he would close the Family Inn/Glen Barn for a day, turning the space into a temporary roller rink, inviting crowds to strap on skates and keep the old dream rolling.

WWII: Altman Answers the Call

As he had during World War I, he became a tireless supporter of wartime charities, lending his flair for event planning to fundraisers, morale boosters, and benefits across Western New York.

In July 1942, he organized a large fundraiser for the Navy Relief Society at Buffalo's Civic Stadium.[581] The event brought together a star-studded lineup, including Sophie Tucker, Paddy Cliff, the 76-piece U.S. Navy Band, the full cast of the Broadway hit Sons o' Fun, and the H.M.C.S. Star Naval Band of Canada. The night also featured eight championship boxing matches.[582]

A crowd of 50,000 spectators attended, prompting The Buffalo Courier-Express to declare it the "biggest combination of entertainment, fun, and talent ever staged in the Queen City.[583] The paper added a poignant note regarding Harry's successful venture: "Did you hear that martial music, Herr Hitler? Did you hear those 50,000 spectators cheer the "Star-Spangled Banner", "God Save the King", and the anthems of the United Nations, Mr. Hirohito?"[584]

That record-breaking attendance was surpassed two years later in May 1944. A free event at Delaware Park Meadows marked the second anniversary of the WAVES (Women Accepted for Volunteer Emergency Service), a special unit of the U.S. Naval Reserve that allowed women to serve in non-combat roles, freeing men for combat duty. The celebration in which Altman helped organize featured 30 Civil Air Patrol airplanes, four bands, and 10 stage acts, drawing a staggering crowd of more than 80,000 attendees.[585]

During the war period, Fort Niagara annually commemorated "Harry Altman Day." Located at the junction of the Niagara River and Lake Ontario in Youngstown, New York, the fort served as a training site for U.S. Army units, preparing soldiers for overseas deployment. On his special day, Harry organized stage shows in Youngstown that included his casino headliners, delivering entertainment and boosting the morale for the soldiers stationed there.[586] c

Altman also contributed to the war effort by hosting bond rallies, including one at the Glen Casino that raised $11,025 in a single night in June 1944.[587] In January 1945, he donated the proceeds of a two-hour floor show at the Glen Casino for the benefit of the Amherst Branch of the American Red Cross. The main attraction was the Mills Brothers. In January 1945, he took on the role of chairman for the "Morale Group," a temporary organization of nightclub and theater owners established to provide entertainment to boost "home-front spirits," and support soldiers on furlough, uplifting disabled veterans.[588]

---

c During WWII, Fort Niagara was one of several locations in the U.S. that housed German prisoners of war (POWs).

Harry was especially focused on supporting military personnel on leave, welcoming them warmly to his two nightclubs and providing them with free admission and free drinks. He recognized that by creating a welcoming environment for these service members, they would likely remain loyal patrons once the war came to an end. The strategy worked with out-of-town veterans returning to Buffalo to patronize Altman establishments.

Figure 140 Harry Altman Day at Fort Niagara
promoted in October 1942
PD

CHAPTER 14—TOWN BARN

The Town Barn, which opened in November 1943, was established partly as a companion to the Glen Casino.

Altman and Wallens operated the Town Barn from Labor Day to Decoration Day, when the Glen emerged from its slumber to provide summer entertainment. The Glen Casino, which accommodated between 800 and 1,000 guests, exuded a rustically elegant ambiance. The Town Barn was designed to host more distinguished clientele and entertainers, boasting seating for 1,200 and using the motto "In the Heart of the Town." Wally Wanger,[589] noted for his work on New York productions like the Latin Quarter, "Artists & Models,"[a] and the Ziegfeld Follies, directed the opening show. Bono and his Orchestra became regulars, and Lenny Paige made his debut outside the Glen as the emcee at this grander property.

Drama unfolded at the Town Barn just a year after its opening, stemming from another incident involving Joe "The Wolf" DiCarlo. It appears that DiCarlo felt slighted at not receiving an invitation to the dinner party celebrating the marriage of Hermine, Harry's younger daughter, to David Goldstein of Canandaigua, NY. The meticulously organized event was held at the Georgian Ballroom of the Stalter Hilton on November 19, 1944[590] and was planned by the Altmans to be a night to remember. They invited the city's elite for a private supper post-ceremony, including figures like Mayor Kelly and high-ranking officials such as Police Commissioner Cannan and Inspector Ryan.[591] The evening's entertainment was headlined by Vic Damone, a talent Harry Altman boasted of discovering. Although Magaddino's presence was not officially documented, it was inferred based on subsequent events that occurred that evening.

As reported by the media, DiCarlo apparently showed up uninvited to the event, introducing

Figure 141 Opening night ad, November 11, 1943

Figure 142 Photo of Souvenir Jacket PD

---

[a] The Lou Walters/Harry Altman failed Broadway musical. (on page 281)

tension among the guests. He was quietly confronted by two individuals reminiscent of film noir gangsters and, after a blunt exchange and physical intimidation in a secluded kitchen, left the venue disheveled and alone.[592]

The disruption continued at the Town Barn, where the after-party was held. When DiCarlo arrived, accompanied by his associates, he triggered a full-blown brawl in this public venue complete with flying chairs and glints of metal handguns.[593]

BIG 'BARN' PARTY ENDS IN A RIOT AS DICARLO ARRIVES

Mayor Reported Almost Hit By Chair as Ex-Enemy No. 1, Bounced From Reception, Returns With Gang

Figure 143 Headline from front page of The Buffalo Evening News, November 22, 1944 PD

A bystander reported that the mayor was nearly struck by a chair, although the mayor later clarified that he had left the dinner at the Statler festivities early and did not attend the after-party.[594] Other observers noted that the police who were present seemed more like bystanders than peacekeepers.[595] By the time additional law enforcement were called in, the melee had already peaked, forcing many guests to flee from the venue.

In a subsequent report by *The Buffalo Courier-Express*, officials who had attended both the supper and the post-event party vehemently denied witnessing any disruptions at either venue.[596] Altman's staff confirmed DiCarlo's presence at the post-wedding gathering at the Town Barn but refuted claims of chaos. Altman stated that reports of flying chairs and drawn guns were "unmitigated falsehoods."[597]

Furthermore, Altman clarified that he was not physically present at the post-event festivities. He told *The Buffalo Courier-Express* that upon arriving at the Town Barn that night, he had retreated to his office and stayed there, not once being called to the event space. "At no time was I ever summoned, and I most certainly should have been if there had been trouble," he asserted.[598]

This conflicting narrative left the community puzzling over the true events of that night. No arrests were made by the police, despite the uproar.[599]

Amidst these tumultuous events, the Town Barn also hosted culturally significant moments. In January 1945, Enrico Caruso Jr son of the famed Italian tenor, made his North American nightclub debut there, bringing international acclaim to the venue.[600]

Figure 144 Newswire story: Enrico Caruso, Jr. makes his first U.S. nightclub appearance
at The Town Barn
PD

A reviewer from *The New York Sun* attended Caruso's opening night performance[601]:

> *"As a dramatic tenor, Enrico Caruso Jr. Is a good 'schmalz' singer, meaning, on a 'sweet' song he's terrific. He opened his North American debut last night at the Town Barn, a Buffalo night club, with a simple melody, 'What a Difference a Day Makes,' and the cash customers loved it. After that he essayed more dramatic numbers, such as the 'Flower Song' from 'Carmen,' that showed a tendency to be flat in the upper register and a harshness that contrasted sharply with the sweetness and melody of his opening song."*
>
> *"The 39-year-old son of the famous dramatic tenor was forced to contend with a capacity crowd that became increasingly noisy. Asked why he had chosen a nightclub in which to begin his professional career here, he answered: 'I thought if I could sing in a nightclub with all its distractions I could sing anywhere. It seems to me a good place to groom for a serious singing career.'"*

Caruso Jr.'s nightclub career was not a long one; he would later stop his vocal performances and become a well-known actor, writer and entrepreneur in Italy.

Figure 145 Headline of Town Barn Fire
PD

On February 13th, barely a month and a half after Caruso's performance, disaster struck when a fierce blaze engulfed the Town Barn, disrupting trolley traffic for three hours and leaving numerous workers stranded at their downtown Buffalo businesses.

The three-alarm fire took place during a "violent blizzard".[602]

Approximately a quarter of the streetcars operated by the International Railway Co. were impacted. The blaze also tested the mettle of more than 200 firefighters who, amid snow and smoke, donned oxygen masks and wielded searchlights to battle the fire.[603]

An overheated stove in the basement's carpentry shop was blamed for the fire that started at 3:30 PM.[604] Altman called in the blaze to the fire department. He estimated that losses to the nightclub amounted to $100,000, with neighboring businesses also incurring significant damage. Fire Commissioner John J. Tubridy tallied up financial losses across the affected stores: $25,000 at Play-More Sporting Goods, $5,000 at Sack's Fur store,[b] and $3,000 at the Town Florists Shop.[605]

Performers lost most of their possessions in the dressing rooms. *The Buffalo Courier-Express* reported that entertainer Betty Reilly[c] had some success in retrieving five gowns and some music sheets with the help of firemen.[606]

Without a downtown venue, *Billboard* announced that Altman would open his Glen Park Casino two months early to accommodate the booking of Arthur Lee Simpkins[d] who was originally bought to appear at Altman's Town Barn on March 31st.[607]

After the Town Barn was destroyed, Altman and Wallens quickly pivoted, designing an entirely new nightclub from the ground up at 681 Main. In less than a year, they relied on an extensive team of architects, designers, and builders to launch the Town Casino on December 29, 1945.

---

[b] The furrier had just moved into the 681 Main Street after being wiped out by fire at its previous location across the street. "An Open Letter," *The Buffalo Evening News*, April 11, 1945, 32.

[c] Reilly was a popular nightclub singer, dancer, and actress of that era, performing with notable orchestras like Xavier Cugat's.

[d] Originally born in South Carolina, Simkins earned the moniker the "Black Caruso" for his exceptional vocal talents reminiscent of the famed opera singer Enrico Caruso.

Figure 146 Interior of the Town Casino
Photo courtesy of The Archives & Special Collection Department of SUNY Buffalo State

CHAPTER 15—THE TOWN CASINO

"An airport hangar fitted out to a maharajah's most luxurious mood."

~ *Jack O'Brian, National Columnist*[608]

When Harry and Harry opened the Town Casino in 1945, they envisioned more than just a nightclub; they aimed to create an unparalleled experience of opulence and entertainment. The sprawling 19,500-square-foot Town Casino quickly became a playground for the elite, a temple of luxury in a city aspiring to grandeur.

Many guests reminisced about the splendor of the experience. According to newspaper reports at the time, upon entering, patrons were greeted by the shimmering sight of white linen tablecloths and waiters in suits, meticulously attired to enhance the feeling of exclusivity and class. Hat check attendants and cigarette girls added touches of old-world charm, reminiscent of an era of genteel sophistication.

The main draw, beyond the sumptuous decor, was the entertainment. A big band, positioned on an elevated bandstand draped in white velvet, played the latest hits, setting the soundtrack for the evening. Performances were staged three times nightly—at 7:30 PM, 10:30 PM, and 1:30 AM—ensuring that the vibrancy of the venue never dimmed.

The main room, capable of accommodating 1,200, was a marvel of architectural ingenuity. With terraced rows of tables, every spot in the grand dance hall offered an unobstructed view of the lavish stage. An article in *The Buffalo Courier-Express* described the casino's interior as a "symphony of color: quilted turquoise velvet walls with mirror button appliqués, coral satin draped valances surrounding the dance floor, all framed by off-white baroque plaster."[609] Gleaming brass rails sectioned off the five terrace levels of seating.

Billboard declared the room a "tremendous space" with a stage that was "capacious, under a high ceiling that accommodated any kind of aerial act, with the orchestra perched on tiered platforms above which another stage was set for grand productions."[610]

The glassed-in cocktail lounge, designed to accommodate 300 guests, dazzled with tufted turquoise plush and mirrored accents. It featured a neon-lit dome and a unique blackout stage for intimate skits, complemented by a revolving stage at the bar's center. The flickering mirror ceiling added a scintillating touch to the lounge, enhancing the already electric atmosphere.

Artists and performers enjoyed first-rate amenities, including 10 separate dressing rooms complete with showers and lavatories, underscoring the Town Casino's commitment to excellence in every aspect of its operations.

Billboard rhapsodized the Town's ambiance, celebrating its unique and opulent character:

> *"When Harry Altman puts a spot on the map, there is never anything halfway about it. He has promoted a long string of successful ventures here, several together with Harry Wallens. His latest layout, a newly built giant theater-restaurant, is really something. Everything about it is super. Spot is just a month old, and biz has been solid every night. Interior decor is lavish, beautiful and strictly class, with service to match. A colorful 90-minute production that can be seen from any part of the huge place, fits right in with the splendid setting. Altman is his own producer."[611]*

> *As for the stage show itself, Billboard reports:*

> *"Town Casino Models, six showgirls, are perfect for providing color. S. A. costumes are beautiful and terping[a] better than adequate. Girls open show with Mexican hat dance; midway do an Oriental nocturne; and close with gorgeously dressed-up parade number. Emcee Lenny Paige, here indefinitely, does a lively job with good gab and pleasing personality. Bono's Band (9) does well in cutting the long show, and equally so for dancing."[612]*

The opening show featured Jerry Cooper, NBC singing star; Jerry Lawlor, singer; The De Marlos, husband/wife premier dancers; Shay & Raymond, "Zanie comedians," Salyman Ali Troupe, acrobats; and Town Casino Girls, dancers.[613]

Billboard reported that H&H, Inc. was on record for owning the Club. A. Irving Milch was the real estate attorney on the deal. Ruben Bodenhorn, who designed several Latin Quarter niteries, was the decorator. Charles E. Speich was the architect. The William Morris Agency was the exclusive talent booker.[614]

The turnaround of the property was quick. The ashes from the Town Barn had been carried away in mid-February 1945; the Town Casino opened on New Year's Eve in time to welcome 1946.

---

[a] Slang for "dancing."

Figure 147 Photo of Town Casino Stage
Photo Courtesy of Marjorie Wallens

Billboard Magazine

Billboard Magazine covered Altman's career since the late 1920s when he was operating the Arcadia Ballroom. Hardly sycophants, Billboard critics served as a vital resource for music industry professionals, offering news, trends, reviews, and industry statistics. Billboard identified what was hot, and what was not.

The year 1952 was considered by experts to be the peak of the nightclub industry's cultural impact; the post-WWII economic boom contributed to a surge in entertainment spending, with nightclubs benefiting as popular venues for socializing and entertainment.

It was during this year that reporter Bill Smith from Billboard dropped into Buffalo to gaze a critical eye on the Town Casino. He was in Buffalo on September 13th to witness the life force that was Sophie Tucker, who brought in a "major production effort that was completely new" to the city "of about 650,000."[615] Smith noted that ticket lines started forming early in the afternoon and continued until the last show at 1:30 AM.[616]

After extolling the "tremendous" showroom, Smith described the Town Casino as a "king-sized Latin Quarter," before diving into the details.[617]

"The Town Casino is a fabulous place. Its grosses are probably high but considering its prices ($3 for a steak dinner; no cover or minimum), the chances are the net is moderate. Usually, the spot has an admission charge, but for [Tucker's] show there was no admission, [though] there was a 60-cent amusement charge placed on the tab."[618]

"The spot has one thing the Latin Quarter doesn't have: a tremendous bar business. The bar is up front, an oval affair in the center of which there's a combo plus three good-looking girl singers who segue from song to song. The show and decor took a lot of guts for Buffalo. Altman, an aggressive host, engineered most of it, showing showmanship ability that is rare outside of the big cities."[619]

Smith then turns his sights to The Glen, "an amusement park about 10 miles out of town.[620]

"The spot is a remarkable operation. Surrounded by a tremendous parking lot (jammed on the night caught) with an entrance where customers walk through a lighted arcade flanked with Bingo and similar games. The park itself has tables, benches and outdoor grills scattered through its more than 10 acres. Patrons come, stay all day, cook their food, use the tables. grills, etc... Much of the area is given over to kid rides of various sorts, none more than a nickel [a ticket]."[621]

"The [Glen] Casino is another big operation within the Park. It consists of a big room, surprisingly well decorated, seating about 1,000, plus a cocktail lounge with talent above a bar doing lively business. The Casino does a large family trade. Pitchers of beer seem to be staple items. The Casino operates on an admission charge basis, 40 to 50 cents, doing three shows nightly and has about two turnovers. The talent budget is about $3,000, and the acts caught were surprisingly good, not only for here but for almost any spot."[622]

In Billboard's national assessment, the Town and Glen secured top ratings.

LET THEM ENTERTAIN YOU

The Town Casino was more than just a venue; it was a legendary stage where countless stars etched their names into Buffalo's nightlife history through unforgettable performances and backstage lore. This iconic nightclub hosted a dazzling array of talent, each act adding another layer to its rich and colorful legacy.

One of Harry Altman's most successful accomplishments was his knack for spotting rising regional performers, acts he believed had the potential to break out nationally. He would sign them to multi-year contracts that, at the time, felt like a windfall for the entertainer. But three years later, when those same artists were headlining national nightclubs and making television appearances, those deals seemed modest at best.

Press releases praised their loyalty to Altman, but in truth, they were fulfilling contractual obligations. In the industry, the phrase "always make time for Harry" became a tongue-in-cheek euphemism for those long-locked bookings. Not every gamble paid off—but when it did, as in the case of Vic Damone, the returns were substantial.

Frances Salerno Ippolito, who served as Altman's secretary for two decades, later pulled back the curtain on how those deals were made. In a 1981 interview with *The Buffalo News* columnist Karen Brady, Ippolito recalled:

"Mr. Altman would tell a performer 'I think you have talent. If you can make it in Buffalo, you can make it anywhere in the world.' And then he would offer the performer a chance to appear at the Town Casino—but only IF he or she promised to come back the following year. It was right in the contract. If the show person could not make it in the next year, he or she had to pay Mr. Altman what he or she would have been paid—sometimes $5000. And remember, this was the 40s."[623]

It was a bold strategy, equal parts beliefs and business, and it helped cement the Town Casino's reputation as both a proving ground and a pressure cooker for rising talent.

What follows are just a few of the stories—some glamorous, some gritty—that illustrate the singular legacy of the Town Casino and its enduring imprint on American entertainment.

SOPHIE TUCKER

During the initial years of operation at the Town Casino, the venue remained open throughout the year. However, a significant challenge arose in July 1946 when intense heat waves deterred patrons from attending performances in the non-air-conditioned space. This climatic issue notably diminished the box office draw for Sophie Tucker, leading Harry Altman to temporarily close the venue.

The review in *Billboard* (7/13/46) memorialized the "hot" performance of "The Last of the Red-Hot Mamas":

> *"Sophie Tucker, headlines, doing a terrific job of selling. Altho spot was covered on a scorching night, with new air-conditioning system not yet working, La Tucker proved herself a real trouper and carried her act thru nobly in spite of unbearable heat under the spots. Customers, inspired by her fortitude, gave out with wholehearted appreciation."[624]*

Figure 148 Autograph signing session with patron Frank E. Freedman and Sophie Tucker
Photo courtesy of the Jewish Buffalo Image Collection, State University of New York at Buffalo

Needless to say, Tucker's attitude was quite heated as she left the stage that night.

While she graciously participated in a charity performance at Perrysburg's Hospital, entertaining patients, and frequently appeared at the Altman nightclubs well into her 70s, she also had a reputation for being ornery. "She was very, very, very difficult," Jerry Coe said in an interview with Kliph Nesteroff about performing at the Town Casino with his comedy partner, Dick Lynn. "The first two weeks we were there we [opened] for Vic Damone. They held us over with Tucker because we were doing so well."[625]

Figure 149 Tucker volunteered to entertain at the Perrysburg Hospital charity event
From left: Altman, Tucker, Wallens and Lenny Paige
Photo courtesy of Marjorie Wallens

With Tucker now part of the show, an issue emerged. Lynn, a stout visual comic, had a sketch that parodied Tucker. Altman wanted the sketch dropped and went backstage to demand its removal.

"Look, we love you guys and you're staying over--but cut the Tucker bit. I don't want problems with this bitch because if she doesn't like it then I'm gonna hear about it," Coe recounted on the "Classic Television Showbiz" blog from April 5, 2012.[626]

"It's not done in a mean-spirited way," Coe explained to Altman. "There is nothing she could take offense for!"

Altman responded, "Please do me a favor and cut the fucking thing. Just take your money and do your act."

Displeased with Altman's verdict, Coe sought advice from Ted Shapiro, Tucker's accompanist and gin rummy partner.

"You do Tucker?" Shapiro asked incredulously when Coe met with him.

"My partner does, and I think it would really work with us both being on the same show."

Shapiro advised, "Listen, keep the number in, but come to the club early and come to the dressing room before the first show. Early."

Coe and Lynn did as they were told, arriving early and went to her dressing room at the Town. Coe described the scene:

"There was a mirror, and it was covered with a giant pair of pink bloomers. That's the first thing you see as you walk into this room," Coe recalled. "This humongous pair of bloomers. She's sitting there at her dressing room table. She doesn't even turn around to look at us. She just sits there at the mirror and says, 'I understand you boys do me? Well... do me good.'"[627]

"And that was it," Coe noted. "We brought her orchids every night for her entrance."

While she graciously handled the parody, Tucker did not react well to a later change in the timing of the lineup. Altman had cut five minutes from Coe & Lynn's act, which required Tucker to start her performance early.

"We assumed--and assumption is the mother of all fuck-ups--that she was told," Coe mentioned. "And she wasn't." When the duo finished their act, they walked backstage and were greeted with language they had never heard before.[628]

"It was absolutely horrendous. The anger she had!" Coe said of Tucker's reaction when she discovered the schedule had been altered at the last minute.[629]

IN BUFFALO — VISIT

TOWN CASINO
681 Main Street
THE NATION'S MOST BEAUTIFUL SHOW PLACE
FAMOUS FOR LAVISH BROADWAY REVUES
COMPLETELY AIR-CONDITIONED BY CARRIER

Figure 150 Promotional sticker for air conditioning
PD

After the Tucker debacle that left her sweating through her bloomers due to a heat wave, Altman had a Carrier air conditioning system installed; its presence was plastered on all the Town Casino advertising and collateral.

Now with the patrons of the Town able to keep cool, Harry returned to operating both casinos during the summer—for a short time.

In July 1946, *Billboard* reported on the change of plans: "Attendance at Altman's Glen Park Casino was waning due to competition from a downtown venue. The operator expressed concerns that the current market was insufficient to sustain both large enterprises simultaneously."[630]

Harry reverted to the initial strategy of keeping the Town Casino open nine months of the year, allowing the Glen to take center stage during the summer.

VIC DAMONE

Figure 151 Damone clowns with Altman and Wallens backstage
Photo courtesy of Brad Altman

Vic Damone's appearances at the Town Casino read like a screenplay—full of high notes, low blows, and a final scene that delivered a twist of fate. The smooth crooner, a favorite of Harry Altman's (who liked to think he helped discover Damone), once found himself entangled in a plot that could rival any gangster film, all recounted in his memoir, "Singing was the Easy Part." [631]

The drama unfolded in 1950 when Damone was headlining at the Town Casino. In his book, the singer refers to Joe DiCarlo as "Johnny D'Angelo," as "the story's still a little sensitive, even after 50 years." [632]

As reported in the book, Damone, just 20, was engaged in 1948 to D'Angelo's daughter, Vincinetta—affectionately dubbed "Franny" in his tales. The engagement went sour after Franny took offense to Mrs. Damone's well-intentioned cooking lessons, calling her a "bitch." This insult was enough for Vic to call it quits, a decision that sparked fury in Franny's father, seeing it as a dishonor to his family (*onore della famiglia*). [633]

The breakup led to an attempt on Damone's life when D'Angelo's henchmen tried to toss him out of a window at the Edison Hotel in New York City. Clinging to a window frame and a necktie, Damone survived, and a mob sit-down quickly followed.[634] The city's most powerful boss at the time, Frank Costello, laid down the law about Damone's survival chances: "We say he lives. That's it. He's part of our family. What's right is right."[635]

But peace was short-lived. At Damone's next appearance at the Town Casino, D'Angelo plotted his next move, placing himself at a table ringside with his wife, daughter Franny and friends for Damone's show. Post-performance, an eerie midnight summons to their table had Damone stuck in a cinematic standoff. "We're sitting there, talking about nothing," Damone recalled. "It's three, four...we're just sitting. I'm not getting up. I can't get up. They have to get up first, then I'll walk out with them and say good night."[636]

As the evening dragged on, the waitstaff lingered awkwardly waiting for the table to disperse. Eventually, Mrs. D'Angelo glanced at her watch and declared, "It's after six. You know we can go to church from here."[637]

The departure of the D'Angelos to St. Michael's Church across the street from the Town offered Damone an escape. He dashed back to the Hotel Statler Hilton, only to be confronted again by D'Angelo who apparently missed Mass. With his charm and quick wit, Damone was able to diffuse the tension, dodging the lurking threat of D'Angelo's baseball bat-wielding companions.[638]

Years later, a peculiar detente was brokered in a Buffalo pub. Damone, having refused to testify against D'Angelo in a federal probe, found himself face-to-face with the old mobster. "D'Angelo took his right hand off the bar," Damone wrote, "held it out to me and looked me dead in the eye. 'It's over,' he said. 'Take a drink.'" With a toast of "Salute," they sealed the peace, and just like that, D'Angelo was gone, leaving behind a cloud of cigar smoke and a story for the ages.[639]

TONY BENNETT

Harry might not have discovered "Anthony Benedetto," but he certainly knew a star when he saw one. He booked the up-and-coming Tony Bennett at the Town Casino starting in 1950, an entire year before Bennett crooned his way to the top of the charts with "Because of You." Bennett followed this initial appearance to Bufalo as a headliner in 1951, 1955, and 1960. His frequent visits to Buffalo became the stuff of legend, but it was not all smooth sailing.

Figure 152 Tony Bennett
PD

The twist in Bennett's tale came to light during a 1995 chat with entertainment reporter Robin Milling, when Bennett shared a chilling encounter from the 1950s—a homicidal stalker had targeted him during a 1950s gig in Buffalo.[640] Altman had unearthed a disturbing pile of letters from a stalker, filled with threats to end Bennett's life. "He was a demented person who called me a communist one night or thought I stole his wife the second night. Each letter was more morbid than the last," Bennett recounted.[641]

The situation escalated when the man threatened Bennett with a sawed-off shotgun, prompting the involvement of the FBI. They sprang into action after one particularly brazen letter when the stalker dared to write, "If you think I'm a coward, here's my address…" Bennett relayed that the police stormed the address only to find the perpetrator absent, but his menacing shotgun stashed in a drawer.[642]

Law enforcement eventually apprehended the man at his home and detained him at the police station, only for him to make a daring escape soon after. "To this day we don't know what happened to him," Bennett revealed.[643] The ordeal left an indelible mark on the singer, teaching him an eternal vigilance that he carried throughout his life, always wary of what might lurk just beyond the footlights.

AL MARTINO

When compared to Damone and Bennett, Al Martino had a lovely time at the Town Casino during the one-week run. As usual, Altman was ahead of the curve, booking Martino in May 1952 before his first number one hit made the charts, "Here in My Heart."

Marilyn Monroe had just wrapped "Niagara," co-starring Joseph Cotton, and caught Al Martino's show at the Town Casino. There are two photos taken after he finished his show that night. "Niagara" director Henry Hathaway was also in attendance.

Martino left the U.S. for the United Kingdom in the mid-1950s after Mob members allegedly bought out his management contract and ordered him to pay $75,000 as a safeguard for their investment. Upon negotiating his return in 1958, Altman was one of the first to book him, helping Martino re-establish his presence on the American music scene. Martino was forever loyal to Harry, playing the Glen Casino as late as 1962.

Figure 153 Niagara film director Henry Hathaway accompanies Marilyn Monroe
to the Town Casino to see the headliner, Al Martino
Photo courtesy of the Al Martino Estate

LIBERACE

One of the entertainment industry's most talked-about breakups of the era unfolded dramatically on the stage of the Town Casino. For years, (Lee) Liberace had captivated audiences with his sparkling costumes and dazzling piano performances, but he had not always been a solo performer. His brother George, an accomplished violinist, had often shared the spotlight, lending classical elegance to Liberace's extravagant shows.

However, their once-harmonious collaboration came to a painful end on an October night in 1958 at the Town Casino. Undercurrents of unresolved tension finally surfaced, prompting the brothers to part ways musically. That emotional evening became their last shared performance, ending with both men leaving the stage in tears.[644]

Mama Liberace, as the public soon learned, was deeply distressed by her sons'

Figure 154 Liberace, a frequent headliner at the Town, crafted and circulated his own eye-catching promotional materials
Photo of postcard courtesy of Neil Parker

separation. Mrs. Frances Liberace, who had steadfastly supported her sons throughout their careers, found herself unable to attend Lee's performances after the duo's split.[645]

Figure 155 : Liberace addresses the audience as his brother, George, and opera star Jean Fenn look on
Photo courtesy of Neil Parker

"I love both of my boys," Mrs. Liberace told a reporter. "They have both been wonderful to me. But I cannot watch either of them perform until they reconcile."[646]

It was reported that the disagreement began after George reacted to Lee's comments about his frozen food business he had as a side business. Lee, performing solo on a television show, responded to an audience member's question about George with a calypso tune: "He was out making a fortune selling pizza pies."[647]

"I'm certainly not making a fortune," George later retorted, suggesting the conflict had been exacerbated by Lee's associates undermining George's efforts. [648]

The family fallout was profound, leading Lee to skip Christmas dinner, deepening their mother's heartache.

"She loved us both very much," George remarked. "Nothing would have made her happier than seeing us back together again."[649]

Regrettably, a reunion on stage never materialized. The 1958 performance at the Town Casino remained their final act together. In his act, Liberace often said out loud: "I wish my brother George was here."[650]

Figure 156 A signed photo of Liberace, gifted to Harry Altman, was proudly displayed in the main office of the Town Photo courtesy of Brad Altman

PHYLLIS DILLER

The Town Casino was no stranger to praise during its heyday—but not everyone was impressed. In April 1961, Phyllis Diller, fresh off her performance at the club, delivered a rare and scathing review. Speaking by phone to entertainment columnist Jack Curtis—who described her as "blonde, daffy, but lovable"—Diller did not hold back.[651] Echoing fellow comic Jack E. Leonard, she quipped, "I liked Buffalo better when it was an animal." As for the club itself? "Actually, the place is a reconverted hangar," she said. "It's nothing but wild. Maybe it was designed by four decorators who hated each other."[652]

The roots of Diller's disdain are not entirely clear. But Leonard may have had his own grudge: years earlier, in 1955, he had been forced to buy his way out of a Town Casino contract after landing a coveted appearance on *The Martha Raye Show*.[653] That kind of move, common in the volatile world of nightclub bookings, may have left some lingering hard feelings.

THE MYSTERY OF THE MANNEQUIN

In the late 1940s and early 1950s, a female mannequin was suspended by wires from the Town Casino marquee, hovering over Main Street and facing the crowd below.

She was not tied to one particular act. She did not change with the seasons or the headliners. Photos show her in place during engagements ranging from Danny Thomas to Josephine Baker. Her presence was not advertised, and no one seems to recall exactly why she was put there in the first place.

In a city still recoiling from the 1942 photograph of Mary Miller, caught mid-fall from the Genesee Hotel[b] the mannequin's position—frozen above the sidewalk—felt oddly familiar. There is no evidence that the two were connected. But in a place where appearance, memory, and mystery often blurred, the echo was hard to miss.

Over time, the mannequin became part of the backdrop, fading from attention. Then, finally fading from view when it was removed from the property.

Yet she remains one of the more curious footnotes in the Town Casino's history: a static figure above a scene in constant motion.

Figure 157 Notable similarities emerge when comparing the marquee images to the tragic leap from the hotel Marquee photos courtesy of The Archives & Special Collection Department of SUNY Buffalo State Hotel image captured by I. Russell Sorgi, The Buffalo Courier Express

[b] The photo was reprinted in Life Magazine, and became a cultural symbol during wartime.

THE LITTLE [ARTHUR] GODFREYS

Arthur Godfrey reigned supreme in the 1950s as America's premier talent discoverer and promoter, wielding his broadcast clout to turn fresh-faced novices into national sensations. With his folksy charisma and an unerring eye for talent, Godfrey's radio and television shows were more than just entertainment; they were star-making machines that defined the era.

His strategic partnership with Altman in the mid-1950s, when both men were at the height of their influence, made national news. The Town secured top talent to headline, and Godfrey was given a safe stage where his protégés could shine beyond the airwaves.

Through "Arthur Godfrey's Talent Scouts" (1948-58), Godfrey created a pivotal platform for young artists eager to break into show business. The format was simple yet revolutionary: ordinary people with extraordinary talents performed live, competing for the affection of both the studio audience and the millions watching at home. Winners, often determined by the applause meter, gained instant fame, and for many, this became the launchpad of their careers.

Godfrey was not content with simply hosting a platform for talent discovery; he integrated these performers into his weekly variety show, "Arthur Godfrey & Friends" (1949-59), providing them with continuous exposure and the chance to refine their craft in front of a national audience. His key regulars—dubbed "Little Godfreys"—were ensemble cast members largely restricted to performing solely on Godfrey's shows, often for months or even years. Performers like Julius La Rosa, Frank Parker, Wally Cox, the McGuire Sisters, Marion Marlowe, and Carmel Quinn were among those who were referred to as "Little Godfreys."

Occasionally, Godfrey bent the rules by featuring professional performers who needed help reaching a national audience. These included Tony Bennett, Connie Francis, Steve Lawrence, Rosemary Clooney, Leslie Uggams, and Janette Davis. The strategy proved successful for the entertainers, Godfrey's ratings, and Altman, who often went on to book many of these performers after their appearances on Godfrey's shows.

Figure 158 Godfrey stands in center with two of his talent discoveries: Frank Parker and Marion Marlowe
PD

Behind the scenes, Godfrey's influence extended further. He was known for his paternalistic, though sometimes controversial, management style, which included maintaining a tight grip on the careers of the performers he discovered. This control was a double-edged sword—while it provided stability and national exposure for emerging artists, it occasionally drew public criticism that eventually diminished Godfrey's influence.

Figure 159 Julius La Rosa
The Archives & Special Collection Department
of SUNY Buffalo State

The beginning of Arthur Godfrey's professional decline was marked in October 1953 when he fired Julius La Rosa, one of his "Little Godfreys," live on the air. La Rosa, a beloved teen idol, was reportedly dismissed for hiring his own manager, as well as for the commercial success of his recordings—both of which infuriated Godfrey.[654]

There was only one king in Godfrey's empire.

In a comment that would haunt him for years, Godfrey told the media that La Rosa had "lost his humility" and had become "too big a star."[655] The backlash was swift and severe, dominating front pages across the country.

To his credit, La Rosa took the hit squarely on the chin. His new manager quickly booked him on The Ed Sullivan Show—Godfrey's chief rival—and began scouting for a nightclub debut. Altman extended an offer, and La Rosa accepted. For one week in January 1954, Buffalo found itself at the center of the entertainment world.

A review in *The Buffalo Courier-Express* captured the excitement:

"Whether Julius La Rosa has humility is something even he doesn't care to discuss anymore. But whatever a whispering voice, a friendly puppy-dog manner, or murmured sweet nothings in Italian add up to, Julius has it. And the sighing ladies, who beseeched the Town Casino last night, apparently love whatever it is."[656]

The reporter noted that La Rosa gave Altman and Wallens a reason to barricade the venue's expensive plate glass windows to prevent enthusiastic fans from breaking them down.[657] While several hundred fans stood outside in the 27-degree cold without a ticket, a cozy crowd of 1,058 patrons enjoyed the performance from inside.[658]

Following La Rosa's show, the Town Casino resumed its regular programming, but Godfrey continued to stew. The public backlash had not subsided, and by late 1954, he began to realize that his strict control over his performers was hurting his image. Seeking a solution, he started exploring venues that would allow the Little Godfreys to perform live, paid appearances—ideally far from the cutthroat talent managers of New York and Chicago whom Godfrey viewed as threats to his influence.

He decided that the Town Casino would fit the bill perfectly. By 1955, Godfrey's relationship with Altman became more visible as three Little Godfreys were booked within the first six months of the year.

For Altman and Wallens, the partnership was financially attractive. Godfrey's performers came with national exposure and a loyal fan base. To accommodate their television commitments, Altman adjusted the club's standard week-long bookings, offering the Little Godfreys weekend-only engagements.

Frank Parker, an Irish tenor known for his versatility and long-standing radio career, was the first Little Godfrey to appear at the Town—"with Godfrey's blessing"—in January 1955.[659] After a successful run, Godfrey sent Parker back to Buffalo in April, despite Parker's own reservations about returning so soon.[660]

"He's the best they ever had in the business. He's the ace," Parker said of Godfrey.[661] Still, he worried about overexposure but gave it his all. At both sets of performances, he delivered the same songs he had sung for years—yet continued to "knock them dead."[662] While in Buffalo, Parker scouted opportunities across the Canadian border to expand his following.[663]

During Parker's first stint at the Town, Altman announced a major booking: the McGuire Sisters, the most popular act in Godfrey's talent stable, would headline starting March 7th.[664] Negotiations were tense. The sisters initially demanded $14,000 a week—a fee Altman refused. Godfrey publicly scolded Harry on his national broadcast for being cheap. Within 10 hours of Godfrey's statement, Altman struck a deal: Christine, Dorothy, and Phyllis would appear for $10,000.[665]

Figure 160 The Harrys with the McGuire Sisters
Photo by Brad Altman

Before the McGuire Sisters arrived, another Little Godfrey made her nightclub debut. Marion Marlowe, a statuesque singer of romantic ballads, had never set foot backstage at a nightclub during her four years on Godfrey's show. She arrived in Buffalo two weeks after Parker. Her appearance proved to be a smash, with customers lined up in a snowstorm to get in.[666]

"I am just the latest one of the family to do a little outside work," Marlowe told a reporter. "Mr. Godfrey just likes to be sure that the auspices will go to the best... that we get the right money, and that such appearances will help our careers."[667]

Accompanied by her fiancé, a producer from Godfrey's show, Marlowe told the press she had "no plan or desire" to leave Godfrey's orbit.[668] But less than four months later, Godfrey fired her—along with eight others—claiming "Arthur Godfrey & Friends" had become too bloated with talent. Her fiancé's responsibilities were also significantly reduced.[669]

To Altman's credit, he capitalized on Godfrey's influence during the broadcaster's peak, and again during his decline. As disillusioned performers drifted from Godfrey's control, they found opportunity and familiarity in Buffalo. One of the first stages Marlowe performed on after her dismissal was at the Town.

"Harry ruined me for everybody else," she told *The Buffalo Evening News* ahead of her return appearance. "He was so nice to me at the time I really needed the confidence. I told him then, and I mean it always—whenever he wants me, I will be delighted to come to Buffalo for Harry."[670]

By early 1956, booking the newly independent Little Godfreys became a thoughtful strategy. Nationally syndicated columnist Jack O'Brian interviewed Altman that February, calling him "one of the best showmen we've ever known."[671]

Altman explained his process for selecting which Godfrey alumni to bring to the Town. On Marion Marlowe, set to appear again in February 1956: "She's not on TV regularly anymore. She appears on Ed Sullivan enough to stay famous—but only for a song or two. She's even more famous now for being fired. People want to see her. They want to hear what she'll say about Godfrey. And she's an outspoken girl."[672]

On the McGuire Sisters, booked for April 1956: "They're hot on records and always in the headlines. Dorothy and [sometimes boyfriend] La Rosa,[c] Dorothy and her husband getting back together, then divorcing—every time La Rosa makes news, the McGuire story resurfaces. Even Phyllis's husband accidentally breaking her jaw—more headlines.[d] They've got a fine act— clean, lively, and entertaining. That's why I hope to get back my $19,000— and a profit."[673]

Figure 161 Richard Q. Lewis—pictured here with Altman and Wallens—was Arthur Godfrey's preferred stand-in during his absences. He used the opportunity as a springboard to launch a successful career in television and nightclubs
Photo courtesy of Brad Altman

---

[c] They had dated during Dorothy's separation from her husband.

[d] Phyllis and her husband would divorce later that year, and she would take up with mafia boss Sam Giancana, who was rumored to have visited the Town when the McGuire Sisters were performing. Dorothy and Sam's relationship lasted 16 years until his death in 1975 of unnatural causes (he was murdered)

COUNT BASIE

Count Basie's long association with Buffalo dates to 1940, when he and the Count Basie Orchestra performed at the Broadway Auditorium on behalf of United Club's Charity Dance. It was part of the Orchestra's first cross-country tour. His inaugural appearance at the Town Casino came in 1948, just three years after the nightclub's grand opening, continuing his rich relationship with the city's jazz scene.

In 1957, Basie returned to an Altman property under the stewardship of emcee Lenny Paige and renowned Buffalo jazz promoter and broadcaster Joe Rico. This time, the venue was the Glen Barn (better known as the Family Inn), located at the rear of the property, as Jerry Vale headlined that week at the Glen Casino. Basie's two evening performances at the Barn, held at 8

Figure 162 Count Basie
PD

PM and 10 PM, featured his orchestra alongside the legendary Joe Williams. The event was were simulcast on WHLD where Rico was a disc jockey.

Though it is unclear if Harry Altman was directly involved in booking these shows—he was known to lease the Barn to outside promoters—it appears that Basie temporarily slipped out of Altman's orbit and into Joe Rico's hands. Basie returned to Buffalo in October 1960, this time gracing the stage at Kleinhans Music Hall, where he and his orchestra were honored for their 25th anniversary, with Rico as promoter.

In 1963, Basie headlined what Rico billed as the "greatest jazz concert in Buffalo history" at the Buffalo Jazz Festival at Offermann Stadium. The festival featured a stunning lineup of jazz legends, including Billie Holiday, Dizzy Gillespie, and Buddy Rich,[e] solidifying Buffalo's status as a jazz epicenter.[f]

Basie's final appearance at the Town Casino came during its twilight in January 1964, shortly after he celebrated his 60th birthday. Speaking with *The Buffalo Evening News*, Basie reflected on his career, noting he would retire "when he had enough bread," though he admitted that composing had taken a backseat. "My ideas are a little webby," he confessed. "A little old-fashioned."[674]

---

[e] Rico's contributions to the jazz world were so significant that artists like Stan Kenton and Basie composed pieces in his honor, including "Jump for Joe" and "Port o' Rico," respectively.

[f] The Rico-Altman relationship was symbiotic. Rico often set up his microphone in the front window of the Town Casino in the early 1960s at Harry's invitation and did live interviews with the stars performing there.

DANNY THOMAS

In an article by *The Buffalo Courier-Express* columnist Bob Sokolsky published after Harry's death; he conjectured that the "Uncle Charlie" Halper character on Danny Thomas's sitcom "Make Room for Daddy" was patterned after Altman.

As reported by Sokolsky: "Danny Thomas and his partner Sheldon Leonard had worked for Harry and knew him well. At any provocation they could spin off multitudes of yarns about him, tales that had to find their way into Thomas' series."[675]

Uncle Charlie,[g] in the 1960s sitcom, was a nightclub owner of The Copa Club where Thomas's character, Danny Williams, performed as a comedian and singer.

Thomas's first appearance at the Town was in January 1949, and he made Altman's Casinos a regular on his nightclub circuit.

Figure 163 Danny Thomas with Altman
Photo courtesy of Brad Altman

---

[g] Charlie was played by Sid Melton, a veteran comic actor of the 50s and 60s. Old episodes of the "Make Room for Daddy" can be found on YouTube.

EDDIE FISHER

Eddie Fisher was a man who could break hearts and make headlines. But, incredibly early in his singing career—October 1947—he appeared for the first time at the Town Casino. This was well before his appearance with Eddie Cantor (1949), his top 10 hit "Thinking of You" (1950), his marriage to Debbie Reynolds (1955), and his scandalous affair with Elizabeth Taylor (1959). Lenny Paige noted in Bob Curran's column in *The Buffalo Evening News* just how early it was in Fisher's career:

"I remember him coming to my room at the Stuyvesant the day before he was going to start here. When I mentioned his tux, he said he did not have one.[676] Without a tux, he couldn't go on, and so I took my brand-new jacket and brought him to tailor Joe Seeburg, and Joe shortened it and gave him some trousers. I never saw the jacket again."[h]

He certainly was not headlining the show (Eleanor Powell was top on the bill), but Altman described him in the advertising as "1947 Singing Discovery Sensation." Harry reported that Fisher was paid $150 for the gig, and "he was tickled to death."

Of course, Fisher went on to mega fame and returned to the Town at least two more times as a headliner.

---

[h] For years, Altman took credit for giving Fisher his first tuxedo. Perhaps Altman compensated Paige for the loss of the tux. Maybe.

Al Capone

Though not an entertainer, the persistent rumor that Al Capone once played poker in the basement of the Town Casino remains one of Buffalo's more colorful urban legends. In reality, the timeline makes this impossible. The Town Casino opened on New Year's Eve 1944—by which time Capone had already been out of the public eye for years. He began serving an 11-year federal sentence for tax evasion in 1932 and was released early in 1939 due to declining health. Immediately upon release, he was hospitalized at Johns Hopkins in Baltimore for treatment of late-stage syphilis, which had severely affected his brain. He then retired to his estate in West Palm Beach where he lived quietly with his wife and grandchildren until his death in January 1947 at the age of 48.

Joni Joseph: A True Star of the Town and Glen Casinos

One would be hard-pressed to say which held a bigger piece of Joni Joseph's heart—the sparkling stages of the Town and Glen Casinos or her favorite performer, Johnnie Ray. Fortunately for Joni, the two often came together.

Joni's devotion to Ray was all-consuming. As president of the Buffalo-area Johnnie Ray Fan Club, she made it her personal mission to greet him every time he came to town. Their meetings were filled with genuine warmth, a reflection of the sincerity that made Joni a favorite among the celebrities she met.

Fortunately for Joni, she did not have to wait long between visits; Ray was a Town Casino regular. Altman proudly took credit for giving him one of his earliest major breaks and, in return, Ray always "spared a week" for Harry, appearing annually at the Town from 1951 to 1956.

Joni had performing ambitions of her own. She was accepted into an acting school in New York City after graduating from Williamsville High School in 1955, but life ultimately called her back to Western New York's southern tier, where she built a career, raised a family, and continued her education. Yet the memories of those casino nights never left her.

The photographs that follow offer a window into Joni's world—a young woman full of life, posing with the stars she admired, capturing a time when the Town and Glen Casinos were alive with music, laughter, and dreams. Through her eyes, we glimpse not just the glamour of a bygone era, but the beating heart of Buffalo's golden age of entertainment.

Photos courtesy of the Estate of Joan D. Joseph

Figure 165 *Joni with Jerry Vale (she is third from left)*

Figure 164 *Joni with the Everly Brothers*

Figure 166 Joni with Sammy Davis, Jr.

Figure 167 Joni with the Four Lads

Figure 170 Joni with Johnnie Ray

Figure 168 Joni and the Quartet

Figure 169 more photos with Joni and stars

ARTISTS ROOTED IN THE COMMUNITY

Altman was never shy about giving new talent a chance. Whether at the Town Casino or the Glen, he regularly offered the stage to aspiring performers, especially those from the local community. Whenever possible, he gave hometown artists the opportunity to "walk the boards" and share the spotlight. Here are a few who rose to the occasion:

BOB LAURENCE (LAUREN HEMEDINGER)

Vocalist Bob Laurence, born Lauren Hemedinger, was a Buffalo native and Bennett High School graduate who emerged as a promising entertainer in the early 1950s. Under the guidance of Altman, he performed at both the Town and Glen Casinos, opening for Sammy Davis Jr in 1952. Known for his smooth vocals and natural stage presence, Laurence brought youthful energy to Buffalo's vibrant nightclub scene at a time when it was attracting national attention.

He began performing early, singing and dancing at public schools #66 and #81—and by high school, he was entertaining at school events, running track, and even "clashing cymbals" during football games. "I tried out for the chorus and stage plays," he said. "The music director liked my voice and had me sing on stage as a freshman for many events."[677] He quickly earned the nickname "The Crooner," and by his senior year, he adopted the stage name Bob Laurence. "Hemedinger was not a great stage name," he explained, though he later joked that after meeting Engelbert Humperdinck in Germany, "Hemedinger may have been a good name after all. Who knew?"[678]

Altman helped secure him gigs outside of Buffalo, including the Catskills, where Bob mingled with emerging stars like Eddie Fisher.

His memories of the Town Casino's dressing rooms remain with vivid clarity. "The old rooms were narrow and dark with the exception of the side lights along the mirrored panels," he said. "Small incandescent bulbs along the sides gave off enough light to facilitate the preparation of stage makeup."[679] The rooms were crowded, busy, and filled with racks of garments—jeweled costumes, net hose, and accessories jammed tightly behind chairs.

"Everyone was subjected to the crowded conditions with the exception of the main artists," he said. Performers cycled through quickly between sets, doing their best to prepare in tight quarters. "The smell of perspiration permeated the room, and garments weighted down with jeweled sequences fell to the floor; room assistants were responsible for gathering them up."[680] There was one bathroom for the entire cast, and performers helped each other with costume changes, snapping buttons and hooking blouses before being called to the wings.

Bob remembers a stagehand poking his head in the doorway for his first performance: "Bob Laurence, you're on in five minutes!" causing "a chill to come over me as I slowly walked to the back curtain." No matter how many times he performed, the nerves never left him. "A lump in my throat and the same-old stage fright came upon me. You would think the feelings would subside—but no."[681]

Figure 171 Bob Laurence performing at the Glen
Photo courtesy of Lauren Hemedinger

When the band, under Moe Balsom's direction, starting the prelude to "Blue Moon," Bob stepped onto the stage. The spotlight erased the crowd beyond the first few rows, and the sound of clinking glasses and soft conversation filled the background. After finishing the first number, he transitioned into "That Old Black Magic" and began to find his rhythm. "I was relaxed and felt great at the time," he said. The set ended with an encore:" I'm Yours."[682]

He was just 18 years old and finding his voice in one of Buffalo's premier entertainment venues. By the summer of 1953, he had earned an invitation to join a backup ensemble supporting various Broadway productions and television specials, arranged through the prestigious Morris Agency in New York City. Just as this promising chapter was beginning to unfold, everything took a sudden turn. "I got a call from my mother," he recalled. "She told me I'd been drafted into the Army. That changed everything."[683]

The military quickly recognized his musical talent and assigned him to perform as a vocalist at special events in Europe. By 1955, he was performing on Amed Forces Network broadcasts. But the Cold War loomed large. "Russia was a threat even then," he said.[684] During a training drill, a live

Figure 172 Bob Laurence Military
Photo courtesy of Lauren Hemedinger

explosive round detonated nearby. "The report (boom) was so loud my ears rang, and I was deafened for two weeks. When my hearing returned, I sustained tinnitus, a loud and persistent ringing in my ears. The condition never stopped from then on."[685]

After being discharged in 1955, Bob returned to music, hoping to resume his career. He released a 45RPM record that sold well using the Hemedinger name, but tinnitus made performing nearly impossible. "I found it difficult to hear the accompaniment when on stage. If an artist cannot hear the band or orchestra, you can be off tempo or off tune."[686] After several years of trying, he stepped away from full-time performing, though he occasionally sang at private events. While hearing problems ended his professional aspirations, Bob remained connected to music in the ways that he could, carrying his talent and love for performing into more personal settings.

MICHAEL BENNETT

The main stages of the Glen and Town Casinos were not the only place future stars were born.

By the age of 11, Buffalo's little Mickey DiFiglia was performing in Mrs. John Dunn's "Little Stars of Tomorrow" dance troupe on Sunday afternoons in the Glen Barn/Family Inn.[687]

By age of 14, the future Michael Bennett already had the makings of a local legend, a potential supernova among the "Little Stars." By the time he got to Bennett High School he knew he was ready to leave the Buffalo dance scene. He left Bennett—adopting his stage name in tribute to his alma mater—to take on the role of Baby John in the U.S. and European tours of "West Side Story."

His career trajectory continued upward, leading him to become an influential American theater director and choreographer. His groundbreaking work on Broadway productions like "A Chorus Line" and "Dreamgirls" profoundly influenced the landscape of musical theatre.

JOANIE SOMMERS

*Figure 173 Joanie Sommers
exiting the plane in Buffalo
Photo courtesy of The Archives & Special
Collection Department of SUNY Buffalo State*

Joanie Sommers, often hailed as "The Voice of the '60s," made a celebrated return to her hometown of Buffalo in 1962, captivating audiences with a week-long stint at the Glen Casino. She had departed for California eight years earlier after clinching a victory in a talent contest on WBEN-TV at the age of 10. The Glen performance, her first in Western New York drew substantial box office success and garnered significant media coverage.

Born Joan Drost and later signed to Warner Brothers Records, Sommers earned national recognition for her rendition of the iconic Pepsi jingle, "It's Pepsi, for Those Who Think Young." Her fame was further cemented by the release of "Johnny Get Angry," a top 10 hit that made her a household name. During her time in Buffalo in July 1962, she revealed in a newspaper interview her willingness to "give it all up for a husband and family of my own," signaling future personal developments.[688]

Just two months later, Joanie, at 21 married 28-year-old talent agent Jerry Steiner in Las Vegas. The marriage, followed by the birth of three children, led her to gradually step back from her music career. After Jerry's unexpected death a decade later, Sommers retreated further from the public eye to focus on her family. In the early 1980s, she embarked on a comeback, diversifying her musical style to include jazz, pop, and American standards, marking a resilient return to her artistic roots.

CHAPTER 16—MANAGING THE TALENT

Feuds with performers over scheduling, salaries, and performance guarantees were the constant headache of nightclub ownership. These challenges often escalated into high-profile disputes, drawing significant public attention to Western New York.

Altman's public feud with the famous shimmy dancer Gilda Gray made headlines when he sued her in New York State Supreme Court for breach of contract. Milch was again the attorney representing the Glen.

According to court documents, Gray had been contracted to perform at the Glen Winter Garden for one week in March 1941 at a salary of $600. Just two days before her scheduled appearance, she sent a telegram that read: "Dear Mr. Altman—I promise on honor to appear at your place for one week gratis after Billy Rose's show[a] closes on condition you release me immediately. Gilda Gray."

Unmoved by her plea, Altman sought a court injunction to prevent Gray from performing anywhere else during the dates she was originally contracted to appear at the Glen.[689]

Altman stated in his complaint that he said he had employed Miss Gray for "her special and unique talent for peculiar and artistic dancing and her ability to execute and perform a certain twist or shimmy of her hips and body in the course of her dancing . . . "[690]

The case was eventually settled out of court, with Gray promising that she would not perform in Erie County for two years unless she fulfilled the week-long engagement at the Glen during that period.[691]

There is no evidence that Gray, whose fame had peaked in the early 1920s during the flapper era, ever performed for Altman. By the time of this lawsuit, her career and health were both in decline. She had suffered a heart attack in 1931 and filed for bankruptcy just three months after her dispute with Harry.

Figure 174 Gilda Gray
PD

As for her Buffalo appearances, press reports indicated that Gray drew strong box office numbers at McVan's Nite Club in November 1943 and was held over for a second week. This happened after the Glen's two-year exclusion window had passed.

---

[a] Billy Rose was a prominent impresario in New York City. His Diamond Horseshoe in Times Square operated out of the basement of the Paramount Hotel.

Figure 175 Cancellation Notice

It can be assumed that Altman recovered the cost of advertising her appearance and its cancellation.

Altman spent much of his nightclub career standing alongside industry heavyweights like Lou Walters of the Latin Quarter and Lenny Litman of The Copa, often locked in battles with the entertainers' union over a host of financial disputes.

The American Guild of Variety Artists (AGVA), affiliated with the AFL-CIO, frequently pushed for contract adjustments, like increasing weekly performer fees (to $35 net in 1942), and demanding that nightclubs cover health and welfare benefits. Altman, frustrated by these demands, once complained, "I can't see having to pay $2.50 a week [for health insurance] when someone like Milton Berle makes ten times the salary of the President of the U.S."[692]

In response to the union's demands, nightclub owners nationally formed the Theater Restaurant Owners Association (TROA).[693] Altman also helped establish the Niagara Frontier Night Club Owners' Association in 1942 to better manage local disputes.

In the ongoing tug-of-war, both the AGVA and TROA claimed victories and losses. When the union threatened a walkout over a funding issue, Altman and Wallens, "paid under protest." For them, keeping their nightclub open remained the top priority.[694]

Altman was most irritated however when a performer he claimed to have "discovered" returned to

*Figure 176 Impresarios Lou Walters and Harry
collaborated on many projects together,
shown here in 1943*
Photo courtesy of The Buffalo Courier-Express

Buffalo to perform at a rival venue. The December 1949 edition of the *Billboard* highlighted the fervent competition among "major talent buyers" like Altman for priority access to nurtured talent.

As noted in the article, Altman was especially furious that two of his early "finds"—Billy Eckstine and Frankie Laine—had returned to Buffalo and performed at a local Lowe's theater.[695] Altman blamed talent management agencies like William Morris and General Artists Corporation for bypassing him.

Altman was so incensed when Eckstine played at Lowe's that he retaliated by booking Xavier Cugat to perform against him during the same week at the Town Casino.

Figure 177 Billy Eckstine had been one of Altman's proudest discoveries, a marquee talent—until their relationship soured
Photo courtesy of Brad Altman

"I threw him out of the box," Altman said of Eckstein's poor box office performance at Lowe's.[696]

He vowed to take similar action against any performer who started with him and later chose to play at a competing venue.

While agency leaders acknowledged that Altman's complaints had some merit and that he was a significant talent buyer, they placed blame on the performers and their personal managers.

"We can suggest certain venues," they admitted, "but we can't force the actors to choose them. They'll go where they think they can get the best deal."[697]

Personal managers, however, found little merit to Altman's complaints.

"If we have a hot act, we're going to make as much money as possible," one manager remarked. The performers' emphasis had to be on broader strategies that extended beyond local allegiance.[698]

"We don't want to hurt Altman," was the consensus, "but we have to protect ourselves."[699]

Handling fragile egos was also an important part of dealing with talent. Altman hired Benny Fields and Molly Picon to perform at the Town in May 1947. Picon, a beloved American actress and singer best known for her roles in Yiddish theater and films, received top billing. Fields, once a popular vaudeville entertainer but now past his prime, was given the "extra added" label. Upon arriving and seeing this, he refused to perform, prompting his wife and former stage partner, Blossom Seeley, to send all his luggage back to New York City.[b]

Altman eventually calmed the situation, but with his wardrobe on route to Manhattan, Fields was not available to perform on opening night. Fortunately, he recovered his wardrobe by day two and completed the rest of the run.

The Billboard later reported that Altman paid Fields "his full salary despite the one-day lag."[c]

---

[b] The story of the Seeley/Fields marriage and career was later made into the movie *Somebody Loves Me* (1952) with Betty Hutton and Ralph Meeker, which revived their careers and led to a string of TV appearances on *The Ed Sullivan Show*.

[c] If *Billboard* said so it must be true.

There were also occasions when Altman faced a far greater challenge—a headliner failing to appear because of personal troubles. Such was the case in 1953, when he was forced to take legal action to compel Dick Haymes, one of the era's leading singers and actors, to honor his performance contract. The dispute made national headlines after Haymes' personal difficulties threatened to derail his scheduled engagement at the Town Casino during the week of November 7, 1953.

Admittedly, Haymes's life was in turmoil during this period. The IRS had garnished his wages due to unpaid alimony; he was embroiled in a highly publicized affair with Rita Hayworth (who would later become wife number four); and he narrowly avoided deportation to his country of birth, Argentina, after leaving the U.S. without the proper immigration clearance.

When Haymes missed scheduled nightclub appearances in Philadelphia and Pittsburgh in the weeks leading to the scheduled Town Casino engagement, Altman demanded that MCA, his talent agency, guarantee his upcoming performance. MCA attempted to reach Haymes at Park East Hospital, where he was reportedly staying, but their efforts were fruitless; the hospital had no record of him as a patient.[700]

After a barrage of calls and letters to the performers' union, Altman successfully voided the pay-or-play contract[701] and enlisted last-minute replacements: a "local singer" (Bill Sullivan, who has since faded into obscurity) and Frankie Scott, dubbed "the undernourished comedian."

As the Glen was beginning to teeter financially in the early 1960s, Altman was handed a possible lifeline. Robert Goulet, who was in the middle of his three-year run as Sir Lancelot in the original Broadway production of *Camelot*, stated publicly that he would start on the nightclub circuit after the show closed.

"I'd like to hit Buffalo's Glen Casino someday," he said in Jack Allen's national column.[702] "I haven't been to Buffalo much despite its proximity to Toronto."[d703]

Harry rushed to his checkbook, offering Goulet $15,000 to appear for a one-week run in 1963. He was turned down, Altman told *The Buffalo Evening News*, because he wanted $20,000.[704] The deal was never made.

The cost of hiring talent—and its effect on nightclub operations—remained a recurring theme throughout Altman's career. As early as 1946, he warned patrons that due to the rising cost of big-name acts, the Town Casino would scale back its bookings for the coming season. He promised plenty of entertainment would remain and that the stars would return "when conditions in the amusement business right themselves."[705]

The stars did return, but the appearance fees continued to rise. In 1952, Altman and Wallens tried to manage expenses by eliminating the third nightly show and replacing it with a novel idea: seating patrons at candlelit tables on the stage itself.

---

[d]Goulet had strong ties to Toronto, particularly due to his training at the Royal Conservatory of Music and his early career performances there, including the world premiere of *Camelot* at Toronto's O'Keefe Centre in 1960.

Performers would work the room and then mingle with guests. The gimmick was short-lived.

By 1956, Jack O'Brian spotlighted the broader financial strain on Buffalo's nightclub scene. The Chez Ami, once a premier venue in the city, had dropped big-name bookings and transitioned into a supper club. Co-owner Jack Grood lamented that the days of booking stars for $1,000 or $2,000 were over.[706] Now, with big-name entertainers flocking to more lucrative television and Las Vegas gigs, the intimate 250-seat venue could not keep up. "You can get cheap acts," Grood admitted, "but they look cheap. They're either inexperienced kids or has-beens, and you can't blame the public for skipping a bad floor show."[707]

In contrast, O'Brian praised the Town Casino, reporting that it was hosting one of the era's biggest stars, Johnnie Ray, for $18,500 a week. Altman credited this coup to having given Ray his start.[708]

By the early 1960s, filling either nightclub was getting difficult to do as the popularity of television rose along with the cost of performers' salaries.

In 1963, just months before the Town's announcement to close, Altman and his trusted emcee, Lenny Paige, openly warned the public about the impending loss of live nightclub entertainment.

"[E]ntertainers today are pricing themselves out of the business," Altman lamented, noting the costs went far beyond hefty weekly salaries: "You sign a contract with a star…and then they start dictating how many musicians they need, what kind of props, and the expenses keep piling up." These rising costs, he explained, force the increase in ticket prices, which impacts sales.[709]

"Soon there's no show," he concluded. "And that's happened not only in Buffalo but across the country."[710]

Paige echoed Altman's sentiments: "No act or performer is worth $35,000 a week, which is what some are asking. A scientist like Mr. Salk who discovered the polio vaccine is worth that kind of money. But a performer who may have made one hit record with more luck than ability, certainly doesn't rate such a salary."[711]

Both men argued that live, on-the-road performances were crucial for entertainers to refine their craft. Paige described nightclubs as "training grounds or schools" for emerging talent.

"Just this past season, Sammy Davis Jr saw Niagara Falls's own Bobby Jones perform on our stage at the Glen," Altman recounted. "He liked him and signed him." Davis later took Jones on tour. [712]

"The point is," Altman continued, "how will young performers like that get their break when there are no clubs left for them to appear in?"[713]

LAST 3 NITES!

★ ★

★ ★

JAYNE MANSFIELD
& Her SATIRE ON BURLESK
With NELSON SARDELLI
★ PLUS ★
The NEWTON BROS.
Direct from JACKIE GLEASON
★ FOR RES. 632-0065

Harry
Altman's ★ GLEN ★
CASINO
Williamsville, N.Y. Thruway Exit 50

Figure 178 Jayne Mansfield Ad
PD

While Altman was typically known for cut-throat negotiating, he spared no expense in 1963 paying top dollar to bring Jayne Mansfield to the Glen Casino for her first-ever solo nightclub performance.[714] Mansfield, one of the era's most prominent sex symbols, was a former Playboy Playmate, film actress, and model.

Her performance at the Glen Casino was billed as a mix of "songs and dances from her latest films, along with a satire on various striptease routines."[715] Henry W. Clune, the noted columnist for the *Rochester Democrat and Chronicle*, covered the much-anticipated opening night. According to Clune, Jayne arrived two hours late, but the audience remained firmly in their seats, unwilling to miss her entrance. When she finally emerged from the wings, Clune described her appearance as "dressed as tight as a pipe wrench... reminding me of nothing so much as that fluffy, pinkish candy on a stick sold at carnival lots."[716]

He said that her stage presence was full of "little gasps; she talked, baby talk, 'Tweet-tweet!'"[717]

Clune wrote:

"She sang a little song about Plain Jane, and then running out of genius, she went among the audience to kiss the bald head of a Brother Elk, to cuddle a Brother Moose, to pretend that she carried a very high torch for a Woodmen of the World"[e] whose "lady friend" gave Jayne "a cold hard eye of disapproval."

"She 'tweeted' up from this audience, in time, and disappeared, in tiny steps, backstage; reappeared, five minutes later in another gown, which she removed, in the semi nebulosity of a cloudy spotlight, in which Plain Jayne announced was a 'take-off' of a strip teaser. And that was that!"[718]

The show was over.

Figure 179 Altman was captivated by Jayne Mansfield's charm and her box office draw
Photo courtesy of Brad Altman

---

[e] Another fraternal organization during that era.

Altman walked over to Clout as they exited the Casino, proclaiming: "That Dame, she can't do a thing! Not a thing! And she wants $18,000 a week!"[719]

Which he paid. Happily.

"He had filled the hall with a performer who apparently couldn't sing, dance or whistle, getting a fee at the door and adding a minimum table charge,"[720] Clune wrote.

She provided everything the impresario ever wanted or needed from a performer.

As Altman's good luck would have it, Mansfield chose the Glen Casino's dressing room later that week to announce her divorce from Mickey Hargitay, turning the venue into a temporary epicenter of Hollywood gossip. She said then that she would be leaving for Juarez, Mexico after the Glen appearances to obtain her divorce from the bodybuilder/actor.[721]

Even with all of his success, Altman still pined for performers who were out of his reach: "Perry Como would fill a ballpark in January, three shows a night," he told *The Buffalo Courier-Express*. "Sinatra? Don't remind me. He'd kill 'em and make me rich! He's got everything."[722] Neither Sinatra nor Como ever appeared in Buffalo for Altman.

Figure 180 The Glen Park dressing room became an unlikely pressroom when wire services announced Mansfield's divorce from behind its curtain
United Press International

MEMORIES OF A BYGONE ERA

Though Perry Como and Frank Sinatra never appeared on the Casinos' stages, many other celebrities were captured in photographs. These images, preserved in the Altman and Wallens family archives as well as in public collections and private fan holdings, are identified when possible.

MEMORIES COURTESY OF MARJORIE WALLENS

Figure 183 Altman and Lenny Paige

Figure 182 All eyes turned to Mae West when she was at the Town Casino

Figure 181 New Years Eve

Figure 184 Buffalo's own Don Mason,
a popular singer of the era

Figure 187 Casino Memories

Figure 185 Johnny Mathis was a popular entertainer at the Town

Figure 186 Nightclub comic Billy Vine

Figure 188 **MEMORIES COURTESY OF JAY WALLENS**

Figure 191 Jack Yellen's ties to Altman and Wallens made Sophie Tucker a frequent performer throughout the years of the Town

Figure 190 Marilyn Maxell was one the most popular nightclub entertainers of the era

Figure 189 Singer/actress Eartha Kitt appeared at the Town Casino in 1954

Figure 192 Rose Marie started in vaudeville as a three-year-old, but found lasting fame as a nightclub performer and television star

Figure 193 **MEMORIES COURTESY BRAD ALTMAN**

Figure 194 Allen & Rossi was a popular American comedy duo comprised of Marty Allen and Steve Rossi

Figure 196 The Four Esquires on the Town stage in 1955

Figure 195 Comic Sam Levenson

Figure 197 British pianist headlined at the Town in 1951

*Figure 201 Jimmy Durante brought his entire variety show cast to the Town Casino, delivering
the venue's most successful box office performance to date
Photo courtesy of The Archives & Special Collection Department of SUNY Buffalo State*

*Figure 200 Eartha Kitt poses with
Lindsey Sapphire Dancers
Photo courtesy of Lauren Johnson*

*Figure 199 Photo courtesy of
The Archives & Special
Collection Department of
SUNY Buffalo State*

*Figure 198 The Three Sons were a popular draw in the early years of the Town
Photo courtesy of Lynette LoCurcio*

CHAPTER 17—THE ONES WHO
SET THE STAGE

B efore the headliners drew applause and the flashbulbs popped, there were others who helped orchestrate the evening's success—some center stage, others just beyond the spotlight's edge. Emcees shaped the mood with quick wit and presence. Orchestra leaders commanded full bands with a flick of the wrist. Show girls dazzled by design, and chorus lines blended choreography and charisma in equal measure. They were a quiet army of workers who set the stage night after night, keeping the show alive.

EMCEES

Altman knew how to pick great talent, and his Masters of Ceremony were no exception. Each brought their unique style to maintain a steady flow of performers onto the stage and keep the audience entertained during quieter moments. Harry actively promoted the emcees who graced his stages, quickly building their individual followings until their names became essential to the night's entertainment.

GEORGIE WALKER

Georgie Walker was Altman's first full-time emcee, commanding the Glen Park stage starting in the mid-1930s. His long sessions on stage were noted in press releases of the era (1942): "Walker is emceeing as usual and keeps himself under the "hundred weight" with his indefatigable efforts in the 3-1/2 hour performances."[723]

His tenure was interrupted when he left to serve in World War II. After seven years, Georgie made his much-anticipated return on opening day in May 1947: "Georgie Walker was a great favorite at the Glen Casino for several years," Altman told *The Buffalo Courier-Express*, "and our reopening party tomorrow night in Williamsville will be a sort of a Welcome Home event in Walker's honor."[724]

He left Altman's service to become a well-regarded disc jockey, first at WJJL-AM and then WEBR-AM where he worked alongside Ed Little and Bob Wells, both an integral part of the radio team that broadcast live from the small studio in the front window of the Town Casino. He also emceed at Chez Ami in the 1950s, and the Glen in the late 1950s where he was billed as the "genial M.C."

LENNY PAIGE

Lenny Paige, renowned for his role as the emcee at both the Town and Glen Casinos, was not merely a master of ceremonies; he was a significant figure in Buffalo's entertainment scene. Esteemed by audiences and respected by the stars he introduced, Paige played an integral role in the local cultural landscape. For more than two decades, Paige's charisma and quick wit not only warmed the spotlight but also illuminated the paths of thousands of performers who stepped out onto the stage. A multi-talented performer in his own right, Lenny could sing, dance, tell jokes, and do impressions of celebrities.

Figure 202 Lenny Paige traveled nationwide as an emcee for walkathons
Photo courtesy of Sheila Paige Roth

Despite receiving offers from Sammy Davis to take his talents to Broadway, and opportunities to join Frankie Laine, Johnnie Ray, and Johnny Mathis on extended tours, Paige remained committed to Buffalo. Occasionally, he would accept out-of-town jobs, which insiders recognized as a sign that Altman had denied one of his infrequent requests for a raise. Lenny would only return to Buffalo when Harry, realizing Lenny's value, would relent and agree to his salary demands (usually on a brisk phone call).[a] This assertiveness highlighted that Paige was not one to be underestimated on stage or off.

Born Leonard Plessner[b] in St. Louis in 1908, Paige developed his stagecraft through the demanding walkathons[c] of the Depression era. Alongside his wife, Florence, and their only child, Sheila,[725] he traveled the walkathon circuit where grueling competitions were coupled with a strong sense of community. ""Our family traveled together from show to show from the time I was six weeks old," Sheila said. "Many of the contestants were on the same circuit and were very good friends."[726]

---

[a] Altman sent press releases to "re-introduce" Paige after his self-imposed hiatuses: "Lenny Paige, who has been on a personal engagement tour since his last appearance, will be the Glen Casino's master of ceremonies." "Glen Casino, Park Open Tomorrow," *The Buffalo Courier-Express,* April 30, 1953, 27.

[b] There were multiple misspellings of his stage name; Lenny often becoming Lennie, and Paige to Page. He responded to all of them with equal aplomb.

[c] A walkathon—often referred to as a "walking marathon" or "go-as-you-please" contest—was an endurance competition where participants walked (or shuffled) in circles or on a track for hours, days, or even weeks at a time.

When the walkathon era died, Paige went out on the road by himself taking a variety of emcee gigs, leaving his family in St. Louis. Lenny's career took a significant turn when he appeared on Altman's radar through an agent's recommendation. "I hear you're a pretty fair emcee," Harry remarked during a phone call to Lenny, who was moments away from stepping onto a stage in Baltimore. "Come up to Buffalo and emcee for me." Lenny

Figure 203 Lenny Paige, wife Florence, and daughter Sheila in St. Louis
Photo courtesy of Sheila Paige Roth

explained that relocating would not be simple, considering his family was settled in St. Louis, but Harry cut him off, saying, "Well, I'm expecting you in Buffalo," and hung up before Lenny could argue.[727]

In 1941, Lenny faced a challenging audition at the Glen Casino. He arrived during a never-ending 8 PM show that stretched past 10:30 PM, with the audience growing increasingly restless. This was Harry's typical strategy, Paige explained.[728] "He kept them there and sold them more beer. Sold them more sandwiches."

Figure 204 Lenny called onto the Glen Casino stage the birthday girls and boys in the audience. Here is Lynette LoCurcio, daughter of long-time trumpeter, Vince Impellitter

Nearing the end of this lengthy session, Harry instructed his emcee Georgie Walker, who was leaving to join the military, to pass the microphone to Lenny. As he took the stage, facing an exhausted crowd, Lenny thought, "I'm going to die the death of a dog."[729]

Fortunately, Lenny was well-prepared with a routine honed from years on the walkathon circuit where he had to make entertainment out of seemingly thin air.

"I did a Hollywood director bit where I'm the director and bring up people from the audience and put them through their paces," he explained. "Well, I got my first laugh. I got my second laugh. The next thing I know the whole evening was rejuvenated."[730]

When the bit began stalling at the 11-minute mark, Altman ran up on stage and said to him "You're my man!" before turning to the audience and announcing, "Ladies and Gentlemen, this is going to be my new emcee!"[731]

Shortly after his audition, Paige found himself working at Altman's downtown nightclub and coordinating the transfer of his family to the Stuyvesant Hotel, their new home in Buffalo. Just as they were getting settled, his new "office" at the Town Barn burned down.[732] Harry immediately pivoted, opening the Glen Casino early that year, and began planning to rebuild the Town Barn's replacement. Paige remained steadfast through it all, along for the entire ride.

Figure 205 Lenny enjoying the limelight with the Town Casino showgirls
Photo courtesy of Marjorie Wallens

Lenny's ability to smoothly transition between acts, captivate the audience, and maintain a lively atmosphere made him beloved by both casual visitors and seasoned performers. His adept handling of any unexpected issues only added to his reputation for professionalism and charm.

Talking to columnist Bob Curran in 1973, Paige recalls facing a difficult moment onstage with Victor Borge, a master at combining classical piano music with his humorous, playful narrative.[733]

"Victor was a great guy who gave me a night to remember," Lenny said. "Before he arrived, he made it clear that he wanted a really good piano. A real concert-type job."[734]

Lenny secured the best Steinway he could find and had it brought to the club. After it was set in place, he realized that he had forgotten to get a piano stool. Rummaging around backstage, he found an old white wooden piano bench and got it onto the stage just before Borge came out.

Victor, Paige said, looked at the Steinway during his entrance onto the stage and beamed. Then, he saw the bench. Without missing a beat, he looked at the audience and said: "Who painted the piano?"[735]

Lenny said that Borge brought the house down and he kept it up for the rest of the night.

"He opened the piano bench and began finding chicken bones and stale bread and all sorts of things inside," Paige said, having never looked at its contents before hauling it to the stage. "I'm sure that many people there that night believed it was part of the routine."[736]

Figure 229 Memories from the era where he entertained at John's Flaming Hearth
Photo courtesy of Sheila Paige Roth

Paige was present when both clubs shuttered at the conclusion of Altman's era and initially retired to Phoenix to be closer to his family. Upon his return to the area, he embarked on another career as the host/maître d' at John's Flaming Hearth in Niagara Falls, New York where he stayed for 25 years (1964-1986).

He was residing in the Glenside Apartments at 42 Spring Street, right next to Glen Park, on the night of the Inferno fire in 1968.

Figure 206 Paige at the Town Casino during its celebrated era
Photo courtesy of Sheila Paige Roth

The lead paragraph of Lenny's interview published on the day after the fire is heart-breaking:

> *"In the 5 AM darkness of Rock Street, the firelight from the Inferno flickered in his face."*
> *"In his hand, the veteran master of ceremonies carried a flashlight."*
> *"In his heart he carried a torch."*
> *"'I introduced some of the world's greatest entertainers from that stage,' he said."[737]*

He finally retired to Arizona in 1986 after undergoing stomach surgery that prompted a pivotal visit from his daughter.

"I did not retire. Sheila retired me," he said. "She came to the hospital and said she was taking me back to Phoenix with her. She really means business."[738]

Paige spent the next four years in Arizona before dying in February 1991 from a heart attack. He was 82.

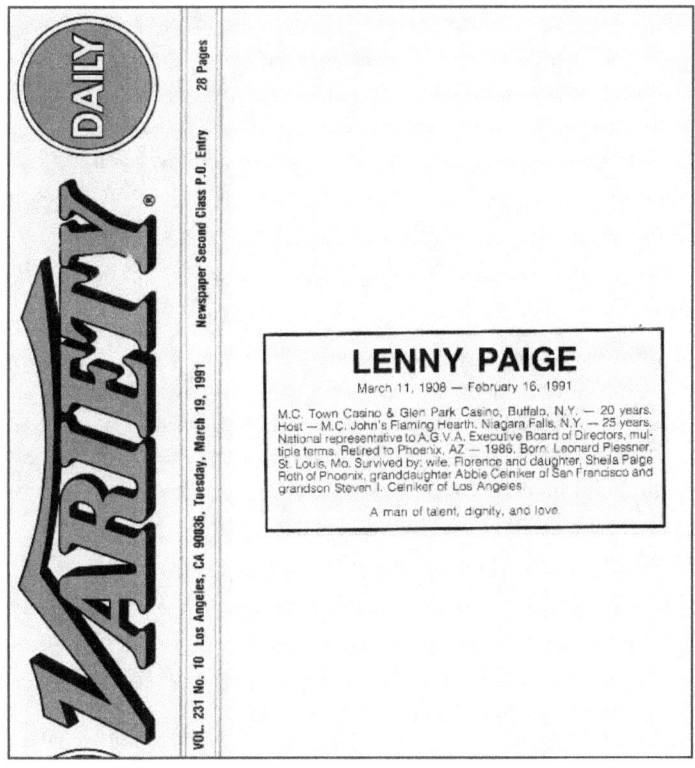

Figure 207 Memorial page for Lenny Paige in Variety
PD

TONY ODDI

Buffalo's limited number of experienced emcees often led them to rotating among various nightclubs and dinner clubs to fill scheduling gaps. Tony Oddi was one such emcee, frequently stepping in to cover gigs at the Town and Glen Casinos when Paige was unavailable. A staple on Western New York stages, Oddi launched his career at 14, winning the "Major Bowes Amateur Hour" contest as a singer.[d]

A native of Lockport, Oddi also served in WWII. He worked at Frank's Casanova and was most notably the emcee at McVan's for more than 16 years. As the nightclub scene began to decline, he transitioned to hosting part-time at the Three Coins Restaurant, where he led the weekly "Bong Show." In a 1976 interview with *The Buffalo Evening News*, he reflected on his 40-year career, remarking, "It's been New Year's Eve every day of my life."[739]

THE ORCHESTRAS

Dance music was a vital component of Harry's entertainment offerings, beginning with his early Mardi Gras celebrations and continuing into his later nightclub ventures. Altman consistently featured orchestras at his events, drawing influence from the prevalent dance trends of the time. His selections were predominantly jazz, swing, blues, and big band music, with the goal of captivating the audience and ensuring a memorable evening.

In cases where the conductor was not widely recognized, Harry would strategically name the orchestra after the venue where they performed. This move turned regular gigs at places like the Bramson Café or the Palais Royal into nightly radio features, serving as a clever marketing tool.

As was the custom of the time, Harry labeled these musical groups as "orchestras" rather than bands, aiming to enhance their elegance and allure for a more refined audience. In addition to supporting the stage talent, the orchestras also played dance music for couples during intermissions between shows. This contributed to a lively and enjoyable atmosphere, encouraging patrons to stay longer and perhaps spend more on drinks and other services offered by the club.

Each season, Harry showcased some of the area's finest musicians in the orchestras he hired for the Glen and Town Casinos. The conductors of these orchestras gained recognition and became well known, turning into notable figures. In exchange for stable, seasonal employment, Harry was able to boost their visibility

---

d The "Major Bowes Amateur Hour" was a popular national radio talent show in the 1930s and 1940s. Participants were amateur performers from across the country who competed for public favor, with audiences voting for their favorite acts by sending in mail-in ballots. Among the show's early discoveries was Frank Sinatra, who appeared on the show with the Hoboken Four and won in 1935.

and appeal. Over a period of more than 30 years, Altman featured just four house bands, each gaining prominence in the main rooms of his nightclubs.

ALLAN BROOKS ORCHESTRA

During Prohibition and the Depression, Altman engaged Allan Brooks in several of his managed establishments, subsequently appointing the group as his primary house band when he opened the Glen Casino. His relationship with the Allan Brooks Orchestra was particularly notable. As a result of two devastating fires on Altman-owned properties in 1936 (Glen Barn, July; Sagamore, December) Brook's musicians lost two sets of instruments in a matter of six months. Despite these challenges, the orchestra was prominently featured at the grand opening of the Glen Casino in April 1937, and they continued to perform there for the next two seasons.

Altman had such high esteem for Sandy Graff, the drummer from Allan's band, that he recommended him to Artie Shaw for a Chautauqua County gig. He even drove Graff to the July 1938 performance at Bemus Point. After the show, Shaw was impressed with Graff's skills and confidently predicted that he would make a significant mark in the swing music industry.[740]

Graff, a native of Niagara Falls, maintained his career in jazz drumming by playing with local bands and working as a session musician. His skills were so well-regarded that in 1942 he was called upon to substitute for Benny Goodman's drummer when he fell ill while on tour in Buffalo.[741]

THE BERNIE SANDLER ORCHESTRA

The next ensemble Altman regularly featured at the Glen was led by Bernie Sandler, a vocalist who conducted a 14-piece band primarily made up of local high school students from Bennett, East, and Masten Park. After a successful one-year run at the Glen, they caught the attention of the Arcadia Ballroom in New York City. In January 1941, as the band prepared to leave for New York, Altman hosted a farewell party at the Glen to mark their final performance there.

"We were doing fine," Sandler recalled, "until 1942...when the big blow came. Six of us received our draft notices from Uncle Sam all on the same day."[742] This sudden turn of events led to the disbandment of the orchestra. After returning from the war, Sandler transitioned to broadcasting, where he became a radio announcer in Buffalo on WEBR-AM. Together with Ed Little, Sandler worked as a staff announcer from the radio booth permanently set up at the Town Casino.

BONO AND HIS ORCHESTRA

The dissolution of Sandler's orchestra left an opening for Americo (Richard) Bono, a veteran trumpeter who began his musical career in the 1920s with the Vincent Lopez Orchestra. He later joined the Paul Whiteman Orchestra with Bing Crosby, and later the Dorsey brothers. Returning to Buffalo in 1927, he started his own orchestra at the Silver Slipper on Pearl Street in Buffalo, managed by his mother-in-law, Minnie Clark.[e]

Bono and his Orchestra became the house band at the Glen for nearly a decade starting in 1942. When the Town Casino opened its doors in December 1945, Bono got the nod to lead the downtown orchestra. He remained there until the early 1950s.

Bono was also at the forefront of the new medium of radio by becoming the director for the Buffalo Broadcasting Corporation (WGR and WKBW-AM). In later years, Bono became a restauranteur, opening several successful spots including The Italian Village, Bono's Red Shutter, and the Club Mayfair. Each of his venues featured the Bono Orchestra and were known for dancing and fine dining.

Figure 208 Americo Bono
Photo courtesy of Clark Bono

[e]As noted in Chapter 8, Minnie Clark, paramour of mobster Joseph DeCarlo Sr., was managing the Auto-Rest roadhouse at Transit and Main Streets in Williamsville when it was raided by the Ku Klux Klan in 1924. Bono was married to Clark's only child, Vera.

MOE BALSOM'S ORCHESTRA

Moe Balsom, a gifted pianist who studied under George Lowry, Arnold Corniellson and Madam Blau, had his first professional engagement at 16 years old at the Iroquois Hotel in 1917.

A member of the Shea's Buffalo Theater Orchestra under the baton of Lou Breese, his first job with Altman was as the conductor of the Mansion House Orchestra in Williamsville. Balsom led the Glen and Town Casino Orchestras from the early 1950s until both closed their doors in the mid-1960s.

Never one to stand on ceremony, he emceed the "Kiddie Amateur Hour" at Glen Park as "Uncle Moe."

Figure 209 Moe Balsom, at far right, with members of the orchestra: (from left) Morris Youngman, Pete Suggs, Vince Impellitter, and Tony Constantini
Photo courtesy of Lynette LoCurcio

Balsom passed away in 1966, four months after Altman's death in May.

Figure 210 Members of Balsom's Orchestra enjoyed some downtime with their guests (Moe is fourth from left)
Photo courtesy of Lynette LoCurcio

Figure 211 The Moe Balsom Orchestra at the Town Casino (left) and the Glen (right)
Photo courtesy of Lynette LoCurcio

SHOW GIRLS AND CHORUS LINE

"Chorus was very important to the show. It would embellish what was on the stage. You take 10 girls with beautiful costumes and prepared choreography—it adds something to the show."

~ *Lenny Paige*

Under the glow of the stage lights, Laverne (Lauren) Johnson moved with a grace that turned heads and held audiences spellbound. She was not just another dancer in the chorus line—she was the kind of performer who made people stop and stare, effortlessly commanding the stage with her poise and precision.

Lauren, as one of the last remaining stars from The Town Casino, embodies the memories and legacy of a bygone era. She danced alongside the best, her beauty and talent making her a favorite among audiences and celebrities. Hollywood stars, jazz legends, and popular singers sought her company, drawn in by her charm and effortless elegance.

For years, she graced the stage in shimmering costumes, high kicking in perfect unison with her fellow dancers, bringing the house down night after night.

Beyond the sequins and spotlights, she lived a life most could only dream of—sipping cocktails with screen icons and sharing laughter with musicians who shaped an era. This glamorous lifestyle was not just confined to one city; it spanned the entire country.

Figure 212 Lenny Paige photographed Lauren Johnson on the stage of the Town Casino
Photo courtesy of Lauren Johnson

Throughout the 1950s, Lauren was a member of the Lindsey Sapphire Dancers, a dance troupe that performed across major cities like Miami, New York, Montreal, and Las Vegas.[743] After three seasons performing at the Town (1953-55), she chose to settle in Buffalo, having fallen in love with Tony DeAngelis, a millwright at Bethlehem Steel whom she met at the Casino's cocktail lounge.[744]

Figure 213 The Lindsey Sapphire Dancers
Photo courtesy of Lauren Johnson

Lauren's journey began in Minnesota where she was born in 1931. Working as a switchboard operator by day, she pursued dance lessons at night, dreaming of a larger stage. After packing up with a friend to New York City, her big break came when she boldly approached the Roxy Theatre doorman[f] asking about auditions. Despite no formal openings, there was a need for two dancers for a production number. The primary qualification would be mastering the routine in four days. Accomplishing that, Lauren was offered spot as a Gae Foster Girl—a Roxyette.[745]

Her time as a Roxyette was intense and demanding, with performances seven days a week, often extending to 12 or 14 hours a day. Despite the grueling schedule and modest pay, she cherished the experience, which included a stint living at the Bristol Hotel near the theatre.[746] After a time, she decided that she wanted something beyond seeing the inside of a theater. She contacted Don Sapphire (Donald Miraglia) at Lindsey Sapphire Dancers, and joined the troupe, which provided better pay and more travel.

Lauren described how the Lindsay Saffire[g] chorus line typically included eight precision-line dancers who had to adapt their routines to keep the show fresh and entertaining. Alongside the line dancers were two showgirls, distinguished by their elaborate costumes adorned with feathers, beads, sequins, and occasionally large headpieces that were prominently featured on stage.

During her time at the Town Casino, she met many celebrities like Andy Griffith, Dorothy Lamore, Nelson Eddy, Johnnie Ray, and Eartha Kitt. She remembered the

Figure 214 Johnnie Ray offers the dancers some advice between shows at the Town Casino
Photo courtesy of Lauren Johnson

---

[f] Situated on West 50th Street just off Times Square, the Roxy was often cited as the most impressive movie palace ever built. The Roxy was a leading Broadway film showcase through the 1950s and was also noted for its lavish stage shows that included a 110-member symphony orchestra, a male chorus, a ballet company, and a famous line of female precision dancers, the "Roxyettes".

[g] In addition to the Lindsay Saffire chorus line, Altman signed yearly contracts for each of his casinos. The GC "Lovelies," The Casino Adorables, and The Casino Glamour Girls where just some of the names he created and promoted in advertisements and press releases.

performers as generous and kind, with Sammy Davis Jr often inviting the dancers out for movies or coffee. She also briefly dated middleweight prize fighter Joey Giambra during this period.[747]

After years of dancing, Lauren transitioned to a quieter life, driving a school bus for 37 years and raising two children with her husband in suburban Buffalo. Yet, the friendships and memories from her dancing days remained a cherished part of her life, a testament to the vibrant and fulfilling existence she led during her early 20s.

Figure 215 Lauren got to meet many celebrities, including Christine Jorgensen; Nelson Eddy, and Zippy the Chimp
Photos courtesy of Lauren Johnson

CHAPTER 18—RUNNING ON PEOPLE POWER

The Town Casino and the Glen Park property employed hundreds of area individuals over the years, forming a workforce that included bartenders, waitstaff, cleaners, and support staff—many of whom moved back and forth between the two venues depending on the season or event schedules. In a statement made by Harry Altman in *The Buffalo Evening News*, he noted that the combined general staff numbered over 100 people, with a remarkable number having been employed for a decade or more.[748]

"For every new hire or five-year veteran," Altman said, "there's a Clyde Urban, our superintendent who's been here 27 years; a Jimmie Phillips, an all-purpose man who's served through two generations; or a Lenny Paige, our master of ceremonies for two solid decades."[749]

The following highlights some of these long-serving individuals—those who might be described as the "lifers" of the Altman operation. These were men who not only spent much of their professional lives within the Town Casino or Glen Park orbit, but who also held key managerial positions that helped shape the day-to-day experience for both staff and patrons.

Figure 216 The Town Casino staff were featured in a brochure the Harrys published on the first anniversary of the nightclub
Photo courtesy of Brad Altman

Figure 240 Harry enjoyed taste-testing menu options that the staff prepared
Photo Courtesy of The Archives & Special Collection Department of SUNY Buffalo State

CLYDE URBAN

Clyde Urban began his long association with the Glen in the mid-1940s, taking on the role of Park Superintendent. He remained a loyal and vital part of Harry Altman's operation for more than two decades. During the height of the summer season, Clyde was the engine behind the park's seamless operation—overseeing the amusement rides, concessions, and entertainment offerings that drew thousands of visitors each week. When the park shut down for the off-season, he shifted gears, managing maintenance and overseeing renovations at the Glen, while also serving as the facility manager at the Town Casino.

For the Urban family, the Glen was more than a place of work, it was home.

Figure 218 Clyde Urban relaxing on the grounds of Glen Park that he helped build
Photo courtesy of Ron Urban

Figure 217 Ron Urban enjoys some winter fun outside the house that his family occupied on park grounds
Photo courtesy of Ron Urban

From 1946 to 1953, they lived on the property in a modest white bungalow nestled near the park's scenic waterfall, a site that today is a favorite backdrop for wedding photographs.

In 1954, as the Glen's popularity continued to rise, the Urban family's bungalow was razed to make room for expanded amenities and guest facilities. They did not move far—just across the street to a house on Glen Avenue, formerly the residence of Amherst Police Chief Edwin Evans. This home, located behind one of the Glen's parking lots, remained in use until the 1970s when it was demolished as part of a transition toward establishing a more natural park setting on the grounds.

Shortly before the devastating fire in September 1968 that destroyed the nightclub portion of the property, the Urban family relocated to Debary, Florida, ending Clyde's 20-plus years at the Glen.

*Figure 219 The view Ron Urban enjoyed from his bedroom in the
back of the family's Glen Park home
Photo courtesy of Ron Urban*

RON URBAN

Ron Urban, son of Glen Park's longtime superintendent Clyde Urban, remembered his childhood as anything but ordinary.[750] Growing up within the park's orbit—first living on the grounds, then just a short walk away—meant the boundaries between home, work, and wonder were always blurred. For the Urban family, Glen Park was not just a business; it was the center of their world. Ron and his six brothers—Clyde Jr., Frederick, Donald, Edward, Glen, and Walter—were raised in the pulse of its daily routine, each taking on odd jobs to help the place run, from sweeping walkways to hauling supplies behind the scenes. Their mother, Olga, anchored the concessions, a familiar and tireless figure behind the counter, keeping things humming with practiced ease.

Amid the scent of popcorn and the glow of carnival lights, Ron found himself surrounded by the rhythms of show business: the music, the laughter, the late-night bustle of crowds. He cherished every moment of it.

One of his earliest brushes with celebrity came when he met the legendary Mae West, a moment he recalls with enduring fondness. Over the years, he encountered a remarkable parade of performers who passed through Glen Park and the Glen Casino. Among them were the comedic duo Dean Martin and Jerry Lewis, the harmonious Four Lads, the ever-hilarious Three Stooges, and musical stars like Sergio Franchi, Al Martino, Paul Anka, Louis Armstrong, Connie Francis, Bobby Rydell, and a young Wayne Newton.

But one of Ron's most cherished memories came in 1963 when he held a baby named Mariska Hargitay—now famous as the star of Law & Order: Special Victims Unit—while her mother, glamorous Hollywood icon Jayne Mansfield, performed at the Glen Casino.

"Jayne was great to work for," Ron recalled. Her appearance marked a new chapter in her career, as she began performing her solo nightclub act after a string of successful films. [See Chapter 15]

Ron also remembered encountering jazz legend Count Basie during a performance at the Glen Barn where Basie's unmistakable swing drew packed crowds.

Growing up, Ron had a hand in several Park traditions. "My dad eventually taught me how to make the Park's soda flavors—orange, root beer, and of course, loganberry," he said. He also helped make the ice cream served across the property, another beloved staple of the Glen Park experience.

By the age of 13, Ron was already contributing to one of the park's most anticipated events: the Fourth of July fireworks show. "I was certified to assist with the display," he said. "We always ended the night with an American flag formation in the sky, using red, white, and blue three-inch aerial shells. I wish I had pictures of it...but I only have the memories."

As he grew older, Ron took on more responsibilities, eventually serving as lighting director at the Glen Casino (1963-64) and even caring for Harry Altman's private property—mowing lawns and clearing snow when needed. Despite all the changes Glen Park has undergone over the years, Ron sees his father's handiwork embedded in its foundations.

"The bridge that connects the two ponds was built by my dad in 1946—the year I was born," he said. "And the retaining wall along the creek? That was his work too."

Ron graduated high school in 1964 in Florida where the family moved upon Clyde's retirement from Glen Park. Ron went on to attend Seminole State College, later serving in the Florida Army National Guard. His career took many paths—from working on the Atlantic Coastline Railroad, to serving as a private investigator, and finding his niche as a certified nutritional manager for hospitals and nursing homes.

Now retired and living in Port Ewen, NY Ron remains active as both an avid fisherman and a dedicated conservationist. His commitment to environmental stewardship earned him a place in the New York State Outdoor Hall of Fame.

"My love for fishing started in Ellicott Creek," Ron said. "In those days you could find panfish, rock bass, black bass and northern pike. Calico bass were stocked for yearly tournaments behind the dam in Island Park, but a few made it over the dam and down over the falls."

Ron still makes regular visits back to Western New York, always stopping by the waterfall that once whispered just outside his childhood home. It is a quiet pilgrimage to a life that few children could imagine, and even fewer could forget.

"I wouldn't script a better life growing up," he said. "Not in a million years."

JOSEPH SWIDLER

Joe Swidler managed the Town and Glen Casinos for more than 20 years. Altman was the showman out front, Swidler was the one who kept everything running behind the scenes. He oversaw nearly 150 staff—waiters, bartenders, cooks, ushers, musicians—and made sure dinner service ran smoothly, the shows started on time, and any problems were handled quietly. He was not flashy, but he got things done. If something broke or someone did not show up, Swidler figured it out before the audience ever noticed.[751]

Born in Syracuse, he started out with the Norton Theatrical Booking Agency in Rochester before Altman brought him on board. He left to serve in the Pacific during WWII, then came back and picked up where he left off. He ran a tight, well-organized operation. Department heads reported directly to him, and everyone knew their role. Staff respected him, and performers trusted him. His daughter, Judith (Swidler) Streeter, who was 10 when her dad died, remembered the long hours he spent at the clubs. After his death from cancer at age 52 in 1958, the clubs remained open, but it took two managers to replace him. Swidler had been the one keeping it all in sync all those years.

Figure 244 Joe Swidler with his young daughter Judy in the early years of the Glen
Photo courtesy of Judy (Swidler) Streeter

BERNARD "BENNY" BUCCI

Benny Bucci began his long tenure at the Town Casino in 1948, starting as a bartender and eventually rising to the role of head steward, a position he held until the nightclub's final curtain call. Earlier in his career, he co-owned and operated the Babe and Benny Restaurant on Grider Street, gaining valuable experience in hospitality and food service.[752]

During the summer months, Benny shifted to the Glen, where he served as both assistant manager and head steward, overseeing all back-of-house food and beverage operations. Perhaps his most enduring contribution was transforming the Glen's Family Inn into a dining destination. He introduced popular concepts like the Chuck Wagon and Smorgasbord buffets, offering generous meals at modest prices.

The Altman properties defined most of Benny's professional life as he died shortly after the Glen closed at the age of 51, following a long illness.

Figure 220 Benny Bucci with Ron Urban at the Glen
Photo courtesy of Ron Urban

JIMMIE PHILLIPS

Figure 221 James F. Phillips, Sr.
Photo courtesy of the Phillips family

James F. Phillips, Sr, a native of Lockport, NY, was one of Altman's first employees at the Glen, hired as the general manager in 1933.

He quickly became indispensable to Harry who referred to him as the "all-purpose man," a title Phillips earned over more than three decades of steady service. Officially, he worked as the house electrician, keeping stage lights and sound equipment in order, but his role went well beyond that. Altman entrusted him with overseeing the daily receipts—much of it in cash—collected from the numerous registers at both the Town and the Glen, a responsibility that underscored the depth of trust between the two men.

Phillips's personal life was more unsettled. He married Frances Styn in 1919, and two years later they welcomed a son, James Jr. Frances died just nine years into the marriage, leaving Phillips with a young child under difficult circumstances. James Jr. went on to establish himself as a respected Buffalo physician, a path shaped more by his own determination than by paternal guidance. He liked to quip that he was "a doctor to the stars," having occasionally been called upon to treat performers from Altman's orbit.

Later in life, Phillips remarried, this time to entertainer Miriam Culligan, who survived him when he died in 1969.

Figure 222 Phillips, far right, at the Town Casino in 1959
Photo courtesy of the Phillips family

JAMES MOSER

Those who worked the concessions at the Glen often recall "Mr. Moser" as a central figure in their time there. Jimmy began at the park in the late 1930s as one of its first carnival game concessionaires[a] and was later hired by the park's management company, Amherst Amusement Corp., when Harry Altman and Jack Gilbert privatized the concessions in 1948. His tenure at the Glen spanned decades—from age 29 until the park's closure following the fire in 1973. He was 62. His time in the 10-acre park was interrupted only by a three-year absence during the 1940s.

"Those of us who worked directly for him in the Games used to say we attended 'Glen Park College,' with Jimmy as our primary instructor," recalled Rev. Robert Mock, who would go on to become a Roman Catholic priest after working summers at the Glen in the early 1960s.[753] According to Mock, Moser took serious employees under his wing and was known to challenge those who were not.

"I was terrified of him during my first year, but over time, we grew close," he reflected. Mock remained connected to Moser for years, even working weekends while home on leave from the Navy and later followed him to Fun & Games Park in Tonawanda, where the concessions were relocated after the Glen closed.[754]

Described by many as unforgettable, Jimmy stood 5'7," with a balding head, a solid build, and a cigar perpetually clamped in his teeth which stained his shirt with tobacco juice. Stern and sharp, he ran a tight operation and reacted swiftly if a cash drawer came up even 50 cents short. "Jimmy commanded respect from the local kids," noted Donald (Sam) Weimer.[755]

Among the younger Glen staff, Moser's past was the subject of frequent speculation. Some believed he had once been a traveling carnival worker—a "carny"—who skirted the edges of the law. Others whispered he was the Mob's printer, imprisoned during WW II for counterfeiting ration coupons. One enduring rumor claimed he had crossed the mob by hoarding some of the fake coupons, and that Altman kept him on staff as a form of protection.

The stories were somewhat rooted in reality. The "carny" legend likely originated from Moser's early work as a games' concessionaire. More significantly, his prison sentence was confirmed to be true. In April 1945, Moser began serving a three-year term after pleading guilty to counterfeiting federal auto use tax stamps.[756]

Moser was raised in Dunkirk and lived in Buffalo when he was arrested by the U.S. Secret Service. News of his plea was widely reported in newspapers across New York State. The investigation had uncovered what the Secret Service described as "a mob engaged in a gigantic conspiracy to flood the state with counterfeit $5 Federal automobile use tax stamps," allegedly led by Michael Chronlois (alias Mike Christy) and Nicoletta Bianchi (alias Mrs. Marie Christy) of Rochester.[757] Moser,

---

[a] Moser owned the darts game, pitch-till-you-win, and penny pitch.

then 34, was described as "the chief distributor" for the Buffalo area and was held on $25,000 bond upon his arrest. [758]

On the eve of his trial, he faced charges for possession of 202 counterfeit $5 stamps and 27,000 gallons' worth of bogus gasoline ration coupons. [759] He ultimately pled guilty and served his sentence, leaving behind his wife, Lora (nee Cardone), and their young son, Daniel, born in 1940.

Upon his release, Moser returned to his family and resumed his duties at the Glen under the supervision of park superintendent Clyde Urban. Each spring he helped prepare the park for opening, and each summer he ran the games section, which included Skee Ball, prize wheels, a shooting gallery with live ammunition, and the ever-popular "Bingo with a Ball" (Fascination). Moser famously called out the play of Fascination with his signature chant: "Roll the ball under the chevron, under the glass, and into the hole. Five in a row wins!"

During the off-season, he was often seen driving Altman around in his Cadillac. Over the years, the Moser family moved closer to the Glen, and Jimmy's commitment to the park deepened. After Urban moved to Florida, Moser took over management of the amusement rides. Even after the Glen closed, he stayed with the games operation as it relocated to Tonawanda—though his cherished Fascination game was lost in the 1968 Inferno fire.

Jimmy Moser passed away on July 4, 1986, at the age of 75. "It was fitting," said Rev. Mock, "because the Fourth of July was always one of the busiest days at the Glen—and one of the few when no one could call off. Everyone worked." [760]

Figure 223 The game Fascination
PD

THE GLEN AMUSEMENT PARK

Clyde Urban and Harry worked deliberately through the 1950s and 1960s to expand Glen Park's grounds and feature new amusement rides. The following photographs capture the park's vibrant life beyond the Casino walls.

Figure 224 Each year, Altman and the Williamsville Jaycees would host a free day at the amusement park for disadvantaged children
Photo courtesy Amherst Bee

Figure 225 View of the Glen from the east side of Ellicott Creek
Photo courtesy of Williamsville High School's yearbook, Searchlight

Figure 227 Actionland promotion

Figure 226 Skee Ball coupon

Figure 228 **PHOTOS COURTESY OF BILL BAUMGARTNER**

Figure 229 **PHOTOS COURTESY OF GEORGE KINDEL**

Figure 230 **PHOTOS COURTESY OF RON URBAN**

Figure 231 The roller coaster that was put in place of the zoo

Figure 233 Most guests entered the property from Glen Avenue

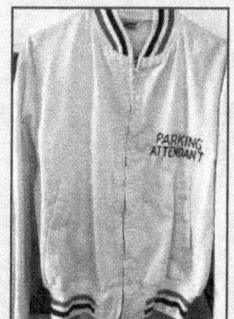

Figure 232 Uniform polo worn by amusement ride attendants during the circus-themed era

Figure 234 The jacket required to be worn by parking attendant
Front and Back views

Figure 235 Murals painted by G. Harold Braner dotted the Glen Park landscape
This set was on the right above the games as you entered the property

Figure 236 Photo is gift of Eleanor Master to the Williamsville Historical Society

Figure 237 Ferris Wheel

Figure 242 Photos Courtesy of the Family of Mark Mattie

Figure 240 Photo courtesy of
Linda Anscombe

Figure 238 Photo courtesy
of Wendy (Gwen) Richdale
Nilson

Figure 241 Glen sign
Photo courtesy of Mike Lorich

Figure 239 Photo courtesy of Elizabeth M. Smith

Figure 243 The Main Street entrance of the Glen
Photo courtesy of Williamsville High School's yearbook,
Searchlight

Figure 247 The final days of the popular swing ride
PD

Figure 244 Ski ball
PD

Figure 246 Car ride
PD

Figure 245 Exiting the Ferris wheel
PD

CHAPTER 19—WHERE THE ENTERTAINERS STAYED

W orking at the Town and Glen Casinos required a week-long commitment from headliners and supporting acts alike, necessitating accommodations that varied greatly in location and amenities.

For A-list stars performing at the Town Casino, Altman predominantly booked rooms at the prestigious Statler Hilton. An alternative downtown lodging option was the Ford/Richford Hotel at 210 Delaware with more than 700 rooms in its three towers.

Figure 248 Hotel Statler
PD

Figure 249 Ford/Richford Hotel
PD

Performers scheduled at the Glen Casino, located more than 10 miles from downtown, often lodged in local motels and tourist homes[b] dispersed throughout the Village. This arrangement offered celebrities a chance to enjoy a quaint, relaxed setting among the villagers who commonly saw them taking leisurely walks along Main Street or visiting nearby shops and restaurants.

While the house orchestras at both Casinos were comprised of area residents, Altman hired out-of-town showgirls and chorus line dancers from well-known talent agencies in New York City. These performers were typically signed for the entire operational season of each Casino, lasting several months, which required

---

[b] Tourist homes, prevalent before the extensive development of hotels and motels, offered travelers lodging through private homeowners who rented out spare rooms. These homes often provided a bed and breakfast-style experience, serving as early precursors to modern B&Bs. In these settings, owners hosted guests, offering a more personal and home-style atmosphere compared to larger commercial establishments.

Figure 250 Glenside Motel,
42 East Spring Street
PD

The tourist home was demolished in the late 1950s to allow the Smith family to build the more-modern Holiday Motel in its place. The Motel featured 17 units with contemporary amenities, and two fully furnished apartments adjacent to it.

securing regional accommodations for them. In 1960, to better support seasonal performers at the Glen, Altman repurposed a commercial building on the edge of the park at 42 East Spring Street,[c] transforming it into Glenside Motel with kitchenette suites.

Patricia (Smith) Riedel's childhood was spent amidst the comings and goings of celebrities, thanks to her parents, Robert K. and Eleanor Smith, Sr., who owned and operated a popular tourist home at 5801 Main Street near Garrison Road.[761]

Figure 251 Village accommodations provided to performers in
the early years of the Glen Casino were at the tourist homes
like this one owned by the Smith family
PD

Figure 252 Photos courtesy of Patricia Riedel

---

[c] The building, which is set on the escarpment above the Glen alongside the Williamsville Mill, escaped fire damage due to efforts of local firefighters in September 1968 when the Inferno was destroyed.

The Smith family, including Pat and her brother, Robert, Jr. (Kenny), lived on-site and became accustomed to the routine that came with their high-profile guests, such as Pat Boone, Enzo Stuarti, Don Rickles, Rip Taylor, Jack Jones, Bobby Darin, the Three Stooges, among others. Notable moments from those years were captured in the guest books of the Holiday Motel.

Figure 253 Bobby Darin and Don Rickles were among the many well-known entertainers who checked into the Holiday Motel during their performance runs at the Glen Casino
Photo courtesy of Patricia Riedel

For the Smiths, hosting celebrities was a daily occurrence and did not stir much excitement. The performers often slept into the afternoon after late-night shows, requiring the family to maintain a quiet environment. Pat recalls the constraints this lifestyle imposed on her social life, noting, "I actually hated my life then, because I did not have the freedom my friends had. I was responsible for cleaning rooms every day after school and missed out on many after-school activities." Now, however, she cherishes those years, understanding its unique privilege.

One regret she has involves Jack Jones, a popular singer of the era, who stayed at the Motel with his first wife and baby. Pat declined the offer to babysit because she had a "hot date." She looks back now and wishes she had stayed home that night.

Figure 254 Jack Jones in front of the Holiday Motel during his week-long run at the Glen Casino
Photo courtesy of Patricia Riedel

*Figure 255 Moe and Larry pose with some local boys during their stay in Williamsville
(circa 1958-59) Jim Adams is the boy on the left
Photo courtesy of Patricia Riedel*

Her parents forged lasting friendships with some guests, notably two of the wives of the Three Stooges with whom they regularly would correspond. Moe Howard would take her brother and friends fishing at the dam in the Village and posed for photos with local kids.

A memorable encounter happened in high school when she talked to Bobby Darin in their driveway. "He had stayed with us a few times, but that time I actually got to talk to him," she recalled. "Back then, you never knew which of these performers would make it big." On that day, Darin joked about his future, saying he would not marry a movie star (he would eventually marry Sandra Dee).[d]

After her parents' retirement, Pat and her husband, Paul Riedel took over hotel operations until it was sold in 2007 and eventually demolished by a local developer.

---

[d]Sandra Dee expressed a similar sentiment in *Parade Magazine* prior to meeting Darin. "The last man I'm going to marry is a man in show business," she said. "They are selfish, unreliable, and make lousy husbands. The Hollywood-type of marriage is not for me. I want all my children to have the same father. I'm going to take a long look before I get married. I'm not going to jump into it." Interestingly, she married Darin three months after they met and had one son. By 1967, after seven years of marriage, their love story was over. She never remarried.

CHAPTER 20—ALTMAN AFTER HOURS

CHARITY EVENTS

As Altman achieved financial stability, his philanthropic endeavors thrived. Throughout his nightclub career, he regularly hosted free lunches and stage shows for residents of the Rosa Coplon Jewish Old Folks Home. He also generously provided an annual Thanksgiving dinner for more than 300 visually impaired individuals in partnership with the Downtown Lions Club. Collaborating with the Williamsville Jaycees Chamber of Commerce, Altman organized special yearly events at Glen Park's amusement area, treating 200 orphans and underprivileged children to a full day of rides, games, and complimentary food.

J.N. ADAM MEMORIAL HOSPITAL

Over the years, Alman would gain recognition for bringing his performances directly to patients in hospital settings.

Beginning in 1937, Altman organized his entire stage company to travel and perform at the Veterans Administration facility in Batavia. More than 40 performers were transported to the hospital by buses donated by the Buffalo Transit Company. This event would become a yearly tradition, garnering support from various organizations throughout the years including *The Buffalo Courier-Express* Goodfellows.

Harry would become well known for his creating the "Mirth Caravan" that travelled every June for nearly 50 years to the J.N. Adam Memorial Hospital in Perrysburg, a rural community 35 miles south of Buffalo.[762]

The hospital, opened in 1912 by J.N. Adams, a former Buffalo mayor and owner of a prominent department store, was built to treat tuberculosis patients.[a]

Figure 256 Entertainers on the grounds of the hospital
Photo courtesy of Marjorie Wallens

---

[a] J.N. Adams would serve as a sanatorium until 1960 when the hospital was converted into a home for developmentally disabled children. It would close in 1993. "J N Adam Facility." *Historic Path of Cattaraugus County*, Historic Path, accessed July 4, 2025. https://historicpath.com/article/j-n-adam-facility-192.

*Figure 257 Moe Balsom's Orchestra members await
their time to entertain on the grounds of J.N. Adam
Memorial Hospital
Photo courtesy of Lynette LoCurcio*

According to Altman, no entertainer ever refused to take part in his caravan, even though "it's pretty tough for show people to finish their regular work at 3 or 4 o'clock in the morning and then get up again at 10 to drive to Perrysburg."[763] To accommodate the large number of acts performing during the two-hour show, Altman said that "the [patients'] beds are brought out on the porch, and we'd stage the show right in the street.

Altman said that his dedication to efforts like Batavia VA and J.N. Adams was born from his own experience of being hospitalized for a few weeks in his early 20s. He vowed then if he ever found himself in a position to do so, he promised that he would spend his spare time trying to make life brighter for similar "unfortunates."[764]

"I take one day a year of lives that are as colorless as hospital bed sheets and doctor it up with a laugh and a song," he said.[765]

He was proud of his staff for pitching in to help. "I wouldn't let them do it without paying them, but they turn right around and donate the money to whichever institution we've just worked for." The support of the Actors Guild of Variety and Local 43 of the Musicians Union was pivotal to the success of these efforts, he said.[766]

"It's a rewarding advocation," Harry told *The Buffalo Evening News*, "I wish I could go to Perrysburg more often. Even with my one day there each year, those people still have 364 monotonous days."[767]

*Figure 258 The audience awaits the start of the performance
Photo courtesy of Marjorie Wallens*

THE FUNORAMAS

Figure 259 Offerman Stadium, home of the Bisons and the annual Erie Club Funorama
PD

One of Harry Altman's most high-profile philanthropic ventures began with dazzling promise but ultimately collapsed under the weight of scandal. Funorama, launched in 1954, was an ambitious annual fundraiser held at Offerman Stadium to benefit the Erie Club, which supported the Buffalo Police Department's Death and Benefit Fund.

Altman, serving as both producer and director, pulled from his deep well of showbiz connections to assemble a star-studded lineup.[768] In its early years, the event drew more than 30,000 spectators and featured marquee names like the McGuire Sisters, Jimmy Durante, and The Four Lads—all of whom volunteered their talents to support the cause. With an executive committee made up of Buffalo's most prominent business and civic leaders, Altman's role at the helm further cemented his reputation as Western New York's preeminent impresario.

Figure 260 Organizers assembled to coordinate the second annual event
Photo Courtesy of The Archives & Special Collection Department of SUNY Buffalo State

Figure 261 Lighter
Courtesy of Brad Altman

For a time, Funorama thrived. But cracks in its polished veneer emerged early. In 1955, during a daytime matinee performance for thousands of children—many from local orphanages—a tragic accident occurred. A donkey, part of the Gritz & Gravy comedy act, slipped and broke its hip before a crowd of 7,200.[769] The on-site veterinarian determined the animal's injuries were too severe, and it was euthanized behind the bleachers. Altman, ever composed, took the microphone to gently break the news to the children.[770] With circus veteran Earl Gritz visibly weeping in full clown makeup, Altman promised the Erie Club would replace the beloved burro.[771] Despite his grief, Gritz went on with the show that day. The moment passed with grace, but in hindsight, it felt like an omen—a dark prelude to the reckoning that would publicly erupt two years later.

Figure 262 John C. Montana Photo courtesy of The Archives & Special Collection Department of SUNY Buffalo State

The downward spiral started in 1956 when the Erie Club presented its coveted "Man of the Year" award to John C. Montana, a respected civic leader, philanthropist, and co-founder of Van Dyke Taxicab, which had grown into the second-largest cab company in the state.[772] An early supporter of Funorama, Montana also served as co-chair of the event's executive committee. His selection as Man of the Year was prominently featured in *The Buffalo Courier-Express*, the event's media partner, which praised his record of public service and business success.

Within a year of receiving the Erie Club's highest honor, Montana's carefully cultivated public image collapsed. In November 1957, he was among dozens apprehended while attempting to flee a law enforcement raid at the now-infamous Apalachin Meeting—an unprecedented gathering of Mafia leaders from across the country.[773] It was held in a small hamlet in the southern tier of New York State. The event, intended to be a discreet summit of organized crime's upper echelon, became a national scandal when authorities exposed its scale. Caught scrambling through the woods, his fur coat tangled on a barbed wire fence, Montana was unmasked as the underboss of the Magaddino crime family.[774]

BUFFALO EVENING NEWS   Mail

MAIL EDITION

BUFFALO 5, N. Y., THURSDAY, MAY 21, 1959   64 Pages—4 Sections—7 Cents

| 27 WHO ATTENDED APALACHIN MEETING ARE ACCUSED BY JURY | Montana, Magaddino and LaDuca Indicted in Apalachin Crackdown |

Figure 263 Headline from May 1959

The revelation sent shockwaves through Buffalo and beyond. Senate hearings soon followed, and the fact that the Erie Club—an organization tied tightly to the city's police department—had recently named Montana its Man of the Year provoked a wave of public outrage and national scrutiny. The stain on Funorama was swift and indelible.

Altman, whose creative vision and leadership had defined the event from its inception, found himself pulled uncomfortably close to the scandal. He and Montana had long shared civic and charitable stages, dating back to the 1920s. Together, they had supported boxing nights at the Broadway Auditorium, served Thanksgiving dinners to the poor at the Palace Royal, and worked side by side on early spectacles like Altman's Mardi Gras parades. Like Altman, Montana was a self-made entrepreneur. Beyond his taxi empire, he owned an auto dealership and other transportation ventures.[775] Politically, he had held office as Niagara District Councilman and counted prominent figures such as Governor W. Averell Harriman and a young Congressman named Richard Nixon among his associates.[776]

But Montana's true skill lay in concealment. His association with the Mafia dated back to at least 1931 when he attended an early national gathering of organized crime leaders alongside Stefano Magaddino.[777] For more than two decades, he had maintained a dual identity—one as a civic icon, the other as a mob boss. That illusion was shattered by his arrest at Apalachin.

MAFIA MAN OF YEAR

There was considerable embarrassment in Buffalo, N.Y., when citizens found that their 1956 "Man of the Year"—John C. Montana—was a guest at the widely publicized 1957 meeting of the Mafia in Apalachin, N.Y. Montana, a wealthy and civic-minded businessman, had kept his Mafia criminal connections a closely guarded secret. This photograph shows him on the happy day when he received Buffalo's award.

Figure 264 The photo of John C. Montana accepting the Erie Club's award was reprinted in newspaper across the country after he testified before Congress
Tucson Daily Citizen, June 27, 1959, 4

Montana's fallout was severe. In Senate testimony following the raid,[778] he was one of the few attendees who did not invoke the Fifth Amendment. Instead, he offered an implausible defense: that he had only stopped at the house where the meeting was held because his car had broken down. He had no idea about the meeting that was being held in another part of the building.

The senators were skeptical and pressed him during several days of testimony. In one exchange with Senator Irving Ives,[b] Montana attempted to explain why he had fled:[c]

> **Senator Ives:** *"One thing that I don't think has been reconciled here at all is Mr. Montana's dash through the woods. I just don't understand it."*
>
> **Mr. Montana:** *"Senator, if I had to do it over again, I probably would not [have run]. I will put it another way: It was just a moment, that is the way my mind went. And I did it, and that is what I did."*
>
> **Senator Ives:** *"But you are a well-balanced individual. After all is said and done, just because somebody yells 'roadblock'... you don't go dashing through the woods, do you? After all, you are a rational person, rather than any other type."*
>
> **Mr. Montana:** *"Well, there is always the first time, Senator. That is what happened."*

The price Montana paid for speaking openly was steep. By breaking the Mafia's code of silence (*Omertà*), he was ostracized by the very organization he had helped lead. His influence vanished. Seven years after being honored as a pillar of Buffalo's civic life, Montana died of a heart attack in his home, a disgraced and diminished figure at the age of 70.[779]

Figure 265 Dizzy Dean signed autographs prior to the 1960 Funorama
From left, Pat McGroder, Harry Altman, Tony Naples, David Naples,
Dizzy Dean and Judge Joseph Sedita
Photo courtesy of Brad Altman

---

[b] Senator Ives, a Republican from New York and vice-chair of the McClellan Committee, played a direct and probing role in the national mafia hearings of the late 1950s.

[c] *U.S. Congress. Senate. Select Committee on Improper Activities in the Labor or Management Field.* Investigation of Improper Activities in the Labor or Management Field: Hearings before the Select Committee on Improper Activities in the Labor or Management Field. 85th Cong., 1st—2nd sess., 1957—1959. Vol. pt. 32, p. 12317.

Despite the lingering scandal, Funorama pressed on. In 1958 and 1959 the Erie Club staged stock-car races at Offerman Stadium as fundraisers, followed in July 1960 by a baseball game between Toronto and Buffalo. Dizzy Dean brought star power to the 1960 Funorama, stepping onto the mound to pitch to Joe DiMaggio, with Joe McCarthy crouched behind the plate as catcher.

Altman attempted a 1961 revival of a stage production, this time in partnership with Pedro Martinez, a former professional wrestler and sports promoter.[780] Altman, ever the optimist, tried to recapture the spirit of the earlier shows, declaring, "It will be like the old-time Funoramas. We uncovered some of the greatest talent of this decade at those shows…"[781]

But the magic was gone. What had begun as a gleaming example of Altman's ability to blend civic pride with show business spectacle quietly faded into memory—overshadowed, in the end, by the company it kept.

"MAN OF THE YEAR?"

The selection of Montana as "Man of the Year" dripped with irony, and it became a focal point of intrigue at the U.S. Senate Committee's hearings about the participants at the Apalachin Meeting. The senators were keen to uncover who had chosen Montana for the Erie Club accolade.

Montana told the senators that Erie County District Attorney John F. Dwyer was part of the selection committee. However, Dwyer quickly refuted this assertion.[782]

Speaking to The Buffalo Evening News,[783] he firmly stated that he had not been involved in the selection process at all. "I had no part whatever in this matter and I don't know how my name can be linked with it," he declared.

Dwyer said that his involvement with the 1956 event was limited solely to being a member of the Ticket Committee and having received the "Man of the Year" award in 1955.

Understandably, no one was eager to admit their participation in the selection process, and no one ever came forward to take credit, including Charles M. Basil who was Erie Club's president from 1952 to 1960.[784]

HORSE RACING

"Mr. Altman has picked a lot of talent in his day, and some horses."

~ Billy Kelly, Sports Editor, The Buffalo Courier-Express

Altman followed horse racing closely, including both thoroughbred and harness racing. When time and season permitted, he could visit any of the five racetracks in Southern Ontario and Western New York[d] with friends and acquaintances. He regularly studied the race form and kept his bookie busy.

Henry Clune, a columnist for *The Rochester Democrat and Chronicle*, recounted joining Altman at Hamburg Raceway in spring 1965:[785]

Figure 266 Altman followed action in the racing form each day
Photo courtesy of Brad Altman

"He was impressive in a homburg and topcoat with a pink silk lining that resembled an opera cloak. Indeed, his general aspect made one think of the late Oscar Hammerstein. He was rather exultant. This night, he declared, he couldn't lose for winning."

"'I got a wonderful thing,' he said. "It's a lock in. The owner just told me. And the price the thing is going off at! Look on the board.' Mr. Altman chuckled. 'It's like a license to steal.' He handed a young lady, who ran his errands, $150. 'Lay it right square on the nose,' he instructed her."

"'Wait,'" I called timidly; and when she turned, I gave her $2 of my own. 'Bet it the same way,' I said.

"We lounged back then, to get rich at our ease. But the horse, which the owner said couldn't lose, with the wire glistening in its eyes, ran out at the top of the stretch and left us empty-handed.'"[786]

---

[d] Batavia Downs, Buffalo Raceway, Hamilton, Fort Erie and Stamford,

Kelly reported regularly in his column on the Harrys' exploits at the tracks.

> *"We can safely say that the Canadian racing season, especially the meets at Hamilton, Ft. Erie and Stamford, were highly successful and eminently satisfactory to Altman and Wallens...their Hot Springs education and study of the science of horse racing apparently was put to good advantage."[787]*

The education in Hot Springs took place annually during the years following WWII. Altman, Wallens and other civic and business leaders from Buffalo visited what was then an "open town" where gambling flourished under local authority approval. It was in competition with Las Vegas for the title of Sin City. Altman seemed to enjoy his time away; according to the Personals column in *The Amherst Bee*, he spent three weeks during racing season at the Arlington Hotel in Hot Springs.

Kelly frequently participated in the trip and reported on his diverse group of fellow travelers that included Joe C. Kerwin, Anthony Vastola, Joe Ryan and Frank Perry. Here are a few short notes about participants who attended the trip in Spring 1950:[788]

John C. Montana was an enthusiastic aficionado of horseracing, even owning thoroughbreds in Canada. *The Buffalo Courier-Express* highlighted Montana's passion for horseracing in a 1946 article about the Kentucky Derby, noting that "John Montana's second interest, after taxis, is racehorses."[789]

Murray Whiteman owned a well-loved music store at 605 Main Street, just a short distance from the Town Casino. Performers visiting Buffalo frequently made their way to Whiteman Song Shop to catch up on gossip. Originally from Brooklyn and with a background in Vaudeville, Murray was a close ally of both Wallens and Altman

James Martin was a Buffalo Police Officer.

Anthony J. Naples was a businessman active in local and statewide Democratic politics. He served alongside John C. Montana as an officer of Frontier Liquors Corporation, a wholesale business. He was also sales manager at Frontier.[790]

Michael Panaro was a noted restaurant owner also known as "Snowball."[791] One of his businesses, "Panaro's Snowball Lounge," was an alleged local mob hangout. In 1967, police arrested almost every member of the Magaddino crime family (except Stefano and his son) in the lounge's basement. The space had allegedly been converted into an illegal gambling hall. The raid became known as "Little Apalachin."[792]

Angelo Acquisto, known in the media as "the trucking tycoon,"[793] was an underboss of the Magaddino crime family until he was caught siphoning off gambling profits from the organization.[794] Outraged, Magaddino swiftly acted, stripping him of his position. The fallout from Magaddino's decision was devastating for Acquisto, who, facing disgrace and potential retribution, took his own life in January 1956.[795]

Members of the group also stopped by to see William J. Dillon and Bill Evans, former Buffalo policemen, who retired to Hot Springs.[796]

A distinctive feature of Hot Springs was the truce among mob members, transforming it into a peaceful retreat for criminals looking to escape retaliation. The Southern Club was the center of activity for the likes of Owney Madden, Lucky Luciano, and Al Capone during their heyday.

Kelly reported on "an incident" on the links that "created considerable talk which endured for days." It involved Angie Acquisto, "the trucking tycoon," and Mike Panaro, "better and more popularly known as 'Snowball.'" [797]

> *"They furnished the gallery at the Hot Springs Country Club with the thrill of the year when Acquisto's drive on the short No. 3 hole stopped a scant 1-1/2 inches from the cup, and Panaro joined the excited Angie in jumping up and down in useless effort to shake the earth sufficiently to cause the ball to drop into the cup for a hole in one. They found out later that the roll was all uphill, and a golf ball, like water, seldom runs uphill."*[798]

During this time, Hot Springs was working its way back to respectability, shifting the city's image toward wholesome attractions like spas, baseball camps, golf courses, and the racetrack Oaklawn Park, known for producing two Kentucky Derby champions. While the major contingent of the annual group was comprised of men, a few wives tagged along to visit the high-end resorts.

By January 1963, the fight against organized crime intensified, leading to a city-wide transformation when Winthrop Rockefeller entered politics. Under his leadership, Hot Springs began distancing itself from its past, redefining itself as a legitimate, family-friendly destination.

As for Altman, the love of racing never ended. In July 1964, Phil Ranallo in *The Buffalo Courier-Express* reported that Harry had purchased a two-year-old thoroughbred named Revelling "for private terms" from Addison-Hall Stables in Ontario.[799] That summer, Harry excitedly shared with his grandson, Steve Goldstein, that he had purchased a horse for him, but Steve never got to see it race.[800] Harry would die before Revelling entered a race.

ALTMAN'S BIG MISS ON THE BIG STAGE

Success, when it came, fueled even greater ambitions. The launch of the Town Barn in 1943 propelled Altman into the national spotlight as an impresario. With a 1,200-seat capacity and a roster of what he called "big-dough performers," the venue's success drew the attention of Lou Walters, founder of the famed Latin Quarter nightclubs in New York, Boston, and Miami, and producer of the *Ziegfeld Follies of 1943*.[e]

It was Walters who encouraged Altman to take a bold leap—and a significant financial risk—by venturing into Broadway musical production. Altman had already shown an interest, having enlisted Broadway producer Wally Wagner to supervise the opening show for the Town Barn, which was rehearsed in a Manhattan studio.[801]

Walters' latest project, *Artists & Models* (1943), was a revue that blended sketches, musical numbers, and comedy.[802] Its lack of a single cohesive narrative, reminiscent of vaudeville, perfectly aligned with Harry's appreciation for varied, dynamic entertainment. This iteration of *Artists & Models* harkened back to its origins two decades earlier, when theater moguls Lee and J.J. Shubert debuted the original in 1923. The early revues were infamous for their risqué content, often featuring topless or nude female performers in elaborate tableaux. However, under Walters' direction, the 1943 version toned down the provocativeness, reflecting the more conservative wartime sensibilities.

Figure 267 Jane Frohman
PD

---

[e] It was during this time that the newspapers started to refer to Altman as "Williamsville's Ziegfeld" for his ability to "put talent together" for community events. *The Buffalo Evening News* also referred to Harry as the "uncrowned king of fun."

Jane Frohman, a renowned singer and actress celebrated for her rich contralto voice, headlined the new musical. She had appeared in the original Ziegfeld Follies, and in films such as *Stars Over Broadway* (1935) and *Radio City Revels* (1938).

In 1943, just prior to the show's opening, Frohman survived a plane crash near Lisbon, Portugal while enroute to entertain U.S. troops during WWII. Due to her severe injuries, her presence on stage for *Artists & Models* was performed in a wheelchair. The cast for the show was extensive and included stars like Jackie Gleason (in his second Broadway appearance), the Four Radio Aces, Ben Yost Singers, Marty May, and Billy Newell. There were 60 models and chorus girls featured in the dance routines.

Figure 268 Playbill
PD

The exact amount of Altman's investment is not known; however, Walters reportedly dropped $200,000[803] (more than $3.6 million in today's dollars) into the show that he co-produced and directed.

Altman's connection with the show was well publicized in Buffalo. The opening night on November 5, 1943 saw a large caravan of local luminaries heading to New York. The list included Buffalo Mayor Joseph J. Kelly, Judge Harry Zimmer, Chief Inspector Thomas W. Ryan, Ben Kerner, Herb Ross and Baxter Smith. New York City Mayor Fiorella LaGuardia attended as a guest of the Buffalo delegation.[804]

Reviews for the show were lackluster, and it closed after 28 performances. Here is a sampling of the show's published reviews:

J.M. Kendrick (*Associated Press*): *Artists & Models* has as its star excellent songstress Jane Frohman—and that's all the good that can be said about the review."[805]

Arthur Pollock (*Brooklyn Eagle*):[806] "The company is a big one, the stage and the theater are big, too, everything looked bright and gay and the spirit is one of hospitality. The entertainment's lacks are those resulting from the producer's evident confidence in the public's love of the commonplace and mediocre.

John Chapman of *The New York Daily News* attributed the poor performance to nightclub operators overstepping their bounds by bringing nightclub-style acts to a Broadway theater audience:[807]

"[The] audience is by in large, sober and demanding. If an act does not happen to be interesting, the audience cannot distract itself by eating, drinking, smoking, or talking across the table; it just has to sit there, and hope things will get better...People who seem witty and talented after midnight in a nightclub don't look so good in the cold gray dawn of an 8 PM Broadway premiere."[808]

LANES, LEAGUES, AND LATE NIGHT

Though best known for owning his own eateries and as Altman's partner in a string of nightclubs, Wallens also pursued a parallel passion: bowling. For Wallens, the sport was not just a pastime; it was a core business interest that he nurtured for decades. Throughout the 1950s, the Wallens family owned and operated Midtown Bowling Center, a 14-lane bowling alley located in the Otto-Kent Building at 640 Main Street (now known as Theater Place).[809] The lanes occupied part of the sprawling 41,000-square-foot complex, sharing an address with Wallens Glass Bar, which had opened in the building in 1940.[810] The location became a dual hub for dining and recreation, particularly as the downtown theater district evolved.

LOST for that week-end date idea?

SHERIDAN LANES, Inc.

announces

OPEN BOWLING
ALL DAY SATURDAY and SUNDAY

3860 SHERIDAN DRIVE   64 AUTOMATIC
(Between Millersport & Harlem)   ALLEYS
TF 9-3900 Open 24 Hours

Figure 269 Sheridan Lanes

But it was in the suburbs where Wallens made his most ambitious mark on the sport. In 1957, he and his two sons invested $1 million to construct Sheridan Lanes in Amherst—a modern showpiece.[811]

Built on a 5.5-acre plot at 3680 Sheridan Drive, the facility featured 500 feet of frontage and parking for more than 600 cars. Inside, the alley boasted 48 state-of-the-art Brunswick lanes (later expanded to 64), all precision-installed to "meet the highest standards of league play."[812] It opened in February 1958 and quickly established itself as one of the premier bowling centers in the region.

In postwar Buffalo, bowling was more than a sport, it was a civic ritual. League teams were drawn from factories, unions, large companies, and small businesses, and alley owners like Wallens catered to this booming clientele. The Sheridan Lanes thrived for decades, with the Wallens family stepping back from management in 1997.[813]

In 1956, Altman decided to carve out his own niche in the sport. Having made his name in the nightclub business, he decided on a hybrid business: part bowling alley, part nightclub, all wrapped into a polished "sports and entertainment center"[814] located in the scenic town of Canandaigua, New York, in the heart of the Finger Lakes.

Opened in 1956, Arrowhead Lanes was a bold $350,000 investment. Featuring 24 AMF-equipped bowling lanes, the venue[815]—advertised as the "Bowling Palace"[f]—also boasted a banquet hall, restaurant, snack bar, and children's playroom. Native American-inspired décor was woven into the carpets and wall designs. But its crown jewel was the Minuet Lounge, a stylish, soundproof nightclub with a revolving stage that could seat 120 patrons. Altman envisioned it as a satellite for the burgeoning talent performing at the Town and Glen Casinos.[816]

Figure 270 Arrowhead Lanes
Photos courtesy of Barney Goldstein

The Minuet Lounge opened with fanfare in October 1956, complete with New York showgirls serving as hosts and a lineup of eight live acts.[817] Over the next four years, it welcomed performers like Don Pacifico, the Wade-Phillips Trio, the Dynatones featuring Barry James, the Chuck Alaimo Quartet, and Joe Christy & His Knights.

The Arrowhead venture was a family affair. Harry served as president of the corporation, while his 26-year-old son Bob, a Syracuse University graduate, was named manager of the facility.[818] Much of the day-to-day management in Canandaigua was overseen by the Goldstein brothers. David Goldstein, married to Altman's daughter Hermine, and his brother Samuel M., both longtime residents of Canandaigua, were instrumental in keeping operations running smoothly.[819]

Arrowhead remained under family ownership for just four years. Bob eventually left to pursue a career in Arizona property development, while David Goldstein moved to Williamsville, stepping into a key role at Glen Park as Harry's likely successor. Unable to match the success of his Buffalo venues, Altman sold Arrowhead Lanes in 1960. However, the building remained in operation as a bowling center, and the Minuet Lounge continued to feature live entertainment.[g]

---

[f] Sheridan Lanes was called the "Palace of Bowling."

[g] Soon after the sale, Geneva's acclaimed local band, Wilmer & the Dukes, performed there. It was just a short 24-minute drive from their hometown. They would later become one of the most popular draws at the Inferno during its heyday from 1966 to 1968.

Figure 271 Opening night festivities at Arrowhead brought together the Altman and Goldstein families
Annabelle Altman is in the center of the photo in the floral dress; Harry is absent
Photo courtesy of Barney Goldstein

While under the new ownership, Arrowhead met a tragic end on August 11, 1965 when a three-alarm fire destroyed the property, resulting in losses estimated at more than $700,000.

PART THREE—THE FINAL ENCORE

*Figure 272 Altman gives a pre-show interview outside the Glen Casino to "Lucky" Pierre Gonneau,
one of the WEBR radio personalities*

---

*"I ask Almighty God for a few more years of health and strength to continue to
bring you the best I can."*

~ Harry Altman, September 1959 at his Testimonial Dinner

CHAPTER 21—THE FINAL YEARS OF TOWN CASINO

1958—A CHANGING OF THE GUARD

The fall of 1958 marked a turning point for the Town Casino. After more than fifteen years as Altman's steadfast partner, Harry Wallens retired, his health declining and energy spent. Wallens had been a pillar of the club's continued success. His departure, along with the death of longtime club manager Joe Swidler, left a vacuum in leadership.

To fill the gap, Altman appointed Lenny Paige as executive manager and brought in Robert M. Lowe as general manager.[820] Lowe, formerly manager of both the Hotel Westbrook and Towne House Restaurant, was tapped not for his nightclub experience but for his banquet and convention savvy—signaling a growing shift in the Town's direction. With fewer sellout nights and a changing clientele, the Town Casino would increasingly rely on private events and large-scale dinners to keep its books balanced.

Wallens had already begun stepping back prior to his official retirement. He closed Wallens Glass Bar in 1955, auctioned off its contents, and guided his sons through the construction of Sheridan Lanes, which opened in 1956. Retirement found him content, spending summers with family at his vacation home on the Canadian shoreline.

Meanwhile, Altman, sensing mounting competition from the up-and-coming Melody Fair (see page 291), bet big on reinvention. That winter, he debuted a full-scale musical revue titled "Curtain Going Up," produced by showbiz veteran David Bines and headlined by The Vagabonds, a well-known comedy-music act.[821] With comedian Mel Leonard as the other familiar name on the bill, opening night drew a full house.[822] For a fleeting moment, it felt like the old magic might return.

"Curtain Going Up" was reported by *The Buffalo Courier-Express* to be a high-octane and modern production. Bines, who had cut his teeth producing for Mike Shea in Buffalo and later choreographed revivals at New York's Palace Theater, "brought a fresh energy to the club."[823] His wife, Ruth Bines, handled choreography for a cast of 35 young dancers and singers, many with Broadway credits, delivering a "whirling blend of music, color, and comedy that blurred the line between Vegas and vaudeville."[824]

Between shows, Jose Gonzales' Cha Cha Band and Moe Balsom's Society Orchestra kept patrons dancing beneath new red, white, and blue canopies. A maple dance floor and a revamped dining area—complete with an 18-foot "chuck wagon" visible from Main Street—reflected Altman's full-court press to draw in foot traffic and create buzz.[825]

The transformation did not go unnoticed. Mayor Frank Sedita offered public praise at the Town's resurgence: "It would be a distinct loss to the city if the club should close. Not only does the Town Casino bring money into the city," he said, "it provides employment for about 150 Buffalonians and helps keep Main Street alive."[826]

But the applause did not last. Despite the investment and innovation, the public's interest quickly faded. That New Year's Eve, once the club's most profitable night, drew the smallest crowd in its history. Just days into 1959, Altman announced a 10-week closure.[827] The losses were too deep, he said. If something did not change, the club might never reopen. His focus might shift entirely to the seasonal Glen Casino, where the summer crowds still came reliably.

The Town, once ablaze with star power, was dimming fast.

MELODY FAIR

In the final years of his life, as performer salaries surged and television became a fixture in American households, Altman grew increasingly vocal in his frustrations—particularly with the rise of community theaters, which he accused of siphoning off patrons from his nightclubs. "A year ago, we were doing fairly well," he remarked in an interview. "Then the community theaters began their upswing, and our business just dropped off completely."

Figure 273 Melody Fair
PD

Community theaters, nonprofit and volunteer-driven, were staging live performances in churches, school auditoriums, and other makeshift venues throughout the region. While the amateur productions were not designed to compete directly with nightclub entertainment, their appeal appeared undeniable.

"The public has a special feeling about these theaters," explained Lenny Paige, who joined Altman in an interview. "The groups use local people, and they get hometown support. It's as if the audience was going out to root for its own ball club."[a]

Altman's frustration may have stemmed, in part, from the meteoric rise of a community theater group that began modestly as the Lake Shore Playhouse in Derby, NY. After staging small productions in rented storefronts, the group made a

---

[a] Altman had once benefited from the popularity of community theater, having rented out the Glen Barn to troupes seeking a venue for their shows during the early 1950s.

daring leap in 1956—launching a summer stock series under a big-top tent near the Wurlitzer Building in North Tonawanda. Rebranded as Melody Fair and led by Lewis G. Fisher, the venture flourished, offering Broadway-style musicals with star-studded casts that often featured performers who had once graced Altman's stages.

For a man who had long anticipated trends in entertainment, Harry saw the shift too late and could do nothing to stop it.[b]

Perhaps the most personal—and painful—rejection came from Dick Shawn, the wildly eccentric comedian. Born Richard Schulefand in Lackawanna, NY, Shawn was the nephew by marriage of Sarah Altman Banditson, Harry's sister. As a boy, Shawn was often found watching rehearsals at his uncle's nightclubs, soaking up the spectacle and dreaming of his own career in show business.

According to Ed Sullivan's syndicated column Little Old New York,[828] a young Shawn idolized the performers on Harry's stage. Though Altman reportedly tried to dissuade him from entering the entertainment world, Shawn refused to back down. Determined to forge his own path he changed his

Figure 274 Dick Shawn
PD

name, allegedly to keep Harry from discovering that he had ignored the advice.

Shawn built his act in the Catskills before graduating to the national stage, earning a reputation for physical, irreverent comedy that blurred the line between absurdity and performance art. He found widespread acclaim on television, on Broadway, and in Hollywood. Two of his most iconic film roles came in the ensemble comedies It's a Mad, Mad, Mad, Mad World (1963) and Mel Brooks's, The Producers (1967), both of which showcased his manic, unpredictable style.

Altman proudly capitalized on Shawn's growing popularity, billing him as a rising star and using their family connection to pack his clubs. Through the 1950s, their relationship appeared mutually beneficial—Shawn had a home stage, and Altman had a marquee name he could promote.

Figure 275 A still from Shawn's break-out movie role, It's a Mad, Mad, Mad, Mad World

---

[b] Nearly a decade after Altman's death, Melody Fair's tent-based operation evolved into a full-scale concert venue featuring an innovative theater-in-the-round design that revolved. With no Altman-run venue to compete, many of his most popular acts found a new weekend home at Melody Fair.

But by the 1960s, the nightclub scene was shifting. Faced with shrinking audiences and competition from television and community theaters, Harry desperately needed help from familiar faces. At a critical moment, he reached out to Shawn, but instead of returning to the Town or Glen, Shawn signed on to star in a production of Do-Re-Mi at Melody Fair, the very venue Altman saw as a threat.

Figure 276 Dick Shawn ad

Shawn gave several newspaper interviews to promote his Melody Fair appearance. In one published July 1963, he remarked that an entertainer "does himself no favors when he tries to play before a hometown audience, especially in a nightclub setting, where he had once performed solo under the glare of a spotlight.[829]

"You get out there on stage and the front row tables are filled with people you went to school with. Nobody thinks of you as an entertainer. They remember you as a schoolmate, as a kid they played ball with, who dated the same girls they did and went to Crystal Beach with. They sit there and sneer and say, 'Show me.'"[830]

Shawn's move to Melody Fair was a bitter blow for Harry. It was not just a personal rejection; it marked a broader shift, a quiet exodus by performers he had once championed. In the coming months, others followed suit—Carmen McRae, Steve Lawrence, Pat Boone—choosing modern venues over Harry's increasingly outdated nightclub model.[c]

---

[c] Shawn's death was as surreal as his comedy. In 1987, during a standup performance, Shawn collapsed face down on stage. The audience at the University of California, San Diego, initially believed it to be part of the act, especially after Shawn had teased "a few unrehearsed surprises" during the show. Tragically, the delay in realizing the seriousness of the situation meant paramedics were not immediately called. Shawn was later pronounced dead at the hospital at the age of 63.

1959—A LONG WINTER

For the first ten weeks of 1959, the doors of the Town Casino stayed shut. The once-glamorous nightclub sat silent, its stage empty, the tables stacked. Altman, ever the optimist, sounded weary. "Business has been bad," he admitted to the press. "Sometimes after the first show is over, there are no more than 25 people in the place."[831] He hated the idea of laying off his staff, some of whom had been with him for more than a quarter-century. "One-hundred thirty people," he said. "They're like family."[832]

By early March, a flicker of Altman's old energy had returned. "It's been a long, hard winter" he told reporters. "I'm going to bring the sun back to Buffalo—at the Town Casino and at Glen Park, too."[833] He had spent the coldest months in Phoenix and noted that even there the nightclub scene had slowed. Still, he sensed a rebound on the horizon. Audiences were coming back to nightclubs across the country; maybe Buffalo would be next.[834]

The Town reopened with a strong lineup: the Ames Brothers, followed by the Three Stooges, Buddy Hackett, Marion Marlowe, Tommy Sands, and the Kingston Trio.[835] Hoping to modernize the club's image and reduce barriers to entry, Altman introduced a new policy: "Dress as you care to!" Gone were the days of tuxedos and evening gowns. Men could now wear sports coats, while women could opt for less formal dresses. The formality that had once defined the Town gave way to something breezier—more like the Glen.

But the glamour days of big-name talent did not last. By May, few of the Town's headliners were household names. Bobby Freeman—billed as "another Johnny Mathis!"—took top billing. Others included Romo Vincent, "the magnificent obstruction" (a self-deprecating reference to his large frame, which he used to comedic effect), and Norman Brooks, known for singing "in the style of Al Jolson." Kathy Linden, a modest chart success, and the comedy duo the Jaye Brothers rounded out the 1958-59 season. It was a barrage of variety—talented but largely unfamiliar acts—offered at bargain prices.

In June, Altman made another bold pivot, extending the Town's season by a month and shifting away from mainstream variety toward more provocative, adult-only fare. He booked *The Jewel Box Revue*, a dazzling and subversive production famously billed as featuring "25 men and one girl."

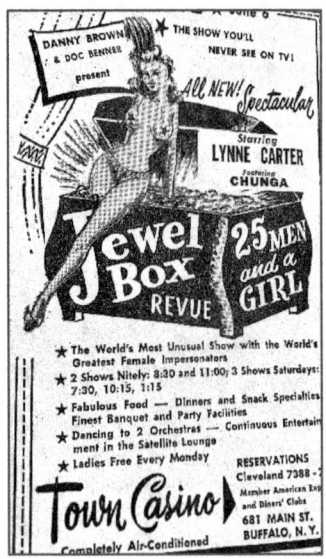

Figure 277 Jewel Box

At its center was Lynne Carter, a renowned female impersonator who had headlined elite nightclubs from Miami Beach to Las Vegas. Sharing the stage was the sultry Chunga, a drag star celebrated for their serpentine grace and lavish costumes. Together, they led a troupe of performers who mastered the art of gender illusion to deliver a show that fused glamour, satire, and musical precision into what was hailed as "the most unique act in show business." The production was a hit, earning an extended run and injecting fresh energy into the Town.

But by mid-July, with the novelty beginning to fade, Altman closed the club and turned to planning the 1959-60 season, opening with crooner Al Martino. The showroom remained active through the fall, though the talent slate leaned modest: comedian Will Jordan; "Buffalo's own singing sensation" Mary Jean Galla; and the patriotic Winged Victory Chorus.

Figure 278 Lynne Carter
in a dress given to them by Josephine Baker
PD

Dinner-and-show packages were heavily marketed, offering a cocktail, full meal, and live entertainment all for just $3 per person. To keep costs low, Altman leaned into multi-act lineups, featuring tumblers like the Seven Sons of Morocco, dance ensembles like the Latin Rhythms, singers such as Ed Dumont, and comedy acts like Hale and Haden.

Marquee names still appeared from time to time—The Four Lads, Morey Amsterdam—but only on weekends. Weeknights were increasingly filled with local performers and budget-friendly variety acts.

In December, desperate to recapture past magic, Altman brought back Eddie Jackson, Jimmy Durante's longtime partner, who had once been a reliable box office draw. For New Year's Eve, he reached even deeper into the nostalgia bag, booking the "Little Godfreys"—Frank Parker, Tony Marvin, and The Mariners, all alums of Arthur Godfrey's once-huge radio show. Altman was relying on the kindness of friends and familiar faces to keep the Town in business.

*Figure 279 Town Casino on the night of Altman's testimonial dinner
Photo courtesy of Brad Altman*

There was one standout event that fall—an undeniable high point in an otherwise uneven season.

On the night of September 13, 1959, nearly 900 civic leaders, entertainers, and admirers packed the Town Casino to pay tribute to Buffalo's premier showman, Harry Altman.[836]

The three-hour celebration, complete with searchlights sweeping the sky, was one of the most elaborate and heartfelt productions of Altman's career. But this time, the spotlight was on him.

The evening's tone was unmistakably sentimental. Comedians Morey Amsterdam and Joey Adams kept the crowd in stitches, but even their wisecracks could not distract from the emotion that underpinned the night. Emcee Lenny Paige guided the program, which was filled with laughter, music, memories and tears.

A pink replica of the Town Casino, made entirely of cake, was wheeled out in Harry's honor.[837] A massive bronze bust of Altman was unveiled. And when the soaring notes of "Ah, Sweet Mystery of Life" filled the room, Harry buried his face in a napkin and wept.[838]

"I miss all my brothers and my mother and my father tonight," he said to the audience. "I'm proud of this crowd that came here tonight. I've made a million dollars' worth of happiness tonight.[839]

In his remarks, Altman deflected praise with humility: "Those things you said about me were probably not really me," he told the audience. "But were the things I tried to do and what I wanted to be."[840]

Figure 315 Direct from the dais: Altman, front center, with (from left) Jackie Bright,
Lenny Paige, Dick Fischer, Morey Amsterdam and Joey Adams
The Buffalo Evening News, September 14, 1959

Proceeds from the $10-a-plate dinner went toward establishing the *Harry Altman Room* at the *American Guild of Variety Artists Home* in Fallsburg, a retirement refuge for performers. It was a gesture of appreciation from the industry he had supported for decades. Comedian Joey Adams, mixing warmth with wit, called Altman "the best showman in any part of the country because he's interested in bringing live entertainment to Buffalo and keeping it here."[841]

Harry had chances to leave; Hollywood offers, including one from longtime friend Sam Goldwyn to try his hand at movie production, had tempted him. But Altman stayed put. "I wanted to stay here," he said, "and do something real."[842]

On that September night in 1959, it appeared clear that he had made a real impact.

Figure 280 Mr. and Mrs. Altman on the night of the testimonial dinner
Photo courtesy of Brad Altman

DICK FISCHER: ALTMAN'S STEADFAST FRIEND

One enduring constant in Harry Altman's life was his friendship with Dick Fischer. United in their devotion to philanthropy and business, Fischer also stood out for his athletic accomplishments, particularly in baseball.

For more than 50 years, Fischer anchored Buffalo's sporting goods trade.[843] He opened his first store in the mid-1930s at 699 Main Street, steps from where Altman built many of his hospitality ventures and less than a block from what would become the Town Casino. Beyond business, Dick scouted major league baseball talent, first for the Brooklyn Dodgers and then the Pittsburgh Pirates.

Figure 281 Fischer's friendship resulted in special baseball moments like this at the Town Casino which hosted a 1958 fundraising dinner for the Damon Runyon Cancer Fund
Photo from left, Altman, Walter Winchell, Roberta Sherwood, Jack O'Brian, Joe DiMaggio and Lee Ann Meriweather (Miss America—1954)
Photo courtesy of Brad Altman

Together, Altman and Fischer became a formidable pair in Buffalo's charitable landscape. They supported the Damon Runyon Cancer Fund, hosted the Lions Club's annual Thanksgiving dinner at the Town Casino, and spearheaded Funorama, where Fischer set a record for ticket sales. He also organized Golden Gloves boxing bouts, raising more than $250,000 for children's toys, and worked alongside Altman on campaigns for the March of Dimes, Courier-Express Goodfellows, and Buffalo State Hospital.

Figure 282 Harry Altman with Dick Fischer
Photo courtesy of Brad Altman

For the Altman and Wallens grandchildren, visits to Fischer's store were magical, an abundance of equipment and sports lore. Fischer's skill as a toastmaster made him the natural choice to chair Altman's 1959 testimonial dinner, a project he had himself proposed. "It's a big job, a lot of work, but I don't mind. I'm glad to help out on a project like this," he remarked. It was Fischer who persuaded Buffalo's business leaders to stage the tribute as a way of saying, "Thank you very much, Mr. Altman...for what you've done for Buffalo."[844]

On behalf of his own personal endeavors, Fischer collected more than 100 awards from civic, charitable, athletic, and business associations. He died in 1983 at age 76.

1960—PIVOT AND PERSEVERE

By the dawn of the new decade, Altman faced a reality no amount of polish could disguise: the Town Casino's once-glittering, 1,000-seat showroom had become more burden than asset. Audiences were harder to impress and even harder to attract. So, Altman did what he had always done best: he improvised.

That winter, Altman jumped at the chance to lease additional space when the storefront next to the Casino became available. He invested $20,000 to convert it into an intimate, 100-seat dining room tailored for a new target: the lunchtime crowd. In the evening, the room could host private events and banquets, an added revenue stream. The move marked a subtle concession: big-name acts and lavish productions were no longer enough to keep the operation afloat.

The early months of 1960 brought little change to the main stage. Revues cycled through, mostly featuring performers who had already made multiple appearances. In February, the club promoted singer Anne Hathaway (no relation to the actress) as a "beautiful song stylist," followed by British circus performer Gene Detroy and his "famous marquis chimpanzee family," advertised as personal friends of Jack Benny.

When it appeared at all, press coverage shifted from promoting upcoming headliners to highlighting the scale and prestige of the banquet bookings.

As Lent approached, the Town entered what had become part of its seasonal rhythm—a forty-day shutdown. The pause gave Altman time to regroup, while Buffalo's predominantly Catholic population observed the season through abstinence from entertainment and other worldly indulgences. When the club opened after Easter, Harry came back swinging.

The spring lineup exploded with top-shelf talent: Connie Francis, Bobby Darin, Paul Anka, and the Ames Brothers, all taking the stage in rapid succession. For a few fleeting weeks, it felt like old times. The seats were full, the energy high, and Altman's confidence was restored. Big names came roaring back that fall. Those gracing the stage included Della Reese, Tony Bennett, Alan King, the Crosby Brothers (Dennis, Phil, and Lindsay), the Kirby Stone Four, Andy Williams (complete with a 23-piece orchestra), Joey Bishop, Connie Francis (again), and Bobby Darin. The roster read like a who's who of mid-century American entertainment.

Harry also doubled down on reinvention, launching a full remodel of the cocktail lounge. It reopened as the Basin Street Room, a tribute to New Orleans jazz culture. Eli Konikoff and his Yankee Six christened the space, followed by acts like The Salt City Six and smooth-voiced crooner Buddy Greco. The strategy was clear: intimate, curated spaces could still draw loyal niche audiences independent of the main showroom.

The remodeled storefront took on a new identity, too. No longer just a dining space, it was rechristened Harry's Melody Lane, decked out in a Gay '90s theme and promoting its "soft lights and great sounds." Buffalo's own Ruth Opler, celebrated as "the city's most beautiful folk singer," opened the venue with a multilingual setlist that ranged from American ballads to Israeli and Spanish songs.[845]

New Year's Eve closed the year on a bittersweet note. Headlining was Frankie Scott, a wiry comic from Western New York once described by University at Buffalo's *The Spectrum* newspaper as looking "undernourished." He was not a big star—but he was local, dependable, and within budget. His appearance reflected Altman's new reality: the Casino could still deliver moments of sparkle, but only through careful, strategic choices. A splashy one-night event no longer justified the cost, especially compared to the value of week-long bookings with reliable talent.

1961—HOLDING THE LINE

The year opened quietly. After the modest success of his fall lineup, Harry Altman again closed the Town Casino for a brief two-week winter reset. When it reopened, it was with a safe, if uninspired, offering: a generically named New York Revue starring familiar favorite Enzo Stuarti. He was followed by a throwback vaudeville bill headlined by Neil Darrow—entertaining, competent, but far from the kind of firepower needed to reignite the club's old magic.

The Basin Street Room had found its groove. Eli Konikoff, whose Yankee Six had opened the space the previous fall, was now a steady presence.

The club entered its now-customary Lenten closure from early February through mid-March. Altman, ever restless, used the break to scout talent on a "western tour in search of topflight talent."[846] He returned with names he believed would "boost Buffalo."[847] Among those booked for the spring were Roberta Sherwood, Pat Harrington, Dario Cassini, Morey Amsterdam, LaVern Baker, and Phyllis Diller.

Diller's appearance, meant to be a highlight, spiraled into a PR disaster (see page 206) when she poked fun at both the City of Buffalo and the Town Casino. For Altman, the remarks hit hard. He had spent years obsessively refining the venue, often investing in lavish upgrades that defied logic. But Diller, famous for her biting wit, had said aloud what insiders were beginning to whisper: the Town's luster was fading.

FALL 1961-SPRING 1962—THE LONG FADE

By the fall of 1961, Harry Altman was still chasing the right formula. The Town Casino remained open, still booking acts, still offering dinners, still giving the appearance of continuity, but attendance continued to drop. What had once been the crown jewel of Buffalo nightlife now flickered dimly at the edge of relevance, its momentum stalled.

Programming followed a familiar, increasingly predictable rhythm. Safe, family-friendly names headlined on weekends. Budget acts filled in the weekdays. Banquets and private parties kept the lights on. There were flashes of vitality—brief sparks that reminded loyal patrons of what the Town had been. Tap legend Eleanor Powell came through on her comeback tour. Enzo Stuarti, a perennial favorite, earned his usual applause. Andy Williams performed for a week, followed by Myron Cohen, the comedian from Grodno, the Altman's' hometown. Chubby Checker brought the Twist craze to the big stage, and the Crosby Sisters closed out the year with a holiday revue that ushered in the New Year with old-school sparkle.

The Basin Street Room remained steady, if subdued, under the direction of Eli Konikoff's jazz ensemble.

Younger audiences still were not coming downtown for weekday nightclub entertainment; instead, they made their appearance on the weekends for the Twist Sessions. For a few hours each week, the ballroom pulsed with youth and possibility as local bands played to clean-cut teenagers in saddle shoes and suits. Older patrons, meanwhile, were tiring of recycled lineups. Even the cocktail-and-dinner crowd, once the financial backbone of the club, was thinning. Across the country, industry was changing. Audiences were trading supper clubs for television sets. Entertainment shifted to suburban lounges with free parking and no cover charges.

On New Year's Day 1962, Altman announced that the Town Casino would close "until further notice." Just five days later, he walked back the uncertainty, telling reporters he was heading to Arizona for a six-week break. The Town would reopen in March, he added, if only because he had already booked Bobby Darin and Joanie Sommers for the spring.[848] The future appeared far from secure. He acknowledged that the club might never return to being a full-scale nightclub. The Glen Casino, with its seasonal crowds and lower overhead, was starting to look like his more sustainable option.

When the Town reopened in March, Altman was in for a surprise: the first night was a sellout. The Winged Victory Chorus shared the bill with Bob Arlen's dancers, delivering a grand and patriotic kickoff. The Basin Street Lounge was rebranded The Casino Club and debuted the Five Jets, marking their first Buffalo appearance. Bobby Darin followed the next week, then the Kirby Stone Four. Altman promised more to come—names like Sammy Davis Jr, Al Martino, and Jackie Mason were "soon to be scheduled."

But before those bookings could materialize, fate intervened.

A single bolt of lightning would bring the nightclub to a stop.

THE FIRE AT ST. MICHAEL'S

Figure 283 St. Michael's Church Fire
Photo courtesy of The Archives & Special Collection
Department of SUNY Buffalo State

On May 23, 1962, a powerful lightning storm struck Buffalo. A bolt hit St. Michael's Church, the 98-year-old Jesuit parish directly across from the Town. Flames tore through the sanctuary in a five-alarm fire, reducing much of the historic structure to charred ruins.

Within hours, Altman stepped forward.

Despite his own struggles, Altman, described in charity circles as a true "mensch," offered the full use of his nightclub to the displaced congregation. "Two or three years if they need it," he said. "The church is more important to the community than my nightclub." [849]

The newspapers made a point of noting that Altman was Jewish, a detail offered with more emphasis than necessary. But labels aside, his gesture was both generous and shrewd. In extending compassion, he also secured goodwill, crafting a moment that would become one of the most enduring and defining stories of his career.

Figure 284 The first mass after the fire at the Town Casino
Photo courtesy of The Archives & Special Collection
Department of SUNY Buffalo State

At the time of the fire, nightclub operations had already been moved to the Glen for the summer season. While the church was being rebuilt, Altman said the Glen would be open year-round.

The transition from nightclub to worship space took one overnight session. Following a private party of 500 persons at the casino Saturday, Altman said the building was "closed up at midnight" so that Casino workmen could "get the place in shape...in time for 6 a.m. Mass."[850]

Removing the tables allowed for use of the building by 1,000 parishioners, about 400 less than the church's capacity.[851] During that first Sunday, eight Masses were held in the "plush, air-conditioned club." One mass was also held every other day of the week.[852]

Praise for this selfless act appeared in the national press, spread by the wire services, and resulted in Altman becoming a hero of sorts. Jerry Evarts, a columnist for *The Buffalo Courier-Express*, reported in June 1962 that Altman had already received nearly 200 letters from as far away as Japan and Tel Aviv "congratulating him upon the benevolent action."[853] His generosity earned him the honor of serving as the grand marshal for Sattler's Santa Claus Parade in November.

But it takes time to rebuild a church, and Altman, despite his generous initial offering, was becoming impatient.

Figure 285 Preparing to repair the altar
Photo courtesy of The Archives & Special
Collection Department of SUNY
Buffalo State

Six months after the fire, Altman groused to *The Buffalo Courier-Express*: "We did not think they would need the place that long, but they're still there. So, we are trying to operate without our downtown location."[854]

To ease Harry's concerns, Rev. James J. Redmond, SJ, pastor of St. Michael's, announced that he had reached an agreement with Altman to vacate the Casino by September 15, 1963.[855]

Redmond also made it known in February 1963 that Altman's benevolence had an expiration date: The rent-free offer extended for only five months. Starting in September 1962 the church was paying $1,500 a month for use of the Casino. The cost of utilities, he said, had always been paid for by the church.[856]

The rental agreement was disclosed in the church's 1962 financial report, Redmond said, because there have been "some misrepresentations of our status in the Town Casino."[857]

"From the very start, the impression was that we were here by the goodwill of the casino owner," Redmond stated. "Of course, [Altman] has his expenses. We sat down and talked things over and agreed on a contract. I think it is better now for both sides that the truth be known."[858]

After a flurry of last-minute efforts to meet the deadline, masses resumed at the newly restored St. Michael's Church on September 12, 1963, coinciding with the Feast of the Holy Name of Mary. The very next day, Harry welcomed 1,000 luncheon guests from Ford Motor Company, showcasing its 1964 vehicle lineup. [859]

"It's all spick-and-span," Altman remarked proudly about the Casino in preparation for the event.[860]

1964—ALL THAT JAZZ

To kick off the new year in 1964, Harry Altman launched one of his boldest late-career ventures: the debut of the "New and Beautiful" Jazz City Lounge.[861] The lounge would replace the Casino Room, creating a space devoted entirely to top-tier jazz. The grand opening on New Year's Day featured none other than Miles Davis and his Quintet, alongside saxophonist Don "Red" Menza. There were three nightly shows at 9:30 p.m., 11:45 p.m., and 1:45 a.m., with Sunday matinees at 3 and 6 p.m.—a full schedule designed to keep the energy alive.

Throughout January, Altman doubled down on the format, booking a steady stream of legends: Maynard Ferguson, Count Basie, Dizzy Gillespie and his band, and vocalist Gloria Lynne. Meanwhile, the main room of the Casino was repurposed for dancing every Friday and Saturday, featuring the Jazz City Five and the Vibratos. On those weekends, the building echoed with music from four separate ensembles, playing across the club's two main spaces.

To attract younger audiences, Altman offered a free bus service from the University at Buffalo, and served dinners in the show bar lounge. The entry price was modest: a $1.50 entertainment charge, with no cover and no drink minimum. It was a generous offer, considering the caliber of talent on stage.

Despite Altman's persistent initiatives to integrate live music throughout the venue and implement creative programming to attract a diverse audience, the momentum was diminishing. The jazz series, while critically praised and beloved by a loyal niche following, failed to generate the consistent revenue needed to keep the lights on. The numbers simply did not add up.

Figure 286 Jazz City ad

In a final, almost defiant bid to stay afloat, or perhaps just to squeeze out whatever money remained in patrons pockets, Altman rebranded the Jazz City Lounge once more. Gone was the refined allure of syncopated rhythms and smoky vocals; in its place, he unveiled the Persian Lounge, a venue now featuring exotic dancers to capture a different kind of clientele.[862]

Figure 287 Persian Room ad

Figure 288 The last marquee under the Town Casino banner
Photo courtesy of The Archives & Special Collection
Department of SUNY Buffalo State

The pivot marked a stark departure from the club's golden years, an unmistakable sign that the glamour of Buffalo's night club era was at its end. By January 1965, after a half-decade of trial and error, Altman surrendered to the inevitable. He announced that the Town Casino would be converted into a banquet hall, a last-ditch effort to salvage a once-glittering institution that had lost $75,000 in just six months.[863] The main showroom would now open only on weekends or for private events.[864] Rising costs for top-tier entertainers and their musicians, he explained, had become impossible to sustain. The bar and cocktail lounge would remain under the current policy, but the golden era of the Town Casino—the era of Rat Pack glamour and sold-out supper shows—was drawing to a quiet, elegiac close.

In June 1965, Altman announced that he was prepared to sell the Town Casino.[865] According to *The Buffalo Courier-Express*, the nightclub impresario had tried nearly everything since St. Michael's parishioners vacated the space in 1963: big bands, jazz legends, burlesque, even teen twist parties. But nothing worked. "He closed the showplace five weeks ago," the paper reported, "with a dying final twist band attraction for teenagers."[866]

Altman did not blame Buffalo. He blamed the changing world. "TV is the monster," he said. "Let's face it—you can sit home with your wife or sweetheart, drink beer, and take your choice of great shows, and it costs you nothing for the show."[867] Beyond the economics, Altman added a personal note: "I'm getting to the age where I'd like to take it a little easy."[868] He was 74.

The asking price for the Casino was $200,000 which included the expansive 19,500 square-foot venue complete with kitchen, bar, tables, and chairs.[869] Altman said there had been a few "nibbles," but no firm offers.[870] The Glen Casino in Williamsville would continue operating, he assured the press. But for the Town, the lights were dimming for good.

SALE OF THE BUILDING TO STUDIO ARENA

In June 1965, a buyer stepped forward. Welles V. Moot Jr., president of the board of trustees for Studio Theater, announced that the theater would buy the building pending final paperwork.[871] The sale price was reported as $175,000, with plans to convert the space into a 550-seat theater and drama school.[872] A bar would remain in the foyer if the State allowed.[873]

Figure 289 The Town Casino transforms into Studio Arena
Photos courtesy of The Archives & Special Collection Department of SUNY Buffalo State

"When Altman hung a 'For Sale' sign in the casino window," *The Buffalo Courier-Express* noted, "he told us, 'It breaks my heart to sell, but that's the nightclub business.'"[874] Still, even as he passed the torch, Harry had one more dream: to build a year-round, 3,000-seat auditorium in the suburbs to rival Melody Fair. "I want to do that before I die," he said. He had already begun speaking with contractors about cost and location.[875]

But that final dream never came to pass.

The Town Casino building, which had once pulsed with the energy of jazz, swing, and the glimmer of spotlights, now prepared for a quieter role—home to the dramatic arts. The Town Casino era was over.

CHAPTER 22—ALTMAN'S LAST YEARS AT THE GLEN

Altman built his nightclub career booking vaudeville and variety acts, showcasing everything from big band and jazz orchestras to classic crooners and the popular tunes of the 1940s and '50s. His annual talent-scouting trips out West often paid off; he had a knack for signing future headliners long before they reached stardom.

During the 1960 season, Altman followed a well-worn booking strategy: mixing dependable box-office names from the past with current pop stars and seasoned Borscht Belt acts. That year alone, the Glen hosted Sammy Davis Jr (who arrived with his trademark Colt pistol),[a][876] Frankie Avalon, The Vagabonds, Rip Taylor, Bobby Darin, The Ames Brothers, Paul Anka, Andy Williams, Johnny Nash, the comic Frankie Scott, and Hollywood duo Linda Darnell and Tom Hayward. The results were not always what he hoped. In particular, Altman expressed disappointment over the lackluster turnout for Andy Williams. In an April 1967 column, Jack Allen recounted overhearing a lunch conversation between Altman and Williams following a sparse opening night.[877]

"I made a mistake," Harry admitted. "It costs $7,500 to have you here for a week, plus $2,500 for the band, and last night the waiters outnumbered the crowd."

Williams, then a staple of television variety shows, reportedly shrugged and replied, "They can see me free on TV. So, what else is new?"[878]

In response to the growing impact of television on live entertainment, Altman broadened his lineup in 1961 to appeal to a more diverse audience. That year's slate included Connie Francis, Bobby Rydell, Dick Gregory, Conway Twitty, Napoleon Reed, Brenda Lee, Neil Sedaka, Chubby Checker, Jack Carter, Dion, Jackie Mason, Al Martino, The Mills Brothers, Paul Anka, and Enzo Stuarti.

The 1962-1963 season brought a major shift. That was the year of the St. Michael's Church fire and Altman's loaning of the Town to its congregation. The Glen, under Altman's management, rose to meet the moment. He increased talent budgets and extended the Glen's performance season. The roster that year featured marquee names such as Jackie Mason, Bobby Darin, Jerry Vale, Sammy Davis Jr,

---

a Sammy's .45-caliber Colt single-action revolver, used in his fast-draw routine during performances, was stolen from the Glen Casino dressing room that year. The Western-style six-shooter was part of a specially engraved matched set gifted to him by the president of Colt Firearms. Whether it was ever recovered is not publicly known.

Betty Johnson, Joanie Sommers, Jack Jones, Al Martino, The Ink Spots, The Smothers Brothers,[b] Morey Amsterdam, and Jayne Mansfield (see page 227).

Altman briefly tested the folk music wave sweeping the nation, branding the experiment a "hootenanny."[879] In August 1963, he booked the Wayfarers, a clean-cut American folk-pop quartet modeled after the Kingston Trio. With polished harmonies and a collegiate stage presence, the group posed no threat to the Glen Casino's core crowd of crooner devotees.[880] Although the Wayfarers would release three modest RCA albums before disbanding within two years, their Glen appearance earned praise. *The Buffalo Evening News* quoted one older patron who nudged his companion and said, "These boys have got it."[881] The group drew warm applause and Altman's endorsement: "They'll be as big as the Smothers Brothers," he declared.[882]

Figure 290 The Eric Andersen Singers,
Glen Park, August 1963
Photo courtesy of The Amherst Bee

The Wayfarers' brief success at the Glen Casino encouraged Harry Altman to try again a week later, this time featuring a local group from Amherst High School led by a young Eric Andersen in his first public appearance. Billed as The Eric Andersen Singers, the group included Andersen, Marilyn Schanzer, Bob Killheffer, and Ev Nienhouse.[883]

They shared the stage with comic George Kirby and pop-jazz vocalist Gene Stridel. Andersen would go on to become one of the most quietly influential figures of the American folk revival. Shortly after leaving Buffalo, he immersed himself in the Greenwich Village scene, where he earned comparisons to Bob Dylan and Joan Baez and built a reputation as one of the era's most compelling songwriters.[884] His 1972 album *Blue River* remains a landmark of the singer-songwriter genre.

In 2012, while visiting Western New York from his home in Norway, *The Buffalo News* interviewed Andersen about a forthcoming documentary on his life titled *The Songpoet*[885]

---

[b] It is worth noting that the performances by the Smothers Brothers, Dick Gregory, and Jackie Mason at the Glen took place years before they became known for the provocative and controversial material that would later define their careers.

"Harry Altman was a smart businessman," Andersen recalled of that first gig. "He listened to me and smelled money. I made enough [from the Glen show] to hitch to California and see the scene and meet the beats—[Allen] Ginsberg and all these people—and it was all from a hootenanny in Williamsville."[886]

Harry continued to book national acts, though with fewer embellishments. Gone were the elaborate three-hour spectacles filled with acrobats and animal acts. In their place were lean, 90-minute shows, typically a main act and an opener. That season began with the Mills Brothers and continued with Joi Lansing, Jerry Vale, Cab Calloway, Enzo Stuarti, The Smothers Brothers, Sergio Franchi, Alberto Rochi, Al Martino, Helen O'Connell (a former Dorsey songstress), Wayne Newton & the Newton Brothers, The Ames Brothers, and Angelo Picardi with Ken Barry.

The final curtain on Altman's classic Glen Casino era fell with a performance by the Buffalo Bills Quartet.[887] Hometown heroes in the barbershop world, the group had already earned national acclaim for their polished harmonies and their starring role in *The Music Man* on Broadway and in the 1962 film adaptation. Their appearance marked more than just the end of a season; it symbolized the close of a golden age of live entertainment at the Glen. By 1965, the venue shifted to generic "All-Star Revues" featuring lesser-known acts, a sign that the once-grand traditions were giving way to a new, less personal era in show business.

Figure 291 Eric Andersen during his commercially successful years
PD

TWIST SESSIONS

The post-war baby boom unleashed a generation of teenagers brimming with energy, autonomy, and unprecedented spending power. It was an audience that would soon redefine American live entertainment. Ever alert to changing tastes, Altman recognized that "the younger set," as he fondly referred to them, was drifting away from the familiar charms of Rat Pack crooners and Borscht Belt comedians. Rock 'n' roll was no longer a fad; it was the future. With cautious curiosity, Altman began to adapt.

In the summer of 1961, he teamed with the Williamsville Chamber of Commerce to host record hops at the Glen Barn, then operating as the Family Inn.[888] These events provided teens a safe, supervised place to dance and enjoy pop music. With only soft drinks on offer, they were designed to be parent-approved alternatives to the rougher edges of youth culture.

By 1962, Altman parted ways with the Chamber and assumed full control of youth programming. He launched his own "Special Twist Sessions,"[889] which featured live music from rising local bands rather than just a DJ. Among those booked were Raven (also known as The Rising Sons) who would later become the house band at the Inferno nightclub, and the Vibratos, a group Altman had first backed at the Town Casino. He called the Vibratos "a fine a group as you'll hear nationally or internationally,"[c] a bold claim for a band that had started as a garage act on Buffalo's East Side, founded by brothers Dick and Jack Terranova.[890]

★★★★★★★★★★★★★★★★★★★★★★★
For the Young Set
SPECIAL TWIST SESSIONS
Fri. 8-12 ★ Sun. 2-6
with the
VIBRATOS
and Special Guest Star
WAYNE NEWTON
99c Admission — No Alcoholic Bev. Served
GLEN PARK FAMILY INN
★★★★ Williamsville, N.Y. ★★★★

Figure 292 Wayne Newton

The Vibratos drew crowds of 2,000 to 3,000 teens for Sunday matinees at the Glen, prompting Altman to run free round-trip buses from neighborhoods across Buffalo. As noted by Bob Paxon, Buffalo music historian, though the group never broke through on a national scale, but their two singles and magnetic performances

---

[c] Dick Terranova, leader of the Vibratos, recalled the group's mutual fondness for performing for Altman. In a *Buffalo Evening News* article dated May 5, 1973 ("Raven Changes its Musical Feathers," p75), he reflected: "When the Vibratos were at the Glen and the Town Casinos, we had people approach us for going out on the road, but we were never interested. We were having fun at the Glen. We had just an unbelievable amount of fun."

Al Fiorella, Dick Terranova, Jack Terranova, Chickie Cicero, Gary Mallaber

Figure 293 The Vibratos

helped launch the careers of several future stars. Initially an instrumental rock 'n' roll band with a guitar-driven sound, they evolved into a vocal group with the addition of singer Kenny Dee, allowing them to deliver everything from slow dances to up-tempo R&B.[891]

The band's lineup became a veritable Who's Who of Western New York's musical talent. Alongside the Terranova brothers were Joe Rogowski on drums, Mike Lustan on guitar, Kenny Dee on vocals, saxophonist Gordy Conklin, and Emil Lewandowski, later known to the world as Cory Wells of Three Dog Night. During one of many lineup shifts, they recruited a teenage drummer named Gary Mallaber, who would go on to perform with Stan & The Ravens, then Raven, and ultimately reach global stages with Steve Miller, Van Morrison, and others.[892] Saxophonist Chic Cicero later formed his own act, Chic and The Diplomats, before gaining a very different kind of notoriety as a prominent figure in the esoteric world of the Hermetic Order of the Golden Dawn, focused on the study and practice of the occult, metaphysics, and ceremonial magic.[893]

Encouraged by the teens' respectful behavior and their adherence to a dress code, Altman leaned further into teen programming. In February 1964, riding the first wave of Beatlemania, he partnered with a promoter to stage a publicity stunt: a search for four young women who could pass as a female version of the Fab Four. Dubbed The Beatletts, the contest began with open auditions at the Town Casino, where admission cost 99 cents.[894] Winners were crowned during a Glen Twist Session and awarded a $100 cash prize. They shared the stage with the Vibratos at several events before disappearing back into the pop-culture ether—one of many passing novelties sparked by the British Invasion.[895]

Ironically, it was the success of the Twist Sessions that led to the Vibratos' departure from the Glen. By 1965, Altman had turned his attention back to reviving business at the Town Casino. He relocated the Twist Sessions downtown, where larger crowds and higher ticket sales could boost revenue.[896] The new format featured three rotating bands at a bargain admission price. But when the Town was ultimately sold to Studio Arena Theatre, the sessions ended for good. They were never resumed at the Glen as Altman's son-in-law David Goldstein had his own vision for teen entertainment: he opened Club Commodore on Genesee Street on Buffalo's far east side, ushering in the next chapter of Buffalo's youth scene.

SALE OF THE GLEN: SPORTSERVICE & LOUIS JACOBS

"Secrets die with the people who keep them."

~ Rebecca Yarros, *American novelist*

By 1965, the sale of the Town Casino to the Studio Arena had transformed Altman's nightlife empire, leaving the Glen Casino as its last standing pillar. Throughout his career, Harry had masterfully curated top-tier entertainment, but as the years passed, he observed a shift in audience behavior. More and more, people chose the comfort of their living rooms, captivated by television broadcasts featuring performers who once headlined in Harry's nightclubs. Moreover, the beloved melodies of the American Songbook were fading, replaced by the bold beats of rock 'n' roll, a change he found difficult to embrace.

Bob Sokolsky, *The Buffalo Courier-Express* entertainment reporter, wrote in Altman's eulogy: "If there is any consolation to be found from Harry's passing, it was that it came in a new show business era that he detested and did not want to understand."[897]

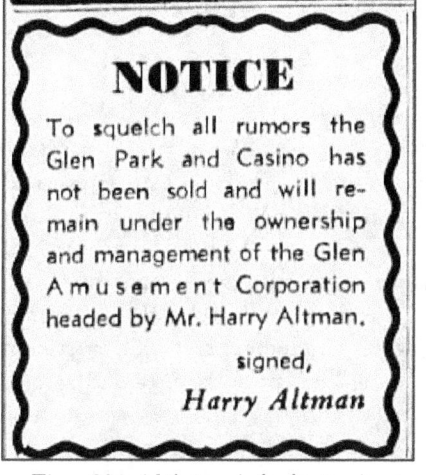

Figure 294 Ad that ran in local papers in April 1965

Behind the scenes, Harry quietly searched for a buyer for the Glen, while publicly downplaying rumors of a sale to avoid undermining the venue's appeal.

Before long, a significant potential buyer emerged.[898] In November 1965, *The Buffalo Evening News* reported that the sale of the Glen to Sportservice Inc. was in its final stages, although "the financial arrangements of the agreement" were not released.[899] A Sportservice spokesman stated that the company would handle all the "administrative functions for Glen Amusement Corp.," while Altman would serve under a 10-year management agreement. At the conclusion of the decade-long period, Sportservice would take possession of the real estate.[d]

---

[d] If reported accurately by *The Buffalo Evening News*, the arrangement meant that Sportservice would operationally take immediate control of Glen Amusement Corp., which owned all above-ground assets at the park. Public records from the period suggest that Emprise (the parent company) assumed control of all the corporations involved with the property in late July 1968, just days before Louis Jacobs died on August 6, 1968 and two years after Altman's death. "Deeds," *Buffalo Daily Law Journal*, August 2, 1968, 3.

At the helm of the conglomerate poised to assume control of Glen Park was Louis M. Jacobs, son of Russian immigrants, who had risen from the city's Jewish East Side to achieve international stature as a trailblazer in the foodservice industry. Since the mid-1930s, Jacobs had led Sportservice,[900] transforming it into a dominant force in concessions and venue management. Today, the company is known as Delaware North—a multi-billion-dollar enterprise still privately owned by the Jacobs family and headquartered in downtown Buffalo.

Altman's decision to sell the Town Casino, soon followed by a management agreement for the Glen, reflected more than just a response to the fading fortunes of the nightclub industry. Though the business was clearly in decline, a deeper and more private reason underpinned his choices: a diagnosis of stomach cancer that cast a quiet but undeniable shadow over his final years. Altman, recognizing his time was limited, was taking the necessary steps to put his affairs in order.

Figure 295 Louis M. Jacobs
PD

Providing for his wife, Annabelle, was a practical priority in Altman's final plans. Married since 1919, she had been a constant presence throughout his long and often complicated public life. Though theirs was not a simple partnership, Altman took seriously his responsibility to ensure she would be financially secure after his passing. Aware of her intention to relocate to Arizona to be closer to their children, Bob and Natalie, he made the necessary arrangements to support that transition and safeguard her future. It was during this period of planning and reflection that Altman's long-running relationship with Louis Jacobs took on new relevance.

For more than 20 years, Altman and Jacobs conducted their businesses mere steps apart on Main Street (681 and 703, respectively). They shared many similarities. Both men were the youngest sons in large Jewish Orthodox families that had immigrated from the Russian Pale of Settlement in 1888. Despite facing personal bankruptcies during the Depression,[901] both rebounded to achieve significant success in their respective industries. Character-wise, they both embodied the tireless entrepreneur archetype, with their keen business instincts sharpened by relentless real-world challenges. Their intense work ethics were also mirrored in their fiery tempers. In a *New York Times* article reflecting on the family's legacy, Louis's son, Dr. Lawrence Jacobs, recalled that his father, when provoked, "had a temper that terrified people."[902]

Bob Sokolsky, in his posthumous tribute to Altman, described Altman as follows:

> *"Demanding, frequently irascible, often abrupt, Harry was not the most beloved figure in the entertainment industry. His rages were monumental and had to be seen to be believed. He ruled with an iron fist in his heyday and those who crossed him— whether that crossing be a comic telling an off-color joke on stage or a waiter not carrying out his duties in the precise form— generally lived to regret It. Yet, those who were privileged to call Harry a friend never had a better ally in any walk of life."*[903]

Their differences were equally striking. Harry relished the local celebrity that came with being a prominent impresario: basking in the spotlight, dressing with flair, and drawing regular media attention for both his business ventures and social appearances. Louis, by contrast, preferred the quiet seclusion of his modest office at 703 Main Street, where he worked across time zones, negotiating deals late into the night with relentless focus. Jacobs seemed far more energized by the intensity of high-stakes transactions than by any desire for public recognition. As *Sports Illustrated* observed, Jacobs had little tolerance for overindulgence:

"His wardrobe consisted of 10 dark suits, each with two pairs of pants, purchased in a bunch once every 10 years. He never had a personal bank account. He did not take vacation trips to Europe. He did not own a summer place. 'The same sun shines in Buffalo,' he said."[904]

Jacobs never courted attention.

As *The Buffalo Evening News* noted in his obituary: "Certainly Mr. Jacobs ranks among the most successful Buffalo businessmen of all time, but little was known about him in the city's business and financial community." He "rarely discussed the Sportservice empire in public and lived much of his later life in a self-imposed isolation."[905]

The motivations behind Jacobs's decision to purchase the above-ground assets of the Glen Park property from Altman in 1965 are unclear. While Harry had many investors over the years, Jacobs' involvement stands out, not only due to his excessive wealth but because the 11-acre entertainment destination in suburban Williamsville could be seen as a questionable investment. It was vulnerable to the same market conditions that had negatively impacted the Town Casino, with attendance at the Glen Casino precipitously falling by the time the deal was signed. In addition, the Glen property did not align well with Sportservice's core business of large-scale catering and concessionaire management.

Jacobs was widely regarded as a pragmatist, a man known for making calculated business decisions rather than sentimental ones. His acquisition of the Glen Park property in 1965, then, raises intriguing questions. Jacobs was not one to invest in faltering ventures, and by the mid-1960s, Glen Park was showing signs of significant decline. Jacobs must have understood the central role Harry played in keeping the operation running. But was he aware, at the time of the deal, that Altman was seriously ill?

The implications are complex. If Jacobs knew Altman was nearing the end of his life, what future did he envision for the Glen Casino without its guiding force? Did Jacob see untapped value in the property itself, approaching the deal as a real estate investment rather than an entertainment venture? Or did he imagine reviving the park with a new vision? One possibility remains difficult to dismiss: was Jacobs, known for his discretion, already involved behind the scenes, his name deliberately absent from corporate records, hidden behind proxies? Or was he acquiring the property from another undisclosed stakeholder, similarly shielded from public view?

A trace of that ambiguity surfaces in a 1995 letter from Janice Hochreiter, a public affairs administrator for Delaware North. Responding to an inquiry about ownership of the Glen carousel[906] which was sold when the amusement park was closed. Hochreiter admitted she was "surprised" to learn that the company had any early connection to Glen Park. She had been told, somewhat vaguely, that Emprise (Delaware North's corporate predecessor) had purchased "part of Glen Park" in the "late 1940s or early 1950s." Her summary of the event was equally nebulous: "We did not own it for long before the interests were again sold.[907]

Tracking the evolution of the Jacobs family's business empire can be a complex task. Delaware North traces its origins to Jacobs Brothers, Inc., a Buffalo-based concession company founded in the early 20th century. As the business expanded into sports venues, it became known as Sportservice, establishing a national reputation as a pioneer in stadium concessions. In 1961, Jacobs created the holding company Emprise Corp. that reflected his broader ambitions. Following regulatory scrutiny of Emprise, the company was dissolved in 1978 and in its place Delaware North emerged, signaling a fresh identity. Today, Delaware North oversees hundreds of subsidiaries across a wide range of industries, with Sportservice remaining a core division that manages food and retail operations at major sports venues across the country.[908]

More recent efforts to confirm any early ties between Jacobs's business empire and Glen Park have yielded no definitive results. The paper trail, if it ever existed, has long since gone cold.[e]

When integrating the Glen under his umbrella of businesses under Emprise in 1965, Jacobs chose one of its existing corporate subsidiaries, Civic Enterprises, Inc.,[f] renaming it Grove Caterers, Inc. Grove Caterers was in existence for only four years before Jacobs died in 1968 of a heart attack while working at his desk. At the time

---

[e] Attempts to obtain information from Delaware North were unsuccessful.

[f] Civic Enterprises was originally a company that was incorporated by Jacobs to manage ice shows in municipal arenas. Jacobs had essentially "invented" the concept of ice shows to fill auditoriums with hungry and thirsty patrons who could purchase their food and drink.

of his passing, the Glen Casino had been leased to David Goldstein, and converted to the Inferno rock n' roll nightclub.

It would now be up to Jacobs' sons, the heirs to his business, to guide the Glen. Just six weeks after Jacobs's death, the Inferno, the former home of the legendary Glen Casino, burned to the ground in one of the largest fires in Erie County history.[g]

As for the relationship between Altman and Jacobs, we can piece together a few key facts. The two men had known each other since at least the 1920s, having run parallel businesses at many of the same venues. Jacobs Brothers, the company founded in 1915 by Louis and his brothers Marvin and Charles, held the concession contract for the Broadway Auditorium during the period when Altman was staging his Mardi Gras carnivals and boxing matches there. In the years that followed, their paths continued to cross, most notably during the annual Funorama events held at Offerman Stadium, where Jacobs provided concession services.[h]

Figure 296 Billboard ad

A 1947 *Billboard* magazine advertisement demonstrated that Sportservice was actively prospecting for concession business in the amusement park industry.

When this advertisement was published, the Glen "amusement park" was still in its infancy with only a few vendor-owned rides and games as entertainment attractions. But by July 1954, Sportservice seemed to have gained a foothold in the industry, as evidenced by its incorporation of Diversified Enterprises.[i] This new company served as an umbrella organization for its "general amusement" ventures, including amusement parks.

Interestingly, 1954 was also the year Altman initiated major expansion efforts at the Glen. This included demolishing Clyde Urban's creek-side home on the property, constructing new public restrooms, extensively renovating the Casino's exterior, and installing numerous mechanical amusement rides.

The financing for these expansions could have been sourced from revenue of the Glen Casinos, or perhaps it was the result of Sportservice's

---

[g] According to Erie County records, Emprise would secure the property ownership of Glen Park just days prior to Jacobs' passing.

[h] Jacobs' company also managed Offerman Stadium, home of the Bison Baseball and donated its use for the Funorama.

[i] Grove Caterers (1965) fka Civic Enterprises (1958) fka Diversified Enterprises (1954).

investment as alluded to by Delaware North's public affairs administrator. Or something else altogether.

But perhaps the most critical connection shared by Altman and Jacobs was their alleged ties to organized crime. Harry was beholden to the Magaddino crew, hosting mob members at his nightclubs and purchasing liquor, linen and other sundries from mob-owned businesses. Louis's associations with organized crime remained concealed from the public until he made a notable investment with two prominent mob leaders involved in the construction of a Las Vegas hotel.[909]

While allegations of organized crime involvement have long surrounded Altman, similar scrutiny was directed at Jacobs. In the early 1970s, national publications, including *Sports Illustrated,* Wall *Street Journal,* and *The New York Times* published detailed investigations into Jacobs' business activities and alleged ties to criminal syndicates.

In 1972, five years after Louis's death, Emprise was federally convicted of conspiracy and interstate transportation in aid of racketeering.[910] The charges stemmed from the company's role in helping businessmen with ties to organized crime conceal their ownership of the Frontier Hotel and Casino in Las Vegas.[911] Due to the alleged sins of the father, a significant burden was placed on his successors, most notably his son Jeremy, to navigate the ensuing legal and public relations challenges.

In the years that followed the conviction, company leaders worked to reshape the corporate narrative, changing the name, rebranding the business, and crafting a new public identity.

Although public records do not definitively confirm joint investments between Jacobs and Altman during the 1940s and 1950s, their lives converged dramatically in their final years with the sale of the Glen. This transaction unfolded publicly amidst a backdrop of burning buildings and swirling rumors, marking a poignant final chapter in their storied careers.

CHAPTER 23—END OF THE ALTMAN ERA

From the moment he produced his first Mardi Gras parade and carnival in 1912, Harry Altman was chasing spectacle. For more than five decades, he carved out a career in show business not by standing still, but by staying in step with the rhythms of a restless nation.

There were ups and downs brought on by history's long march: World War I, the Spanish Flu, the free-spending twenties, Prohibition, Depression, war again. There were new fads and fleeting fancies—jazz came and went and came again. There were blues singers, torch singers, sweet music, hot music. And through it all, Altman stayed the course. He pivoted from one genre to the next with a producer's intuition and a gambler's nerve.

He believed in clean, compelling entertainment: music, comedy, and stagecraft that could draw crowds and hold attention without stooping for shock. But prosperity has a way of calling in its debts, and at times, Harry made decisions that suggested pressure came from forces beyond his stage lights. Still, he steered as best he could, keeping the curtain rising even when the ground beneath him shifted.

He divested both the Town Casino and the Glen Casino in 1965. The Town closed its doors for good to accommodate the downtown building's new operator, The Studio Arena Theatre. The Glen was expected to remain under Harry's management, at least on paper, for a decade; his death in 1966 would not allow him to fulfill his promise to Lou Jacobs and Sportservice.

Faced with the collapse of his nightclub empire, Altman tried to adapt. Embracing the adage "if you can't beat 'em, join 'em," he made one last course adjustment in an attempt to outshine his nemesis, Melody Fair. In 1963, he began work on the Glen Park Playhouse that he planned for a newly remodeled Family Inn.

Altman rallied local civic leaders[912] to support the project.[a] Even as his health deteriorated over the next few years, he remained a hands-on force, managing operations and directing decisions from his hospital bed. It was one final attempt to reclaim relevance in a world that was moving on without him.

As business at the Glen Casino increasingly declined, he decided to abandon the Family Inn as the performance venue for the new theater, shifting his attention to transforming the nightclub. His inspiration was Paris's famed Folies Bergère, with intimate tables and cabaret-style seating in a space that could accommodate more than 1,000 people.

---

[a] Altman assembled a group of male business leaders—self-described theater enthusiasts—who pledged their support by helping to draw audiences and sustain the venue's 1,000-seat venue.

The first and only show Altman lived to see opened on May 3, 1966, a month ahead of its planned June debut, to accommodate his rapidly failing health.[913] The production was a throwback, a love letter to the Gay Nineties—the nostalgic American vision of the 1890s, with its vaudeville, barbershop quartets, and gaslit charm. It harkened back to the century of his birth and to men like Michael Shea, a cultural forerunner in Buffalo who believed good entertainment should be within reach of the common man. One could say Harry picked up that mantle and carried it further.

The Playhouse's debut production was the campy melodrama "Dirty Work at the Crossroads," described at the time as a "gay-nineties" musical satire designed more for laughter and levity than high art. Publicity for

Figure 297 Playhouse opening announcement April 22, 1966

the show promised a return to a merrier age of theater that was free from what Altman called "the miasma of problem-situation pieces."[914] The cast and crew were drawn from various community theater troupes to present what Altman referred to as "cabaret-style production."[915] He was careful to distinguish his effort from that of traditional musical theater that he reviled. "If I can't have a nightclub the way I want it," he said, "I'll give them a cabaret theater—and I want to make it good."[916]

Although Altman did not witness much of the premiere, he did leave his hospital bed to be at the opening.[917] "He went out with performers on the stage and the appreciative audience in the seats," reporter Bob Sokolsky wrote. "It was the only fitting finale he could have been given."[918]

Figure 334 Harry Altman Photo courtesy of Amherst Bee

Altman died five days later on May 8, 1966, at Buffalo General Hospital after a three-week stay.[919]

He was 75.

By that time, he had moved from his long-time residence on Mill Street into the Carriage House Apartments on East Spring Street in the Village.

The funeral was held at Temple Beth El in Eggertsville, his life-long synagogue, where Rabbi Milton Feierstein honored Harry's "many generosities, his enduring devotion to live theater, and his passion for helping those in need.[920] He was remembered for not just his money, but his time—to veterans, to performers, to strangers who needed a break. He hosted Thanksgiving dinners for the blind.

He brought lunches and laughter to hospitals. He made phone calls, covered costs, and opened doors without expecting headlines in return.

He was buried at Brith Shalom Cemetery in Cheektowaga, laid to rest among family.

He was survived by his wife, Annabelle; their children, Natalie, Hermine, and Robert; and six grandsons, each of whom would go on to establish careers beyond Western New York.

The Gas Light sputtered on. After "Dirty Work" finished its two-week engagement, it was followed by a second production, "Carnival of Comedy."[921] However, shortly after its opening, cast and crew received a phone call: theater operations would "cease immediately."[922] But the writing was on the wall before that. Immediately following Altman's passing, the Playhouse lounge[b] was quickly converted from its nostalgic 1890s aesthetic into a more modern "go-go club format."[923]

After his death, while Annabelle Altman was publicly presented as the new figurehead of Glen Park, it was her son-in-law David Goldstein who stepped in behind the scenes to salvage what he could. The Goldstein family moved into Harry and Annabelle's former home at the edge of the park.

In a sign of waning resources, the Glen Casino began advertising "all-star" shows early in the season without revealing who would perform. It was a gamble, relying on the venue's past reputation to draw crowds. When that strategy fell flat, the schedule was scaled back to Saturday-only dances featuring regional acts like Bobby Jones & His Entertainers, a jazz standout from Niagara Falls. Emceeing was generally left to Ray Vohwinkle,[924] a former area nightclub owner who leaned heavily on audience interaction to fill performance gaps.

In a bid to draw in any crowd, the Glen returned to its "spend as you like" model, offering free admission with the hope that patrons would spend on 99-cent pitchers of beer and sandwiches.

By the end of the 1966 season, the Glen Casino, worn down by months of small crowds and fading cultural relevance, had ceased its usual programming. A new era was about to begin at the Glen—one marked by uncertainty, improvisation, and a louder, far less formal atmosphere than ever before.

---

[b] Over the years, the Casino lounge was refitted under various themes, including the Glenorama Room, the Cocktail Lounge (1954), and the Continental Room.

EPILOGUE

THE LONG GAME

Success did not come early—and it never came clean.

Harry Altman was not born into money, did not inherit a stage, and had no place in Buffalo's old-guard circles. He was the youngest child of Eastern European Jewish immigrants who fled persecution and remade themselves in America, changing their names upon arrival. He came of age in one of Buffalo's dense ethnic ghettos, where ambition was measured in small, stubborn steps forward.

For more than three decades, Harry carved out a career on the margins: renting civic auditoriums, booking acts, managing ballrooms and skating rinks, and learning the restaurant business through persistence and reinvention. He built his reputation in the background, where the spotlight was brief and the profits were narrow. Every show, every season, every night on the floor became part of his training. By the time he opened the Glen Casino and Town Barn, he was no novice. He was a seasoned operator with instincts honed by necessity.

He helped reshape Buffalo's cultural life, bringing national talent to a city long overlooked. His venues were not just places to eat or be entertained; they were stages for transformation, where ordinary people could feel part of something grander, even just for a night.

There were two sides to Harry: the man who booked stars and the man who made quiet deals. He operated in a world where glamour brushed against power, where ambition demanded trade-offs, and where success often came with strings. He made those bargains, and carried the weight that came with them.

History has not always been kind to him. The spotlight he once built moved on. His name faded, misremembered, or erased altogether. But here, it returns to focus, not to glorify, but to give him back what time tried to take: his place on the stages he built.

There is no force more lasting than memory committed to print and here, at last, he is remembered.

APPENDIX

THE ROCK 'N' ROLL YEARS (AND BEYOND)

CLUB COMMODORE

While Harry Altman paid lip service to the cultural wave that was Rock 'n' Roll with his Twist sessions and occasional Hootenannies, his heir apparent, David Goldstein, recognized its potential to cultivate a new generation of patrons. Determined to tap into this burgeoning market, Goldstein partnered with Williamsville native Kevin Elliott to open a venue in August 1965 designed specifically to appeal to young audiences hungry for the music of their era.

Together, the duo launched Club Commodore, located at 2285 Genesee Street near the Cheektowaga town line. The building, once the Commodore Movie Theater, had been transformed into a vibrant dance space by removing the seats and creating an expansive floor plan capable of accommodating more than 600 dancers. Conveniently situated near bus routes, the club became a hub for Friday night and Saturday afternoon and, in time, Sunday afternoon/evening concerts, showcasing local bands and occasionally hosting special guest performers.

Figure 298 Club Commodore sign

Drawing on strategies pioneered by Altman to attract younger crowds, Club Commodore offered free bus service from high school parking lots, suburban malls, and inner-city neighborhoods. The club's affordable admission fee of $1 to $1.25 fit neatly into the budgets of its youthful patrons, ensuring a steady stream of eager attendees. Goldstein further bolstered the club's appeal by advertising directly to parents, emphasizing the alcohol-free environment and the safe, supervised setting for their kids, a move that promoted community support.

The Club Commodore was managed by Elliott, while Goldstein continued overseeing operations at the Glen Casino and amusement park, taking on greater responsibilities as Harry's health deteriorated.

During the approximately 14 months the Club Commodore was in business, dozens of bands would take to the stage. The Rogues, managed by Goldstein/Elliott, would serve as the house band. Others who appeared included Cavemen, The Twiggs, Road Cyclones, Squires, Rodents, The Bitter End, Just Us Five, The Unleashed, Kahns, The Knorks, Crestwoods, Londonaires, The Spectres, Sinnerman, Lonely Souls, Root of All Evil, Madmen, and the Vibratos. Perhaps the most notable national act to grace the stage in November 1965 was Joey Dee and The Starliters who had the mega hit "Peppermint Twist."[925] During this era, the band's guitarist was Jimi Hendrix who was starting to experiment with the image that would become his trademark: a fringe jacket among a group otherwise known for wearing suit jackets.[926] The club began to lose traction in the fall of 1966 when neighbors began to complain of the commotion caused by the club's patrons.[927] One evening, police officers, accompanied by the K-9 Corps, arrived to enforce a newly imposed restriction on the club's occupancy. Previously, the club was licensed to accommodate up to 650 guests but the fire department had recently revised the maximum capacity to 385.[928]

"For nine months we operated with no problems," Elliott told *The Buffalo Evening News*. "Then all of a sudden the neighbors did not want the young people in the neighborhood—and this happened."[929]

Elliott said the crowd of young people were "disappointed and puzzled" by having to leave the property.

"The police brought the dogs, and that was unnecessary and unfortunate," Elliott said.[930]

Later that month, a petition signed by more than 250 residents was filed with the Buffalo City Common Council protesting the operation of the club. The petition stated that most residents in the vicinity are "under great tension and stress" because of the appearance of "participants on motorcycles" from other parts of the state and Canada. "They are boisterous, they create a lot of noise after 11 PM and throw bottles and beer cans on streets and lawns," the petition stated.[931]

Just days later, law enforcement was back at the club. This time, they arrested 21 patrons for disorderly conduct. The cases were later dropped.

The second police intervention prompted the club owners to announce their decision to terminate the lease on the building. "We're now searching for a larger space where we won't disturb the neighbors," Elliott stated.[932]

Fortunately, there was another opportunity that would soon arise to fit the bill. It would end up making a lot of noise. It was called the Inferno.

Figure 299 College Dance sign

THE INFERNO

Figure 300 The Inferno Banner

With Harry's passing in 1966, and the entire Glen now under the ownership of Sportservice, Goldstein had a chance to create an entirely new vibe at the Williamsville club. A freshly signed lease in hand, Goldstein began booking acts that would have played in Harry's nightmares.

The east end of the Casino building that once served as the cocktail lounge was now the Inferno. The huge performance space that once could seat 800 people was renamed Hell's Half Acre.

For a time, just in case the destination was not obvious, the name "Glen Casino" was draped atop advertisements and posters that promoted shows at the Inferno.

But once the rock audience had discovered its new home, ties to the Casino were abandoned. The building's neutral exterior was painted the color akin to "the Devil's red" and a new banner logo was created featuring a smoldering fire with the appropriate color palette.

Glen Casino had become a historical footnote; the building that once entertained tables of demure audiences looking for a 90-minute stage show followed by orchestral dancing was now a fully tricked-out rock 'n' roll club. While the Inferno's lifespan was relatively brief (1966-1968), its significance as a proving ground for early rock/R&B performers enhanced Buffalo's reputation as an important concert destination.

The club's vast size (1,000 patrons plus) attracted up-and-coming national acts seeking a solid payday in a city with a thriving music scene. Canadian concert goers—attracted to the area because of the great music, ease of travel across the border, money taken at par,

Figure 301 Glen Casino's - The Inferno

Figure 302 Inferno poster

and the lower legal drinking age—were often in plentiful supply. All nationalities benefited from the cheap beer (35 cents for a 32-oz draft), the ample free parking, and the club's roster of performers.

On big concert nights (Wednesdays through Sundays), patrons would often queue at the entrance door hours before show time. As the time was nearing for the club doors to open, the young patrons often formed a line that snaked through the concessions area and onto Glen Avenue, crossing the bridge and heading toward Mill Street.

Local bands thrived in the spotlight of the Inferno's popularity, finding opportunities to grow their fan base and showcase their talent. Emerging acts with potential but limited audiences could perform in the Inferno's "small room" at the east end of the building. This intimate space was separated from the expansive Hell's Half Acre by a soundproof wall of thick glass. Patrons in the smaller area gathered around a massive horseshoe-shaped bar where bartenders served the venue's only hard liquor and bottled beer.

Above and behind the horseshoe bar was a raised stage where bands played and go-go dancers performed, creating a dynamic focal point for the crowd.

Figure 303 Go-Go Dancer
Photo courtesy Pamela Taylor Kneis

Skilled local musicians were invited to perform on the big stage on nights when national acts were not booked or as opening acts for headliners. While some of these musicians had experience, many were college-aged, cutting their teeth in garages and late-night rehearsals.

Raven's guitarist, John Weitz, not yet 18, was legally prohibited from performing in venues that served alcohol. To get around the restriction at the Inferno, the band rigged a 200-foot guitar cable that connected to the stage amplifier, allowing Weitz to play his music from inside a parked car outside the club.

While extraordinary music could often be heard from these area bands, their membership seemed somewhat nebulous. Musicians and vocalists often traded places, requiring local rock historians to ponder long and hard to provide an accurate line up of a particular band in any given month.

ODE TO KEVIN ELLIOTT: GTM

Every spotlight casts a shadow.
And Kevin?
He was pure wattage.
Cane, sunglasses, a towering cowboy hat—
always the center of attention.
An elongated Eldorado idling out back,
its trunk packed with Blue Nun,
ready for whatever came next.

Truth did not follow him—
it chased,
gasping to keep up.
Facts blurred at the edges,
burned out by the brightness.
We still talk about him.
Not just because we remember,
but because we can't agree.
Promoter?
Performer?
Prophet or imposter?
An argument could be made for any—or all.

Figure 304 Kevin Elliott
Photo courtesy of Pamela Zepp Moore

The cult of personality doesn't get built,
it bursts to life.
And Kevin?
He was at the center of it all,
laughing in the fallout,
feeding the blaze.
Research the man,
you'll lose the thread.
Research the myth,
you just might find something better.

Now pour a glass.
Blue Nun, of course.
And drink to the question
that always gets asked,
but never answered:
Did he really do all that?

Even decades later, Kevin Elliott's name still surfaces on social media; whispers, shoutouts, and stories laced with disbelief and affection. His antics, his presence, his sheer unpredictability remains part of Buffalo's rock 'n' roll folklore.

He died in August 1998 in Key West, Florida, the owner of Boston Billy's Restaurant, though his name never appeared on the liquor license or incorporation documents. Still, ask anyone who was there, and they will tell you: it was **his** place, no question.

Kevin was a big man on a bigger frame, his gait forever altered by polio. One leg, he said, stretched to 6'3," the other only 5'6," yet the disparity never slowed him down, least of all on the dance floor. "He could dance your shoes off!" someone once marveled.

Toward the end, the stories only got wilder. "They were pulling him around Key West in a rickshaw," a friend reported—half-laughing, half-serious, as was always the case with Kevin.

Kevin Elliott's connection to Harry Altman might be more urban legend than fact. Some say it was Kevin who convinced Altman to transform the old Casino nightclub into a rock 'n' roll haven, a bold pivot in Buffalo's nightlife history. If there is any truth to that claim, one might joke that Harry chose to avoid facing the music. By the time the Inferno opened its doors in fall of 1966, Altman was dead, safely in the ground in a soundproof vault.[a]

Still, Kevin played a very real, and vital role as promoter of the infamous Inferno nightclub, operated by Goldstein. The club threw its doors open to rock bands, roaring crowds, and an endless flow of Iroquois beer in Hell's Half Acre. The big room hosted acts who were already legends or were just about to become them.

Fueled by Kevin's manic, magnetic energy, the nightclub was electric. For many young men tossing back 35-cent drafts under the club's flickering lights, it would be their final nights of freedom before the draft board came calling. Some would later learn of the nightclub's fate not from friends, but from the pages of Stars and Stripes. "The Inferno Burns."

Kevin drove a customized "limo" that cruised around town with a license plate bearing just three letters: GTM. The same initials sparkled from the gold-and-diamond chain around his neck, his personal motto: "Get Their Money." And get it, he did. Fifties and hundreds spilled out of his pants' pockets like confetti. But Kevin gave back, too, always with an entourage in tow, the car's trunk packed with four or five cases of Blue Nun. Inside the vehicle: echoes of laughter, stories half-told, and a blizzard of McDonald's hamburger wrappers carpeting the floorboards.

---

[a]Perhaps to ward off Altman's spirit, when the Inferno first opened men had to wear coats and ties and women were expected in dresses or skirts. "That lasted for about two weeks" before changing over to casual dress, Sam Weimer, Inferno bartender and informal historian, recalled.

Kevin made the rounds, gliding from one hotspot to the next like a man on tour. At each stop, screwdrivers (the vodka-and-orange-juice kind) were ordered on his dime for the entire room, hundreds of cups lining the bar in a citrus-scented salute. One competitor remembered the night Kevin and his entourage rolled in with a clawfoot bathtub and asked the staff to fill it to the brim with the cocktail.

Unorthodox? Sure. Unforgettable? Absolutely.

But that was Kevin.

After the Inferno went up in flames, Kevin—often partnering with Goldstein—moved on to new ventures. The names of the places have faded, their identities blurring into a haze of business cards, backstage passes, and dimly lit memories.

When Kevin died at age 57, he left behind two final requests: that his friends pay ten dollars for the honor to attend his funeral luncheon, and that his ashes be sifted into pepper shakers as parting gifts. The souvenirs have become part of the folklore; the story talked about whenever his memory is shaken.

No headstone etched in granite,
no plaque on a wall—
just stories passed like sacred gossip
in the corners of old bars.
His legend outlived the limo,
outshined the chain,
outranked the myth.

He always knew how to
Get Their Money—
and gave us
one hell of a story in return.

PERFORMERS WHO PLAYED THE INFERNO

Figure 305 Inferno ad

Fortunately for Goldstein, the nightclub required little in the way of advertising.

Aside from the occasional listing in the University at Buffalo's *Spectrum* newspaper, most of the club's weekly crowds, often numbering in the thousands, arrived thanks to word of mouth. The following list was compiled through extensive research and with the invaluable insights of Bob Paxon and Sam Weimer. It aims to document performers across the venue's key spaces: the Inferno (smaller room), the main stage (Hell's Half Acre), and the popular Sunday matinee soul sessions.

Butterfield Blues Band	Beau Geste & The Legions
1910 Fruitgum Co.	The Peeple
Screamin' Freeman Williams & the Showstoppers	Individuals
Bobby "Blue" Bland	Sam the Sham & the Pharaohs
Human Beinz	Barbara St. Clair & The Pin-Kooshins
Leroy Taylor	Sly & the Family Stone
The Drifters	The Rising Sons (Tony Galla)
Moving Violations	The Box Tops
Brenton Wood	The Happenings
Wilmer & the Dukes	Freddy Cannon
The Vibratos	William Bell
Willie and the Knight Cats	The Contours
The Pilgrims	Etta James
Harold Smith & The Largos	The Ronettes
The Untouchables	The Tokens
Road Runners	The Shangri-Las
The Bold	The Foundations
Earl Levitt	Patti Labelle & the Bluebells
Sweet William	Esquires
Tommy Roe	Wayne Cochran & the C.C. Riders
	Jimmy Ruffin

Al Green
Wilson Pickett Revue
Brian Hyland
Percy Sledge
Jr. Walker and the All Stars
Ike & Tina Turner Revue
Kim Weston
Lesley Gore
Arthur Conley
Jackie Wilson
The Beacon Street Union
Bobby Hebb
Johnny Maestro & the Brooklyn Bridge
The Fantastic Four
Fontella Bass
Mar-Keys
Bar-Kays
Shirelles
Gladys Knight & the Pips
Fantastic Johnny C.
The Parliaments
The Leaves
The O'Kaysions
Chris Montez
The Intruders
Goldie and the Gingerbreads
John Fred & the Playboys
Gary Puckett & the Union Gap
Friend & Lover
Every Mother's Son
Rose Garden
Rare Earth
Cannibal and the Headhunters
The Delfonics
Ten Wheel Drive
The Tymes
The Murmaids
The Dells
Chuck Berry
The Platters
Betty Everett
James Cotton Blues Band

The Hesitations
Jimmy Jones
The Hollywood Argyles
J. Frank Wilson & the Cavaliers
Mary Wells
Lou Christie
Bob Seger System
American Breed
The Five Stairsteps
Jimmy Soul
The Fifth Estate
Five Americans
Soul Survivors
Mandala (Toronto)
The Coasters
Mike St. Shaw and the Prophets
Ben E. King & the Drifters
Jerry Butler Jr.
The Marvelettes
Ohio Express
The Valentinos
Zombies
Martha & the Vendellas
J.J. Jackson
The Angels
Len Barry (1,2,3—formerly of the Dovells)
Lemon Pipers
Mike Finnigan & the Serfs
Jay & the Americans
Joey Dee & the Starliters
Strawberry Alarm Clock
Dee Dee Sharp
Jimmy Gilmer and the Fireballs
Twiggs
Jay & the Techniques
Grant Smith and the Power (out of Toronto)
The Exciters
Keith
The Elgins
Little Eva
Scarecrow (out of Long Island)

The Duprees
Freddie Scott
Robert Knight
Dyke & the Blazers
Cliff Nobles
Danny & the Juniors
The Chantels
Tyrone Davis
Curtis Lee
Terry Stafford
Gene Chandler
Emotions
Bill Haley and the Comets
King Curtis and the Noble Knights
The Capitols
Barbara Mason
The Crystals
Chiffons
Gary (US) Bonds

Barbara Lynn
Edwin Starr
Barbara Ann Lewis
LaVern Baker
Bobby Lewis
The Outsiders
The Toys
The Velvelettes
Bobby Womack
Ruby & the Romantics
Classics IV
Orlons
The High Keys
Johnny Taylor
Isley Brothers
James and Bobby Purify
Clarence Carter
Eddie Floyd
Bubble Gum Machine

REGIONAL BANDS THAT PLAYED THE INFERNO

by Buffalo Music Historian, Bob Paxon (aka "Bob the Record Man")

WILMER & THE DUKES

Active Years: 1958-1974

Members: Wilmer Alexander Jr.—Lead Singer, Saxophone
                    Ronnie Alberts—Drums
                    Ralph "Duke" Gillotte—Keyboard, Vocals
                    Monty Alberts—Bass/Bob Egan
                    Doug Brown—Guitar

Albums: "Wilmer & the Dukes" (Aphrodisiac Records, 1969)
(Chuck Mangione and Gap Mangione also worked as musicians and arrangers)

Singles: "Give Me One More Chance"/ "Get It"
                    "I'm Free"/ "Heavy Time"
                    "Living in the U.S.A"/ "Count on Me"

Perhaps no local band blazes as bright in the minds of Inferno regulars as Wilmer & the Dukes, hailing from Geneva, NY.

They were the archetypal frat "party-animal" band, blowing up many college and frat house shows on the upstate and central New York circuit during their most popular period (1961-1970). Their legacy was thought to have been immortalized in one of the most popular cult film classics of the era.

Ivan Reitman, who attended college in Toronto and later produced *National Lampoon's Animal House*, is believed to have modeled the film's fictional band, Otis Day & the Knights, on Wilmer & the Dukes. According to local lore, Reitman saw the group perform at the Inferno while he was a student at McMaster University.

Wilmer & the Dukes was a huge hit as the house band at the Inferno, starring every Wednesday night in the big room to a sold-out house. They also appeared occasionally on Sundays when the club hosted R&B/Soul Days.

Figure 306 Wilmer & the Dukes photo

WILMER
ALEXANDER
JR.
AND THE
DUKES

Wilmer and The Dukes

WILMER - Sax
RON - Drums
RALPH - Organo
MONTY - Bass

Figure 307 Wilmer & the Dukes Poster

Junior Walker was a great artistic influence on Wilmer and may have, indirectly, affected the course of the band's future. Wilmer was the opening act of a special Thursday night show at the Inferno featuring Jr. Walker and the All Stars. It is during that evening when Walker is thought to have shared with Wilmer how Motown had sabotaged his release of "What Does it Take to Win Your Love?" This may have ultimately led to Wilmer not signing with Motown when the label later showed interest in him. He went on to record, instead, with local label Aphrodisiac.

Their sound was a fusion of rock 'n' roll and soul, as displayed on their signature song, "Give Me One More Chance" written by guitarist Doug Brown. It was the band's first release on Aphrodisiac 260 and their only hit. In the U.S., it placed moderately on the *Billboard* and Cashbox Top 100 charts in 1968. It did better in regional markets (including Buffalo, Rochester and Syracuse) and MUCH better in Canada.

Cover songs appearing in their act included "Reach Out" and "I Can't Help Myself" by The Four Tops; "Shotgun" & "Road Runner" by Jr Walker & the All Stars; and "Baby Let Me Bang Your Box" by Doug Clark and the Hot Nuts.

The fact that they were an interracial band does not seem to have raised eyebrows. This may not have been the case when they started, though. In the late 1950s, when they were playing mostly black clubs, the racial dynamic of the band probably stood out more and may have been part of their novelty.

After the Inferno was destroyed in 1968, the band became regulars at

Figure 308 Wilmer & the Dukes Album Cover

Gilligan's in Cheektowaga. In fact, Wilmer & the Dukes was the opening act on the first night at Gilligan's on March 16, 1969. Other performers appearing on that bill included The Serfs.

The band was inducted into the Rochester Hall of Fame in 2015. The music of Wilmer and his mates lived on through a tribute band that played and recorded as The Legendary Dukes with some of the original members.

(TONY GALLA &) THE RISING SONS

Active Years: 1965-1968

Members: Tony Galla—Vocals/Bass
Mike Bell—Keyboard/Jimmy Calire (& Sax)
John Weitz—Guitar
Tom Calandra—Bass
Fred Meyer—Drums/Gary Mallaber

Singles: "In Love"/ "Guys Go for Girls"
"There's Nothing Going for Us"/ "I'm Feeling Down"

Tom had appeared with The Galla Family (the siblings, plus their mother!) on Ted Mack's Original Amateur Hour in the late 1950s, where—though only a child—he dominated the performance with a great lead vocal on "Why Do Fools Fall in Love." Look for it on YouTube, you will not be disappointed!

He later recorded with his siblings as The Sherwin Trio for the local Sahara label. His older brother, trio member Armando (better known as Mondo), had also achieved some local fame as an Elvis-type vocalist on the sock hop circuit.

The Rising Sons played in a style like Stan & The Ravens—a mix of R&R, R&B and bluesy Soul. They even hung around the garage studio on Poultney Avenue that was co-run by Gary Mallaber and Tom Calandra, who, at the time, were members of Stan's group.

Along the way, Galla hooked up with WKBW-AM disc jockey Joey Reynolds and cut this record for Swan in 1967, "In Love" b/w "Guys Go for Girls." Some pressings credit Tony Galla only, some Tony Galla & The Rising Sons, but some sources credit studio players with providing most of the backup.

A hit in some regional markets (the biggest being Philadelphia, and of course Buffalo), "In Love" failed to click nationally, but due to lots of local radio play they were able to raise their profile significantly. The Rising Sons became the house band at the Inferno.

At this point Calandra and Mallaber jumped ship from Stan's band, joining The Rising Sons in time to cut their next record, "There's Nothing Going for Us" b/w "I'm Feeling Down" for the local Upstate label.

It should be noted that in the 1970s "In Love" was discovered by the Northern Soul dance crowd in the UK, and only became more popular as time went on, spreading to the rest of Europe where it's now considered a classic. In fact, it is probably in the Top 30 all-time favorite Northern Soul songs to connoisseurs, making Tony Galla a well-known name in the foreign soul scene. Locally it is fondly remembered by their many fans, and Tom still performs it live, though I suppose for many it was just a step on the way to the big ROCK success he was to have with Raven.

Figure 346 "In Love" 45 Record

RAVEN

Active Years:	1967-70
Members:	Tony Galla—Vocals, Harp Jimmy Calire—Keyboard John Weitz—Guitar Gary Mallaber—Drums Tom Calandra—Bass
Albums:	"Raven" (Columbia Records, 1969) "Live at The Inferno" (Discovery Records, 1969; recorded 1967)
Singles:	"Feeling Good"/ "Green Mountain Dream" "Children at our Feet"/ "Here Come a Truck"

The band Raven, that gave us the much talked about "Live at The Inferno" album in 1969, was the result of the successful merger of band members from The Rising Sons and their local rival, Stan and the Ravens.

Figure 309 The day-after photo from the September 1968 fire is used as the cover art for the "Live at the Inferno" album

As The Rising Sons, they released a 45 for Upstate Records in 1968. After changing their name to Raven, the group got a major label deal with Columbia Records, with whom they put out their first eponymous album.

"Raven," their first album, sold fairly well, and they started playing some big shows, opening for bands like Led Zeppelin, Johnny Winter And, Procol Harum, and Jethro Tull. They moved to New York City where they played the Fillmore East and Steve Paul's The Scene, the hangout for musicians Jimi Hendrix and Janis Joplin, with whom they became acquainted.

At some point Columbia released a single from the album. It does not seem to have sold well, but their sound really was not right for the AM radio market anyway. They toured the UK where they were well received and did some more recording for Columbia, from which a second single was released with songs that may have been recorded for a second album.

Figure 310 Raven

The A-side was a Tom Calandra composition, "Children at Our Feet," which has a mild Gospel feel and something of a conservation theme. Unfortunately, it is kind of bland and not "AM Radio" material. The B-side is not hit material either, but it is something else again!

"Here Come a Truck" is a real odd track written by guitarist John Weitz. It instrumentally is a straight-ahead rocker with a bit of a West Coast feel. But the vocals and lyrics are bizarre. I do not know what they were going for here, unless it was meant as a joke; but it would be odd to waste a shot at chart success on anything less than their best material.

Maybe they were just rebelling after being told to do something more commercial. "Truck" sounds nothing like any of the other stuff they did.

Figure 311 Columbia ran an article promoting "Raven" in the Cash Box magazine in October 1969

Somewhere around this time, Raven broke up and/or the record company gave up on them. That is almost the end of the story except years later a second album came out, "Raven: Live at The Inferno." The material is similar to the released Columbia LP (with some of the same songs) but more raw and energetic in their performance.

The good news is that most of band members from Raven had subsequent careers in music, ranging from star-level to low-level to behind-the-scenes notoriety. But the original band remains the true sound of Buffalo 1960s music to those who followed them back in those heady days.

Tom Calandra - Played locally-made jingles and parody songs for WKBW; formed "the legendary" BCMK Studio; and recorded many local musicians there. Tom died in 1998.

Gary Mallaber - Became one of the top drummers in the world with credits too lengthy to mention here. Suffice to say he did lengthy spells with The Steve Miller Band (in the days of their biggest successes), and Van Morrison, as well as work with Bruce Springsteen, John Lennon, The Beach Boys, Bob Seger, Gene Clark, Bonnie Raitt—the list goes on. Most recently he was on tour with A.J. Croce.

Tony Galla - Continued playing music locally and elsewhere; did some acting; and released albums in many styles including Italian music. Most recently, he has been working as a Blues singer and guitarist.

Jim Calire - Joined America and became their longtime musical director (working with their producer George Martin). Oddly, with America his main instrument became the saxophone. His son Mario was the drummer for The Wallflowers.

John 'JR' Weitz - Led a high-energy jazz/rock trio in the Buffalo area, probably the first local fusion band. After moving to California, he worked in audio design, receiving many patents. Sadly, he passed away at age of 63 in 2012.

TWIGGS / TWIGS

Active Years:	**1966-1969**
Members:	**Gordon (Blake) Kapsar—Vocals & Toys (percussion)**
	Glen Skadan—Bass
	Paul Vastola—Lead Guitar
	Robert Frederico—Guitar
	Tom Gentile—Drums
	Bob Federico—Rhythm Guitar
Singles:	**"Moon Maiden"/ "Flowers and Beads"**

Twiggs began in 1964 as a group of Cleveland Hill High School students performing under the name New Castle 5. As their sound matured, so did their identity—they eventually rebranded as Twiggs and built a steady following at local bars and teen events, including regular gigs at the Glen and Town Casinos. Their early performances were rooted in blues and rock, but they later embraced the acid-infused psychedelia that became their trademark sound.

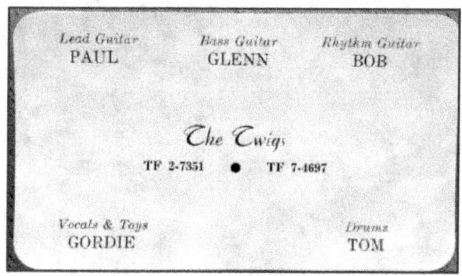

Figure 312 Twiggs Business Card

A standout moment in the band's early career came when Chuck Berry asked them to back him on the Inferno's main stage—without so much as a rehearsal. Arriving just before showtime in a red Cadillac, carrying nothing but a brown paper bag, Berry simply told the band: "You know the music; you only need to know the key." Twiggs rose to the occasion and powered through the performance.

By 1969, the band adopted a new name—Magic Ring—shifting their focus toward original material and studio work. The name was inspired by Tolkien's *The Lord of the Rings*. Core members Gordon (Blake) Kapsar, Glen Skadan, and Paul Vastola carried over from Twiggs, and were later joined by Derek Hillburger (keyboards), Bill Friday (drums), and eventually Jim "Woody" Knoblock (drums). The group was managed by Steve Goldstein, whose father, David Goldstein, operated both the Inferno and Gilligan's.

Magic Ring soon found themselves sharing stages with major acts. They opened for Cactus the night of their live album recording and later traveled to New York City to record at Electric Lady Studios, where they cut their only record: the acid rock 45 "Moon Maidens," released under their former name, The Twiggs. In 1971, they scored a high-profile opening slot for The Doors at the Peace Bridge Exhibition Center.

Of note: lead vocalist Gordon "Blake" Kapsar came from a musically accomplished family. His father, (Jack) Gordon L. Kapsar, founded the Jack Gordon Trio, a group that frequently performed at the Town Casino. He also played with the Gordon Robinson Orchestra, a swing and dance band known for backing major touring acts.

Figure 313 Twiggs Album Cover

BARBARA ST. CLAIR & THE PIN-KOOSHINS

Active Years: 1965-1972

Members: Barbara St. Clair—Vocals
Jake Jakubowski—Organ / Ronnie Davis-Keyboard
Bill Phillips—Bass / Carmen Castiglione
John Culliton Mahoney—Guitar
Ron (Tabby) Zalewski—Drums
Ernie Corallo
Tony Galla
Jimmy Claire
Joe Ford
Herman Young
Andy LaPella
Freddy LaPella

Singles: "Share Your Love"/ "Make it Easy on Yourself"

Barbara St. Clair started singing professionally as a teenager in the Buffalo vocal group The Supremes, recording one 45 alongside members (Dr.) Lonnie Smith and Grover Washington.

Coming under the guidance of Buffalo DJ Lucky Pierre, she worked the local record hop scene until becoming part of The Sessions. This bunch—who had the then-popular typical girl group pop/soul sound—came together for a "session" produced by Joey Reynolds (hence their name).

The Sessions cut a version of Joey's song he had previously produced with Tony Galla, "Guys Go for Girls." In this case, they changed a few words, as appropriate, but saved money on producing the record by re-using the backing track from Galla's single!

In the early '60s, The Sessions performed at places like the Town Casino and Glen Casino with back-up musicians. With her knowledge of the club scene and relationships with hip musicians who could cross genres, Barbara and group became one of Buffalo's premium club bands: The Pin-Kooshins (or The Pin Koo-shins, or Barbara St. Clair &...).

The Pin-Kooshins became one of the house bands at the Inferno. In fact, they lost all their equipment that was inside the building the night the fire destroyed the club. The music community came to their rescue and gave a benefit at The Mug on Hertel Avenue to raise money to replace the burned gear.

In time, membership became somewhat elastic, with great Buffalo players like Ernie Corallo (of Stan & The Ravens) and Tony Galla and Jimmy Calire (of Raven) spending time in the group.

Clubgoers were treated to duets of the great soul voices of Barbara and Tony, and it is a shame they did not cut records from these lineups. Barbara, of course, went on to form the legendary Houserockers in 1975, which included Jay Beckenstein and Jeremy Wahl, and is said to be the genesis of superstars Spyro Gyra.

The Pin-Kooshins made only two 45s. The one on Janus Records is not very memorable, but their Mercury Records release—from about 1972—is a two-sided gem. Recorded at Buffalo's Act One Studio, "Share Your Love" was the local hit, a quiet but moving soft rock/soul heartbreaker.

"Make It Easy on Yourself" is an up-tempo soul mover with all the right elements to appeal to dancers—a loping bass, Hammond organ, and tight drums.

Despite the story being local lore, the band was not the last to play the Inferno on the night of the fire, although their equipment was stored in the building while they were recording in New York City. That distinction goes to the Brass Buttons.

Figure 314 The Pin-Cooshins

BRASS BUTTONS

Active Years: 1968-1969

Members: Gene Cornish—Guitar
Bob Guglielmino—Drums
Jay Capozzi—Lead Vocals
Eric Thorngren—Vocals, Guitar
Joe Graziano—Keyboard
Danny Labatte—Saxophone
Mike Julian—Bass

Single: "My Song"/ "Hell Will Take Care of Her"

While not considered a "local band," Brass Buttons did have Western New York connections as Gene Cornish, lead guitarist, became a Rochester boy early in his life after moving from Ontario.

He joined Joey Dee & The Starliters but he also found time to lead The Unbeatables, who recorded one LP and several 45s for tiny, upstate NY label, Dawn Records. And, of course, he went on to fame with the (Young) Rascals. The Rascals are not as well remembered today as many of their peers, but at one time they were one of the biggest-selling bands in America, a hit-making machine.

But Gene never cut ties with his hometown and in 1968 he produced a 45 for Rochester's own Brass Buttons. Jay Capozzi had previously played with The Show Stoppers (very popular locally in their time but mostly remembered today as the starting point for Bat McGrath and Don Potter). Eric Thorngren had previously led his own band, Eric & The Chessmen.

Like so many bands, the Brass Buttons played a lot of shows—— but took only one shot at the black plastic (a 45) and went away. Gene wrote the A-side for their Cotillion single, "My Song" and Capozzi wrote "Hell Will Take Care of Her."

A few years later, after the Rascals broke up, Gene Cornish and Dino Danelli joined with Brass Buttons' Thorngren and John Tauri (a later-day member) to form Bulldog, who recorded two good but little-known LPs for Decca. In later years, Eric Thorngren became a prominent producer, under the monicker *ET*.

Figure 315 Brass Buttons

THE INFERNO FIRE

When *The Buffalo Evening News* hit doorsteps at dinner time on Monday, September 26, 1968, reporter Bob Buyers captured the huge blaze with a front-page lead that read like a line from a Hollywood script:

"A fire that lit the sky in the best show-business tradition early today destroyed the Inferno…"[933]

The story was carried by newspapers across the country partly because of the building's legacy of hosting A-list entertainers, but mostly because a nightclub called the Inferno had been consumed by flames in the most spectacular of fashions.

The fire broke out in the early hours of that Monday morning, just hours after a concert by the Brass Buttons had wrapped on a humid Sunday night. The building had originally opened in 1936 as the Glen Casino after a previous fire had destroyed the Ritz Barn. The building measured 158 by 285 feet, totaling more than 41,000 square feet of space.[934]

Around 2:30 a.m., porters finishing the usual overnight cleanup smelled smoke and ran to Goldstein's nearby home on Mill Street, just around the corner. Goldstein had been at the club earlier that night, around 10:15 p.m., to sign a few checks. Now, alarmed by the porters on his doorstep, he placed the emergency call at 2:40 a.m.[935]

By the time firefighters arrived, it was too late.

The first to respond were members of the Williamsville Fire Department/Hutchinson Hose Company. Flames were visible behind the west side of the building. Roger Walker, a firefighter who lived directly across the street at 156 Glen, rushed over after hearing the alert on his home receiver and saw smoke pouring from cracks around the doors.[936]

The fire appeared to have started in the club's general office area, a walled-off room within the all-wood-frame structure. Newspapers first reported that when firefighters forced the door of the office open, the air rushed in and the fire exploded.[937]

Other reports suggested an exhaust fan over the office door activated, pulling in oxygen and causing an immediate flashover, sending flames shooting over the firefighters' heads and into the adjacent main dance hall. Others said it was simply the act of opening the door that fed the fire.

Tom Wutz, the firefighter who led the first team of firefighters into the building, described the moment with haunting precision:

"As soon as we opened the office door, the air rushed in and the fire just backflashed. It was instant—heat and smoke hit us like a wave. We couldn't see, couldn't breathe. We had to get out fast. After that, it was out of control, flames shooting through the roof."[938]

As Wutz retreated, he watched a ball of fire rip through what he said was a "glass-walled hallway" between the two showrooms, engulfing the interior in seconds.[939]

The *Amherst Bee* captured the chaotic beauty of the blaze: "The flames shot a hundred feet in the air at times as residents nearby ringed the hill watching the firefighters save the Glenside Apartments with a curtain of water."[940]

Despite the hour, onlookers gathered. Some wept.[941]

The *Bee* continued: "In spite of the early morning hours there were a number of young adults who added their tears to the general dampness at the fiery end of the dance hall. Monday evening young people continued to stream down the hill to stand and shake their heads at the sadness of it all."[942]

By 3:05 a.m., Chief Irv Lorich of the Williamsville Fire Department began calling in mutual aid. Within two hours, firefighters from 13 departments had arrived: Main-Transit, Snyder, Cleveland Hill, Getzville, Transit, Eggertsville, Harris Hill, Swormville, Kenilworth, North Bailey, Clarence, Clarence Center, and U-Crest.[943]

Figure 316 Firefighters
Photo courtesy of The Archives & Special Collection Department of SUNY Buffalo State

At the height of the battle, more than 200 firefighters and 25 trucks fought the blaze, pumping two million gallons of water into the Inferno. Hydrant pressure remained strong throughout, with Arthur A. Wolf, Williamsville's public works superintendent, feeding stored water into the system. Four companies pumped from Ellicott Creek in a continuous relay.[944]

Chief Lorich ordered equipment into position to protect the historic Williamsville Water Mill and the nearby 12-unit Glenside Apartments, perched on the escarpment above on E. Spring Street. Residents were evacuated as flames crept dangerously close.

The fire was declared under control at 6:50 a.m., though volunteers remained on site through the afternoon. By 2:00 p.m., more than 25 firefighters were still on duty, some having worked nearly 13 hours. *The Amherst Bee* reported: "The charred ruins of the Inferno, in symbolic fashion, smoldered all day Monday. [The firefighters returned] late in the evening when the ambers rekindled a blaze."[945]

Figure 317 The Inferno Stairs
Photo courtesy of The Amherst Bee

Hutchinson Hose would later describe it as the largest fire in Amherst history in terms of manpower and equipment deployed.[946]

In the days that followed, investigators from the New York Fire Underwriters, insurance adjusters, and law enforcement combed through the debris. The final ruling: "A fire of unknown origin."[947]

Figure 318 Ruins are still smoldering the day after the fire
Photo is one of the series made famous on the cover of Raven's "Live at The Inferno" album
Photo courtesy of The Archives & Special Collection Department of SUNY Buffalo State

But theories abounded. Some pointed to the condition of the building—its brittle wood frame, aging glass fuse wiring, and the increasing demands of electric guitars, amplifiers, keyboards, and stage lighting. Others whispered a darker theory: arson.

The debate endures.

Alongside the nightclub, a popular game pavilion called Fascination was also lost, putting an end to the familiar chant of "Bingo with a Ball." The amusement rides were untouched.

One small relief for Goldstein: the weekend's house receipts, locked in a safe, were recovered unharmed. So too were Jimmy Moser's silver coins, which he had swapped nightly from the game booths.

Figure 358 The Inferno Closed Sign

Figure 319 Aftermath 1968 Clean-up was underway in January 1969 at the former site of the Glen Casino/Inferno
Photo courtesy of The Archives & Special Collection Department of SUNY Buffalo State

GILLIGAN'S

Even before the Inferno was reduced to ashes, Goldstein and Elliott were planning their next move—a new rock 'n' roll venue farther east on Main Street in Clarence, NY. As of September 18th, just days before the fire, the Clarence Town Board had approved a change-of-use permit application to convert a former bowling alley at 8700 Main Street (near Connection Dr.) into a restaurant with dancing.[948]

News of this permit appeared in the final paragraph of the Amherst Bee's September 23, 1968 article covering the Inferno fire. Goldstein, when pressed, dismissed the report, claiming he would abandon the plans due to unresolved issues with parking and sanitary sewer capacity.[949]

* * * * * * * * * * * * * * * *

But once the Inferno was gone, Goldstein and Elliott found themselves without a music venue and the search for a new space began in earnest. They knew the next location had to check several boxes: it had to be sizable, situated outside a residential zone; equipped with ample parking; and easily accessible via a major highway to draw crowds from Buffalo and the surrounding suburbs.[a]

They eventually identified a promising site at 2525 Walden Avenue—a former lumber supply facility across from the GEX/Super Flea (now Walmart), barely a mile from the I-90. Located in the Town of Cheektowaga, just east of the Depew village line, the property seemed ideal on paper. But its proximity to Depew caused many Village residents to be wary of a loud, youth-driven nightclub. The need for a zoning variance nearly derailed the project before it could begin.

The permit application, submitted under the corporate name 2525 Inc., described the venue as a "pizzeria with entertainment," a vague description that made no mention of plans for a full-scale music venue. Cheektowaga Town Supervisor Daniel E. Weber took issue with the omission, publicly rebuking Goldstein—who headed the corporation—for submitting the request under "false pretenses."[950] Unfortunately for Supervisor Weber, the permit had already been quietly approved at an earlier board meeting, slipping through with little notice. By the time the issue drew attention, Goldstein had the permit in hand. Despite two additional attempts, Weber could not gather enough votes to have it rescinded.[951]

---

[a]Attracting Canadian patrons was also part of the strategy as New York's lower drinking age of 18 appealed to Canadians, whose legal age was 21 at the time

Weber's latest scolding galvanized local opposition. Concerned citizens, including the newly formed Depew Action League, began organizing against what they feared would become another Inferno-style nightclub in their backyard. In a February 1969 Letter to the Editor,[952] one member of the Depew Action League wrote:

"...[O]nly amusements which add to the moral fiber of our community should be allowed to open here and we do not think that this dancehall has any place in Cheektowaga or Depew...We urge the Cheektowaga Town Board to adopt a very restrictive dancehall ordinance as soon as possible to control this situation. We prefer this place isn't allowed to open."[953]

But the opposition came too late. With the permit secure, Goldstein and Elliott moved forward. In March 1969, roughly six months after the fire that destroyed the Inferno in Glen Park, they opened Gilligan's, proudly promoted as being under the "Same management as your old favorite... The INFERNO!"

The opening night was March 26, 1969.

The club launched with a bang, featuring Wilmer & the Dukes as the headlining act. The beloved band returned every Wednesday night, quickly establishing Gilligan's as a go-to destination for live music. In a notable moment of reconciliation, Barbara St. Clair & The Pin-Kooshins—who had lost their equipment in the Inferno fire—returned to the fold and performed at Gilligan's in June 1969.

Gilligan's drew even larger crowds than its predecessor. By then, more baby boomers had reached the legal drinking age, and the music itself took on a harder edge—whether due to shifting audience tastes or the emerging influence of David Goldstein's oldest son, Steve, who was beginning to shape the club's musical direction.

Figure 320 Advertisement for Opening Night at Gilligan's

As for the legacy of this unforgettable venue, local music historian Bob Paxon captures the spirit of Gilligan's in his own words:

Deep Purple toured on both "In Rock" (July 1971) and "The Book of Taliesyn" (May 1969), and certainly had the joint rocking as it was known to be one of the loudest bands on tour. In one city, three patrons were knocked unconscious as a result of standing too near the band's 10,000-watt Marshall PA system. (In terms of ear-splitters, Deep Purple faced stiff competition from Blue Cheer who travelled with four Marshall stacks each (guitar and bass)).

Cactus recorded a live album at Gilligan's (not released until decades later. but it's killer), with local band "Magic Ring" (formerly Twiggs) opening for them. "The Crazy World of Arthur Brown" played there with Vincent Crane (later of Atomic Rooster) and Arthur's "helmet of fire."

You could say Gilligan's was Buffalo's version of The Fillmore, except it did not feature many "hippie bands." They had more underground, acid rock, and hard rock performers. Although Gilligan's offered plenty of mainstream acts like Joe Cocker, Chicago (the same week their first "Chicago Transit Authority" album came out), Ricky Nelson and even Tiny Tim, I view it as a kind-of Buffalo's Grande Ballroom... without the acid.

At some point the Goldsteins must have realized that some of these bands had outgrown their club... or that by gathering up a few of them, they could do big business at bigger venues. They created Iron Spur Music Inc and put on shows like Rod Stewart & Faces with Cactus and Audience at the Aud.

Gilligan's shut its doors in 1972, to be followed by Uncle Sam's, a national franchise group owned locally by the Goldsteins. To confuse matters further, a club name "The Inferno" received a reprise at the former lumber yard around 1985, long after its namesake in Williamsville burned in 1968.

THE LAST DAYS OF GLEN AMUSEMENTS

Following the demolition and cleanup of the charred remains of the Inferno in the fall and winter of 1968, Emprise Corporation, through its subsidiary Sportservice Corp. announced plans to revive part of the property for the 1969 summer season.

Spokesman Jack Zander told reporters that "two or three or more amusement rides" would be installed on the footprint where the nightclub once stood. The nearby structure known as the Family Inn, situated beside the Glen Avenue bridge would serve as an event venue.[954]

As in previous years, Glen Park's maintenance crew spent the winter months preparing amusements for the upcoming season. Each fall, the rides were dismantled and stored in the Family Inn). During the coldest months, staff would clean, repair, and repaint the pieces—signage, themed murals—in preparation for the park's spring reopening.

YEARLY CLEAN-UP

As had been the custom for many years, Jimmy Moser was called in as soon as April rolled around to clean up the park with his young team of men.

Patrick Hasburgh,[955] a member of the cleaning crew, said that participating in the work was almost "magical.

"It was the circus before the gates opened," he said. "We got to see behind the curtain; I loved it."

In the early days of the cleanup, he saw "large drifts of icy snow melting in the early sun revealing picnic tables and piles of dead leaves from the previous fall."

He remembers that the removable components of the amusement rides were "stacked everywhere—painted horses, miniature helicopters, bumper cars, and flying cages."

"It seemed that everything needed painting and a good scrubbing; but for a teenager in Western New York, it was a coveted job: keys to a childhood kingdom," Hasburgh said.[956]

THE AMUSEMENT PARK'S FINAL RIDE

After four years of amusement park operations following the Inferno's demise, Emprise permanently shut the gates at the end of the 1972 summer season. The company began liquidating the rides and preparing the prime real estate for sale. By the spring of 1973, most of the amusement rides had been sold to Fun-N-Games Park in nearby Tonawanda, NY.[957] The Family Inn (aka The Old Barn), once the home of live shows and buffet dinners, would no longer host events. It was repurposed as a storage facility for fuel tanks, landscaping tools, signage, cleaning supplies, and other remnants of park maintenance.

Figure 321 The park's mural in the final days
Photo courtesy of Kathleen Venezia

By September 1973, Glen Park had been essentially shuttered for a year. Since then, the only visitors to the grounds were police patrols, maintenance crews, and occasional trespassers. Over the months, the outbuildings around the park, left abandoned on cracked and crumbling asphalt, were weathered by harsh Western New York winters and the daily intrusions of gatecrashers, who left graffiti, broken bottles, and piles of trash. The property appeared desolate.

In June 1973, Hutchinson Hose responded to a call at the park after vandals started a rubbish fire. Investigators suspected the perpetrators "might have had other designs."[958] Paint thinner had

Figure 322 Final Days

been poured onto the ground and set alight. Firefighters called the overall condition of the property "a mess."[959]

Two days later, another blaze broke out, destroying the old hot dog stand and damaging a large willow tree. Three five-gallon containers—formerly used to hold flammable liquids—were found nearby. One firefighter was treated for injuries sustained at the scene.

Then came September 8, 1973, a day that would mark the final blow to Altman's Glen. The Old Barn, once a bustling venue that could accommodate up to 800 patrons, erupted in flames.[960]

While the 1968 fire that destroyed the Inferno had been dramatic, the 1973 blaze that consumed The Old Barn proved far more dangerous. "There may have been more apparatus at the Casino fire, but [The Old Barn] was tougher to fight," said Hutchinson Hose Fire Chief Evor G. Williams.[b]

Amherst police spotted the fire just before 7 p.m. and called it in. Williams, riding on the first Hutchinson Hose

Figure 323 Fire from the Bridge
Photo courtesy of Hutchinson Hose Fire Department

truck to arrive, found flames sweeping through the complex of vacant buildings.[961] The Snyder Fire Department responded to the initial alarm. Main-Transit and Eggertsville joined the fight at 8 p.m. following a second alarm, and Getzville arrived within minutes of the third.

The building's position below the Glen Avenue bridge allowed firefighters to approach from both ground and air. But early in the battle, two Hutchinson Hose teams were nearly killed when the combustible materials stored in the barn caused a sudden flare-up that caught the firefighters by surprise.

"It was a scary place, a real 'hot spot' for us," Williams said. He recalled having a dozen or more men inside the barn when the flames began "jumping through the building."[962]

"They dropped the hose and ran like hell," he added. Three firefighters were burned during the narrow escape.[963]

---

[b] Appreciation is due to David Sherman, who provided much of the narrative in this section through his research and earlier publication: *Rough and Ready: Hutchinson Hose Volunteer Fire Company, Williamsville, New York,* Established February 16, 1856, ed. David Sherman (Williamsville, NY; Lifetouch, 2006).

Also at risk were the crews atop Hutchinson Hose's new $98,000 aerial scope, positioned on the bridge directly over the barn.[964]

"No one heard my message not to put the scope there," Williams said. "They were fried like fish in a pan." The men in the aerial scope's bucket, dangerously close to the burning barn, suffered burns.[965]

In total, eight firefighters were injured in the blaze that night. The new aerial scope sustained damage, with its side warning lights and dome light melting from the heat.[966]

Other fire departments that joined the effort included Clarence Center that used its tanker to prevent embers from landing on Mill Street rooftops. Harris Hill firefighters drafted water from Ellicott Creek. In total, it took two hours and 20 pieces of firefighting apparatus to bring the blaze under control.[967] Once the smoke cleared, it could be seen that the building had been reduced to twisted steel and ashes.

Figure 324 Ruins of The Old Barn
PD

Arson was never in doubt. In the days that followed, a Snyder Volunteer Fire Department captain suggested that children seen running from the area may have started the blaze.[968] But Williams quickly dismissed that idea: "It spread out of control too quickly to have started by them," he said.[969]

The arsonists knew what they were doing. Investigators found accelerants and multiple ignition points, as well as smaller fires in nearby outbuildings—clear signs of a coordinated effort to wipe the slate clean. As a new day dawned, it was apparent that they had succeeded. The three-alarm blaze marked the final chapter for Altman's Glen, leaving behind only blackened ruins.

Figure 325 Once the demolition crews were finished, all that was left was the bridge that Clyde Urban had once built that took patrons from the games area to the amusement rides
Photo courtesy of Grever & Ward

The *Amherst Bee* captured the moment with somber poetry: "Today, the park, which gave years of pleasure to old and young alike, lies desolate, abandoned to the ravages of time. Where once the park was thronged with patrons shouting and laughing, silence now reigns."[970]

In the years that followed, the future of the Glen became a source of bitter dispute among the Village of Williamsville residents. One side wanted to privatize the land for residential development; the other fought to reclaim it as a passive park, reimagined with sculpted hills, greenery, and tranquil reflecting pools. Either choice would dramatically depart from the Glen that Altman had built, a flat expanse of black asphalt, nearly at creek level, broken only by a few towering trees that dared not interfere with the amusements.

For more than 40 years, Altman's Glen had been a place of lights, laughter, and spectacle—and, in its fiery end, a place of silent ruin. After a bruising three-year battle in the mid-1970s, the residents of Williamsville chose natural conservation over profit, ensuring the land would remain open to anyone seeking a serene and reflective experience.

Harry, the ultimate showman, would have understood. He always recognized a good stage when he saw one. In this final act, Glen Park no longer hosts orchestras or grand performances. Instead, the gentle music of the falls has become the star of the show. The park's eleven acres, once bustling with crowds, have been carefully restored to a place of natural beauty, open and welcoming.

Here, within these pages, memories are rekindled. Harry's vision endures—a legacy preserved in photographs and words, held close in memory and offered to those who seek to understand what once was.

To this place, to Harry, to the spirit that lives on: *L'chaim.*

TABLE OF FIGURES

INDEX

SOURCES

1 Encyclopedia Judaica, 2nd ed., s.v. "Kiddushin," vol. 9, cols. 1188—1198, accessed April 28, 2025, https://www.eleven.co.il.

2 Yannay Spitzer, "Jewish Occupations in the Pale of Settlement," Yannay Spitzer (blog), September 30, 2012, https://yannayspitzer.net/2012/09/30/jewish-occupations-in-the-pale-of-settlement/.

3 Dubnow, Simon. *History of the Jews in Russia and Poland*, Vol. 3. Philadelphia: Jewish Publication Society of America, 1916.

4 John Doyle Klier, *Imperial Russia's Jewish Question, 1855—1881* (Cambridge: Cambridge University Press, 1995), 64.

5 Irving Howe, *World of Our Fathers: The Journey of the East European Jews to America and the Life They Found and Made* (New York: Harcourt Brace Jovanovich, 1976), 5-7.

6 Selig Adler and Thomas E. Connolly, *From Ararat to Suburbia: The History of the Jewish Community of Buffalo* (Philadelphia: Jewish Publication Society of America, 1960), 169.

7 Adler and Connolly, *From Ararat to Suburbia*, 188.

8 "Canal Street, Buffalo," Discovering Buffalo One Street at a Time.

9 "Canal Street, Buffalo," Discovering Buffalo One Street at a Time. "Canal Street, Buffalo, 'The Wickedest Street in the World,'" Discovering Buffalo One Street at a Time, March 31, 2014, https://buffalostreets.com/2014/03/31/canal-street-buffalo/.

10 "Canal Street, Buffalo, '" Discovering Buffalo One Street at a Time."

11 Eagle Preserving Co. Sues Five Insurance Companies," *Buffalo Courier*, March 21, 1909, 21.

12 "Beaten in One Suit, He Sues Another," *Buffalo Courier*, January 26, 1910, 6.

13 "Altman's Insurance Actions Dismissed," *Buffalo Courier*, May 30, 1910, 7.

14 "Witness Tells of Gasoline Sprinkling Just Before Fire at Altman's Place," *Buffalo Courier*, December 17, 1909, 6.

15 "Altman Again Sues Insurance Company," *Buffalo Courier*, March 15, 1910, 8.

16 "Another Altman Case on Trial," *Buffalo Enquirer*, May 14, 1910, 6.

17 "Altman Gets a Verdict," *The Buffalo News*, March 16, 1910, 17.

18 "Altman Loses Insurance Case," *Buffalo Courier*, March 26, 1910, 7.

19 Ibid.

20 "Truth or Lie," *Buffalo Enquirer*, January 26, 1910, 1.

21 "Chief Witness Has a Bad Memory," *The Buffalo Commercial*, March 14, 1910, 11.

[22]"Fire Was Planned, Says Young Altman," *The Buffalo News*, December 18, 1909, 8.

[23] "Another Altman Case on Trial," *The Buffalo Enquirer*, May 14, 1909, 8.

[24]"Must Go Thirsty or Drink Water," *The Buffalo Commercial*, May 20, 1909, 13.

[25] Ibid.

[26] Ibid.

[27] "Held Up in Her Home," *Buffalo Evening News*, December 18, 1898, 1.

[28] "Criminal Work," *The Buffalo Commercial*, January 18, 1899, 14.

[29] Ed Sullivan, "Little Old New York," *Albany Times Union*, May 1, 1955, R4.

[30] Adler and Connolly, *From Ararat to Suburbia*, 34.

[31] "Charles Altman, 80, Dies; Former Produce Dealer,." *Buffalo Courier-Express*, July 1, 1965, 24.

[32] "Harry Evans Weds," *The Buffalo Times*, December 23, 1901, 2.

[33] "Harry Evans Will Wed Miss Altman," *The Buffalo Enquirer*, December 20, 1901, 11.

[34] Ibid.

[35] "Morris Altman Weds Miss Minnie Bergstein," *Buffalo Courier*, November 16, 1911, 6.

[36] "Morris Altman Guides Jewish Home 25 Years," *Buffalo News*, October 23, 1933, 54.

[37] "A Conversation with the Parents of the Jewish Opera Singer, Thelma Altman." *The Forward*, December 1941.

[38] Ibid.

[39] *A People at Risk*, Library of Congress. https://www.loc.gov/item/2021669796/.

[40] "Stars and Area Folk to Honor Harry Altman" *The Buffalo Courier-Express*, August 1959, 59.

[41] Adler and Connolly, *From Ararat to Suburbia*, 187.

[42] Chana Revell Kotzin, *Jewish Community of Greater Buffalo* (Charleston, SC: Arcadia Publishing, 2013).

[43] Adler and Connolly, *From Ararat to Suburbia*, 187.

[44] Ibid.

[45] Hall-Saladino, Samantha, "Gloversville in Hollywood Part 1: Samuel Goldwyn." *Fulton County Historian* (blog). December 5, 2017, https://fultoncountyhistorian.wordpress.com/2017/12/05/gloversville-in-hollywood-part-1-samuel-goldwyn/.

[46] Cynthia Morey, Gloversville History, Facebook post, January 31, 2014, accessed January 24, 2024, https://www.facebook.com/groups/GloversvilleHistory/.

[47] "Goldwyn and Gloversville—Focus on History," *The Daily Gazette*, September 8, 1923, 6.

[48] Peter Betz, "Goldwyn and Gloversville—Focus on History," Gloversville History (Facebook page), September 8, 2013,

https://www.facebook.com/permalink.php/?id=350171255121746&story_fbid=
357152361090302.

[49] "Samuel Goldwyn Quotes," BrainyQuote, accessed April 29, 2025,
https://www.brainyquote.com/quotes/samuel_goldwyn_1210640.

[50] "Dictionaries Take Beating," Rome Sentinel, December 2, 1946, 10.

[51] O'Brian, Jack. "Broadway." *Morning Pioneer*, December 6, 1946, 7.

[52] Ibid.

[53] Rick Falkowski, *Historic & Influential People from Buffalo & WNY* (Volume II), 278.

[54] "Altman Rites Are Tomorrow," *The Courier-Express*, December 20, 1936, 8.

[55] "Mardi Gras Carnival of the Cabaret Club to Be a Mammoth Joyfest," *The Buffalo Times*, November 4, 1912, 4.

[56] "American Night Draws Big Crowd to Auditorium," *Buffalo Courier*, May 23, 1913, 6.

[57] "2000 Children to Participate in Games at Auditorium Tonight," *The Buffalo Evening News*, May 24, 1913, 13.

[58] Ibid.

[59] "2000 Children to Participate in Games at Auditorium Tonight," *The Buffalo Evening News*.

[60] "Mardi Gras Dance Marks Hallowe'en," *Buffalo Courier*, October 26, 1913, 45.

[61] "Mayor to Open Mardi Gras," *Buffalo Enquirer*, October 29, 1913, 12.

[62] "Real Mardi Gras," *The Buffalo Enquirer*, October 21, 1913, 7.

[63] "Tango Contest at Mardi Gras," *The Buffalo Enquirer*, October 25, 1913, 2.

[64] "That Mardi Gras," *The Buffalo Enquirer*, October 29, 1913, 3

[65] "Mardi Gras Festival," *The Buffalo Times*, October 31, 1913, 6.

[66] "Grotesque Parade Brilliant Success; Thousands Laugh," *The Buffalo Enquirer*, August 20, 1914, 8.

[67] "'Studes' will Swell Fun at Mardi Gras," *Buffalo Courier*, October 25, 1914, 78.

[68] "Chase and Kelly are Appointed as Judges," *The Buffalo Times*, October 18, 1914, 54.

[69] "Mardi Gras Dance Tonight," *The Buffalo Enquirer*, October 30, 1914, 9.

[70] "Valuable Prizes at Mardi Gras Dance," *The Buffalo Times*, Oct 1, 1914, 8.

[71] "Great Crowd at Mardi Gras," *The Buffalo Enquirer*, October 31, 1913, 9.

[72] "Marriage Licenses," *Buffalo Courier*, March 17, 1915, page 5.

[73] "Crystal Beach to Open on Next Saturday," *The Buffalo Enquirer*, May 22, 1915, 9.

[74] "Fifteen Hundred in Grotesque Parade," *The Buffalo Enquirer*, October 28, 1915, 11.

[75] "Parade and Mardi Gras of Enquirer a Huge Success," *The Buffalo Enquirer*, November 2, 1915, 3.

[76] Ibid.

[77] "Enquirer's Grotesque Parade to be Held Tuesday, October 31st," *The Buffalo Enquirer*, September 13, 1916, 3.

[78] Ibid.

[79] "Parade Entries Close Tonight," *The Buffalo Enquirer*, October 25, 1916, 3.

[80] "All Ready for the Enquirer's Parade Tonight," *The Buffalo Enquirer*, October 31, 1916, 1.

[81] "Enquirer's Grotesque Parade," *Buffalo Enquirer*, September 13, 1916, 3.

[82] "Court Calendars—Equity Term," *Buffalo Courier*, April 18, 1916, 12.

[83] "Halloween Masquerade," *The Buffalo Times*, October 10, 1917, 41.

[84] "Engagements Announced," *Buffalo Courier*, January 4, 1916, 5.

[85] "Annual Grotesque Parade Conducted by Enquirer will be held October 31st," *The Buffalo Courier*, October 22, 1916, 71.

[86] "Buffalo Enquirer Grotesque Parade Tomorrow Night," *The Buffalo Enquirer*, October 30, 1916, page 3.

[87] "Parade Entries Close Tonight," *The Buffalo Enquirer*, October 25, 1916, 3.

[88] "Anson is Here," *The Buffalo Enquirer*, October 31, 1916, 12.

[89] Robert H. Schaefer, "Anson in Greasepaint: The Vaudeville Career of Adrian C. Anson," *The National Pastime* 28 (2008), 11.

[90] "Anson is Here," *Buffalo Enquirer*, October 31, 1916.

[91] "Thousands Attend Mardi Gras," *The Buffalo Enquirer*, November 1, 1916, 7.

[92] "Wilson Before Congress at 8 PM," *The Buffalo News*, April 3, 1917, 1.

[93] Jacek A. Wysocki, "Behind the Great War: 'Home Fires Kept Burning—1917—1918,'" *Western New York Heritage Magazine*, 36.

[94] Wysocki, "Behind the Great War," 44.

[95] Ibid.

[96] *History of Buffalo and Erie County, 1914—1915*, ed. Daniel J. Sweeney (Buffalo, NY: Committee of 100, under authority of the City of Buffalo, 1916), 59.

[97] "Aid Concert for Base Hospital," *The Buffalo Enquirer*, April 26, 1917, 2.

[98] "Cantors Give Fine Concert for Hospital," *The Buffalo News*, May 10, 1917, 5.

[99] "Big Show for Boys at Fort Niagara," *The Buffalo Enquirer*, September 20, 1917, 1.

[100] "Fourth Annual Grotesque Parade," *The Buffalo Enquirer*, September 13, 1917, 11.

[101] Ibid.

[102] "Final Plans for the Big Parade," *The Buffalo Enquirer*, October 1, 1917, 9.

[103] "Final Plans for the Big Parade," *The Buffalo Enquirer*, September 25, 1917, 5.

[104] "Mutt and Jeff at Masquerade Dance," *The Buffalo Enquirer*, October 29, 1917, 7.

[105] "Grand Ball," *The Buffalo News*, December 13, 1917, 2

[106] "Buffalo in the American Influenza Epidemic," *Influenza Encyclopedia*, University of Michigan Center for the History of Medicine, 2016, https://www.influenzaarchive.org/cities/city-buffalo.html (accessed May 21, 2025).

[107] "New Flu Cases Drop to 569 for Day; 1010 Deaths," *The Buffalo Courier*, Oct. 26, 1918, 5.

[108] "Buffalo in the American Influenza Epidemic," *Influenza Encyclopedia.*

[109] "Hallowe'en Ball is Postponed Until Thursday, November 7," *The Buffalo Enquirer,* October 28, 1918, 2.

[110] "The Hallowe'en Dance is Postponed Until Thursday Nov. 7th," *The Buffalo Times,* October 27, 1918, 27.

[111] "Parade Tonight Before 'Dance of the Allies,'" *The Buffalo Enquirer,* November 7, 1918, 6.

[112] "Girls Wanted for 'Dance of the Allies,'" *The Buffalo Enquirer,* November 6, 1918, 9.

[113] Ibid.

[114] "Big Crowd Attends 'Dance of the Allies,'" *The Buffalo Courier,* November 8, 1918, 13.

[115] "Victory Dance Next Monday If Peace is Declared," *The Buffalo Enquirer,* November 9, 1918, 14.

[116] Ibid.

[117] Ibid.

[118] "Victory Dance Next Monday," *Buffalo Enquirer,* November 9, 1918.

[119] "Rally in Square," *The Buffalo News,* October 17, 1918, 2.

[120] "Ex-Entertainer Harry E. Webb Dies in Florida," *The Buffalo News,* October 19, 1967, 3.

[121] Ibid.

[122] "Great Crowd at the Victory Dance," *The Buffalo Enquirer,* November 12, 1918, 9.

[123] Ibid.

[124] Ibid.

[125] Ibid.

[126] "Big Victory Chanukah Fete Tomorrow Night at Broadway Auditorium," *The Buffalo Enquirer,* December 3, 1917, 3.

[127] "'Dance of the Aces' a Big Success," *The Buffalo Enquirer,* December 13, 1918, 13.

[128] "'Dance of the Aces' Thursday at Auditorium, *The Buffalo Enquirer,* December 7, 1918, 5.

[129] Ibid.

[130] "Invite Stage Folk to Leady 'Victory March' at Dance," *Buffalo Courier,* December 19, 1918, 7.

[131] "Farewell Party for Miss Rosen of Toledo," *The Buffalo* Enquirer, December 10, 1918, 12.

[132] "Rosen-Altman," *The Buffalo Enquirer,* February 28, 1919, 11.

[133] Ibid.

[134] "Ed Hyman's Career Parallels Growth of Movie Business," *The Buffalo News,* April 6, 1949, 72.

[135] "Mardi Gras Co. Has Ambitious Plans on Foot," *The Buffalo Enquirer,* September 27, 1919, 6.

[136] Ibid.

137 "Mardi Gras Dances to Start September 13," *Buffalo Courier*, August 24, 1919, 43.

138 Preservation Ready Sites ,"Elmwood Music Hall," Accessed May 21, 2025.

139 "Bolton's Band, Fresh from Field of War, to Play Dance Music," *Buffalo Courier*, September 7, 1919, 64.

140 "Six Thousand at Mardi Gras Ball," *The Buffalo Enquirer*, October 3, 1919, 15.

141 Ibid.

142 Ibid.

143 Ibid.

144 "$500 in Prizes at Masquerade on Hallowe'en," *The Buffalo Enquirer*, October 18, 1919, 6.

145 "Mardi Gras to Celebrate Hallowe'en," *The Buffalo Times*, October 26, 1919, 39.

146 "Annual Mardi Gras Ball this Evening at the Auditorium," *The Buffalo Times*, October 2, 1919, 17.

147 "Hero at Peace Dance Tonight," *The Buffalo Enquirer*, November 11, 1919, 8.

148 "Little Miss Altman," *The Buffalo Enquirer*, December 5, 1919, 19.

149 "News from Here, There, Everywhere," *The Glovers Review*, January 1920, 35.

150 "The Port Side Column," *The Buffalo Enquirer*, March 29, 1920, 1

151 "Civic Stadium Scene of Big Navy Relief Show Tonight," *Buffalo Courier*, July 20, 1942, 18.

152 "Elaborate Preparations for Mardi Gras Ball," *The Buffalo Enquirer,"* September 25, 1920, 5.

153 Ibid.

154 "Mardi Gras Ball on October 6th," *The Buffalo Times,* September 12, 1920, 46.

155 "Windows Smashed, Much Other Damage about City," *Buffalo Courier*, December 19, 1921, 2.

156 "Incorporations," *The New York Times,* October 7, 1925, 42.

157 Ibid.

158 "Jolson Girls Show New Boot Styles," *The Buffalo Evening News*, December 16, 1923, 9.

159 "3-Alarm Fire Sweeps Seneca Street Block, $100,000 Loss." *The Buffalo Enquirer*, December 31, 1924, 1.

160 "Women's Show Shop to be Opened in City," *The Buffalo Courier*, December 13, 1925, 14.

161 "Joins Firm," *The Buffalo Times,* November 4, 1926, 22.

162 Preservation Ready Survey of Buildings Downtown, Northland and Fougeron/Urban Survey Areas, City of Buffalo, Erie County, New York (Buffalo: Panamerican Consultants, Inc., 2013), 112, https://buffaloah.com/surveys/PresReady/PresReady.pdf.

163 "$200,000- Bramson Building, Inc.," *The Buffalo Courier*, April 13, 1924, 82.

164 "Thirty-fifth Year in the Restaurant Business," *Buffalo Jewish Review*, November 14, 1924, 17.

[165] "Bramson's Café Opens with Dinner for 200 Guests," *The Buffalo Courier*, April 13, 1924, 80.

[166] Ibid.

[167] "Bramson's Café Opens," 80.

[168] Ibid.

[169] "Bramson Restaurant is Opened Today," *The Buffalo Enquirer*, April 11, 1924, 8.

[170] "File Liabilities List," *The Buffalo Enquirer*, August 20, 1924, 12.

[171] "Noted Building to be Replaced," *The Buffalo Evening News*, May 7, 1940, 8.

[172] "Altman Friend to Many in Area," *The Buffalo Courier-Express*, May 10, 1966, 23.

[173] "Roller Skating Every Night," *The Buffalo Times*, March 22, 1924, page 14.

[174] "Wes Barry's All-Star Act to Opens at Arcadia Ballroom on Monday," *Buffalo Courier Express*, March 4, 1927, 18.

[175] Ibid.

[176] "Wes Barry Here in Person," *Buffalo Courier Express*, March 7, 1927, 5.

[177] "New Arcadia Ballroom to Open Saturday Night," *Buffalo Courier Express*, September 2, 1927, 7.

[178] "New Arcadia Ballroom," *Buffalo Evening News*, September 2, 1927, 24.

[179] "Ballroom Notes," *The Billboard*, November 17, 1928, 27.

[180] Bill Coleman, *Trumpet Story* (Boston: Northeastern University Press, 1991). 44

[181] Bill Coleman, "Trumpet Story," 52.

[182] Ibid.

[183] "Former Arcadia Ballroom Heads to Open New Pavilion," *Buffalo Courier Express*, July 29, 1928, 4,

[184] "Bus Terminal Here is Second Largest," *The Buffalo Evening News*, May 1, 1931, 21.

[185] "Art Landry at Ritz," *The Buffalo Times*, September 30, 1928, 48.

[186] "New Ritz Ballroom," The *Buffalo Times*, August 26, 1928, 19.

[187] "Roller Rink at Park Made into Dance Hall," *Rochester Times Union*, May 28, 1932, 8.

[188] "Daily Hammer," *The Buffalo Times*, October 26, 1928, 26.

[189] "New Ballroom Opened: Patrons Tax Capacity of Downtown Dance Palace," *The Courier-Express*, October 27, 1928, 9.

[190] Ibid.

[191] "On the Fence," *The Buffalo Times*, October 26, 1927, 32.

[192] "Safe Blowers are Amateurs, Police Think," *The Courier-Express*, October 30, 1928, 1.

[193] "I'm Thankful!" *The Buffalo Times*, November 18, 1928, 9.

[194] "Fenton, Friend of Poor, Widely Known," *The Buffalo Enquirer*, January 31, 1924, 9.

[195] Ibid

[196] Ibid.

[197] "Harry Altman Dies; Club Owner," *The Buffalo Courier-Express*, May 9, 1966, 1.

[198] "Speedy Anderson Found Guilty," *The Buffalo Courier*, April 9, 1921, 12.

[199] "Rum Trade Barred in Robbery Trial," *The Buffalo News*, September 9, 1930, 1.

[200] "Near Pain at Palais Royal When 20 Dry Agents Pay Call," *The Buffalo News*, January 3, 1930, 1,

[201] Ibid.

[202] Ibid.

[203] Ibid.

[204] Ibid.

[205] "Orchestra to Play at Dinner for Poor," *The Buffalo News*, December 22, 1930, 16.

[206] "Midnight Show Adds $5,000 to Fund for Needy," *The Courier-Express*, February 7, 1932, 22.

[207] "Two Escape Injury in Bomb Explosion," *Buffalo Evening News*, May 21, 1932, 3.

[208] Ibid.

[209] Ibid.

[210] "New Dance Center will Open Tonight," *The Buffalo Times*, September 5, 1931, 8.

[211] "Park Central Ballroom to Open for Season Tonight," *The Courier-Express*, September 19, 1932, 14.

[212] "New Glen Colosseum Now Open to Public," *Lockport Union-Sun & Journal*, October 10, 1934, 5.

[213] Marathon Dancers at Beach Get Hour Cut," *Buffalo Courier Express*, August 1, 1928. 1.

[214] Ibid.

[215] Ibid.

[216] "Twenty-five Couples Accepted for Sea Breeze Dance Marathon," *Democrat and Chronicle*, September 9,1928, 20.

[217] Ibid.

[218] "Dozen Couples, Eyes on Heaven, Girls Feet Weary, Cut to Eleven," *Rochester Democrat & Chronicle*, September 13, 1928, 15.

[219] "Tireless Cupid Gets in Shot as Marathon Die-Hards Lag On," *Rochester Democrat & Chronicle*, September 16, 1928, 19.

[220] "Five Couples Fight Fatigue as Marathon Enters Seventh Day," *Rochester Democrat & Chronicle*, September 17, 1928, 15.

[221] Ibid.

[222] "Dance Marathon at Danceland—Sea Breeze Park—September 1928," (Rochester, NY: Public Relations Department at Seabreeze, 2022).

[223] Winning Marathon Teams Paid Off in Secrecy; Each Couple Gets $250," *Rochester Democrat & Chronicle*, September 19, 1928, 2.

[224] Ibid.

[225] "Dancers in Dreamline Two Ways Plodding in Sea Breeze Marathon," *Rochester Democrat & Chronicle*, August 24, 1932, 15.

226 "Derby Dancers to Beat Cops to Last Waltz," *Rochester Times-Union*, September 4, 1932, 9.

227 "Derby Dancers,' 9.

228 Ibid.

229 "7 Couples Complete 20 Days Dancing; Get $35.72 Apiece," *Rochester Democrat & Chronicle,"* September 11, 1932, 7.

230 Ibid.

231 "Marathon Amusement Company is Chartered," *The Buffalo Evening News,* November 16, 1932, 28,

232 'Incorporations," *Buffalo Evening News,* September 17, 1936, 39.

233 "Buffalo Men are Nabbed in Detroit," *The Buffalo Enquirer*, December 6, 1918, 14.

234 "90 Indicted in Drive on Liquor; Source of Poison Bootleg Found," The *Buffalo Evening News,* July 29, 1926, 1.

235 "Main Street Property Sold," *The Buffalo Times*, March 4, 1923, 56,

236 "Arthur J. Block Buys 625-6377 Main Street," *The Buffalo Evening News*, October 7, 1925, 14.

237 "Incorporations," *The New York Times*, September 26, 1925, 37.

238 "Wallens Corned Beef Shop," *The Buffalo Jewish Review*, October 31, 1930, 2.

239 "Dinty Moore's, Inc., *The Buffalo Evening News*, November 20, 1930, 18.

240 "Beer for Local Eating Places, Homes Today," *The Courier-Express*, April 7, 1933, 1.

241 "Bankruptcies," *The Buffalo Evening News*, October 1, 1935, 26.

242 "Legal News," *The Niagara Falls Gazette*, August 17, 1934, 25.

243 "Business Names," *The Buffalo Evening News,* April 13, 1934, 10.

244 "Nightclubbing," *The Buffalo Evening News,* September 30, 1936, 18.

245 "Flames Sweep Big Ballroom on Main Street," *The Buffalo Courier-Express,* December 10, 1936, 1.

246 "Dance Hall Fire Ties Up Traffic," *The Buffalo Evening News,* December 10, 1936, 17.

247 "Arson Reports Denied by Fire Commissioner," *The Buffalo Courier-Express,* December 20, 1936, 1.

248 Ibid.

249 "Jinxed Orchestra," *The Buffalo Evening News,* December 11, 1936, 36.

250 "Grave to Gay," *The Buffalo Evening News,* February 8, 1937, 17.

251 "Hickory Steak House Opening October 3d at 360 Main Street," *The Buffalo Courier Express,* September 20, 1935, 18.

252 "Gay Party Savarin," *The Buffalo Times,* October 4, 1935, 34.

253 "Savarin," *The Buffalo Times,* September 12, 1935, 20.

254 Ibid.

255 Ibid.

256 "Back Again," *The Buffalo Times,* September 15, 1935, 36.

257 "Racket Rumor Inquiry Begun by Police Head," *The Buffalo Times*, February 5, 1937, 1.

258 "Higgins Holds City's Crime Showing Good," *The Buffalo Courier-Express*, March 11, 1937, page 1.

259 "Women to Seek Better Policing," *The Buffalo Evening News*, March 11, 1937, page 1.

260 "Racket Rumor Inquiry Begun," 1.

261 Ibid.

262 Ibid.

263 Ibid.

264 Ibid.

265 Ibid.

266 "Savarin Café, Buffalo," *The Billboard*, October 30, 1937, 20.

267 "Slam-Bang," *The Buffalo Courier-Express*, December 11, 1937, 26.

268 "A Daring Revelation," *The Buffalo Times*, February 24, 1939, 19.

269 Ibid.

270 "Kay Fears, Milk Bather, wants to be a Nun," *Oklahoma Tribune*, March 12, 1939, 51.

271 Ibid.

272 "Once Over Lightly," *The Buffalo Courier-Express*, March 4, 1939, 6.

273 "Legal Notice," *The Buffalo Times*, February 9, 1934, 17.

274 'Elks Make Merry at Annual Outing," *The Buffalo Enquirer*, June 19, 1919, 12.

275 Ibid.

276 "200 Investment in Grove Started Harry Altman Career," *The Buffalo Evening News*, July 1, 1960, 14.

277 Ibid.

278 Prominent Business and Professional Men (Buffalo, NY: *Buffalo Times*, 1918).

279 George M. Bailey, *Illustrated Buffalo: The Queen City of the Lakes* (New York: Acme Publishing and Engraving Co., 1890), 185.

280 "Burying Paupers," *Buffalo Daily Republic*, July 10, 1885, 4.

281 "Another Point Scored," *The Buffalo Morning Sunday News*, July 26, 1885, 1,

282 "Buying Paupers," 4.

283 "Monopoly in the Grave," *The Buffalo Morning Sunday News*, July 5, 1885, 1,

284 Ibid.

285 Ibid.

286 Ibid.

287 "Pauper Burials," *The Evening Telegraph*, July 14, 1885, 1.

288 *Illustrated Buffalo*, 185.

289 "Debs in Buffalo," *The Buffalo Express*, September 23, 1898, 7.

290 "Eugene V. Debs Here," *The Buffalo Evening News*, September 23, 1898, 1.

291 "Burial Reform," *The Buffalo Commercial*, August 5, 1899, 5.

[292] "Low Price, No Pomp," *The Buffalo Express,* August 22, 1899, 7.

[293] Ibid.

[294] *Illustrated Buffalo,* 185.

[295] Laura Helmuth, "The Disturbing, Shameful History of Childbirth Deaths," *Slate,* September 10, 2013, https://slate.com/technology/2013/09/childbirth-deaths-in-history.html.

[296] "Achievements in Public Health, 1900-1999: Healthier Mothers and Babies," *Morbidity and Mortality Weekly Report* 48, no. 38 (1999): 849—858.

[297] "City Hall Briefs," *The Buffalo Evening News,* February 18, 1902, 1.

[298] "Cars Bought First Night," *The Buffalo Express,* February 15, 1910, 5.

[299] "Our Day's Outing," *The Buffalo Evening News,* September 25, 1915, 11.

[300] Ibid.

[301] "Grand Picnic," *The New Age,* August 18, 1917, 5.

[302] "Elks Make Merry at Annual Outing," *The Buffalo Enquirer, June* 19, 1919, 12.

[303] *U.S., City Directories, 1822-1995: Buffalo, New York, City Directory, 1922,* 239.

[304] "Firemen's Convention Opens in Williamsville," *The Buffalo Times,* July 29, 1924, 1.

[305] Eric Herschthal, "The KKK's Attempt to Define America," *The New Republic,* January 16, 2018, https://newrepublic.com/article/146616/kkks-attempt-define-america.

[306] Shawn Lay, *Hooded Knights on the Niagara: The Ku Klux Klan in Buffalo, New York* (New York New York University Press, 1995), 77.

[307] Ibid.

[308] Daniel Robert Kowalski, *The Ku Klux Klan in Buffalo, New York, 1922—1924: A Class Study* (master's thesis, University of North Carolina at Greensboro, 1972).

[309] *Hooded Knights on the Niagara,* 64.

[310] Thomas Hunt and Michael A. Tona, *DiCarlo: Buffalo's First Family of Crime,* vol. I (2013), 136.

[311] "Klan Says It Will Close Roadhouse This Week," *Buffalo Commercial Advertiser,* March 17, 1924, 1.

[312] Ibid.

[313] *Hooded Knights on the Niagara,* 71.

[314] "The Ku Klux Klowns," *Heacocks,* April 1924, 15.

[315] Hunt and Tona, *DiCarlo,* 136.

[316] *Hooded Knights on the Niagara,* 76.

[317] Kowalski, 58.

[318] Ibid., 61.

[319] Ibid.

[320] "Mortician is Buried in Hand-Carved Casket," *Springville Journal,* February 1, 1940, 4.

[321] Ibid.

[322] Ibid.

[323] *Thomas M Cardina, 1881—1964*, MyHeritage Family Trees, accessed June 2, 2025, https://www.myheritage.com.

[324] "Kensington Theatre," *Cinema Treasures*, accessed June 2, 2025, https://cinematreasures.org/theaters/21525.

[325] "Event Tomorrow at Uptown Theater to Announce Funds for Restoration of Bailey Avenue Landmark," *Views of Buffalo*, February 27, 2014, https://viewsofbuffalo.blogspot.com/2014/02/event-tomorrow-at-uptown-theater-to.html.

[326] "New Theaters," *The Billboard*, November 14, 1925, 36.

[327] "Glen Amusement Pk," *The Buffalo Times*, July 4, 1925, 58 https://www.newspapers.com/paper/the-buffalo-times/9188/.

[328] Ibid.

[329] 'Glen Amusement Pk.," 58.

[330] Ibid.

[331] Ibid.

[332] "Ideal Picnic or Outing Grounds," *The Buffalo Evening News,* July 7, 1927, 28.

[333] Ibid.

[334] "Red Cross Benefit Performances at the Capitol Opening Night," *The Niagara Falls Gazette*, October 1, 1926, 19.

[335] "$200 investment in Grove Started Harry Altman's Career," *Buffalo Evening News*, July 1, 1960, 7.

[336] Ibid.

[337] Ibid.

[338] Ibid.

[339] Steve Goldstein Interview by Susan Fenster, May 20, 1921.

[340] Maron (Dykstra) Carubba (Menno and Edna's granddaughter) Interview by Susan Fenster, July 7, 2023.

[341] Ibid.

[342] "Glen Art Theatre," *Cinema Treasures*, accessed June 3, 2025, https://cinematreasures.org/theaters/61559.

[343] "New Theater in Williamsville Lists Fine Films," *The Buffalo Evening News*, March 13, 1959, 13.

[344] "Keller Leases Glen Theater," *The Buffalo Courier-Express, July 15,1965, 15.*

[345] "Ibid.

[346] "Glen Art Fire Destroys Theater and Book Shop," *The Buffalo Evening News*, November 12, 1970, 1.

[347] Michael Wutz interview by Susan Fenster, March 3, 2021.

[348] "J.H. Pardee Found Dead in Automobile," *The Buffalo Evening News,* November 15, 1931, 1.

[349] Ibid.

350 "Pardee Buys Erie Beach," *The Buffalo Times,* July 31, 1926, 13.

351 "Erie Beach: Canada's First Atlantic City—Episode 1" YouTube video, 10:06, posted by "History Lives Here," October 30, 2019, https://www.youtube.com/watch?v=Q5FQHlaouUQ

352 "J.H. Pardee Found Dead," 1.

353 *Amherst Bank v. Thomas Cardina,* New York Supreme Court, September 10, 1930.

354 Dan Byrne, "What is a nominee director?" *The Corporate Governance Institute,* accessed June 3, 2025, https://www.thecorporategovernanceinstitute.com/insights/lexicon/what-is-a-nominee-director/.

355 "Plan New Amusement Park at Williamsville," *Lockport Sun & Journal,* March 30, 1931, 4.

356 "Plan Amusement Park," *The Buffalo Courier-Express,* March 29, 1931, 17.

357 Ibid.

358 "Williamsville Amusement Park to Have Pool, Beach," *The Buffalo Courier-Express,* April 4, 1931, 15.

359 Ibid.

360 Ibid.

361 "Altman General Manager of Glen, Williamsville, NY, *The Billboard,* May 2, 1931, 44.

362 "Village will Fight Sunday Dance Case," *Buffalo Evening News,* May 15, 1931, 11.

363 Ibid.

364 Williamsville Bans Sunday Dancing; Legal Battle On," *The Buffalo Courier-Express,* May 11, 1931, 1.

365 Ibid.

366 Ibid.

367 "Col. Rogers Now Claims Pole Sitting Record," *The Buffalo Evening News,* September 1, 1931, 1.

368 "Shipwreck Kelly Leaves Post to Join Stricken Wife," *The Billboard,* August 1, 1931, 37.

369 Ibid.

370 "Names Features Which Proved Profitable at Glen for 1931," *The Billboard,* February 6, 1932, 38.

371 Ibid.

372 Ibid.

373 "Opening Dance of the Season," *The Bee,* April 8, 1932, 3.

374 "Big, Decoration Day Program," *The Buffalo News,* May 28, 1932, 20.

375 "Dancing Partners Wed in Lion's Cage," *The Buffalo Evening News,* May 5, 1931, 13.

376 Ibid.

377 Ibid.

378 Ibid.

[379] "Gets Verdict for Jury in Williamsville," *The Buffalo Courier-Express*, December 23, 1932, 1.

[380] Ibid.

[381] "Young and Old Enjoy Games at N.Y.C. Outing," *The Buffalo News*, July 13, 1934, 23.

[382] "Glen Park Memories," *The Amherst Bee*, July 21, 1976, 39.

[383] Ibid.

[384] Ibid.

[385] Ibid.

[386] "Bankruptcy Petitions," *The Buffalo Evening News*, February 9, 1934, 17.

[387] "Mortgages," *The Buffalo Law Journal,* November 14, 1934, 5.

[388] Certificate of Incorporation, *Williamsville Amusement Corporation*, May 3, 1934, New York Department of State, Division of Corporations.

[389] "Valentine E. O'Grady, Former Internal Revenue Deputy, Dies," *The Buffalo Evening News,* January 8, 1951, 7.

[390] "Alleged Bigamist's Son Arrested for Running Booze Still," *The Buffalo Commercial,* August 22, 1922, 3.

[391] "Lee Healy Dies; Buffalo Attorney," *The Buffalo Evening News*, July 2, 1956, 19.

[392] "Glen Park Casino will Open Saturday; Music by Robinson," *The Buffalo Courier-Express,"* March 27, 1935, 16.

[393] Ibid.

[394] "Prospect Bright for Successful Fair," *The Lawrenceburg Press*, July 28, 1938, 1.

[395] "Altman Reports Increase is Big for Williamsville," *The Billboard*, July 4, 1936, 38.

[396] Ibid.

[397] "Fire Sweeps Thru Williamsville Park," *The Billboard,* July 11, 1936, 1

[398] Fire Loss $12,000 at Williamsville Amusement Spot," *Lockport Union-Sun & Journal,* July 1, 1936, 1.

[399] "Glen Park Fire Burns Pavilion," *The Buffalo Evening News*, July 1, 1936, 7.

[400] Ibid.

[401] "I'm All Ears," *The Buffalo Times,* July 10, 1936, 19.

[402] "Snake Charmer Featured on Program at Glen Park," *The Buffalo Courier-Express*, July 2, 1936, 8.

[403] "Williamsville Permit Tangle Stirs Williamsville Folk," *The Buffalo Evening News,* July 22, 1936, 19.

[404] Ibid.

[405] Ibid.

[406] Ibid.

[407] Ibid.

[408] Ibid.

[409] Ibid.

[410] Ibid.

[411] "Mansion House," *The Amherst Bee*, February 24, 1938, 12.

[412] "Williamsville Landmark to Come Down," *The Buffalo Evening News*, October 10, 1957, 6,

[413] "Stompin' at the Glen," *The Buffalo Evening News*, April 7, 1937, page 34.

[414] Ibid.

[415] "Casino at Glen Park Opens this Saturday," *The Lackawanna Herald*, April 8, 1937, 1.

[416] Ibid.

[417] *Glen Barn, Old-Fashioned Barn Dance*, advertising card, Williamsville, NY, 1937.

[418] "Glen Park 45% Under '37," *The Billboard*, September 17, 1938, 11.

[419] Ibid.

[420] Ibid.

[421] "Gene Krupa's New Orchestra Will Play at Glen Park May 3," *The Buffalo Evening News*, April 18, 1938, 15.

[422] Sammy Davis Jr, Jane Boyar, and Burt Boyar, *Yes I Can: The Story of Sammy Davis, Jr* (New York: Farrar, Straus and Giroux, 1965), 39.

[423] "Make Your Date for Decoration Day," *The Sun and the Erie County Independent*, May 26, 1938, 8.

[424] "This is a Trying Out Point for His Recordings, Sammy Davis, Jr Says," *The Buffalo Evening News*, September 12, 1955, 20.

[425] Ibid.

[426] Ibid.

[427] Davis, *Yes I Can*, 49.

[428] "YouTube Tues: Eddie Cantor and Sammy." Posted on *sammydavisjr.info*, published ca. 8 years ago. Accessed June 7, 2025.

[429] Ibid.

[430] "Casino Plans College Reunion.," *The Buffalo Courier-Express*, June 15, 1952, 27.

[431] "Held Over Second Big Week," *The Buffalo News*, June 28, 1952, 20.

[432] "This is a Trying Out Point," 20.

[433] "The Homeowner," Rochester Democrat & Chronicle, October 24, 1955, 15.

[434] "Theater Notes," *The Buffalo Courier Express, June 8, 1962*, B-10.

[435] Ibid.

[436] Ibid.

[437] Ibid.

[438] "Harry Altman will Manage Island's Park," *The Buffalo Courier-Express*, January 1, 1938, 5.

[439] Ibid.

[440] Ibid.

441 Ibid.

442 "A New Ferry Service," *The Evening News (North Tonawanda)*, May 14, 1938, 7.

443 Ibid.

444 "Features 2004," Isle de Grande (Grand Island, NY), "Features 2004," www.isledegrande.com/features-2004.htm, accessed June 7, 2025.

445 Ibid.

446 "Giants Train at Night," *The Buffalo Evening News*, July 26, 1938, 20.

447 Ibid.

448 "Talun's Shoes Blamed by Danno for Defeat," *The Buffalo Evening News*, July 30, 1938, 6.

449 "New Winter Garden Glen Park," *The Buffalo Evening News*, October 13, 1938, 30.

450 Ibid.

451 "Glen Winter Garden," *The Buffalo Courier-Express*, February 1, 1941, 24.

452 Ibid.

453 "Night Clubs," *The Buffalo Evening News*, January 23, 1941, 16.

454 "The Hay Mow," *The Buffalo Courier-Express*, April 16, 1938, 24.

455 "Three Buildings Burn, Attracting Thousands, in Clarence Section," *The Daily News (Batavia)*, November 14, 1938, 1.

456 Ibid.

457 "New Wagon Wheel Roller Rink," *The Buffalo Evening News*, September 30, 1938, 35.

458 "Incorporations," *The Buffalo Evening News*, January 31, 1941, 34.

459 "See, for example, incorporation of Leon Sales, Inc.," *The Buffalo Evening News*, November 9, 1946, 6.

460 "Obituaries," *Lackawanna Leader*, February 17, 1955, 10.

461 "Altman Reports Increase is Big for Williamsville," *The Billboard*, July 4, 1936, 38.

462 Ibid., 61.

463 Ibid., 54.

464 "Boulder Park," *Boulder—Howland Amusements*, accessed June 19, 2025, https://freepages.rootsweb.com/~howardlake/history/amusement9/boulderny.html.

465 Ibid.

466 Cindy Henning Hanks, *Boulder Amusement Park: The Biography of a Carousel*, (Firefly Publication, 2003), 64.

467 Hanks, *Boulder Amusement Park*, 28.

468 "Williamsville Glen Per Capita is Down," *The Billboard*, September 4, 1940, 42.

469 Linda M. Bartash-Dawley, *Horses in Motion: The History of Carousels in Monroe County, New York* (2013), 11.

470 Arlen Ettinger interview by Susan Fenster, June 16, 2021.

[471] Frederick Fried, *A Pictorial History of the Carousel* (Vestal, NY: Vestal Press, 1964), 51.

[472] Anne Dion Hinds, *Grab the Brass Ring: The American Carousel* (New York: Crown Publishers, 1990), 10.

[473] Interview with Ettinger.

[474] Ibid.

[475] Ibid.

[476] Hinds, *Grab the Brass Ring*, 5.

[477] Janine Rebbie Matscherz interview by Susan Fenster, December 10, 2021.

[478] "E.J. Morris: The Forgotten Carousel Builder," *The Carousel News & Trader*, March 1989, 5.

[479] Ibid., 6.

[480] Ibid., 8.

[481] Ibid.

[482] Interview with Matscherz. She is the current (2025) operations manager for PTC, Inc. and the archivist at the company is when this research was undertaken.

[483] "1904 Fort Erie Carousel will Run Again at Falls,"|*Niagara Falls Review*, June 17, 1975, 6.

[484] Richard Lohr interview by Susan Fenster, September 29, 2020.

[485] Ibid.

[486] Ibid.

[487] Linda M. Bartash-D-awley interview by Susan Fenster, November 20, 2020.

[488] Bartash-D-awley, *Horses in Motion*, 12.

[489] Interview with Lohr.

[490] Ibid.

[491] "Historic Preservation," *ICC Commonwealth*, accessed June 20, 2025, https://www.icc-commonwealth.com/historic-preservatio

[492] "'Before is the Easy Part at Williamsville Depot," *The Buffalo Evening News*, September 23, 1989, 5.

[493] "1904 Fort Erie Carousel," 6.

[494] Ibid.

[495] Interview with Lohr.

[496] "1904 Fort Erie Carousel," 6.

[497] "Arcade Review and History: Skyquest Arcade at the Basement of the Skylon Tower, Niagara Falls, Ontario, Canada." *Arcade Heroes*, May 4, 2016. Accessed June 20, 2025. https://arcadeheroes.com/2016/05/04/arcade-review-history-skyquest-arcade-basement-skylon-tower-niagara-falls-ontario-canada/.

[498] Interview with Arlen Ettinger.

[499] Ibid.

[500] Ibid.

[501] Ibid.

[502] Example, "The Splendid Corey Collection," *The Carousel News and Trader,* June 1988, 4-8.

[503] Ibid.

[504] "Rogene Corey," *The Carousel News and Trader,* January 1989, 13.

[505] *Fairground Fantasy,* auction catalogue, Guernsey's Auctions, April 2, 1989.

[506] Ibid., 4.

[507] Ibid.

[508] "Auction Results," *The Carousel News and Trader,* June 1989, 11.

[509] Ibid.

[510] "The Newly Married Sprouses" *The Buffalo Courier-Express,* July 2, 1942, 13.

[511] "Bride, 78, Said There'll Be No Little Sprouse," *The Buffalo Courier-Express,* July 4, 1946, 6.

[512] "May-December Romance Marches On," *The Buffalo Courier-Express,* June 8, 1957, 1.

[513] "Bride, 78," 6.

[514] "Altitude Hits Show Folk Hard," *The Detroit Free Press,* March 20, 1942, 18,

[515] Ibid.

[516] "Night Clubs," *The Buffalo Evening News,*" September 24, 1943, 28.

[517] "Altitude Hits Show Folk," 18.

[518] "Frank Fontaine Gathers Laughter," *The Morning Union,* October 22, 1955, 22.

[519] "Don Romero Added to Glen Program," *The Buffalo Courier-Express,* September 2, 1942, 6.

[520] Ibid.

[521] Ibid.

[522] "$200 investment," 7.

[523] "Nightclubs," *The Buffalo Evening News,* September 26, 1945, 13.

[524] "Concesh Op Deals in Real Estate." *The Billboard,* October 17, 1960, 62.

[525] "Native Son Revives Memories with Sammy Davis Tribute," The Buffalo News, May 1, 2016, 19.

[526] Ibid.

[527] Ibid.

[528] "Entertainment Keeps Bingo Games Going," *The Buffalo Evening News,* April 9,1954, 12.

[529] Ibid.

[530] "Williamsville Resident Charges Park is Noisy," *The Buffalo Evening News,* April 21, 1954, 62.

[531] Ibid.

[532] "Entertainment Keeps Bingo," 12.

[533] Ibid.

[534] Ibid.

[535] Ibid.

[536] "Concesh Op Deals," 62.

[537] Ibid.

[538] Ibid.

[539] "Baa, Baa Black Sheep." *The Buffalo Courier-Express*, July 15, 1953, page 15.

[540] Ibid.

[541] "Llamas, Aoudads, Give Buffalo Zoo a Sheepish Look," *The Buffalo Evening News*, October 7, 1957, 29.

[542] "Buffalo Area News Highlights," *The Buffalo Evening News*, September 6, 1956, 45.

[543] "Glen Patrons are Assailed," *The Buffalo Courier-Express*, August 8, 1956, 5.

[544] Ibid.

[545] Ibid.

[546] Ibid.

[547] Ibid.

[548] "Buffalo Area News," 45.

[549] "Incorporation Certificates," *Buffalo Law Journal*, February 3, 1943, 3.

[550] "Pre-Yule Deb Set for Buff Casino; Plans Name Shows," *The Billboard*, December 15, 1945, 35.

[551] "A. Irving Milch, Attorney, is Dead; Aided City Probe," *The Buffalo Evening News*, September 19, 1951, 87.

[552] "Game Operators Trial Opens Today," *The Buffalo Courier-Express*, April 20, 1954, 19.

[553] "Levitt Disclaims Knowledge of His Tax Returns," *The Buffalo Evening News*, April 22, 1954, 10.

[554] "Gambling Squad Testifies Before Probers," *The Buffalo Evening News*, March 29, 1951, 1.

[555] "LaGuardia Wins Slot Machine Victory; Highest Court Voids Old Ban on Seizures," *The New York Times*, May 22, 1934, 1.

[556] "Levitt Disclaims Knowledge of His Tax Returns," *The Buffalo Evening News, April 22, 1954, 10.*

[557] "Levitt Says Dead Attorney," 25.

[558] "Levitt's Lawyer Pleads for Reversal, New Trial," *The Buffalo Evening News*, April 27, 1954, 14.

[559] "Witness Says Levitt Admitted Income from 16 Machines," *The Buffalo Evening News*, April 21, 1954, 61.

[560] "Levitt Fined $2000 by Knight; Prison Term is Suspended," *The Buffalo Evening News*, May 11, 1954, 17.

[561] "Tax Court Calendar Lists Cases for May Session Here," *The Buffalo Evening News*, February 25, 1955, 12.

562 How the Mafia Used to Control the Music Industry," *ClickTrack*, accessed June 21, 2025, https://www.clicktrack.fm/p/how-the-mafia-used-to-control-the.

563 "The Intriguing History of the American Mafia: From Immigrant Roots to Organized Crime," *Vocal*, accessed June 21, 2025, https://vocal.media/criminal/the-intriguing-history-of-the-american-mafia-from-immigrant-roots-to-organized-crime.

564 John Roos, "How Prohibition Put the 'Organized' in Organized Crime," *History.com*, January 14, 2019, updated May 28, 2025.

565 Frank X. Schwab, Wikipedia, last modified June 2025, https://en.wikipedia.org/wiki/Frank_X._Schwab?utm_source=chatgpt.com

566 "Dead Man's Hand Seen Upper One in Police Hunt for Joe DiCarlo," *The Buffalo Courier-Express,* November 5, 1939, 1.

567 Ibid.

568 Thomas Hunt and Michael A. Tona, "Chapter-by-Chapter Summaries for the Books," *DiCarlo: Buffalo's First Family of Crime*, BuffaloMob.com, accessed June 30, 2025.

569 "Dead Man's Hand," 1.

570 Joseph DiCarlo (Nov. 1, 1899—Oct. 11, 1980)," *BuffaloMob Blog* (blog), August 2013.

571 *BuffaloMob Blog*, accessed June 30, 2025, https://buffalomob.blogspot.com/2013/.

572 *The People of the State of New York v. Leonard Mordino*, Appellate Division of the Supreme Court of New York, Fourth Department, July 12, 1977.

573 Roadhouses, Resorts, Up Against That Gas Snag Again, Stalling on Tee-Offs," *The Billboard,* May 29, 1943, 4.

574 "Altman's Famed Funhouse Moves to Handier Spot," *Tonawanda News*, May 10, 1943, 5.

575 "Gourmands," *The Buffalo Courier-Express,* February 28, 1943, 8-D.

576 "'Barn's' Opening Set for Thursday," *The Buffalo Courier-Express,* November 7, 1943, 6-B.

577 "Part 1010—Suspension Orders [Suspension Order S-295] GLEN AMUSEMENT CORPORATION," *Federal Register*, April 27, 1943, 5446.

578 "Business Zoning at Main and Kensington Approved," *The Buffalo Evening News*, April 7, 1942, 13.

579 "Part 1010," 5446 .

580 Ibid.

581 "Navy Show Stars Rank High in Theater," *The Buffalo Courier-Express*, July 19, 1942, 4.

582 Ibid.

583 "Crowd of Navy Relief Show Surpasses Mark of 50,000." *The Buffalo Courier-Express,* July 21, 1942, 1,

584 Ibid.

585 "The Daily Pictorial," *The Buffalo Courier-Express,* July 31, 1944, 8.

586 "Harry Altman," *The Buffalo Evening News*, October 26, 1942, 14,

[587] "Individual Sales in 5th War Loan Reach 23% Mark," *The Buffalo Evening News*, June 20, 1944, 1.

[588] "Morale Group Formed to Serve in Buffalo Area," *The Buffalo Evening News*, January 13, 1945, 3.

[589] "Barn's Opening," 6-B.

[590] "Big 'Barn' Party Ends in a Riot as DiCarlo Arrives," *The Buffalo Evening News*, November 19, 1944, 1.

[591] Ibid.

[592] Ibid.

[593] Ibid.

[594] Ibid.

[595] Ibid.

[596] "Denials Made of Brawl at Main St. Club," *The Buffalo Courier-Express*, November 22, 1944, 11.

[597] Ibid.

[598] Ibid.

[599] Ibid.

[600] "Night Club Debut,"*Associated Press Wire Story*, January 9, 1945.

[601] "Caruso's Son is Singing in Nightclub." *The New York Sun*, January 9, 1945, 7.

[602] "Storm, Fire Tie Up City's Traffic," *The Buffalo Courier-Express*, February 14, 1945, 1.

[603] Ibid.

[604] "Traffic Paralyzed by Three-Alarm Blaze Wrecks Town Barn," *The Buffalo Evening News*, February 5, 1945, 5.

[605] "Storm, Fire," 1.

[606] "Traffic Paralyzed," 1.

[607] "Simpkins to Head Glen Park which Opens Ahead of Sked," *Billboard Magazine*, March 24, 1945, 28.

[608] Ibid.

[609] "Casino Makes Its Debut to Capacity Tune," *The Buffalo Courier-Express*, December 30, 1945, 3-B.

[610] "Altman, Wallens Have Fine Buffalo Spots with Solid Acts, Low Tabs," *The Billboard*, September 20, 1952, 17.

[611] "Town Casino, Buffalo," *The Billboard*, February 9, 1946, 39.

[612] Ibid.

[613] "Casino Opens Doors Saturday," *The Buffalo Courier-Express*, December 25, 1945, 17.

[614] "Pre-Yule Deb Set for Buff Casino; Plans Name Shows," The Billboard, December 15, 1945, 35.

[615] "Altman, Wallens," 17.

[616] Ibid.

617 Ibid.

618 Ibid.

619 Ibid.

620 Ibid.

621 Ibid.

622 Ibid.

623 "Town Casino Rising Again Tonight," *The Buffalo Evening News*, September 23, 1981, 17.

624 "Town Casino, Buffalo," 44.

625 Kliph Nesteroff, "An Interview with Jerry Coe," Classic Television Showbiz (blog), April 5, 2012.

626 Ibid.

627 Ibid.

628 Ibid.

629 Ibid.

630 "Buffalo Niteries Hit by Heatwave." *The Billboard*, August 3, 1946, 41.

631 Vic Damone with David Chanoff, *Singing Was the Easy Part* (New York: Macmillan + ORM, 2009).

632 Ibid.

633 Ibid.

634 Ibid.

635 Ibid.

636 Ibid.

637 Ibid.

638 Ibid.

639 Ibid.

640 "Lost Tony Bennett Interview: Pop Icon Recalls Shotgun-Toting Stalker—Who Might Still Be at Large," Robin Milling, *Blog Talk Radio*, July 21, 2010.

641 Ibid.

642 Ibid.

643 Ibid.

644 "The Liberaces Feuding?" *The Austin Daily Herald*, December 27, 1958, 19.

645 "Frozen Pizza Adds a Chill to Liberace Family Feud," *The Buffalo Evening News*, October 24, 1958, 14-II.

646 Ibid.

647 Ibid.

648 Ibid.

[649] "Well-Rounded Talkers Join Godfrey Tonight," *The Buffalo Evening News*, December 30, 1958, 16.

[650] "Spooktacular Display Pleases Ghouls and Gals," *The Roanoke Times*, October 31, 2001, 4.

[651] "As I See It," *The Buffalo Courier-Express*, May 4, 1961, 39.

[652] Ibid.

[653] "The 'Show-Off Program' Showed Gleason as Masterful Bigmouth," *Chronicle Tribune*, February 3, 1955, 23.

[654] "The Night Arthur Godfrey Fired a Singer on Live Radio," *Winnetoba Radio*, accessed June 30, 2025, quoting *The Night Arthur Godfrey Fired a Singer on Live Radio*, published online (retrieved via search).

[655] "'Charming Rascal' Receives Ovation at Show for Navy," *Binghampton Press and Sun Bulletin*, October 24, 1953, 1.

[656] "Feminine Sighs Sweep Casino as La Rosa Croons," *The Buffalo Courier-Express*, January 5, 1954, 15.

[657] Ibid.

[658] Ibid.

[659] Ibid.

[660] "TV's Part as Educator as Emphasized by Parker," *The Buffalo Evening News*, April 23, 1955, 9,

[661] Ibid.

[662] Ibid.

[663] Ibid.

[664] "McGuire Sisters to Appear Here," *The Buffalo Evening News*, January 20, 1955, 12.

[665] "McGuire Sisters to Get $10,000," *The Buffalo Courier-Express*, January 20, 1955, 1.

[666] "One 'Little Godfrey' to Miss Program for Next Four Weeks," *Bristol Virgina-Tennessean*, Wednesday, February 9, 1955, 2.

[667] Ibid.

[668] Ibid.

[669] "Agents Planted False Account of Marion Marlow-Puck Case," *The Buffalo Evening News*, May 17, 1955, 12.

[670] "Marion Marlowe Reveals She Has Brand New Routine," *The Buffalo Evening News*, February 3, 1956, 6.

[671] "Video Has Puzzling Effect on Night Club Business," *The Buffalo Courier-Express*, February 19, 1956, 27A.

[672] Ibid.

[673] Ibid.

[674] "Everyone Taps When Count Basie Sits at the Piano," *The Buffalo Evening News*, January 23, 1964, 58.

[675] "Altman Friend to Many in Area," *The Buffalo Courier-Express*, May 10, 1966, 23.

[676] "Lenny Paige Fondly Recalls Town Casino's Yesterdays," *The Buffalo Evening News*, March 14, 1973, 49.

[677] Lauren Hemedinger interview by Susan Fenster. February 22, 2022.

[678] Ibid.

[679] Ibid.

[680] Ibid.

[681] Ibid.

[682] Ibid.

[683] Ibid.

[684] Ibid.

[685] Ibid.

[686] Ibid.

[687] Kelly, Kevin, *Michael Bennett: A Life in the Theater.* New York: Harper & Row, 1989, 15.

[688] "A Report in Depth of the U.S. Economy," *The Buffalo Evening News*, August 20, 1962, 24.

[689] "Gilda Gray, Famed 'Shimmy Dancer,' to appear in Court," *Tonawanda Evening News* March 18, 1941, 10,

[690] Ibid.

[691] "Gilda Gray, Altman Settle Trouble Out of Court," The *Buffalo Evening News*, March 25, 1941, 1.

[692] "Night Club Owners Paying Benefits to Avert Strike," *The Buffalo Evening News*, December 5, 1952, 66.

[693] Ibid.

[694] Ibid.

[695] "Opposition Books Arouses Altman; Agents in Middle," *The Billboard*, November 12, 1949, 45.

[696] Ibid.

[697] Ibid.

[698] Ibid.

[699] Ibid.

[700] Ibid.

[701] Ibid.

[702] "Goulet's Star Rises on Stage, TV," *Buffalo Courier-Express*, April 5, 1962, 18.

[703] Ibid.

[704] "Series on Cancer Begins Tonight," *The Bufalo Evening News*, April 24, 1963, 47.

[705] "Town Casino Alters Policy," *The Buffalo Courier-Express*, January 16, 1946, 18.

[706] "Video Has Puzzling Impact on Night Club Business," *The Buffalo Courier-Express*, February 19, 1956, 27A.

[707] Ibid.

[708] Ibid.

[709] "From My Window," *The Buffalo Courier-Express*, May 10, 1953,16..

[710] Ibid.

[711] Ibid.

[712] "Night Clubs Doomed by Community Theater?" *The Buffalo Courier-Express*, October 7, 1962, 10B.

[713] Ibid.

[714] "Jayne Mansfield to Appear Here," *The Buffalo Evening News*, April 18, 1963, 52.

[715] Ibid.

[716] "Greatest Human Being," *Rochester Democrat and Chronicle*," May 5, 1963, 2M.

[717] Ibid.

[718] Ibid.

[719] Ibid.

[720] Ibid.

[721] "Mansfield to Head to Mexico," *UPI TELEPHOTO*, April 22, 1963.

[722] "Video Has Puzzling," 27.

[723] "Summer Programs to Open at Casino," *The Buffalo Courier-Express,* June 14, 1942, 17.

[724] "Veteran Emcee to Return to the Glen," *The Buffalo Courier-Express*, May 8, 1947, 10.

[725] Interview with Sheila Paige Roth by Susan Fenster, March 15, 2022.

[726] Ibid.

[727] Newberg, Rich (Producer, Writer, Reporter), "Play It Again Buffalo!" *B&ECPL Digital Collections*, accessed July 1, 2020, http://digital.buffalolib.org/document/

[728] Ibid

[729] Ibid.

[730] Ibid.

[731] Ibid.

[732] "Lenny Paige Fondly Recalls Town Casino's Yesterdays," *The Buffalo Evening News*, March 14, 1973, 11.

[912] Ibid.

[734] Ibid.

[735] Ibid.

[736] Ibid.

[737] "A Sad Night at the Inferno, But Memories Linger in Ashes," *The Buffalo Evening News*, September 23, 1968, 1.

[738] "Paige Returning to Phoenix," *The Amherst Bee*, December 10, 1986, 24.

739 "Look—Up on the Stage: Is It Really Tony Oddi?" *The Buffalo Evening News*, June 12, 1973, 17.

740 "Glen Park Drummer Plays in Artie Shaw Band," *The Amherst Bee*, July 14, 1938, 1.

741 "News Nuggets," *The Buffalo Evening News*, April 27, 1942, 16.

742 "Broadcaster Pushes Big Band Era Sound," *The Buffalo Courier-Express*, April 8, 1967, 10.

743 Interview with Laverne (Lauren) Johnson by Susan Fenster, March 15, 2021.

744 Ibid.

745 Ibid.

746 Ibid.

747 Ibid.

748 "$200 investment," 7.

749 Ibid.

750 Interview with Ron Urban by Susan Fenster, June 11, 2021.

751 Interview with Judy (Swidler) Streeter by Susan Fenster, May 5, 2025.

752 "Obituary of Bernard A. Bucci," *The Buffalo Evening News*, March 27, 1969, 10.

753 Interview with Rev. Robert Mock by Susan Fenster, October 9, 2021.

754 Ibid.

755 Interview with Donald (Sam) Weimer by Susan Fenster, May 5, 2020.

756 "Two Are Sentenced," *The Buffalo Courier-Express*, May 1, 1945, 7.

757 "Feds Arrest Eleven in Gas Stamp Racket," The Daily News, July 18, 1944, 6.

758 Ibid.

759 "Bogus Coupon Trial to Open," *The Buffalo Courier Express*, April 18, 1934, 1.

760 Interview with Rev. Robert Mock

761 Interview with Patricia (Smith) Riedel by Susan Fenster on February 21, 2022.

762 "No One Ever Refused to Join Mirth Caravan, Asserts Altman," *The Buffalo Evening News*, July 15, 1949, 12.

763 Ibid.

764 "As I See It," *The Buffalo Courier-Express*, August 1, 1950, 13.

765 Ibid.

766 Ibid.

767 "No One Ever Refused," 12.

768 "Funorama Here July 5th to Be Best Yet," *The Buffalo Courier-Express*, May 5, 1957, 33,

769 "15,000 View Funorama Show, Hold Memorial for Police," *The Buffalo Evening News*, July 3, 1954, 6.

770 Ibid.

771 Ibid.

772 "John C. Montana," *Wikipedia*, last modified November 25, 2024. Accessed July 4, 2025. https://en.wikipedia.org/wiki/John_C._Montana.

[773] Wire Fence Aided in Raid in Apalachin; Buffalo's Man of 1956 was Snagged on It, U. S. Agent Testifies at His Trial," *The New York Times*, November 14, 1959, 44.

[774] Ibid.

[775] "John C. Montana," *Wikipedia*.

[776] "Just Stopped at Apalachin for Tea, Says Buffalo VIP," *New York Daily News*, December 21, 1957, 161.

[777] "John Montana: July 1, 1893—March 18, 1964." *Buffalo Mob*, September 2013. Accessed July 4, 2025. https://buffalomob.blogspot.com/2013/09/john-montana-july-1-1893-march-18-1964.html.

[778] The U.S. Senate Select Committee on Improper Activities in Labor and Management (the McClellan Committee) (1957-1960).

[779] "John C. Montana Dies Following a Heart Attack," *The Buffalo Evening News*, March 19, 1964, 14.

[780] "Police Show Mixes Songs and Wresting," *The Buffalo Evening News*, July 15, 1961, B-7.

[781] "Funorama Committee Plans All-Out Ticket Sales Drive," The Buffalo Courier-Express, June 29, 1961, 20.

[782] "Dwyer Disclaims Having a Part in Montana Award,." *The Buffalo Evening News*, July 3, 1958, 4.

[783] Ibid.

[784] "Charles M. Basil, Erie Club President," *The Buffalo News*, October 13, 1995, 10.

[785] "Seen and Heard," *The Rochester Democrat and Chronicle, December 18, 1965, 22.*

[786] Ibid.

[787] "Before & After," *The Buffalo Courier-Express*, September 9, 1948, 21.

[788] "Before & After," *The Buffalo Courier-Express*, March 21, 1950, 18.

[789] "Before & After," *The Buffalo Courier-Express*, May 4, 1946, 14.

[790] "Anthony Naples, Democratic Party Leader," *The Buffalo News*, May 9, 1992, 34.

[791] Michael F. Rizzo, *Gangsters and Organized Crime in Buffalo: History, Hits and Headquarters* (Charleston, SC: The History Press, 2012), 98.

[792] Ibid., 100.

[793] "Before & After," *The Buffalo Courier-Express*, March 21, 1950, 18.

[794] Ibid., 118.

[795] Ibid.

[796] Ibid.

[797] Ibid.

[798] Ibid.

[799] "'Win Again' Does It Again," *The Buffalo Courier-Express*, July 24, 1964, 15.

[800] Steve Goldstein Interview by Susan Fenster, May 20, 1921.

[801] "'Barn's Opening Set for Thursday," *The Buffalo Courier-Express*, November 1, 1943, 6-B.

[802] Hischak, Thomas S. *Broadway Plays and Musicals: Descriptions and Essential Facts of More Than 14,000 Shows through 2007*. Jefferson, NC: McFarland & Company, 2009, 248.

[803] "Little Old New York," *The Daily News*, November 29, 1943, 66.

[804] "New Altman Show to Open in Gotham," *The Buffalo Courier-Express*, November 5, 1943, 11.

[805] "Froman Good, Revue Dull," *Omaha World-Herald*, November 14, 1943, 74

[806] "'Artist and Models' and Jane Frohman Arrive at the Broadway Theater," *Brooklyn Eagle*, November 6, 1943, 12 .

[807] "Jane Froman Stars in 'Artists and Models' and It's Not So Hot," *New York Daily News*, November 6, 1943, 140.

[808] Ibid.

[809] "Buffalo Group Buys Midtown Bowling Center," *The Buffalo Evening News*, December 8, 1959, 45.

[810] "Announcements," *The Buffalo Courier-Express*, October 15, 1940, 23.

[811] "Incorporations," *The Buffalo Courier-Express*, January 22, 1957, 17.

[812] "Grand Opening of Sheridan Lanes," *The Buffalo Evening News*, February 14, 1958, 32.

[813] "Sheridan Lanes Wants You Back!" *The Buffalo Evening News*, August 29, 1997, 69.

[814] "Arrowhead Lanes Sports Top Management Staff," *The Daily Messenger*, October 9, 1956, 3.

[815] "Alleys to Open in Canandaigua," *Rochester Democrat and Chronicle*, May 13, 1956, 3B.

[816] "Kelgers' Corner," *Rochester Democrat and Chronicle*, October 14, 1956, 66.

[817] Ibid.

[818] "Arrowhead Lanes Sports Top," 3.

[819] Ibid.

[820] "Town Casino to Open with New Manager," *The Buffalo Evening News*, September 4, 1958, 21.

[821] "Town Casino's Fall Season Brings Bines Back to Town," *The Buffalo Evening News*, April 15, 1958, 19.

[822] "Town Reopening Draws Capacity House," *The Buffalo Courier-Express*, September 15, 1958, 5B.

[823] "Town Casino's Fall Season," 19.

[824] Ibid.

[825] Ibid.

[826] Ibid.

[827] "Altman to Close Casino 10 Weeks, Then Try Again," *The Buffalo Evening News*, January 2, 1959, 7.

[828] "Little Old New York," *Albany Times Union*, May 1, 1955, B-4.

[829] "Home Town Audience Tough, Shawn Claims," *The Buffalo Courier-Express*, July 16, 1963, 6.

[830] Ibid.

[831] "Altman to Close Casino," 19.

[832] Ibid.

[833] "Ames Brothers Booked to Re-Open Casino," *The Buffalo Evening News*, March 2, 1959, 41.

[834] Ibid.

[835] Ibid.

[836] "900 Honor Harry Altman," *The Buffalo Courier-Express*, September 14, 1959, 18.

[837] Ibid.

[838] Ibid.

[839] Ibid.

[840] Ibid.

[841] "Leaders from Various Fields Pay Tribute to Harry Altman," *The Buffalo Evening News*, September 14, 1959, 20.

[842] "Stars and Area Folk to Honor Harry Altman," *The Buffalo Courier-Express*, August 23, 1959, 13-C.

[843] "Dick Fischer Dies; Was Leader in Athletic, Civic, Charity Affairs," *The Buffalo News*, May 15, 1983, 63.

[844] "Dinner Will Honor Harry Altman for Service to Buffalo," *The Buffalo Evening News*, August 22, 1959, A-13.

[845] "Casino Folk Singer a Lure to Talent Scouts," *The Buffalo Evening News*, September 10, 1960, 7.

[846] "25 on Bill for Casino Opening," *The Buffalo Courier Express*, March 16, 1961, 27.

[847] Ibid.

[848] "Casino Closed Until March 17," *The Buffalo Courier-Express*, January 6, 1962, 4.

[849] "Church Burns, Masses Held in Nightclub," *The Geneva Times*, May 28, 1962, 1.

[850] Ibid.

[851] "St. Michael's Parish to Use Town Casino for Services," *The Buffalo-Courier Express*, May 26, 1962, 4.

[852] Ibid.

[853] "As I See It," *The Buffalo Courier-Express*, June 25. 1962, page 47.

[854] "Nightclubs Doomed by Community Theater?" *The Buffalo Courier-Express*, October 7, 1962, 10B.

[855] "St. Michael's Opening by Summer Expected." *The Buffalo Evening News*, November 12, 1962,12.

[856] "Loss of Parishioners and Income Reported by St. Michael's Pastor,"
The Buffalo Courier-Express, February 4, 1963, 7.

[857] Ibid.

[858] Ibid.

[859] "The Town Quick Changes to Show Business." *The Buffalo Evening News*, September 13, 1963, 46.,

[860] Ibid.

[861] "Jazz City Premier Opening," *The Buffalo Courier-Express*, January 1, 1964, 48.

[862] "Casino to be Made into Banquet Hall," *The Buffalo Courier-Express*, December 16, 1964, 43.

[863] "Town Casino to Become Banquet Hall," *Tonawanda News*, December 17, 1964, 3.

[864] Ibid.

[865] "Town Casino, Famed Night Spot, for Sale," *The Buffalo Courier-Express*, June 21, 1965, 8.

[866] Ibid.

[867] Ibid.

[868] `Ibid.

[869] Ibid.

[870] Ibid.

[871] "Town Casino Sold: Altman Discloses Auditorium Plans," *The Buffalo Courier-Express*, August 15, 1965, 10A.

[872] Ibid.

[873] Ibid.

[874] Ibid.

[875] Ibid.

[876] "Pistol Stolen from Singer.," *The Buffalo Courier-Express*, July 31, 1960, 2-B.

[877] "Sophisticated, Simple Best Describe Williams," *The Bufalo Courier-Express*, April 10, 1967, 22.

[878] Ibid.

[879] "Speedy Repertoire of the Wayfarers Covers Wide Range," *The Buffalo Evening News*, August 6, 1963, 26.

[880] Ibid.

[881] Ibid.

[882] Ibid.

[883] "ACHS Grads to Sing at Glen Casino," *The Amherst Bee*, August 22, 1963, 14.

[884] Buffalo Music Hall of Fame. "Eric Andersen." Buffalo Music Hall of Fame Inductees, class of 1999. *Buffalo Music Hall of Fame*, n.d. Accessed June 13, 2025.

[885] Lamont, Paul, and Scott Sackett, directors. *The Songpoet*. Produced by Toward Castle Films and Skipping Stone Pictures; in association with The Center for Independent Documentary, 2019.

[886] "An American Folkie; Documentary will Follow Long Career of Legendary Singer-Songwriter Eric Andersen, Who Got His Show at a Williamsville Hootenanny," *The Buffalo Evening News*, 2012, 23.

[887] "Buffalo Bills Quartet To Open Season at Glen Casino," *The Buffalo Evening News*, April 23, 1964, 18.

[888] "C of C in Williamsville Plans Dances for Youths," *The Buffalo Evening News*, June 15, 1961, 5.

[889] "Open All Year," *The Buffalo Evening News*, November 2, 1962, 25.

[890] Interview with Bob Paxon by Susan Fenster on March 14, 2022.

[891] Ibid.

[892] Ibid.

[893] "About the Ciceros," *Golden Dawn Shop*, accessed June 30, 2025, https://www.goldendawnshop.com/about-the-ciceros/

[894] "Buffalo is Looking for the Answer to the Beatles!" *The Buffalo Courier-Express*, February 19, 1965, 6.

[895] Ibid.

[896] "Night Clubs," *The Buffalo Evening News*, January 6, 1965, 60.

[897] "Altman Friend to Many in Area," 23.

[898] "Glen Casino Being Sold, Altman Says," *The Buffalo Courier-Express*, November 24, 1965, 1.

[899] "Altman Sells Glen Casino," The Buffalo Evening News, November 24, 1965, 61.

[900] https://d.docs.live.net/cd3284d4c7fdb6e5/Documents/Book/Harry Altman-9-4-25-Chapter 2-end of Part One edits.docx

[901] "Jacobs Brothers' Schedules Filed," *The Buffalo Evening News*, February 16, 1932, 25.

[902] *"The Past Haunts Brothers Who Own Convicted Sports Empire."* New York Times, October 7, 1977, 38.

[903] "Altman Friend to Many in Area," 23.

[904] ""What has Louie Wrought," *Sports Illustrated*, February 29, 1972, 48.

[905] "Louis Jacobs Dies at Work in Office; Sportservice Head," *The Buffalo Evening News*, August 7, 1968, 49.

[906] Janice Hochreiter (Administrator, Public Affairs, Delaware North Corporation) to Linda M. Bartash, letter, May 1, 1995.

[907] Ibid.

[908] "Delaware North Companies Incorporated." *Encyclopedia.com*, published by International Directory of Company Histories. Accessed July 4, 2025. https://www.encyclopedia.com/books/politics-and-business-magazines/delaware-north-companies-incorporated

[909] "Dope Inc.," Arizona Political Secrets (blog) July 2008. http://arizonapoliticalsecrets.blogspot.com/ 2008/07/dope-inc.html?m=1, Accessed September 2, 2025.

[910] "Emprise Corp. Loses Plea for U.S. Pardon,'" *New York Times*, September 29, 1977, 1.

[911] Ibid.

[912] Gaslite Theater to Open Soon at Glen Park," *The Amherst Bee*, May 9, 1963, 2.

[913] "Glen Park's Playhouse's 1st Show Opens May 3rd," *The Buffalo Courier-Express*, January 18, 1966, 18.

[914] "Gaslite Theater to Open," 2.

[915] "Frank M. Moltz," *The Sun and Erie County Independent*, April 27, 1966, 5.

[916] "Altman Friend to Many," 23.

[917] Ibid.

[918] Ibid.

[919] "Harry Altman Dead at 75; Buffalo's 'Mr. Show Business,'" *The Buffalo Evening News*, May 9, 1966, 3.

[920] "Rabbi Feierstein Lauds Altman for Service to Mankind," *The Buffalo Evening News*, May 10, 1966, 13.

[921] "Glen Park Playhouse Lasts Month," *The Buffalo Courier-Express*, June 4, 1966, 8.

[922] Ibid.

[923] Ibid.

[924] "As I See It," *The Buffalo Courier-Express*, June 1, 1965, 25.

[925] Interview with Bob Paxon.

[926] Ibid.

[927] "Limit on Occupancy Blamed for Trouble." *The Buffalo Evening News*, September 10, 1966, 5.

[928] Ibid.

[929] Ibid.

[930] Ibid.

[931] "Petition Protests Club Operation," *The Buffalo Evening News*, September 30, 1966, 4.

[932] "Dance Sponsor Seeks New Site After Trouble," *The Buffalo Evening News*, October 1, 1966, 3.

[933] "Glen Park Casino Destroyed by Fire," *The Buffalo Evening News*, September 23, 1968, 1.

[934] [934]"Inferno Lost in Flames as Young Fans Weep, and Firemen Cool it All," *The Amherst Bee*, September 23, 1968, 1.

[935] Ibid.

[936] "Inferno Lost in Flames," *The Amherst Bee*, September 23, 1968, 1.

[937] Ibid.

[938] Interview of Thomas Wutz by Susan Fenster on February 2021.

[939] Ibid.

[940] "Inferno Lost in Flames," 1.

[941] Ibid.

[942] Ibid.

[943]Ibid.

[944] Ibid..

[945] Ibid.

[946] "Glen Park Casino Destroyed," 1.

[947] "Twenty-five Years Ago," *The Amherst Bee*, September 24, 1993, 11.

[948] "Inferno Lost in Flames," 1.

[949] Ibid.

[950] "Effort Fails to Kill Plan on Pizzeria," *The Buffalo Courier-Express*, January 26, 1969, 1.

[951] "300 Protest Town Permit for Pizzeria," *The Buffalo Courier-Express*, January 31, 1969, 24.

[952] "Letters to the Editor," *The Lancaster Enterprise*, February 6, 1969, 4.

[953] Ibid.

[954] "Glen to Have Dance Center," *The Buffalo Courier-Express*, October 27, 1968, 11.

[955] Interview with Patrick Hasburgh on May 7, 2022 by Susan Fenster.

[956] Ibid.

[957] Interview with Rev. Robert Mock.

[958] "Two Glen Park fires started by vandals," *Amherst Bee,* June 27, 1973, 1.

[959] Ibid.

[960] "Fire Officials Probing Blaze at Glen Park," *The Buffalo Evening News*, September 10, 1973, 13.

[961] Ibid.

[962] Ibid.

[963] Ibid.

[964] Ibid.

[965] Ibid.

[966] Interview with Michael Wutz.

[967] *Rough and Ready, 59.*

[968] "Casino Fire Cause Probed," *Buffalo Courier Express*, September 11, 1973, 4.

[969] "Fire Officials Probing Blaze at Glen Park," *Buffalo Evening News*, September 10, 1973, 3.

[970]"Empty Shells of Building Monument to Better Days," *Amherst Bee*, November 6, 1973, 6.

www.ingramcontent.com/pod-product-compliance
Lightning Source LLC
Chambersburg PA
CBHW070904130626
46555CB00001B/12